AF394787

SEASIDE
PHOTOGRAPHER

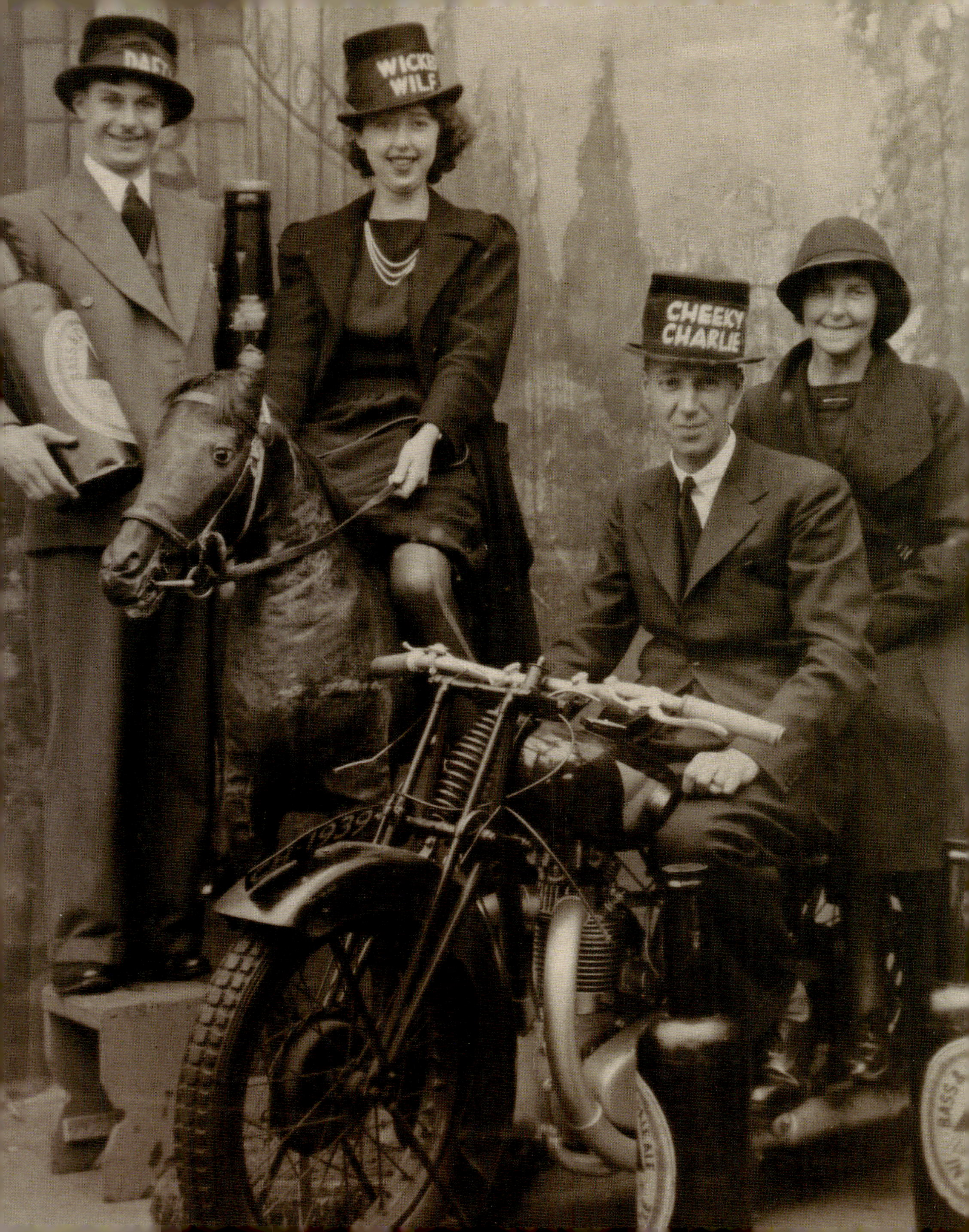
DAFT
WICKED
WILF
CHEEKY
CHARLIE
BASS
1939

VAL WILLIAMS

KAREN SHEPHERDSON

SEASIDE PHOTOGRAPHED

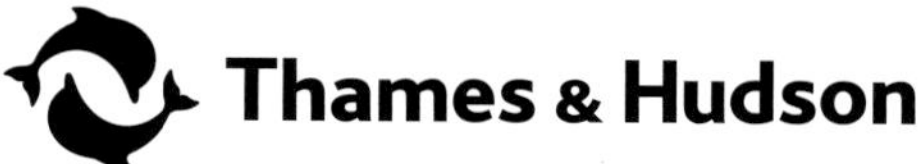

Thames & Hudson

with 208 photographs

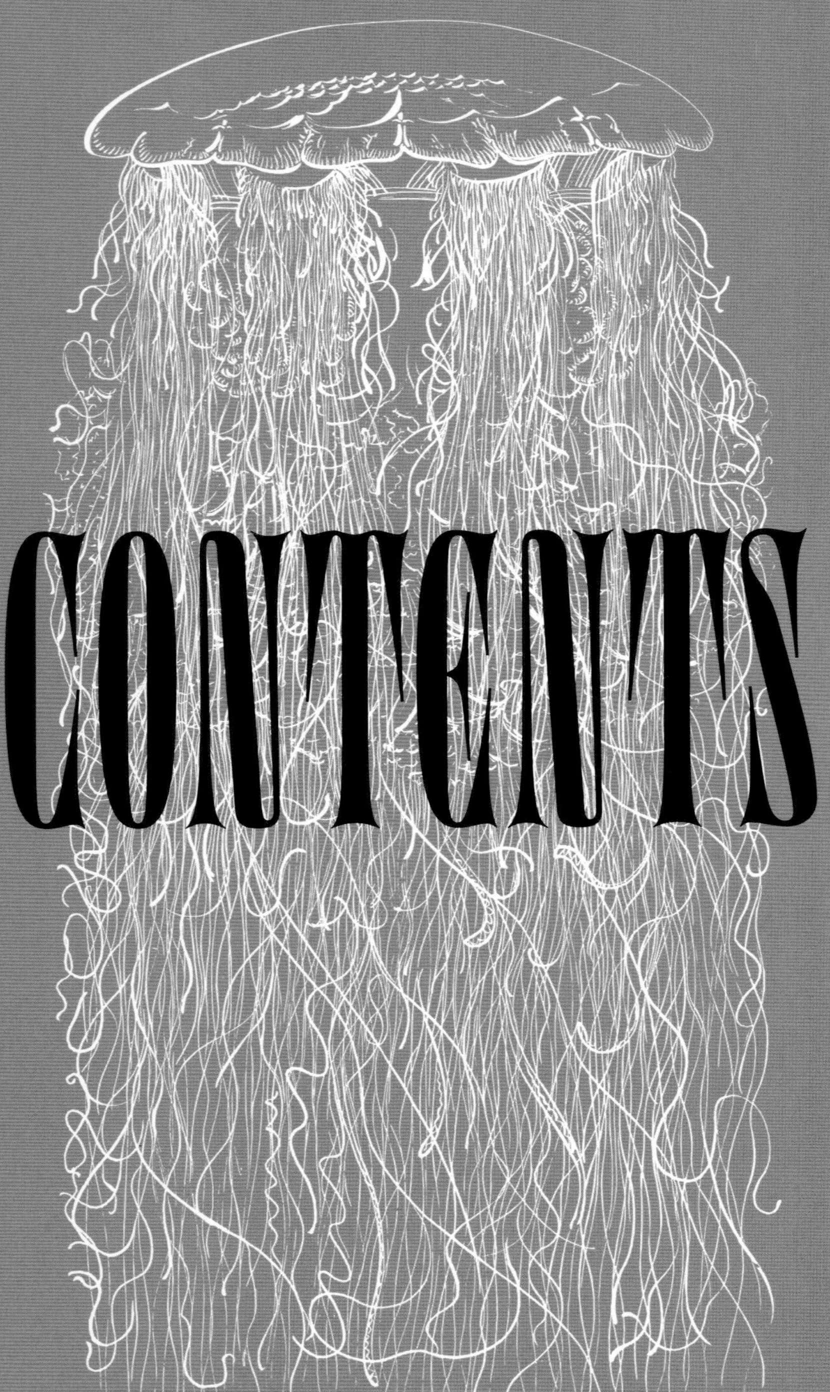

CONTENTS

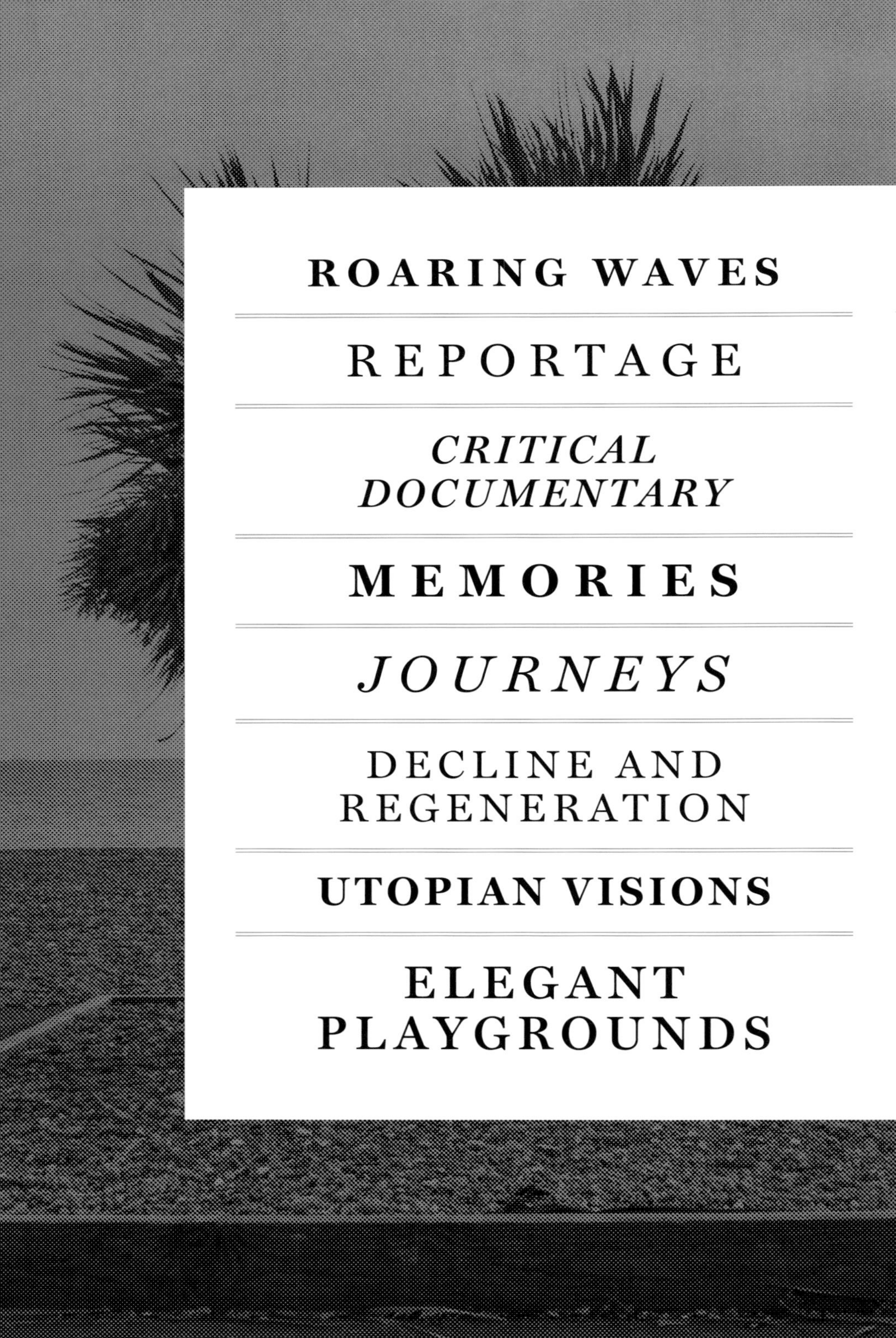
ROARING WAVES
REPORTAGE
CRITICAL DOCUMENTARY
MEMORIES
JOURNEYS
DECLINE AND REGENERATION
UTOPIAN VISIONS
ELEGANT PLAYGROUNDS

DO YOU WISH
YOU WERE
HERE?

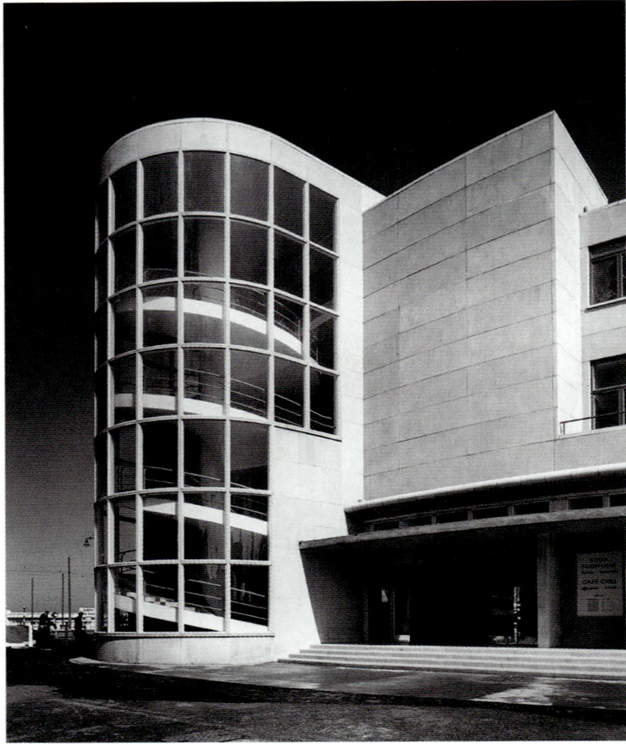

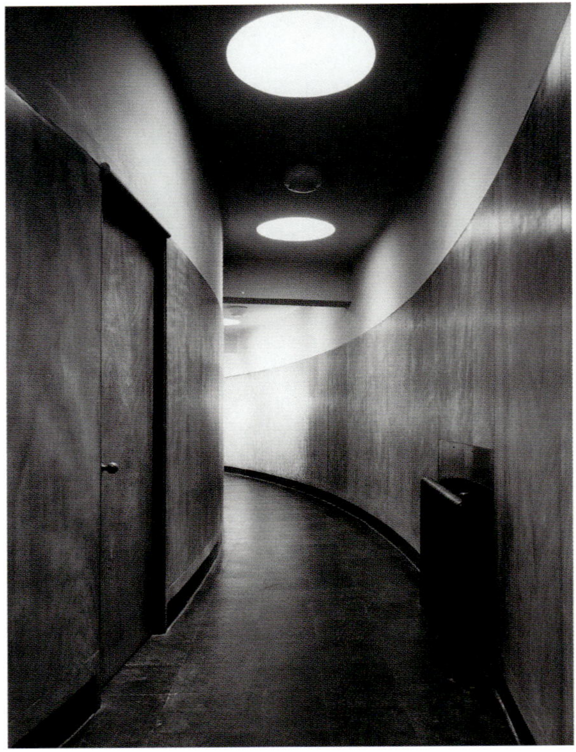

How has the seaside been photographed? From the roaring waves of the nineteenth century through the reportage of the 1960s and the critical documentary of the 1980s and 1990s, to what is perhaps the more intimate work of the last ten years. No one can tell it exactly the way it is. We all have a vision of the seaside that is uniquely our own. Memories, false and real, are aided and abetted by photography, a unique, fascinating, but in the end unreliable source of evidence. And time changes everything. What remains are a set of substantial fragments, thoughts along the way, obsessions, records, constructions, journeys. Ours for the taking.

The British seaside has always been a metaphor for the state of the nation. Decline and regeneration have become seaside descriptors and the coastal population is a complex one – new sets of urban colonizers repurposing seaside buildings and spaces, visitors, émigrés, retirees, all living alongside longstanding citizens whose occupations stretch across the national norm. In the 1930s, photographers such as Alfred Cracknell were commissioned to photograph the new seaside of gleaming modernist buildings (above). What we now often see as ghosts of their former selves were once utopian visions of elegant playgrounds by the sea. In July 1936 the *Architectural Review* commissioned the distinguished émigré László Moholy-Nagy to produce an entire issue on the seaside, including a series of his own photographs made on the south coast. Fifty years after he photographed it, in its gleaming modernist glory, Bexhill's De La Warr Pavilion had been

ABOVE: LEFT AND RIGHT
Alfred Cracknell
Blackpool Casino,
1939

OPPOSITE
László Moholy-Nagy
Architectural Review,
July 1936

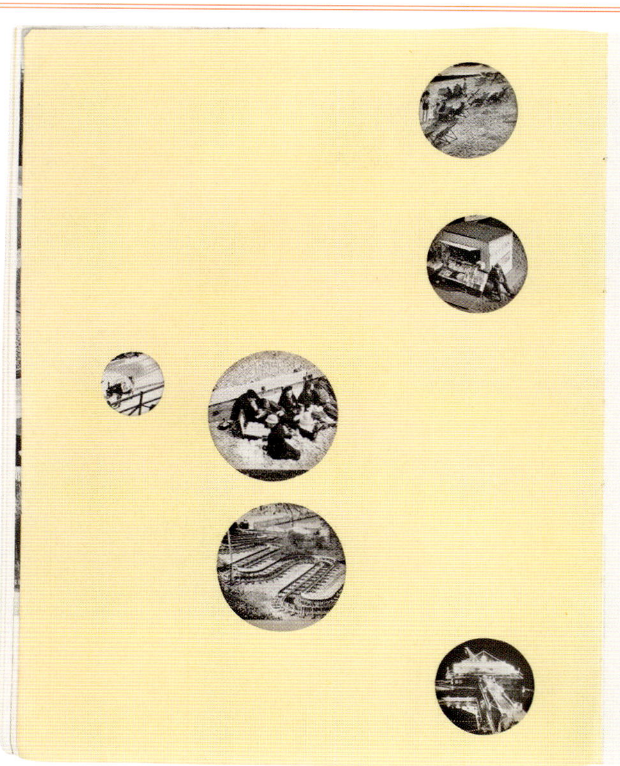

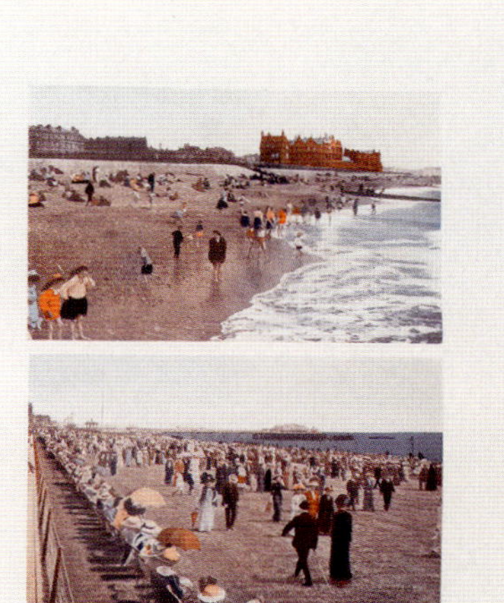

bore ample witness to His Majesty's long association with the quarter-deck. He was particularly partial to piers and when at Brighton was frequently to be seen on the celebrated Chain Pier.

By the time that that amiable and eccentric monarch had left his throne for realms where, as we are told, there will be no more sea there will presumably be no more piers, every summer saw the coasts of Great Britain invaded by a steadily increasing army of the Middle Classes. The seaside's proudest era had begun.

The Victorians have suffered as no other generation has suffered from the hasty generalizations of latter day critics; they are accused and praised, applauded and condemned en masse, as though they were as completely undifferentiated as a flock of sheep; but if there is one characteristic more generally applicable than another, it is that as a class they knew what they wanted with a terrifying certainty that can only evoke the admiration of their descendants. What they wanted at the seaside were plenty of facilities for healthful relaxation attended by all those comforts to which they were accustomed at home. To satisfy these demands the seaside resort as we know it today came into being. Rows of comfortable lodging-houses sprang up, equipped with that great architectural discovery of the period, the bow-window, which enabled the meticulous visitor constantly to reassure himself as to the actual and immediate presence of the ocean; that admirable invention the bathing machine (why, oh why, did we ever forsake it for that wretched substitute the stationary hut?) was at hand to insure that his womenfolk should be able to enjoy the healthy pastime of sea bathing, with the requisite modicum of decent privacy; and his spiritual wants, in all their fascinating variety, were catered for by innumerable churches of all denominations and in every known style of ecclesiastical

11

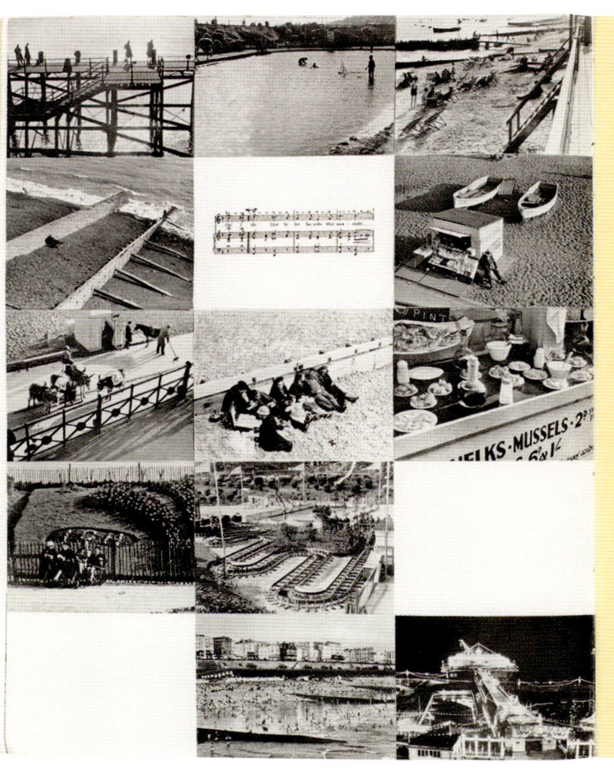

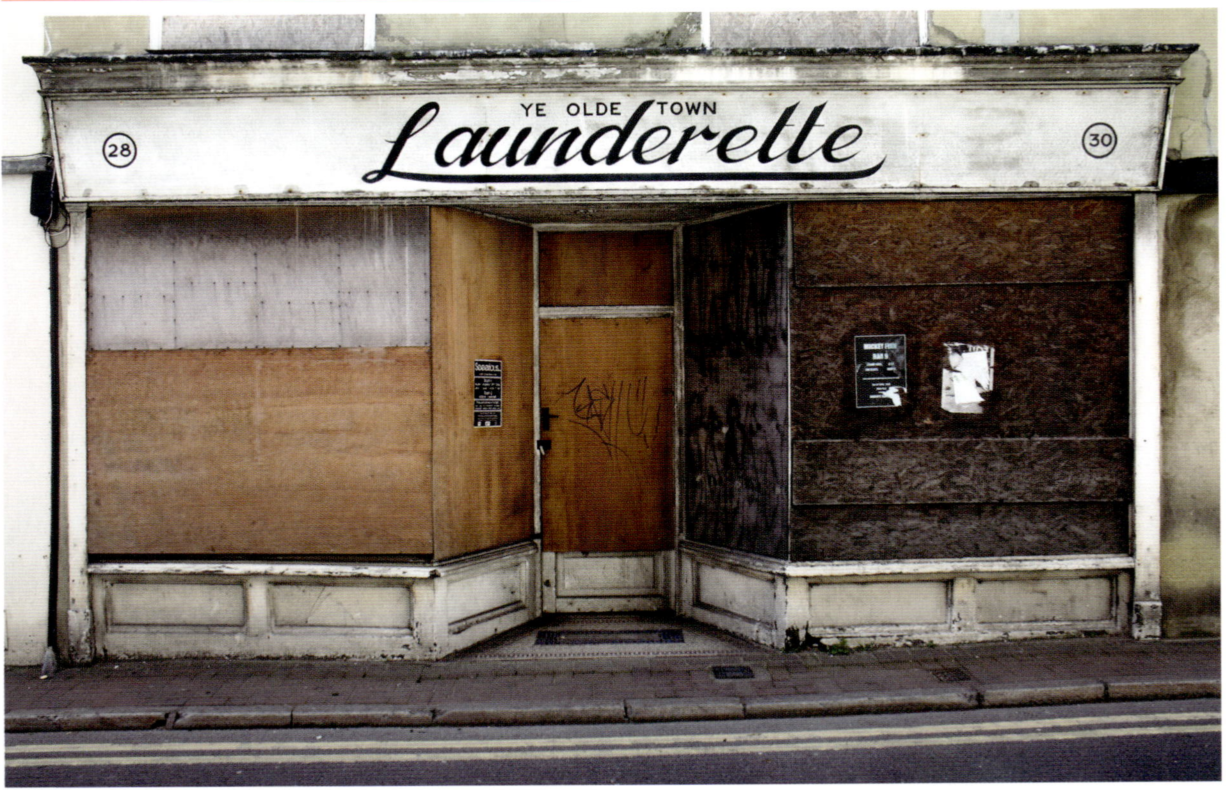

HANNAH BLACKMORE
*Vacant, Launderette,
King Street, Margate,*
2011

overwhelmed by carpeting and civic signage – photography preserved its past. As a built structure, the British seaside is perplexing – elegant modernism stands beside the higgledy-piggledy of seasonal stalls and entertainments, while suburban stretches turn their backs to the sea.

But there are, of course, many other ways of looking at our coast, and at the phenomenon of the seaside. It has become a setting for a bleak description of national life and identity. In 1998 young British novelist Matt Thorne published *Tourist*, a novel about sex, drugs and dissoluteness in Weston-super-Mare. Following on from films such as *Wish You Were Here*, David Leland's 1987 tale of frustrated youth and predatory sexuality, *Tourist* perpetuated and expanded upon the notion of the seaside as a place of last resort, a stumbling block to real life. Thorne's is one of many kinds of views of the British seaside, and perhaps one of the most persuasive. We will see echoes of it in Stuart Griffiths's remarkable documenting of the rave scene in nineties Brighton. In the English seaside, we may perceive glorious failure, rackety decay, a playground for our thoughts and, as seen in many contemporary television crime dramas, a site for misdemeanour. In his 2010 book *Wish You Were Here: England on Sea*, Travis Elborough, who grew up in the retiree town of Worthing, noted:

… it was to spend formative years at what felt like the wrong end of the line: biologically, chronologically and geographically.

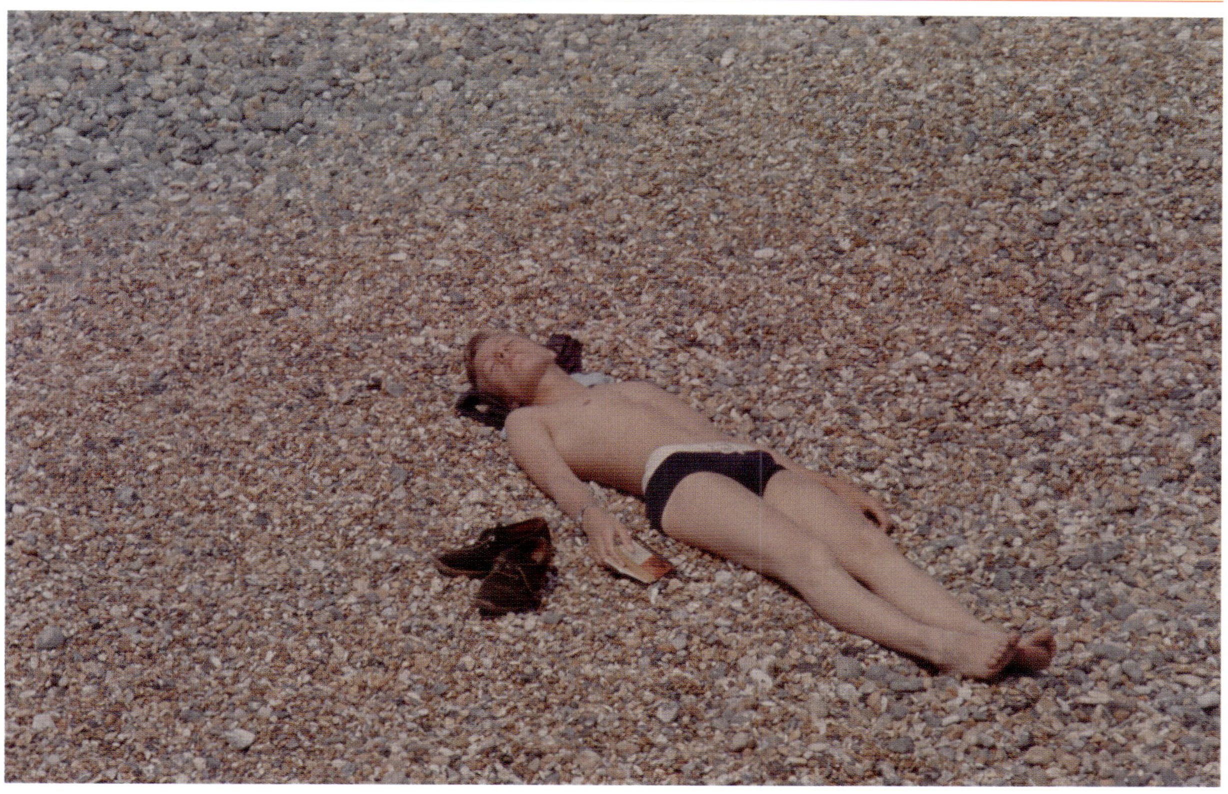

ABOVE

ERIC PATTERSON
Eastbourne,
Summer 1969

FOLLOWING PAGES

JULIA HORBASCHK
Worthing Palms,
July 2017, from the series
Time for Trees

Any town where the most urgent appointment of any week for the bulk of its inhabitants is with a post office counter is bound to suffer from a degree of lethargy. And as a child, inactivity, immobility, is just much more unbearable. Rather like being trapped on a planet with a different gravitational field, every action was so heavily weighted against you.[1]

Away from this vision, attractive as it is, of the British seaside as a place of phantasmagoria and broken dreams, we find the work of photographers whose delight in working at the seaside, and whose belief in it, are clear. Photographer Henry Iddon grew up in Blackpool and makes photographs that explore its idiosyncrasies – a hotel left intact down to the folded napkins on the breakfast table by a departing owner (pp.153–4) – while Hannah Blackmore, brought up in Ramsgate, has made a loving, if mournful, document about disused shops on the Kent coast (opposite). Apart from the photo reporters who flocked to the coast from the 1940s to the 1960s, most of the photographers in this book have a personal tie to the place they photograph. Iain McKell honed his skills working as a seaside photographer in his hometown Weymouth in the 1970s, as shown in this chapter's portfolio section (pp.16–23). Some, like Barry Lewis, Dafydd Jones and Daniel Meadows, made their own work while employed by Butlin's holiday camps, while Chinese–British photographer Grace Lau used photography

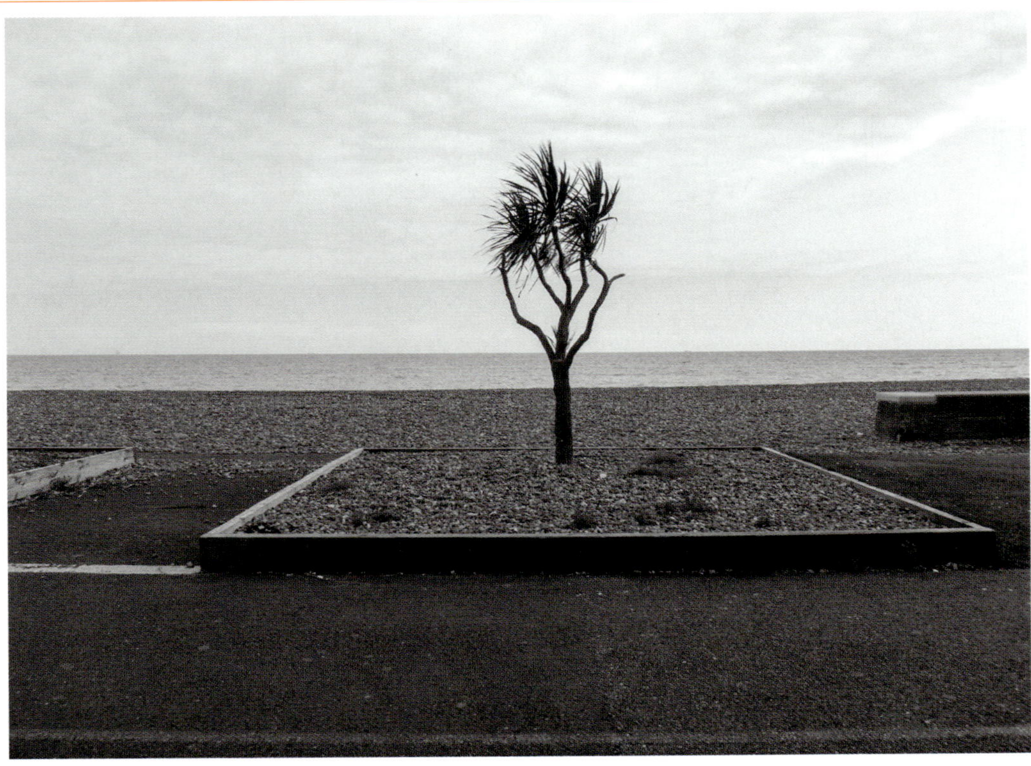

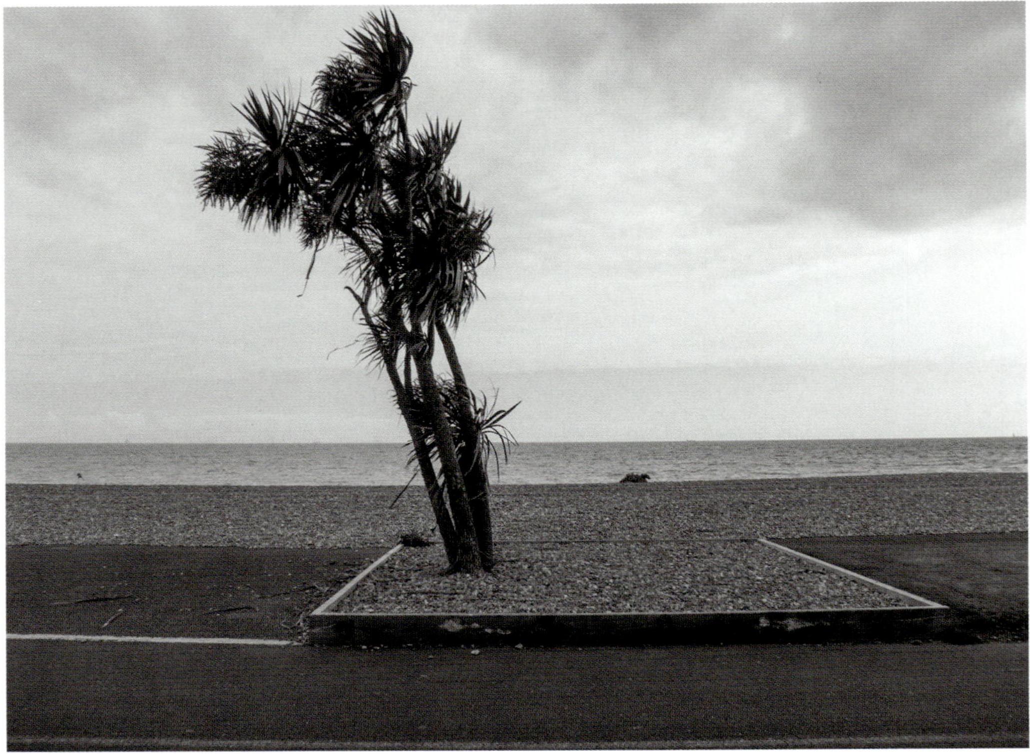

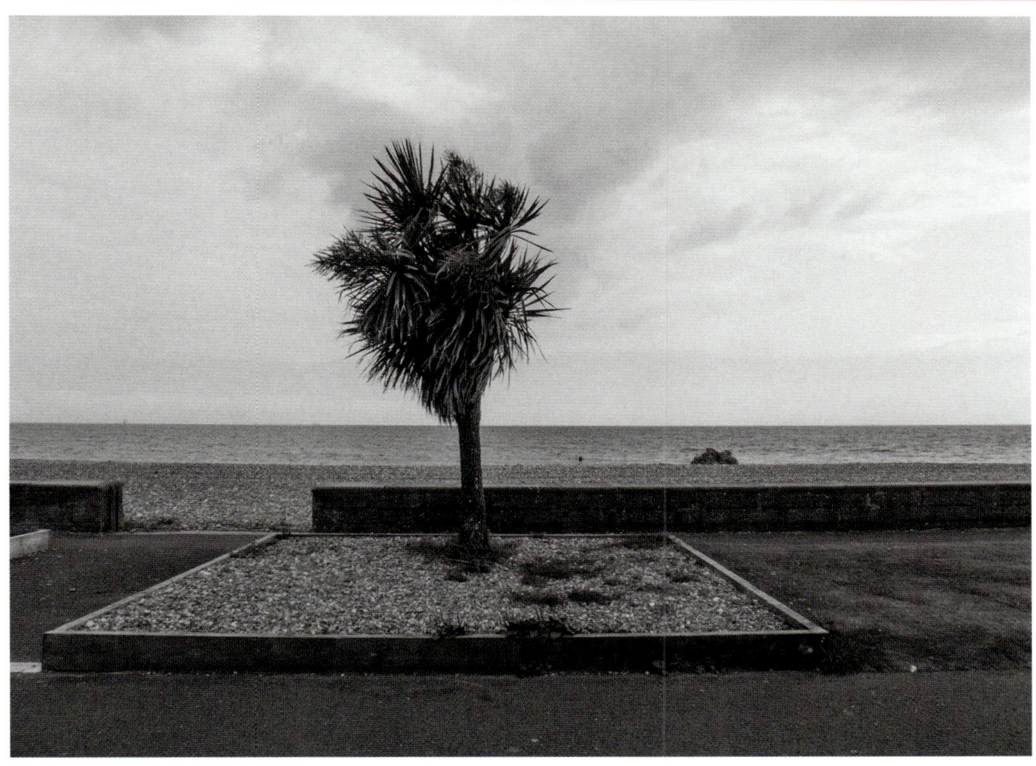

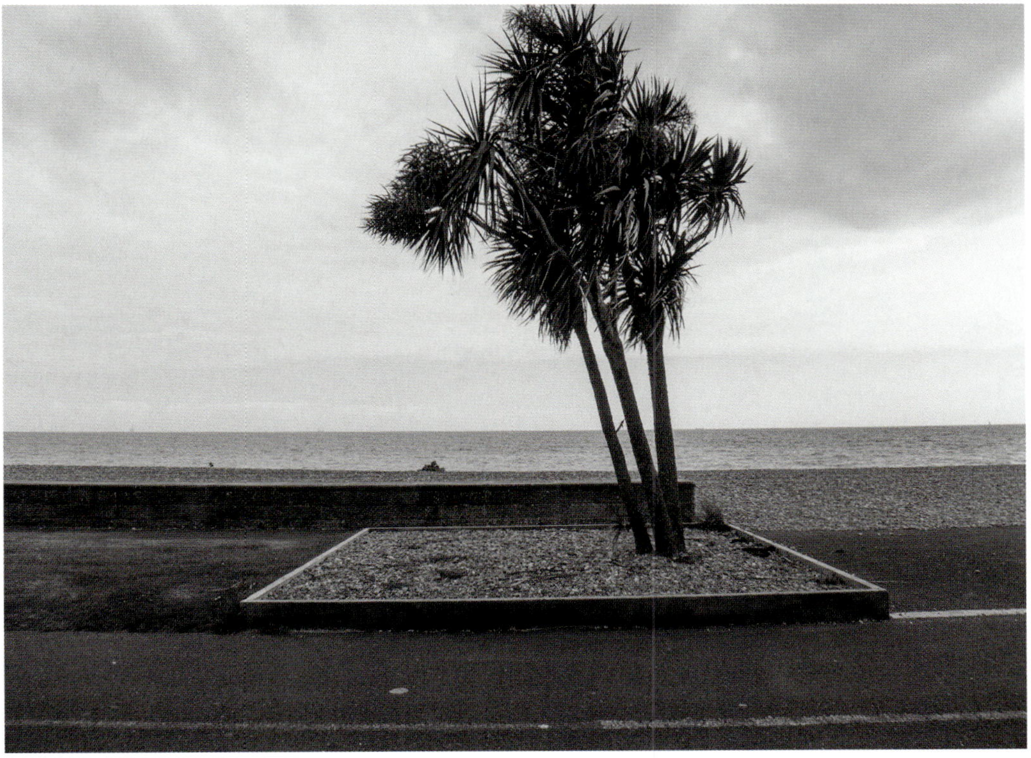

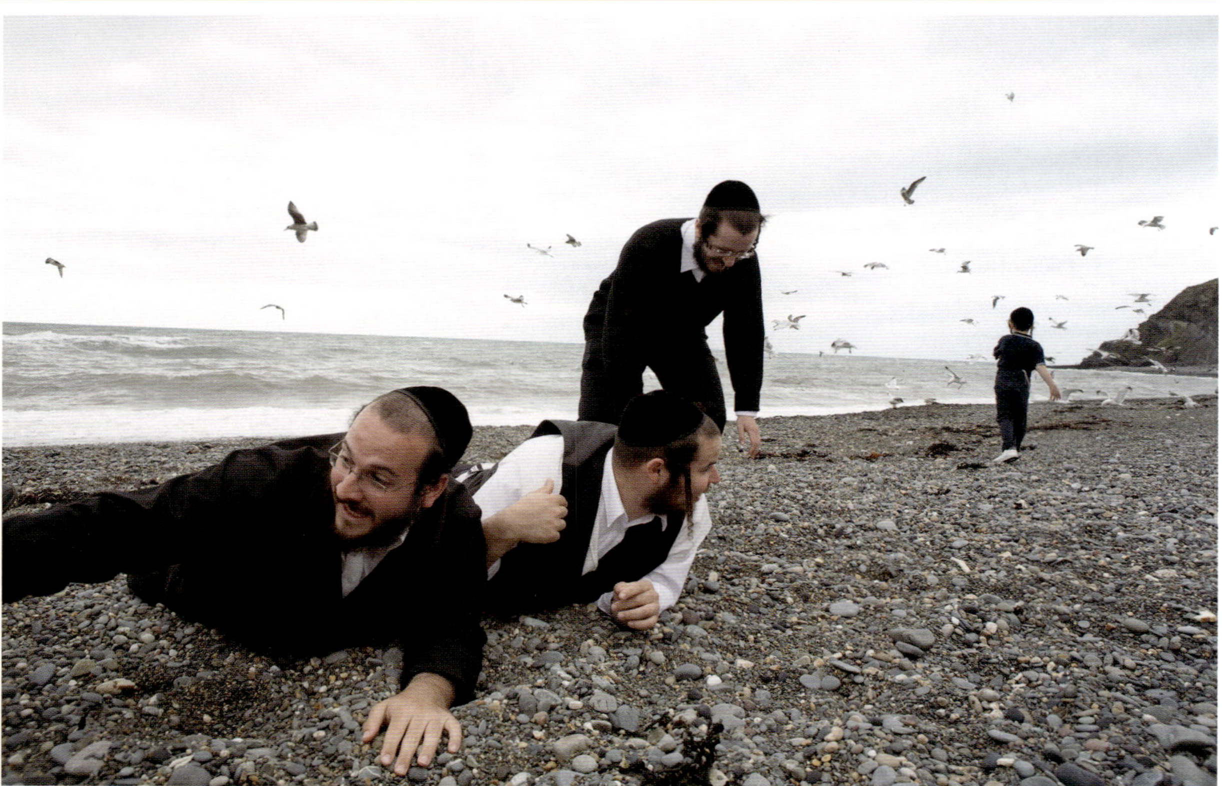

to map a new place and to carve out an identity within it (pp.172–5). For others, the comedy of the seaside is presented via photography – the abandonment of social mores as men undress for the knobbly knees completion, the terrible comedy of the seaside stag night.

We have a multitude of different visions of the seaside – many conjured up by photographs. Some of these are intended to persuade us to visit, trading carefully edited views of what we will find when we arrive. Others are driven by the need to make news, and show us the seaside as an economic or social phenomenon – in the process either of declining or regenerating. Yet more are simply personal, marking the synergy of family or friendship. For many, the seaside has been a haven and a place of light and seclusion. Composer Benjamin Britten and tenor Peter Pears created a private place by the sea that they lovingly documented, while Eric Patterson's slides, discovered by Jess Kohl in a vacated London flat in Canonbury, gaze at young men photographed at a distance (p.11). Patterson's images are infused with longing as bodies are revealed and performed in the open air. Kohl remarked:

> These beautiful images range from holiday photos, to family photos, to hardcore gay erotica. One thing that is clear from the slides is that Eric was a promiscuous man in an age where being queer was totally unaccepted. His appreciation for the male form runs throughout his photos.

CHLOE DEWE MATHEWS
Hasidic Holiday: the Annual Trip to Aberystwyth, 2008

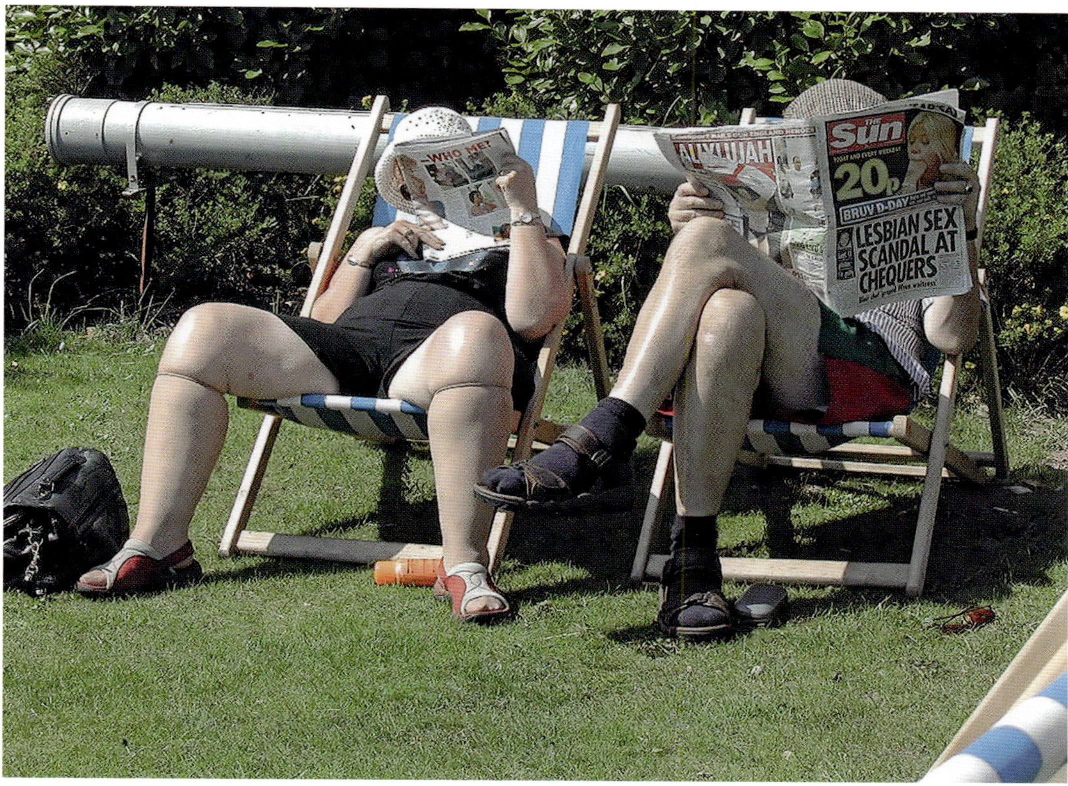

THE CARAVAN GALLERY
Lesbian Sex Scandal,
Skegness, 2002

Photo reporters and groups of critical documentarists have also been attracted to the seaside because this public parade provides its myriad photo opportunities, all set against a background of seafront shabbiness that shows up so well in photographs. Yet within a framework of critical documentary, Chloe Dewe Mathews's finely crafted photographs not only bring us information, but convey the energies and joys of community gatherings. In her photographs of Orthodox Jews holidaying in Aberystwyth, we see the seaside as a canvas choreographed with action and annual rituals played out (opposite).

In the past, the photographic seaside postcard was a way of signaling that we were really there. The Caravan Gallery maps Britain through picture postcards, exposing the grime and glee of the British seaside as it refuses to conform. Out of season, the seaside is gaunt and a little sad; at peak time it is crowded and raucous.

For photographers, dereliction and decline have always been attractive. A boarded-up shop, as can be seen in Blackmore's series on Ramsgate and Margate (p.10), is more interesting in surface and texture than a thriving one. Likewise, Julia Horbaschk's wind-battered palms on the Worthing seafront (pp.12–13) say much about the civicness of the seaside, as planting battles against the salt-laden winds. Photographers' visions are necessarily partial ones – they follow their noses, sniff out the strange and the unusual, the comic and the melancholy. They do not necessarily picture things the way that they are. [VW & KS]

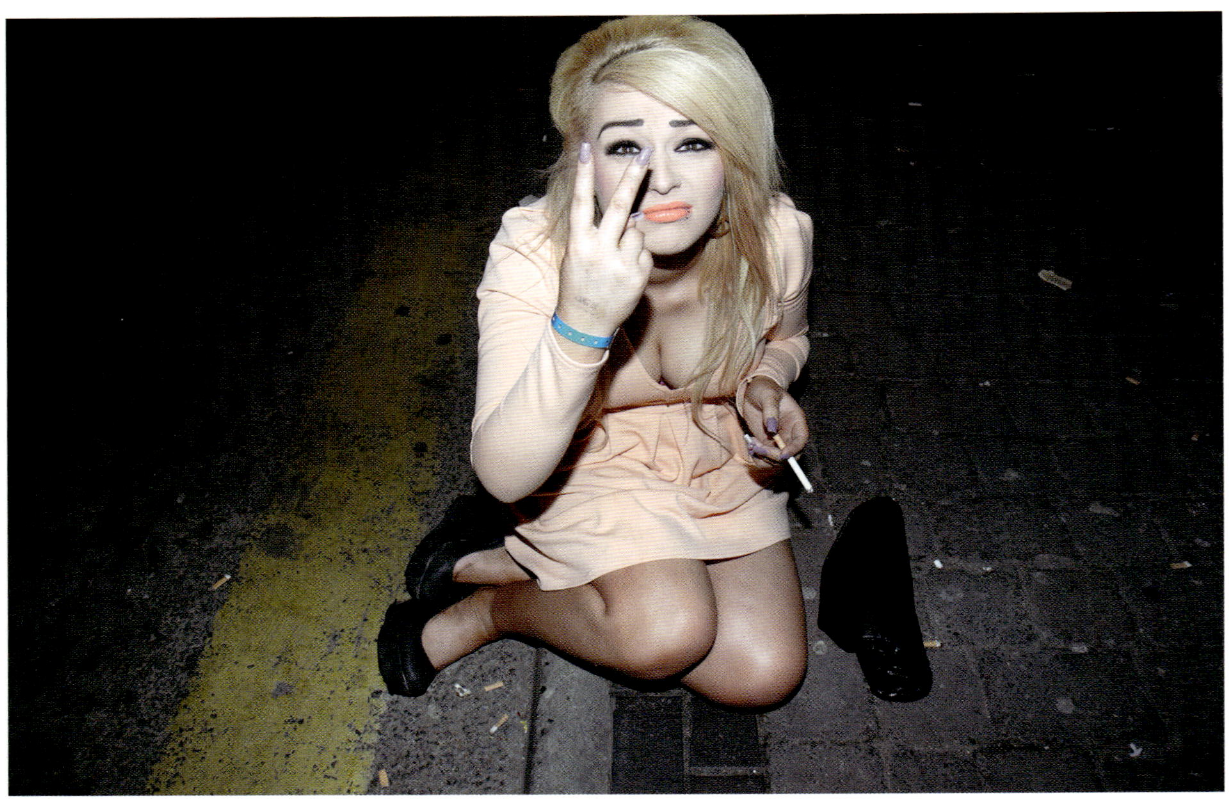

In the Gutter, Blackpool, 2014

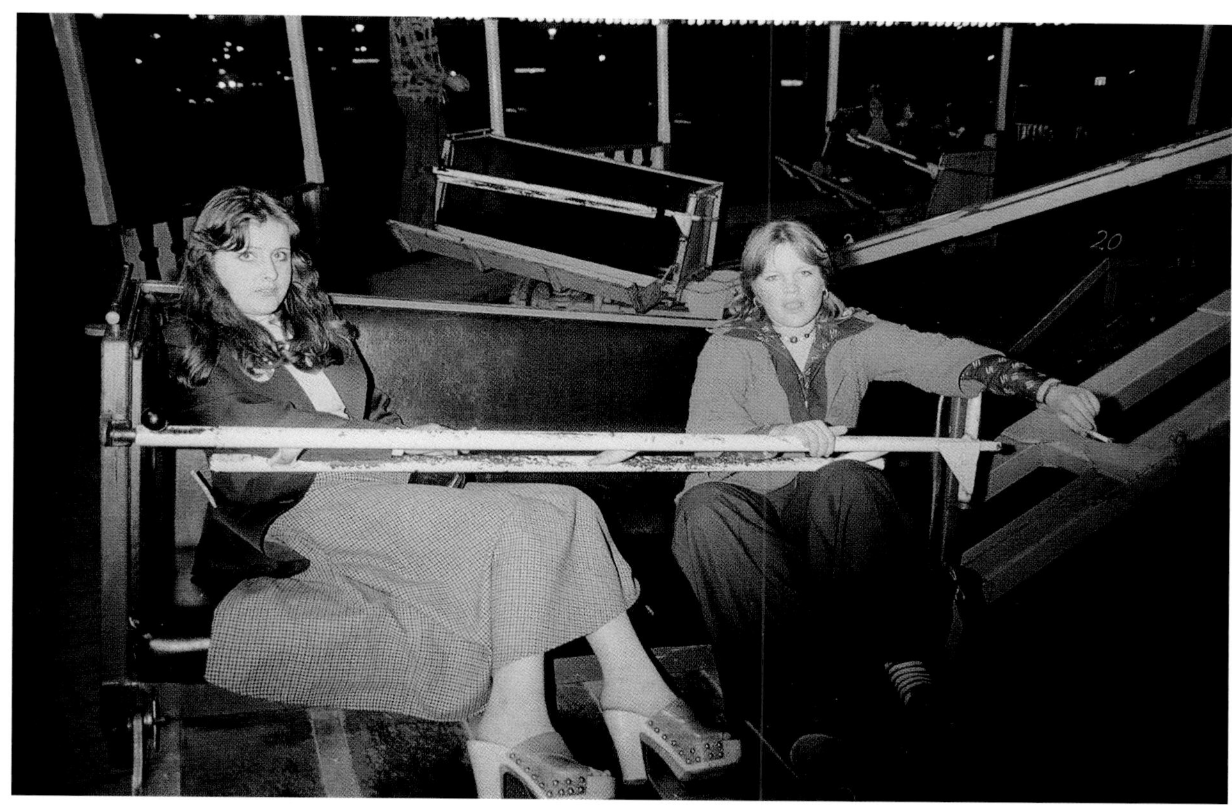

Preston Fair, Weymouth, 1976

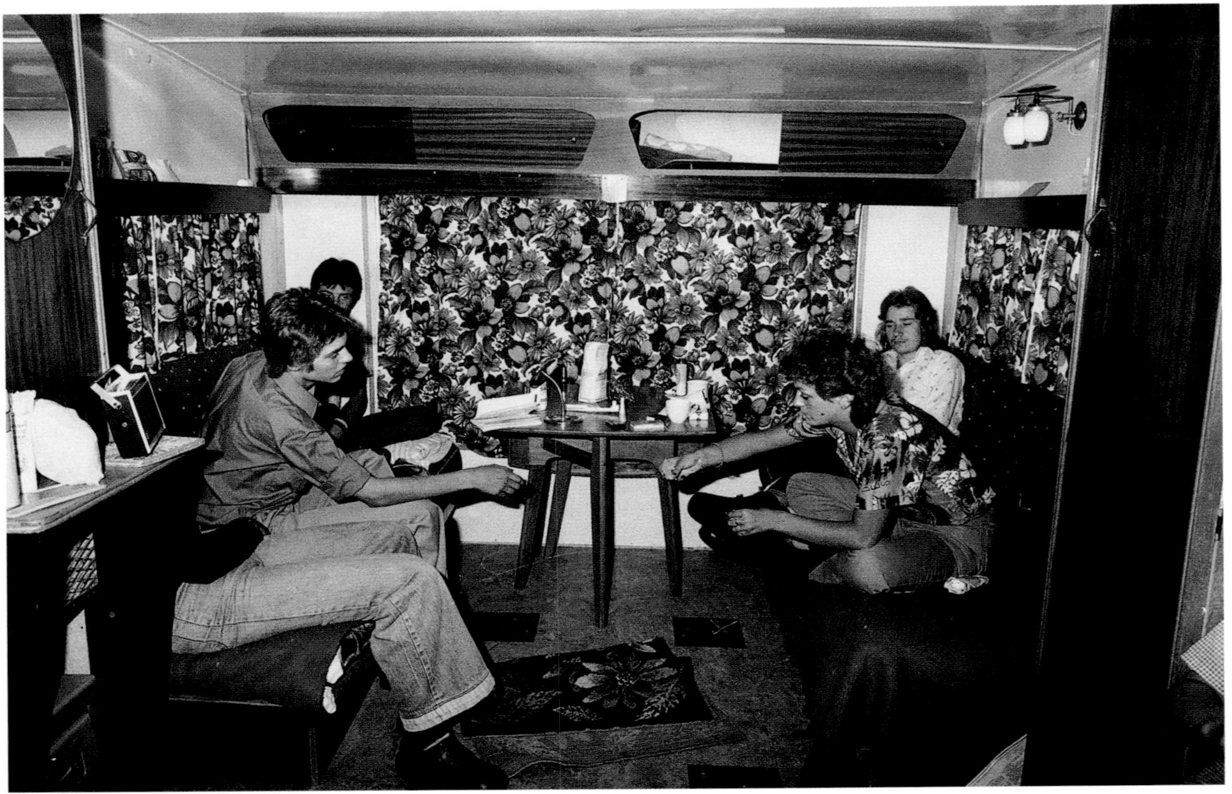

Sea View Caravan Park, Weymouth, 1976

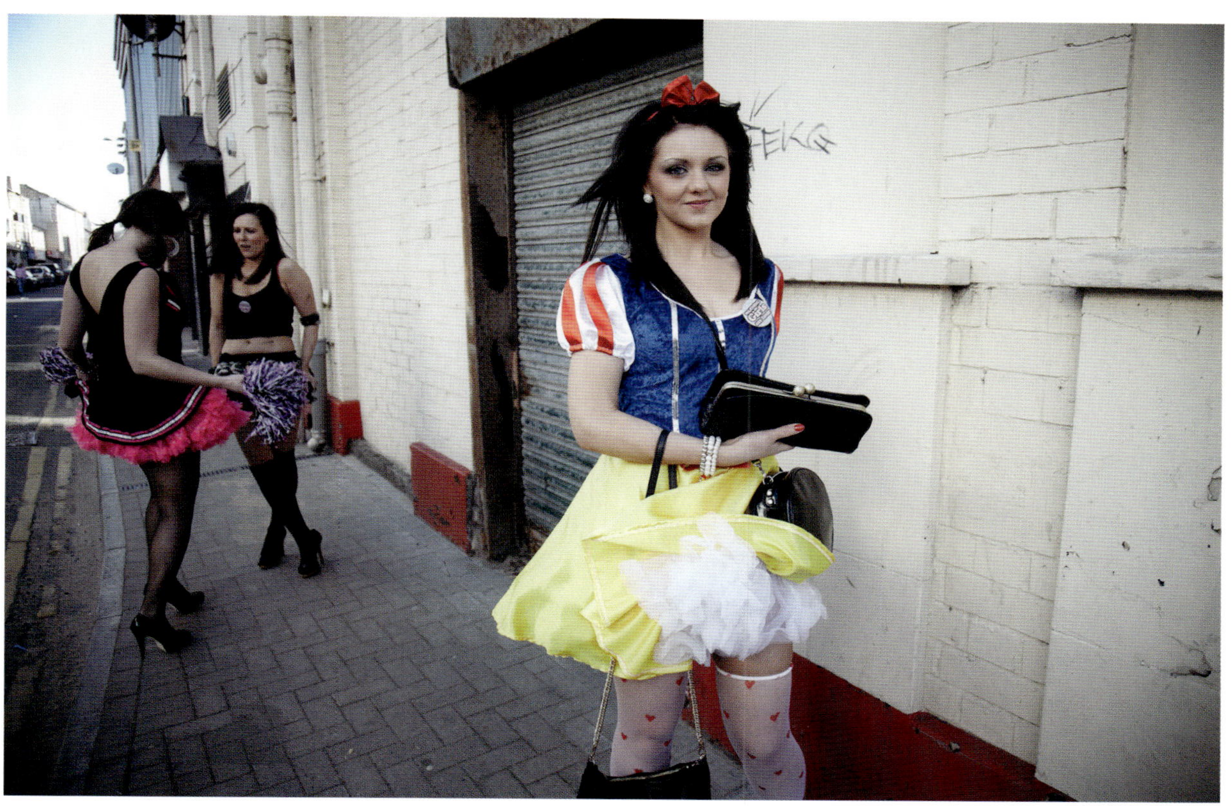

Snow White, Blackpool, 2013

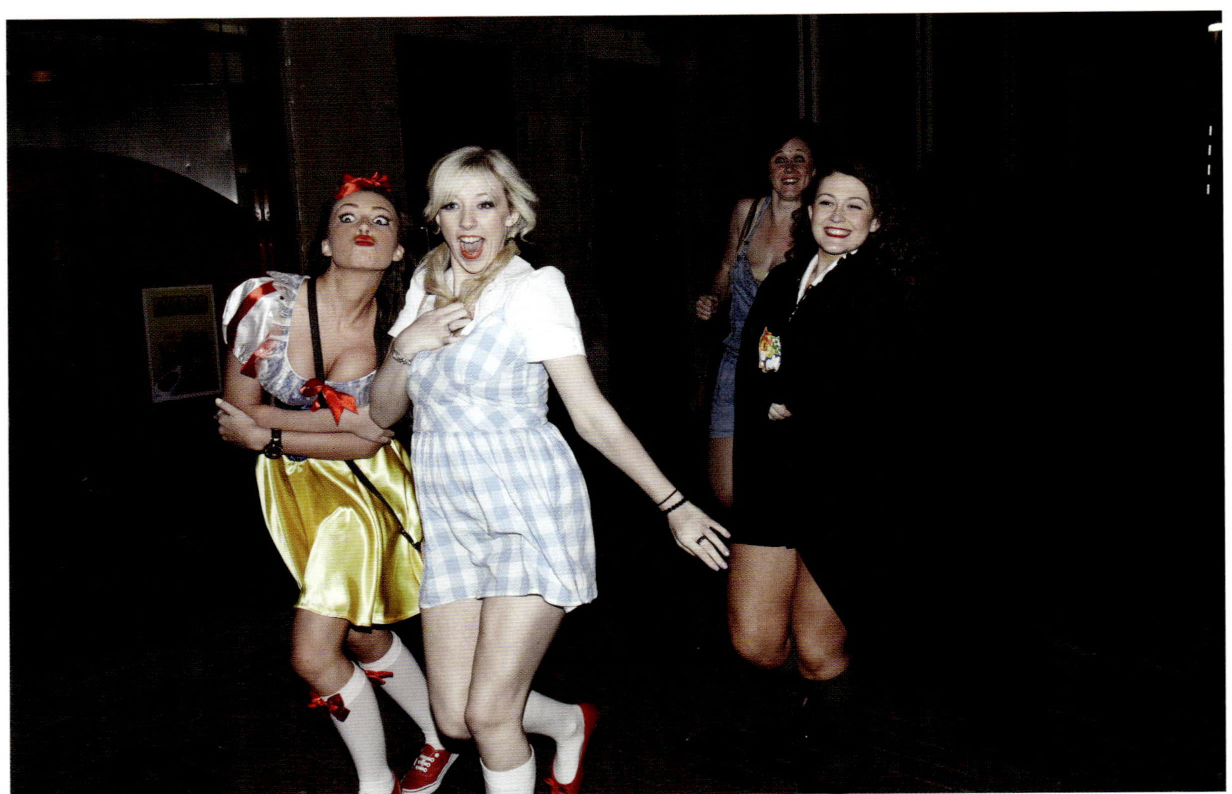

Women Running, Blackpool, 2013

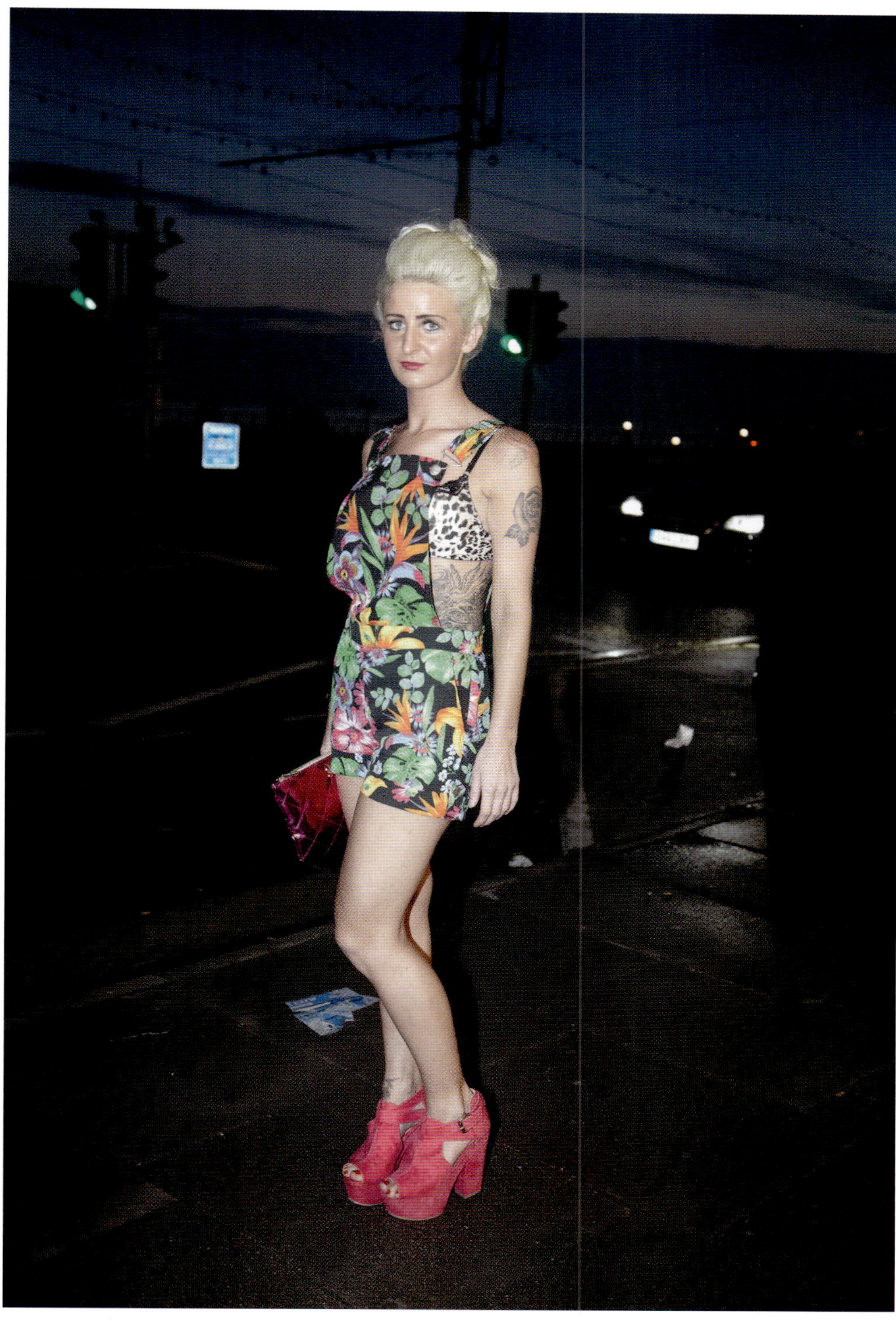

Woman at 'Twilight 1', Blackpool, 2015

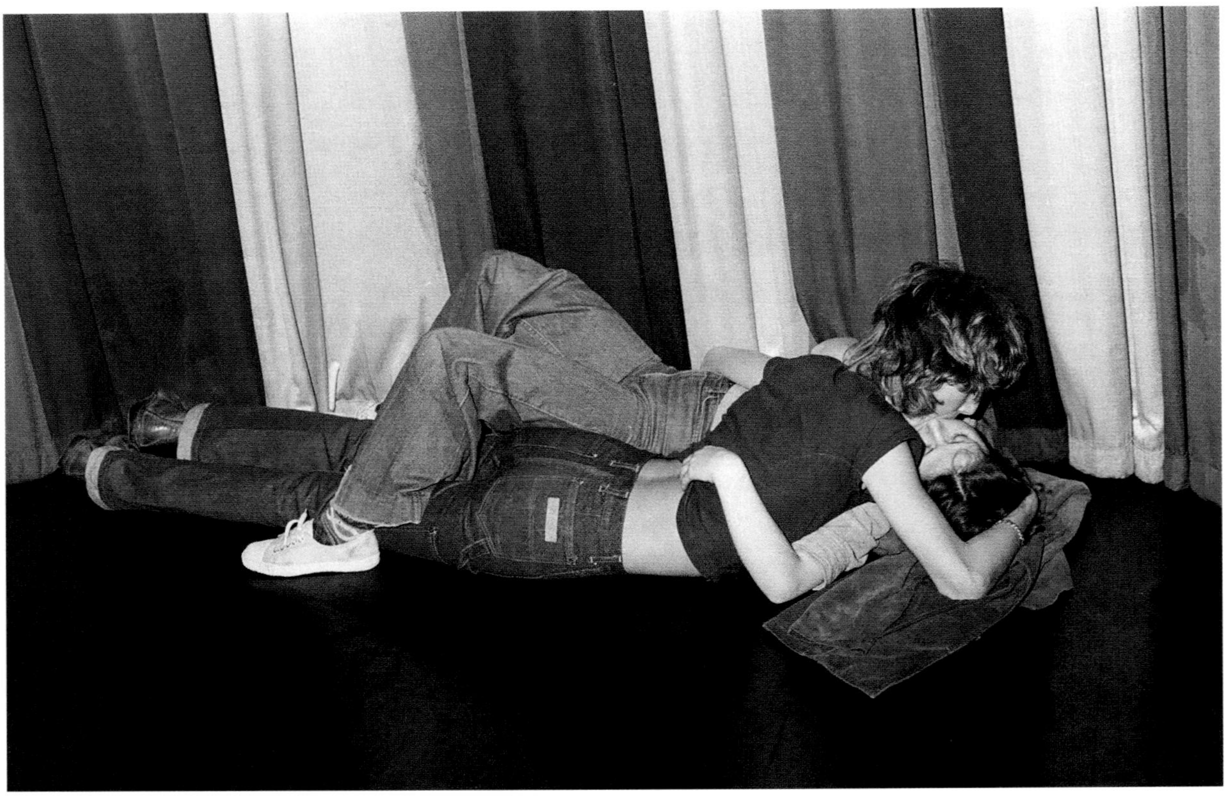

The Pavilion Disco, 1976

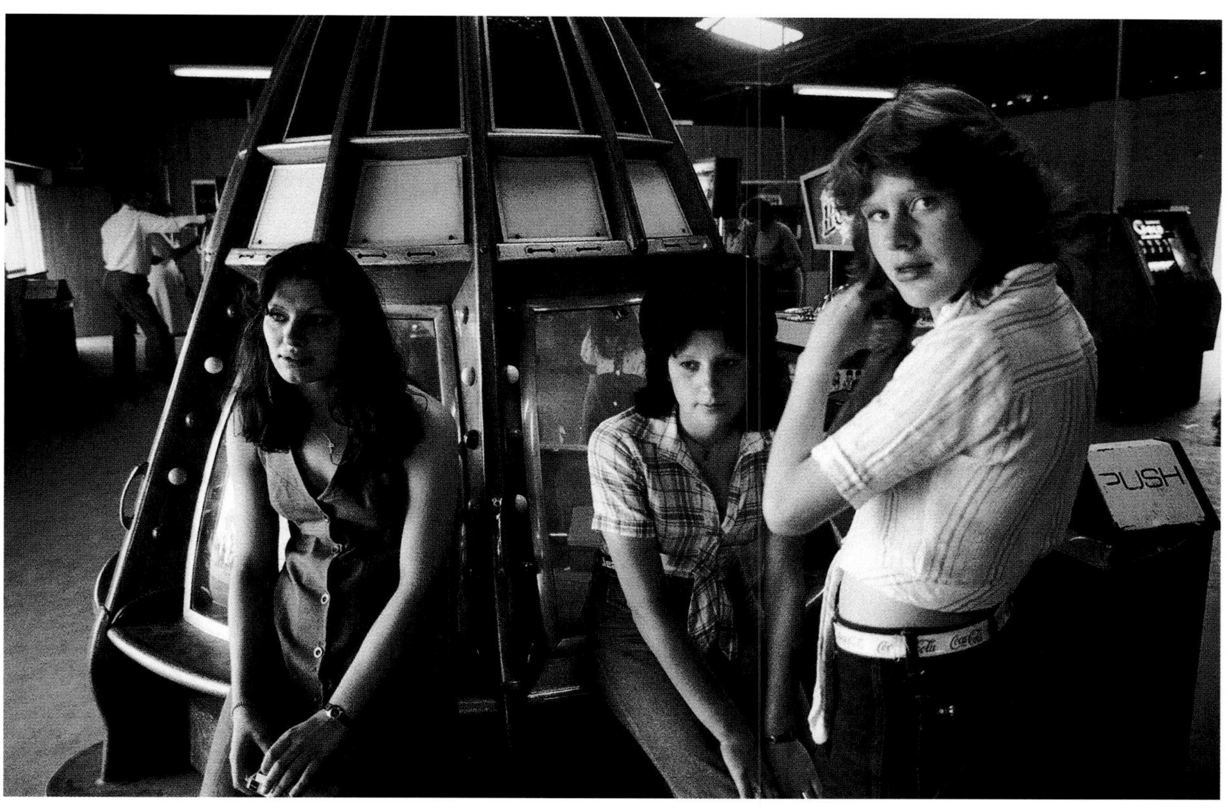

Three Girls on Holiday, Bowles Cove, Weymouth, 1976

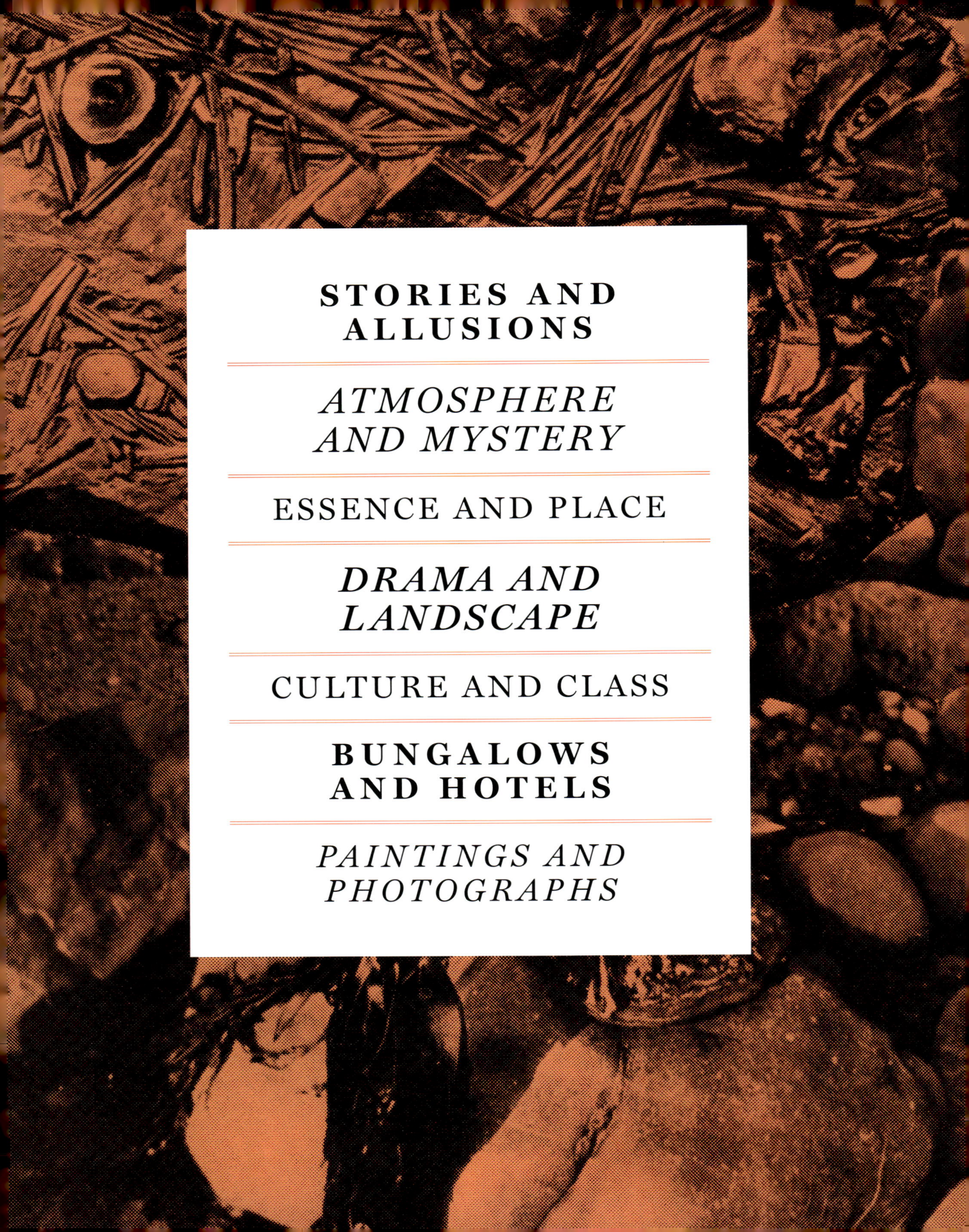

SHELL STORIES

EDITING THE SEASIDE FROM
THE THIRTIES TO THE EIGHTIES

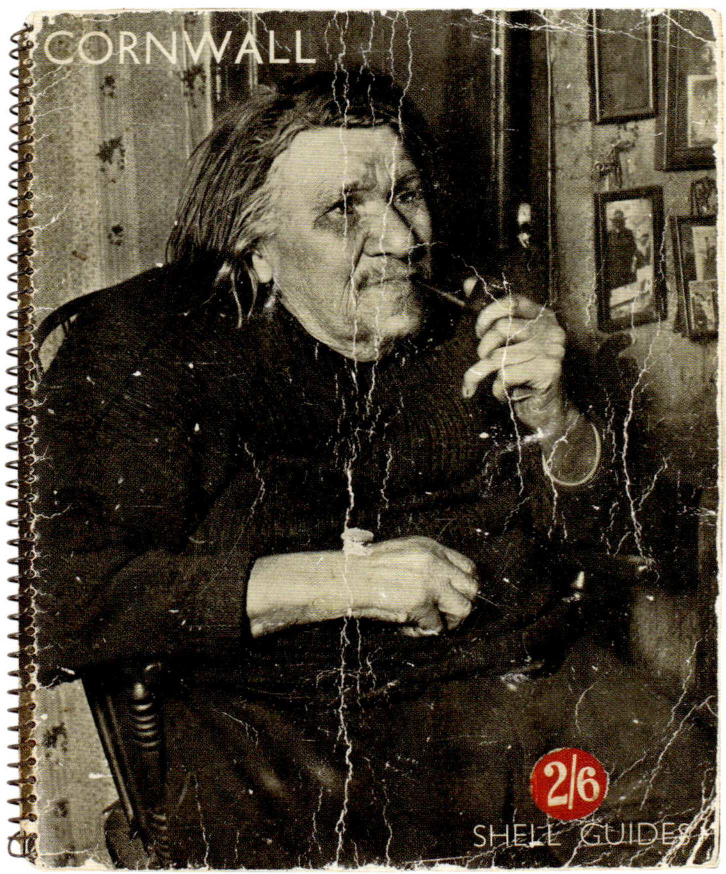

MAURICE BECK
Cornwall: A Shell Guide,
1934

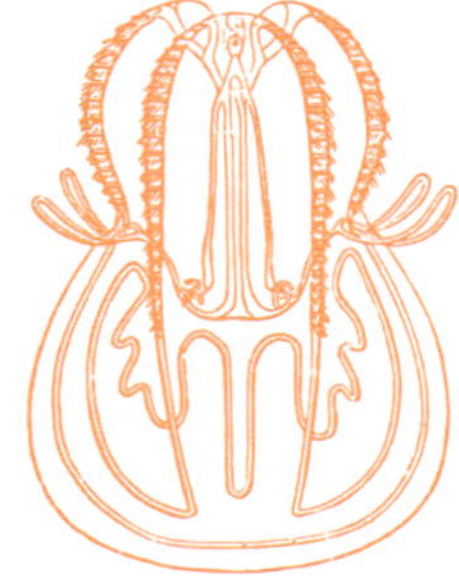

sixty-three pages of photography, design, diagrams and writing spirally bound. The cover was bold and modern: a full-bleed portrait of a fisherman by *Vogue* photographer Maurice Beck (who was the principal photographer for the early guides) and a sans serif typeface. *Cornwall* is a remarkable publication in terms of photography and design. From the fisherman on the cover (left) to Beck's modernist still life of shell and sand, through to the eccentricity of the double-page spread 'the road to Cornwall' and Beck's two double-page photographs of a Cornish churchyard and a wrecked fishing boat, the Cornish seaside is presented as a dramatic and enticing visual spectacle (opposite). In *Cornwall*, Betjeman and Beck created a formula that would endure, and a vision of the coast that remains at the centre of the national imagination. As lecturer David Heathcote[1] has noted:

> the strength of the guide [Cornwall] lies in its serendipitous view and fascination with the local rather than well-established 'sights'. There is, for instance, a full-page image of a back alley in Polperro [opposite, below] that is purely about the picturesqueness of the juxtaposition of stone walls.[2]

Beck's photographs were as modern as the guidebook formula would allow. But the uncompromising front cover and the meticulously realized endpapers, showing a mussel shell on a wave-furrowed beach (opposite, top), demonstrate that in picturing a county (which, by the late 1940s, had become one of England's most popular destinations for the independent, motorized tourist) photographers could be quite free to range around genres, from portraiture to close-up abstraction, from picturesque street scenes to photographs of industry. By the time he came to contribute to the guides, Beck was already a well-known photographer. In 1925 he was head of *Vogue*'s studios in London with fellow photographer Helen MacGregor. Beck and MacGregor's modernist credentials had been established in the mid-1920s, when they

In the early 1930s, poet John Betjeman, then assistant editor of the *Architectural Review*, was invited to devise and edit a new kind of guidebook for the aspirant, independently minded, car-owning middle classes. Betjeman and Jack Beddington, Shell's ambitious and innovative head of publicity, agreed on a new format, in which photographs would be at the core: telling stories, making allusions, creating atmosphere and mysteries. The British seaside counties were a prime focus – Cornwall in 1934, Devon in 1935 and Dorset in 1936.

The Shell Guides were born out of an appreciation of the fragile architectural and environmental fabric of the British Isles, and Betjeman's fear of despoliation and destruction as times changed and society modernized. For his first guide, published in 1934, Betjeman chose Cornwall, and produced

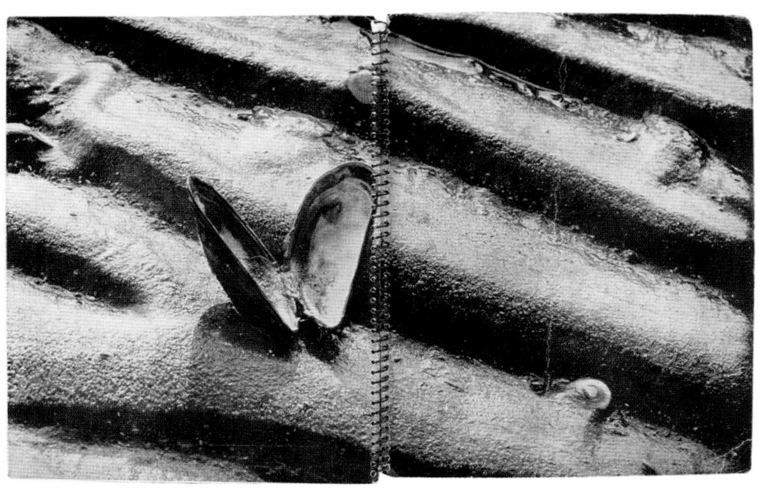

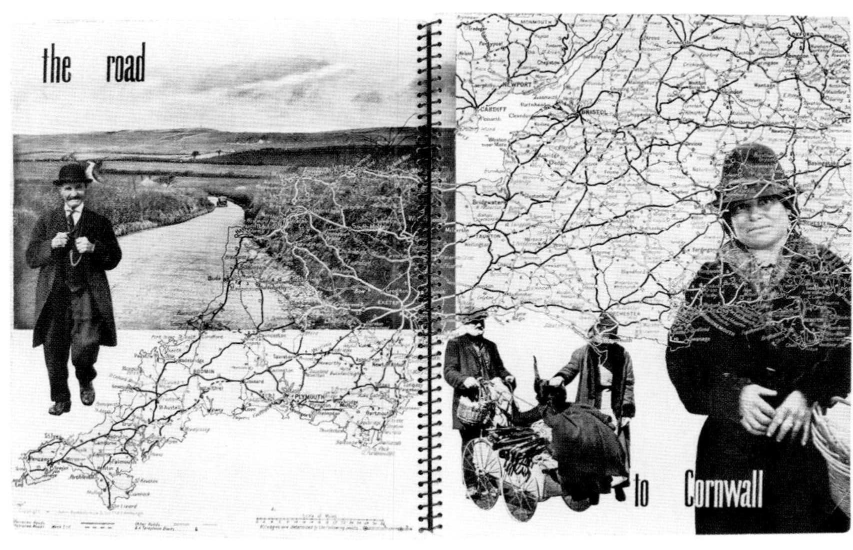

ABOVE, RIGHT AND BELOW

**PHOTOGRAPHER UNKNOWN,
POSSIBLY MAURICE BECK**
Cornwall: A Shell Guide, 1934

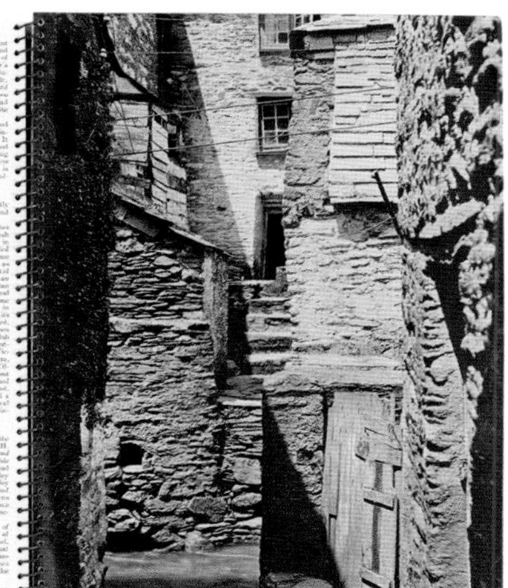

photographed avant-garde luminaries – the writer Virginia Woolf in 1924, photographer Cecil Beaton and socialite Stephen Tennant in 1927 and the dancer Laurie Devine in 1928. Beck had also worked with London Transport on a series of startlingly modern instructional posters in the early 1930s and had contributed photographs to Shell-Mex and BP's publication *Lubrication*. This adopted the spiral bindings that so distinguished the early Shell Guides and suggested informality, ease of opening and modernity.

Betjeman was a discerning commissioner of photographers and artists, seeing them as central to the guide, and soon began to employ them as editors. Beginning with Beck (who worked on *Cornwall*, 1934, and *Devon*, 1936), he also employed Edwin Smith and *Country Life* photographer A. F. Kersting in these early editions. In 1936 Paul Nash's *Dorset* appeared, with photographs by Nash, Beck and Edwin Smith. These early guides proposed that photography was an expression of the imaginary – and could convey the essence of place and the drama of landscape. They insisted that photography could narrate and express rather than illustrate. Released from the notion of 'the view', photography became modern, bold, dynamic and purposeful.

Significant as Nash and Beck were to the development of the new tourist vision of England, by far the most important photographer and editor for the Shell Guides was the artist John Piper. In 1937 John and Myfanwy Piper accompanied Betjeman on a trip around Devon and Cornwall, mapping out the work they might do for the guides, and convincing Betjeman that they were kindred spirits.[3] Piper was already a skilled photographer when he joined the guides. He admired Bill Brandt and Nash, and as writer David Fraser Jenkins remarked:

The photographs of Piper and Brandt share a dramatic chiaroscuro, sometimes to the extent of blackening out most of the image. Brandt's distortion of perspective is more extreme (and would not have been appropriate for the Shell Guides) but both of them often brought up the foreground close to the lens ... to give a confusing base to the composition ...[4]

Piper had taken up photography as a teenager, beginning with a No.2 Brownie. He later bought a Zeiss IKON IDEAL camera, a small top-of-the-amateur-range bellows camera that used 9 × 12 cm plates,[5] which he later had converted so that he could use film packs.[6] Piper was aware of advances in the technology of photography, changing from Kodak film to the Italian company Ferrania, which produced larger film packs and was also the favourite film manufacturer for the Italian cinema industry.[7]

A prolific and multi-skilled artist, Piper produced paintings, drawings, stained glass, ceramics and photographs. In his lifetime, he made thousands of images, both for the Shell Guides and as research for artworks. In the 1960s, when Piper became editor of the Shell Guides, he was joined by his son Edward, who contributed many photographs. Together, their photographic vision of the British counties is probably the most pervasive and substantial of the post-war years, dwarfing the output of their photographic contemporaries. The Pipers' view of the British seaside remains in the national consciousness and their photographs are remarkable, deep and dark, challenging seaside cliché. As art historian Frances Spalding noted:

What began as one of the pleasures of his childhood became in adulthood a passion. And there were many aspects of the sea that he loved: remote and empty beaches; rocky coastlines; the gaiety of coastal buildings; the romance of lighthouses; ... fisherman's huts and signal masts; and the elegant sweep of the grander seaside resorts such as Brighton and Scarborough.[8]

Piper was particularly engaged by the remote seascapes that he found in his trips around the north of England, including

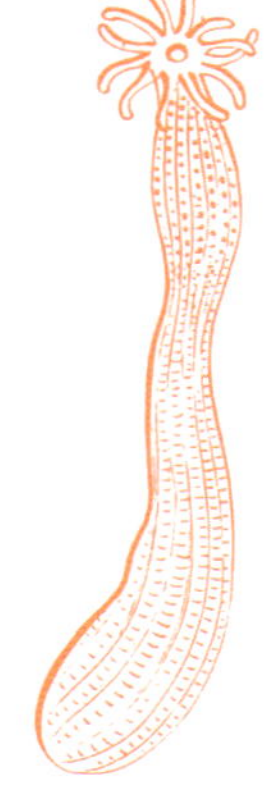

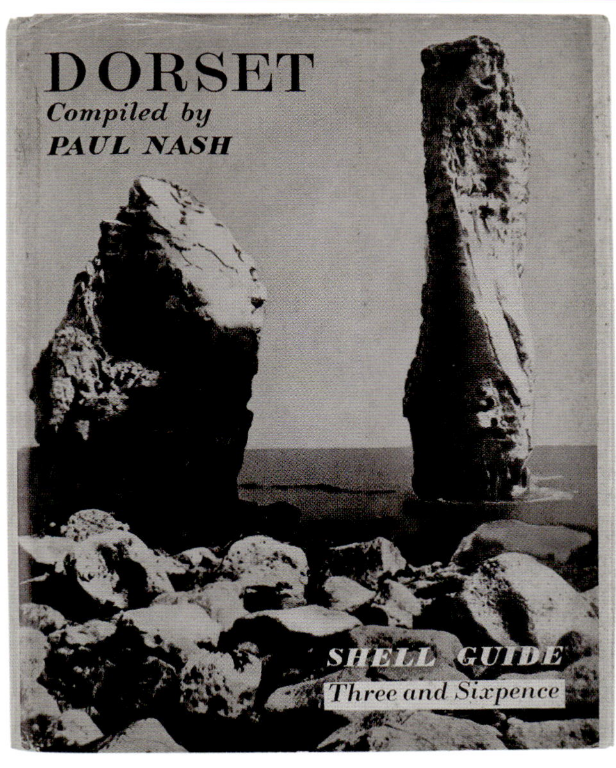

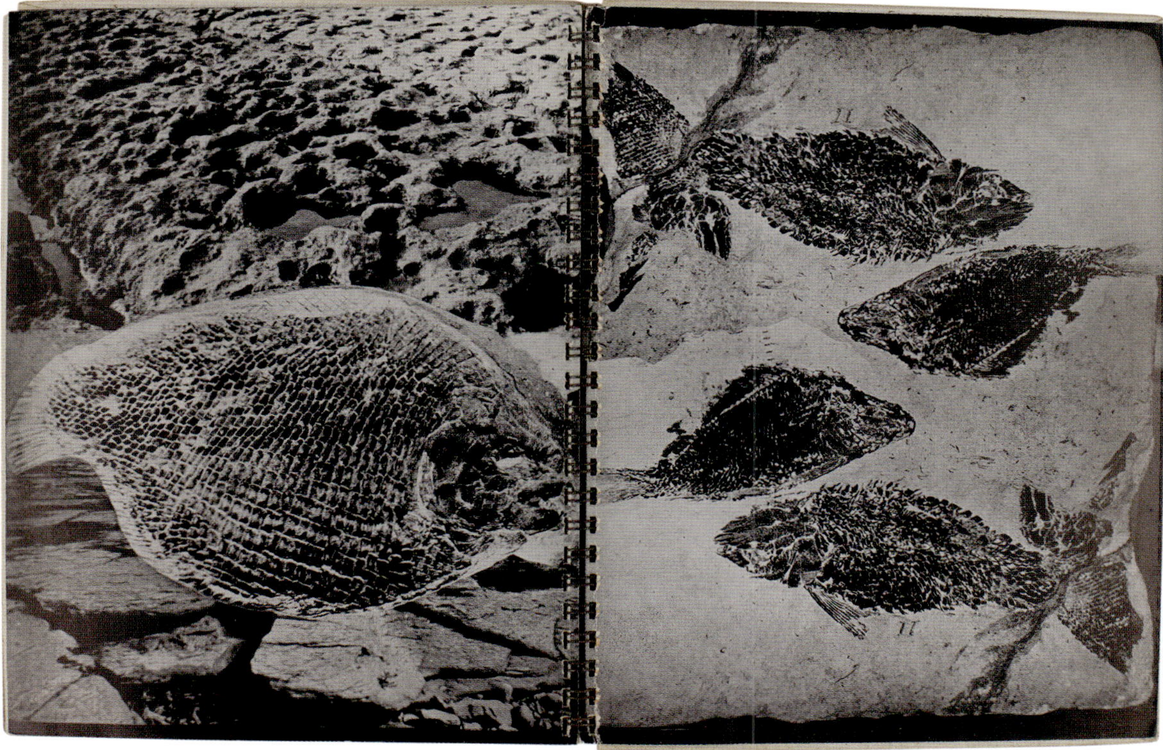

Spurn Point in East Yorkshire, where he made a series of photographs. Piper's essay 'The Nautical Style' first appeared in the *Architectural Review* in January 1938 and was republished in an anthology of Piper's writings in 1948:

> There is a lively sense of style about sea – coast building in England with its maritime pride and efficiency. The tarred look-out tower that rises above the vegetable garden wall at a seaside hotel, the pole with its black cones hoisted halfway along the jetty or beside the harbour master's office, the old lighthouse on the edge of the cliff, the new lighthouse on the rising ground behind – all these have something about their design and construction.[9]

For many British artists and writers, the seaside resort became a place of tension, where cultures and class clash. The guides encouraged people to travel to the seaside by car, but it was these very same people who, enthused by the well-written prose and exciting photographs, would build bungalows, create a need for new hotels and create traffic jams. From the mid-1930s to the 1980s, the guides presented the seaside as an architectural and natural vision, uncluttered by the razzmatazz of entertainment and consumption.

While Piper's editorial and photographic relationship with Shell Guides was a long and rich one – he edited the guides from 1962 to 1984 – it was another artist–photographer whose edition has remained the symbol of the guides' synthesis of writing, photography and illustration: Nash's *Dorset* was made over two years and published in 1936.

Nash had lived with his family in Kent during the early 1920s, moving to Iden on Romney Marsh in Sussex with his wife Margaret and later to Rye. Like Piper, who was a frequent visitor to the area, Nash was much taken by the starkness of the coastline. Piper took many photographs in Rye in the 1930s, and Nash's series of paintings and photographs of the restraining sea wall at Dymchurch are a testament to his fascination with this remote and eerie coastline. Rye, an ancient and picturesque town, was also home to a number of artists and bohemians – including the painter Edward Burra and writer Una, Lady Troubridge – and had also found itself in the novels of H. G. Wells and Rudyard Kipling.[10] Although both Piper and Nash discovered other seaside places – Piper became interested in Brighton and Nash in Swanage – the exposed Kent coast, with its smattering of small towns, the eerie desert of Dungeness and the unique background of the Romney Marsh, played an important part in their visual and creative development. Then, as now, this corner of Sussex and Kent was an isolated and harsh place to live. In 1933, in search of a smaller house and a better climate for Nash's asthma, Margaret and Paul left New House in Rye for the Isle of Purbeck.

Nash photographed *Totems*, *Old Shipyard*, *Rye Harbour* in 1932, shortly after acquiring his first camera. *Woodstack and Barns* demonstrated his grasp of the medium with its concentration on mass, form and detail. Nash was knowledgeable about photography and admired the work of the modernists László Moholy-Nagy and Man Ray. Betjeman, with great perspicacity, invited Nash to compile, write and illustrate the Dorset Shell Guide. In Swanage, Nash met the Surrealist artist Eileen Agar, with whom he had a passionate friendship, and the two began to experiment with photography and montage around the Dorset coast.

Nash came relatively late to photography, having been introduced to it by the pioneering modernist sound radio producer, Lance Sieveking.[11] His first (and only) camera, a No.1A pocket Kodak series 2, was given to Nash by his wife Margaret before they crossed the Atlantic on a visit to New York in 1931.

Nash was no doubt spurred on to make the Dorset photographs by his Shell Guide commission from Betjeman, but as his grasp of the medium grew firmer, he began to make bolder experiments with still life and perspective. The deep connection with Agar

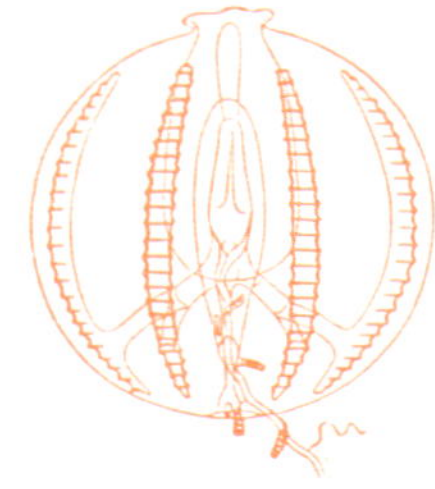

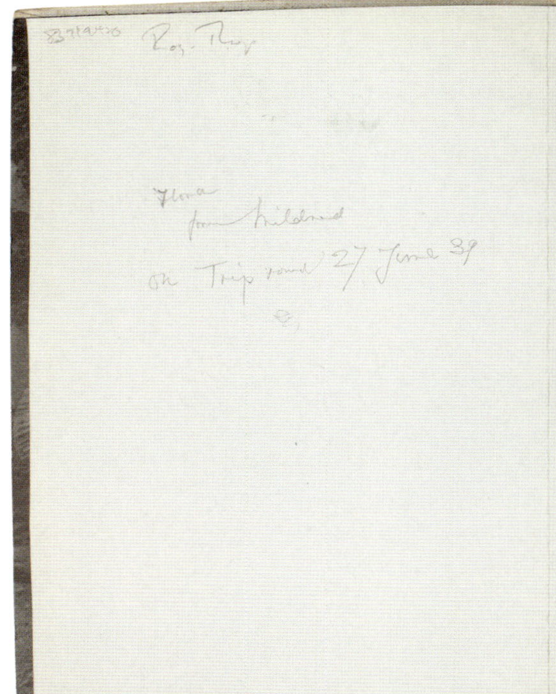

DORSET

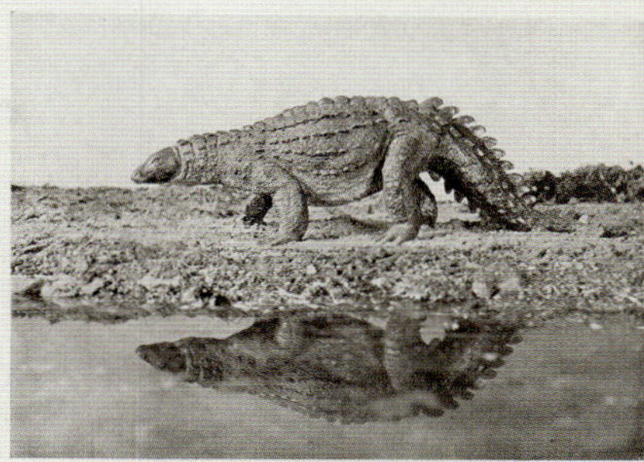

SCELIDOSAURUS HARRISONI : FORMER NATIVE

SHELL GUIDE

COMPILED
AND WRITTEN BY PAUL NASH

FABER AND FABER LIMITED
24 Russell Square
London

---

church. Look up at the curious carving of Virgin and Child and the beautiful golden vane. Powerful haunt of legends: the healing spring of St. Augustine at the end of a dark grove, and so on. But on the hill above the town the huge ancient design of the naked Giant, 180 ft. high, tends to diminish the importance of mediævalism.

Puddletown : 6, 13 : Neat and gay little houses and cottages, white walls, and bright gardens on the street. One of the most interesting churches in Dorset. Well situated on rising ground. Many good gravestones covered with incredible lichens. The bush yews are clipped into the form of chalices. Interior contains many distinguished features — slender brown stone pillars, lovely carved wood roof, font of very good simple Norman type, shaped as a tumbler glass decorated by vine trellis carving, and very fine Jacobean gallery. Here also is the Athelhampton chapel containing effigies of the Martin family. The one illustrated is particularly beautiful, wrought in alabaster with tints of faded blue.

Weymouth : 9 : Attractive eighteenth-century watering - place where George III. bathed to music. Now almost obliterated by various advertising devices or simply unsuitable painting. But Weymouth Harbour has a more permanent charm, and the great bay is seldom dull. Here ships of the Fleet are constantly in view. Their inevitable dignity and chilling mien give Weymouth a look of rather dubious frivolity. The surrounding country is of great beauty. A monster chalk cut of King George on horseback on the downs has certain comical distinction. Poxwell Manor is one of Dorset's architectural gems well restored.

Portland : 9 : To pass on from Weymouth to Portland is to experience a transformation indeed. Magnificent drive on winding road from Chesilton to Easton. Very interesting eighteenth-century church with fantastic graves and monuments. Pennsylvania Castle, the home of the Penns, must be seen in its rocky dell of trees. A description of Portland occurs in the main article, but the island should be thoroughly explored, as both coast and interior are intensely interesting. Note the buildings, stone porches especially; the views from the heights are unequalled in Dorset.

BEAMINSTER (pronounced Beminster) : 5 : Market town of Marshwood Vale and centre of grazing country. A town of warm yellow stone buildings, sunny and kind, dominated by one of the greatest church towers in England. Of this town, in this place, it is appropriate to quote from William Barnes a few lines which seem typical of his poetry, his attitude, and the Dorset tongue :

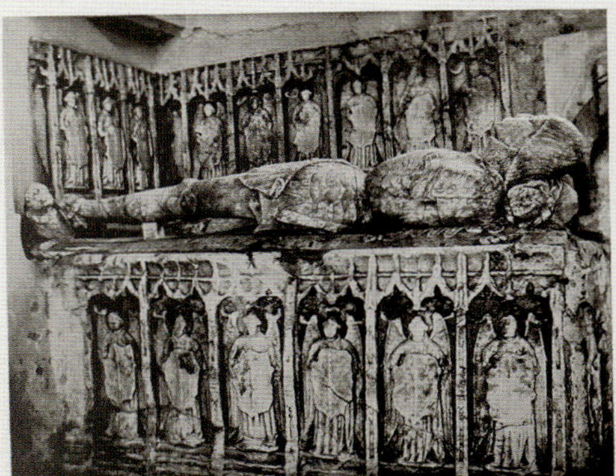

An alabaster tomb in Athelhampton Chapel, Paddletown.

" Sweet Be'mi'ster that bist abound
Wi' hedges reachen up between
A thoosan' vields o' zummer green,
Where elems lofty heads do show
Their sheádes vor hay-meakers below,
An wild hedge-flow'rs do charm the souls
O' maidens in their evenin' strolls."

Manor Houses in the Neighbourhood. Parnham House, Melplash, and Mapperton. Mapperton is one of the gems among Dorset manors, a lovely decorative building virtually unimpaired.

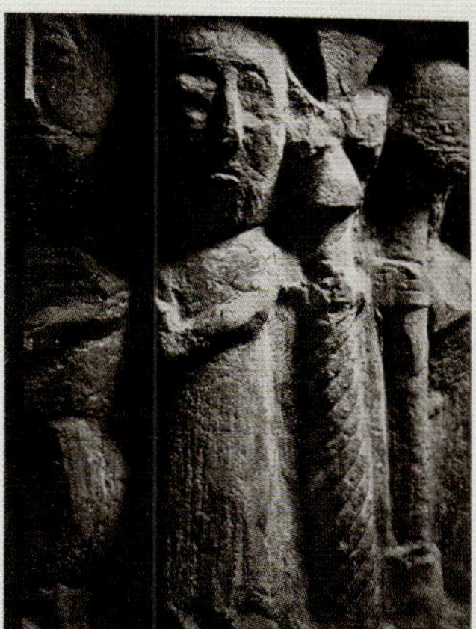

Part of a Saxon font at Toller Fratrum, near Dorchester.

Bridport : 4 : Gate to the West. A delightful town set back from a wide street of fine red-brick houses. Formerly had a busy life and considerable importance. The making of nets and ropes still goes on, and there is a slight coasting trade. The sea lies 2 m. distant at West Bay, which is being developed from a quiet watering-place into something different. On every side the country is magnificent. The coast rears up a shaggy orange cliff which slopes backwards in tumultuous downs, ribbed with dark hedge lines. Across the coast road, inland, downs continue ample movement, revealing many barrows and other earthworks in their course. Here and there sudden pyramids are thrown up—actually conical in form and sometimes topped by clumps of trees.

Charmouth : 4 : The second invitation to the West following Bridport. Enchanting village of pretty Regency houses with bow windows winking in the sun. Rather romantic in history. Between here and Lyme Regis several landslips have taken place, complicating the scenery very pleasantly. But main characteristics persist from here to Lyme rather heightened in beauty. Here the voice of Jane Austen should break in :

" Charmouth with its high grounds and extensive sweeps of country, and, still more, its sweet retired bay, backed by dark cliffs, where fragments of low rock among the sands make it the happiest spot for watching the flow of the tide; for sitting in unwearied contemplation."

These dark cliffs are mines of the most frightening fossils. Here Miss Mary Anning in 1811 discovered her gigantic reptile. Where the Char trickles into the sea strange bones have been found of elephants, rhinoceros. On the other hand, Charles II. missed his boat here in escaping to France, and Harriet Wilson wrote her memories. A place full of odd contrasts.

Lyme Regis : 4 : The steep hill descending to the port of Lyme Regis reveals prettily built-up tiers of Regency villas looking out over business-like structures of the Cobb, with its beautiful lines and precarious footing, where Monmouth landed and Jane Austen's Louisa Musgrove tumbled. No one visiting Lyme must pass through without driving down to the Cobb, reached by a narrow road about ½ m. beyond the actual town. Lyme has an ancient history dating from 774, and has always been a place of interest, even of importance. If you are sensitive to haunts, here are many. Beyond everything, Lyme is a place of real distinction and charm, invaded but not yet spoilt by " development." Beyond lies Devon.

Sherborne : 3 : Historic town on the northern border. Once the capital of Wessex. Two Saxon kings lie buried here. Both King Charles and Cromwell were present at its siege during the Civil War, and so on. Its very beautiful abbey is mainly Perpendicular, with roof of superb fan tracery encrusted with heraldic bosses and coats of arms in bright colours. The town itself

during his years in Swanage, together with the inspiration of the coast, undoubtedly gave him confidence to vary his methods, ranging from intense study of detail, in, for instance *Stones and Seaweed*, c.1935,[12] which was used in the Dorset Shell Guide. *A Lamp-post in Swanage* (1935–6, Tate Archive) is startlingly modern with its juxtaposition of a lamppost with a municipal litterbox, likewise, *Open Window, Garden Hut, Scarbank, Durlston Head, Dorset*.[13]

Even when Nash produced images more likely to be recognized as 'views', for instance *Slipway, Beach at Swanage*, c.1935–6,[14] rocks, stones and slipway assume the monstrousness that makes Nash's photographs of the British seaside so intriguing. Though he never quite came to terms with Swanage, thinking it a place of such 'extreme ugliness architecturally that the inhabitants look out to sea',[15] later he 'began to discover that Swanage was definitely ... surrealist'.[16] One of the consolations of Swanage was that, like Rye, it was home to a distinct artistic community, including the photographer Helen Muspratt and Eileen Agar (see Chapter III).

The Nashes were dogged by ill-health and family worries, and they had very little money. Nash (like Piper), would often resort to commercial design and writing work to augment the couple's funds. But like Piper, Nash took every creative task seriously, and he set about compiling *Dorset: A Shell Guide* with dedication, turning it into a work of art. After the vicissitudes of Rye, living in Dorset was paradisiacal, for a time at least. The Nashes were lent a small manor house by a friend and patron.[17] Another new friend, Janet Russell, drove the Nashes around Dorset,[18] as Paul entered a phase of great creativity, producing many photographs and drawings and the monumental collage made with Agar – *Swanage*, 1936.

However idyllic Dorset appeared to be in Nash's photographs, the reality was rather different. He complained of trippers and encroaching mass tourism when he wrote to his friend Ruth Clark in the 1930s: 'and all this time Swanage was getting us down. Every

day it seemed more unbearably vulgar. The people who live there, my God, the people who come there on the buses and steamers – beyond belief.'[19]

In his introductory text to the post-war edition of *Cornwall*, Betjeman mourned the loss of the Cornwall of his childhood: 'Roads were only partially metalled and in the lesser lanes the rock showed through on the surface. Everyone in the village had oil lamps and candles. A journey to the nearest town and back was a day's expedition'.[20] If Betjeman glimpsed the irony of editing a guidebook specifically designed to encourage motorists to drive to Cornwall, this did not deter him from exposing its secret mysteries to all comers. A tight group of photographers worked on the guides, including Edwin Smith, whose photograph of pebbles formed the endpapers of the revised *Cornwall* in 1964. Benjamin and Piper were frequently at odds with Shell's advertising department, as Betjeman despaired of the quality of Cornwall's resorts, and Piper chose not to photograph them. Of Polperro, Betjeman wrote: 'gift shops abound and the place is more like a new film set than an old Cornish fishing port,' and saw it as a place of interlacing car parks, dominated by cars.[21]

Though Nash shied away from photographing people, he was attracted to both wide seascapes, resorts (though usually photographed from a distance) and details of seaside life, from driftwood to street furniture. Nash's passionate friendship with Agar was clearly a spur to his creativity as the two explored Purbeck together, and Nash's commitment to photography was not simply driven by the needs of the guide. Nash's Swanage photographs are joyful and full of invention, and he was intrigued by the strange street furniture of Swanage, imported from London by the developer George Burt as he cleared parts of London for new property development schemes.

In his short essay 'Seaside Surrealism', originally published in the *Architectural Review* in April 1936, Nash explores the presence of Burt's architectural salvage from the point of view of a shipwrecked visitor.

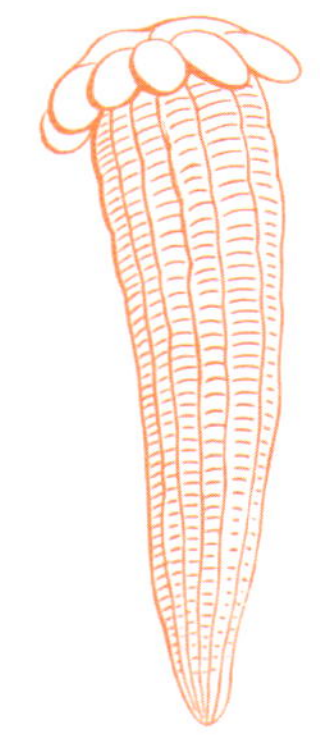

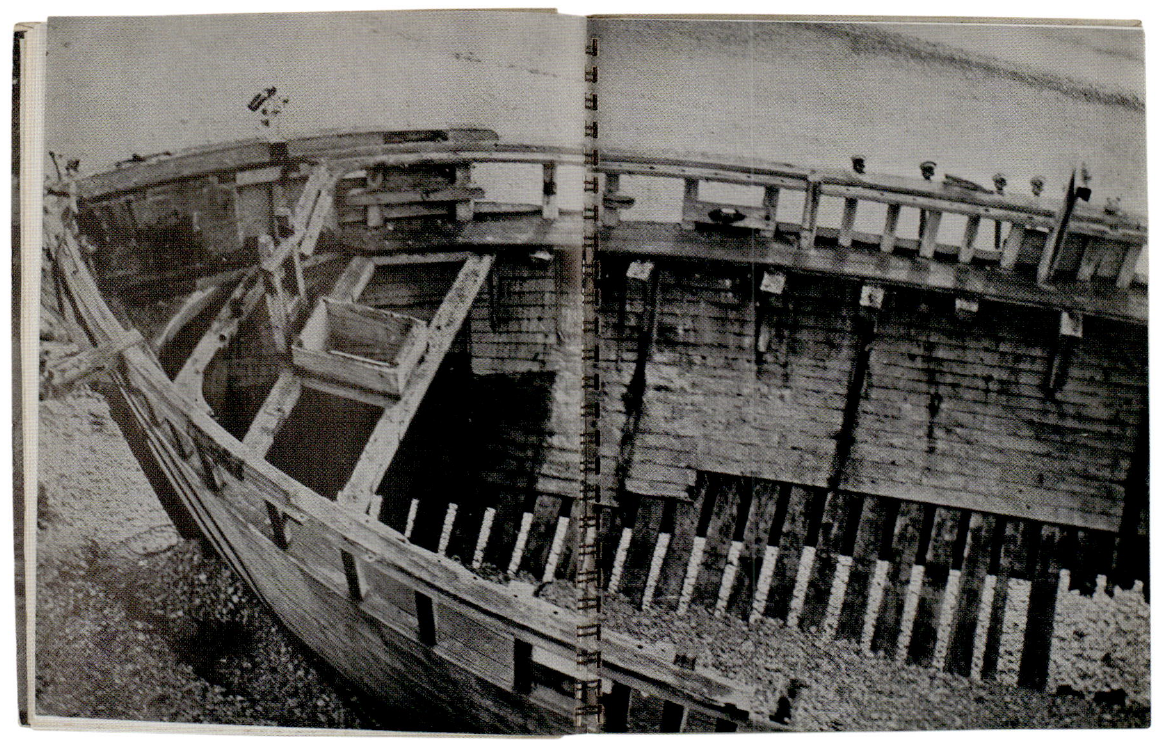

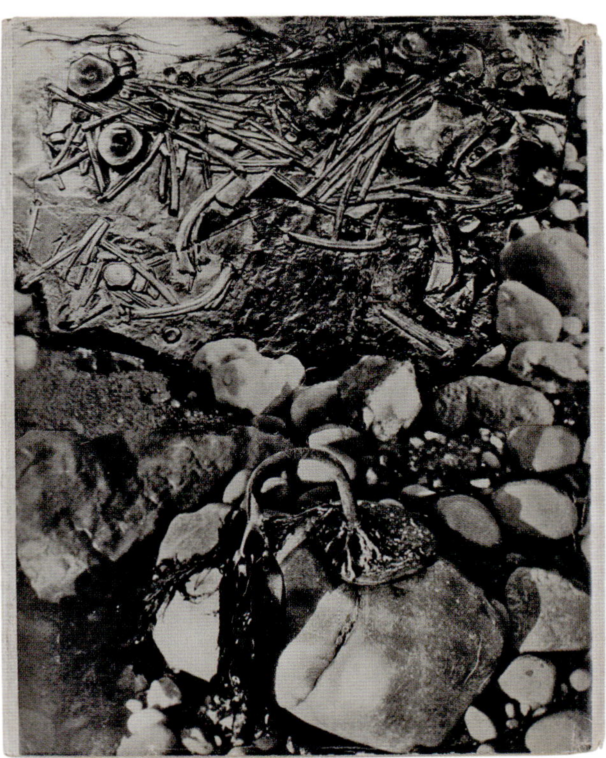

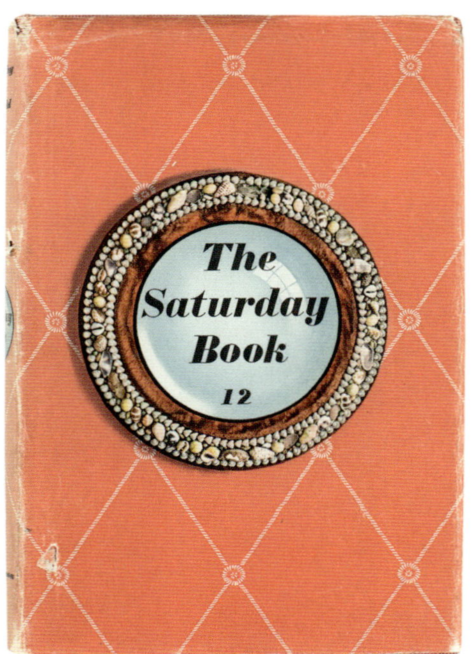

A façade of a building built by the architect Sir Christopher Wren and shipped down to Swanage to become the frontage of the town hall, a set of swanlike benches, lamp-posts bearing the names of prominent London locations, a clock tower without a clock, an inscribed stone globe. The accidental surrealism created by George Burt and John Mowlem's architectural salvage, and captured so carefully by Nash's camera, was something to be both satirized and admired. 'Seaside Surrealism', while it is whimsical, summed up the contradictions of seaside life for those artists and photographers who lived or worked on the coast. For Nash, Piper and Smith, who all depended at some point in their careers on topographical photography to make their livings, there was always the tension between wanting to extol the old and also needing to represent the new.

In their 1952 article 'Beside the Seaside' for *The Saturday Book*, illustrated by a meticulously collaged set of photographs and reproductions of paintings, sculpture and folk art, Smith and writer and partner Olive Cook presented their own view of the seaside, with illustrations that included Smith's

The Saturday Book,
No. 12, 1952

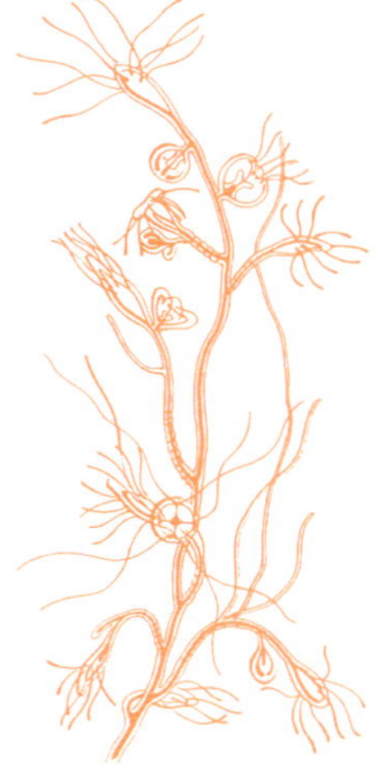

photograph of a fossil fish used in Nash's 1936 *Shell Guide to Dorset*. Though somewhat peripheral within the Shell Guides group, at *The Saturday Book* Smith was instrumental in its design and content. The picture section, laid out as a frontispiece and twenty-one pages of illustration plus a short text, is a rare example of Smith and Cook's own particular take on the English seaside, often obscured by the many commercial commissions that they both took on throughout their careers. 'Beside the Seaside' was far more personal than much of the commissioned work they did, and the miscellany format of *The Saturday Book* was liberating:

> The pleasures of this strange world are those of form, colour and texture. Soft sand is patterned with delicate curves and ridges by the receding wave, and mirrors the sky, the white breasts of gulls and the darting motion of the sandpiper. Every tide exposes some new, enchanting shell shape; pink yellow and orange fans; large striated Venus shells; razors, lime green, purple and brown, shining as though freshly varnished; white and violet tops tipped with pink; augers like unicorn horns ... many marvels, as well as the gaiety of the concert party and the brass bedstead and rose-decked wash-basin of the old-fashioned lodging house, make up this special world into which we step when the train draws up at the seaside platform.[22]

Though the text for 'Beside the Seaside' was a hotchpotch, the power of the piece lies in the visuals, which are elegant and complex. Aquatint and engraved seaside views are out of the ordinary – a giant sturgeon tied to a boat, giant shells, fish with outsized eyes and, at the bottom of the page, Smith's fossilized fish (opposite). To the right of these are four photographs (uncredited but almost certainly by Smith) of sea anemones, pebbles, seaweed and wave marks in wet sand. Lithographs of fantastical sea creatures by Philip Gosse are

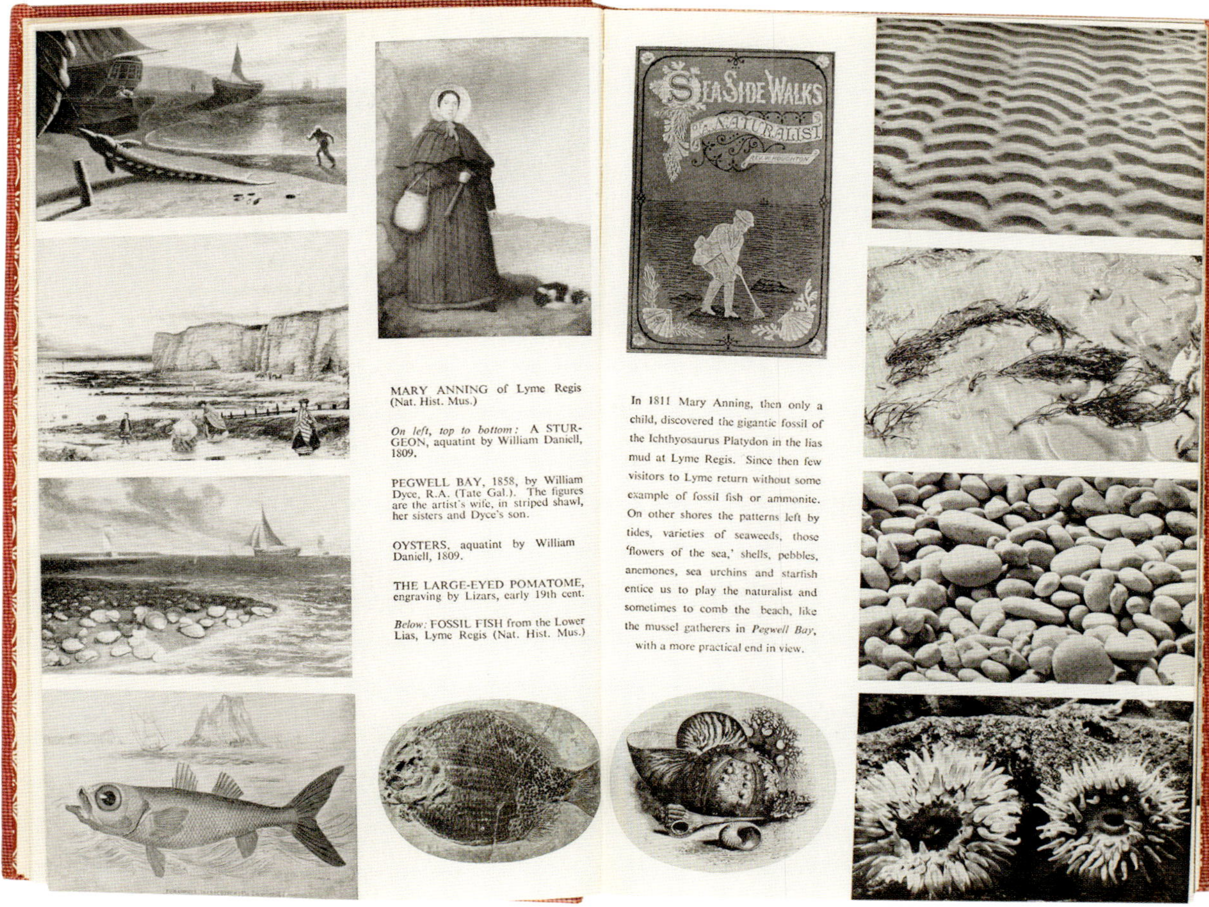

MARY ANNING of Lyme Regis (Nat. Hist. Mus.)

On left, top to bottom: A STURGEON, aquatint by William Daniell, 1809.

PEGWELL BAY, 1858, by William Dyce, R.A. (Tate Gal.). The figures are the artist's wife, in striped shawl, her sisters and Dyce's son.

OYSTERS, aquatint by William Daniell, 1809.

THE LARGE-EYED POMATOME, engraving by Lizars, early 19th cent.

Below: FOSSIL FISH from the Lower Lias, Lyme Regis (Nat. Hist. Mus.)

In 1811 Mary Anning, then only a child, discovered the gigantic fossil of the Ichthyosaurus Platydon in the lias mud at Lyme Regis. Since then few visitors to Lyme return without some example of fossil fish or ammonite. On other shores the patterns left by tides, varieties of seaweeds, those 'flowers of the sea,' shells, pebbles, anemones, sea urchins and starfish entice us to play the naturalist and sometimes to comb the beach, like the mussel gatherers in *Pegwell Bay*, with a more practical end in view.

carefully positioned, and later, photographs by Smith dominate the layout, including an interior of a simple hotel room, complete with brass bed and chamber pot. Smith and Cook paid homage to the seaside postcard, folk art, Punch and Judy shows, fishermen's huts and Pierrots. Smith's photograph *Beach Photographers' Properties* on the last page of the illustrations is an ambivalent gesture to 'tradesman' photographers – *Me and My Gal* at Brighton is an empty portrait stand, thrown into sharp relief by the weather-beaten beach structures in the background, and is on a par with the early Shell Guides for its acknowledgment of the vernacular, the natural and the sublime.

Of the central group of Shell Guide photographers, Nash, John (and later Edward

EDWIN SMITH
AND OLIVE COOK
'Beside the Seaside',
The Saturday Book,
No. 12, 1952

Piper) and Smith, Edwin Smith has received the least acclaim, classed as a journeyman photographer rather than (like the others) an artist using photography This is expressed clearly in David Fraser Jenkins's introduction to *John Piper: A Painter's Camera* (1987):

Edwin Smith's are more professional; crisp throughout, unmarked, show the major interest in the place, and no doubt are afterwards archivally stored and identified. The effect of Piper's depends more than do Smith's on their printing, and go beyond the record or the interesting contrast, to become one item in the range of a landscape painter with an original point of view.[23]

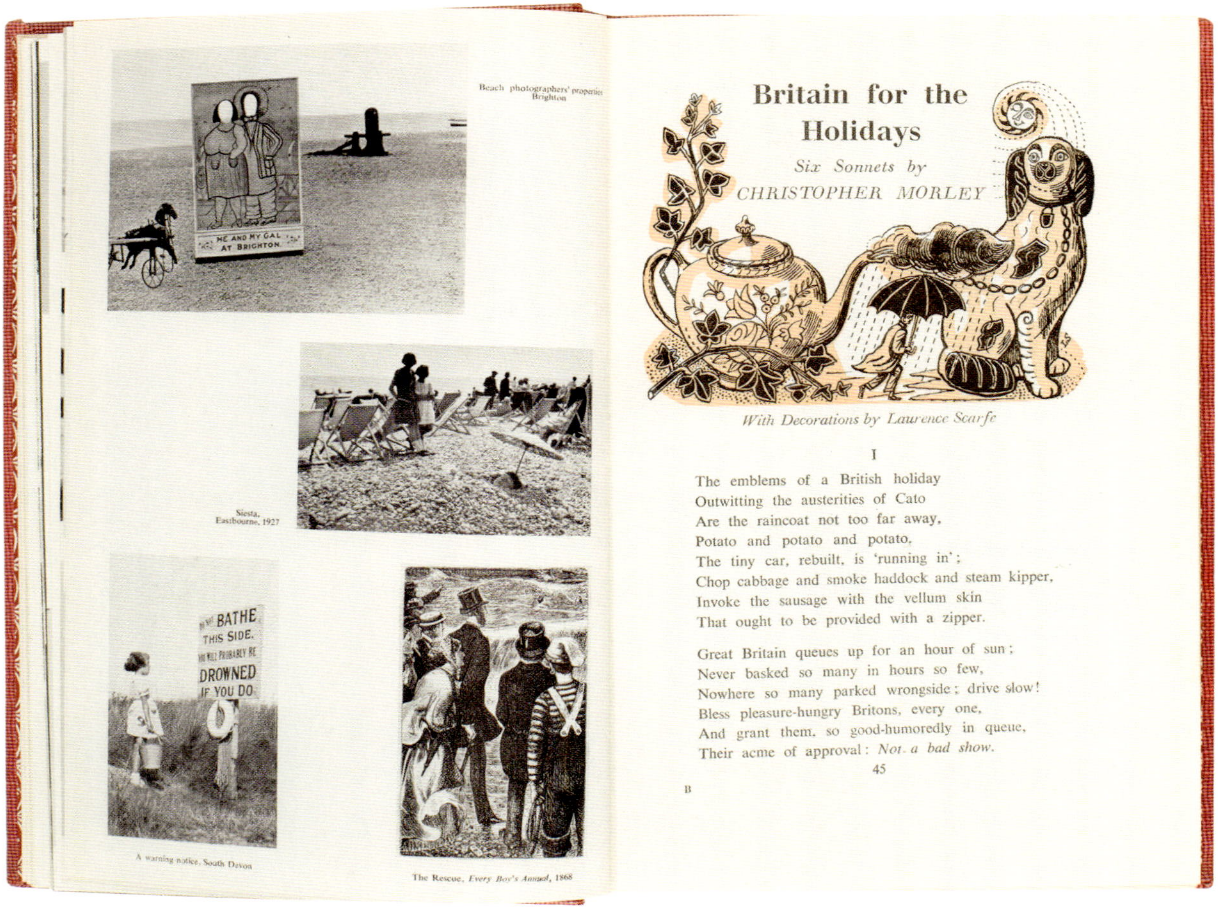

Beach photographers' properties, Brighton

Siesta, Eastbourne, 1927

A warning notice, South Devon

The Rescue, Every Boy's Annual, 1868

Britain for the Holidays

Six Sonnets by
CHRISTOPHER MORLEY

With Decorations by Laurence Scarfe

I

The emblems of a British holiday
Outwitting the austerities of Cato
Are the raincoat not too far away,
Potato and potato and potato,
The tiny car, rebuilt, is 'running in';
Chop cabbage and smoke haddock and steam kipper,
Invoke the sausage with the vellum skin
That ought to be provided with a zipper.

Great Britain queues up for an hour of sun;
Never basked so many in hours so few,
Nowhere so many parked wrongside; drive slow!
Bless pleasure-hungry Britons, every one,
And grant them, so good-humoredly in queue,
Their acme of approval: *Not a bad show.*

45

B

The Shell Guides, under the editorships of Betjeman and Piper, were always more than tourist guidebooks. They discussed both the built architecture and the natural environment of the counties they covered, many of which included the coastline. Both were inspired and opinionated editors – quite often Shell would step in and ask them to moderate their criticisms of specific buildings. They were inventive in their use of contributors – documentary photographer Roger Mayne and playwright Anne Jellicoe were commissioned to illustrate and write the 1975 edition of *Devon*.

Their attitude to the seaside was ambivalent – Piper certainly preferred to photograph in deep countryside and the guides concealed much of the 'real' seaside of the 1960s and 1970s. But theirs was a view that, for better or worse, has remained central to the British imagination, a romantic sense of being an island, of remoteness, of secret places. When we look at *Dorset*, *Cornwall* or *Devon*, perhaps we are seeing something which was never really there: a collection of components for a very English Shangri-La. [vw]

ABOVE, OPPOSITE AND PAGES 38–9

EDWIN SMITH AND OLIVE COOK
'Beside the Seaside',
The Saturday Book,
No. 12, 1952

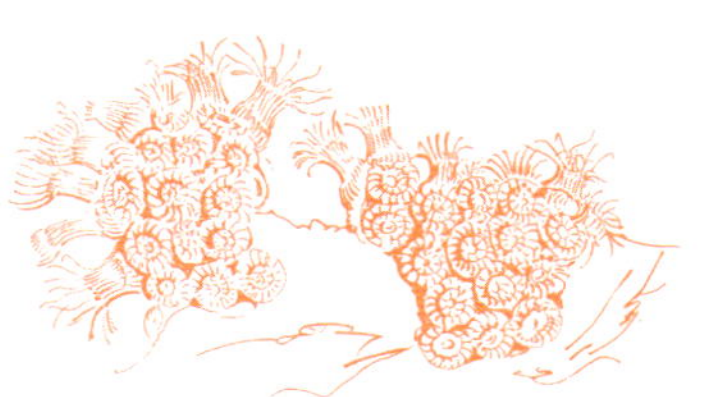

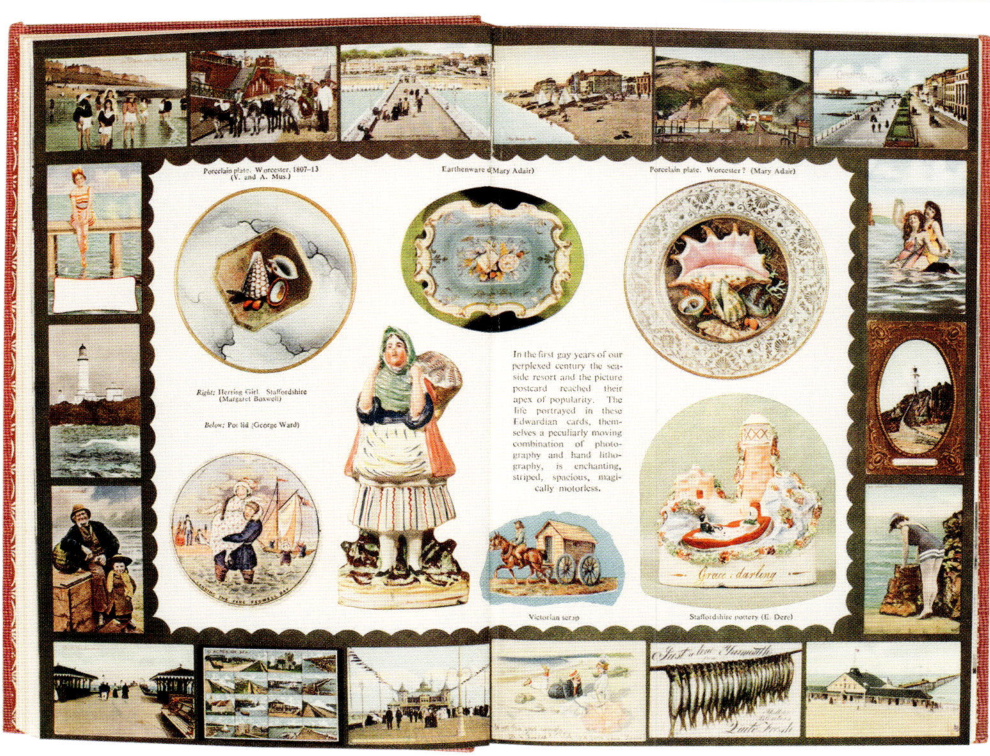

Porcelain plate. Worcester, 1807–13 (V. and A. Mus.)

Earthenware (Mary Adair)

Porcelain plate. Worcester? (Mary Adair)

Right: Herring Girl. Staffordshire (Margaret Boswell)

Below: Pot lid (George Ward)

In the first gay years of our perplexed century the sea-side resort and the picture postcard reached their apex of popularity. The life portrayed in these Edwardian cards, themselves a peculiarly moving combination of photography and hand lithography, is enchanting, striped, spacious, magically motorless.

Victorian scrap

Staffordshire pottery (E. Dere)

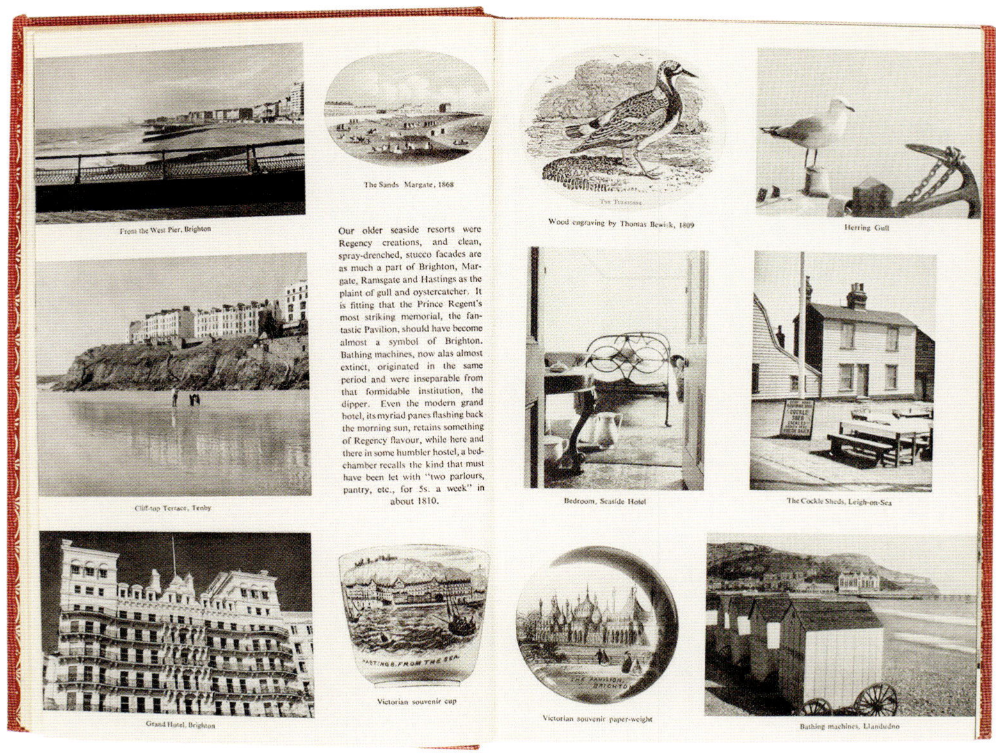

From the West Pier, Brighton

The Sands Margate, 1868

Wood engraving by Thomas Bewick, 1809

Herring Gull

Our older seaside resorts were Regency creations, and clean, spray-drenched, stucco facades are as much a part of Brighton, Margate, Ramsgate and Hastings as the plaint of gull and oystercatcher. It is fitting that the Prince Regent's most striking memorial, the fantastic Pavilion, should have become almost a symbol of Brighton. Bathing machines, now alas almost extinct, originated in the same period and were inseparable from that formidable institution, the dipper. Even the modern grand hotel, its myriad panes flashing back the morning sun, retains something of Regency flavour, while here and there in some humbler hostel, a bed-chamber recalls the kind that must have been let with "two parlours, pantry, etc., for 5s. a week" in about 1810.

Cliff-top Terrace, Tenby

Bedroom, Seaside Hotel

The Cockle Sheds, Leigh-on-Sea

Grand Hotel, Brighton

Victorian souvenir cup

Victorian souvenir paper-weight

Bathing machines, Llandudno

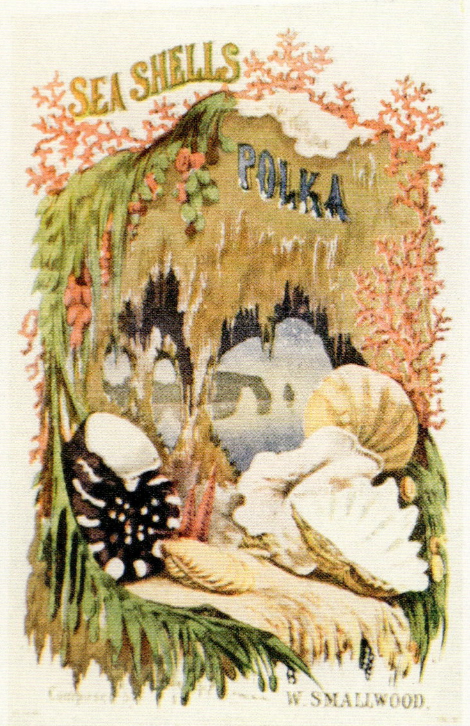

Lithographed Song Cover, late 19th century
(Barry Duncan)

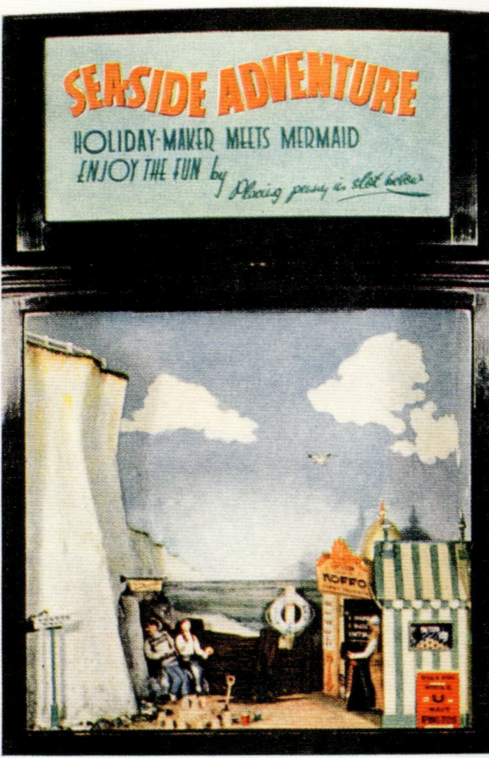

Seaside Slot Machine, by Mr Leonard Lee
(British Automatic Company)

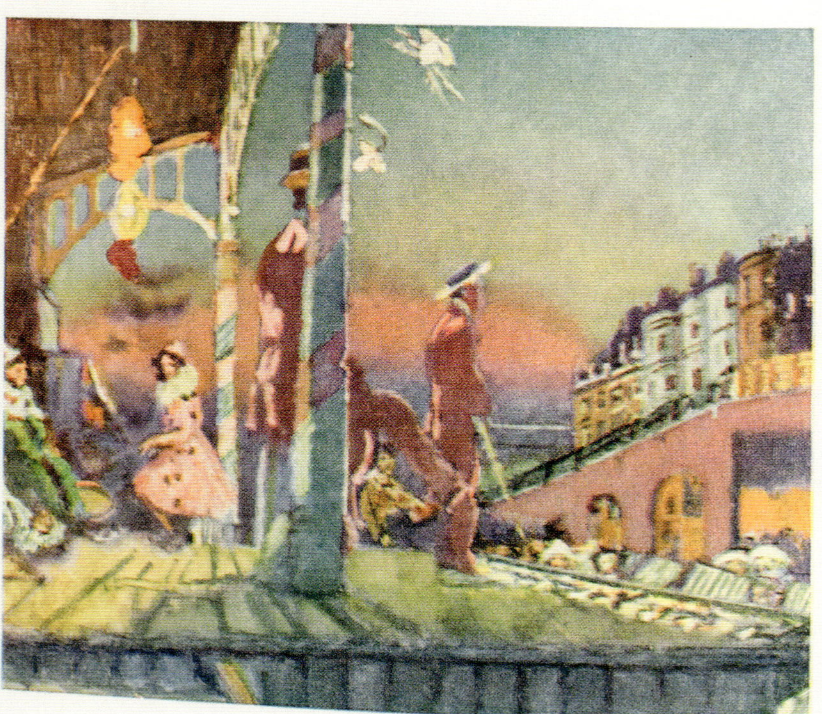

Brighton Pierrots, by W. R. Sickert (Morton H. Sands)

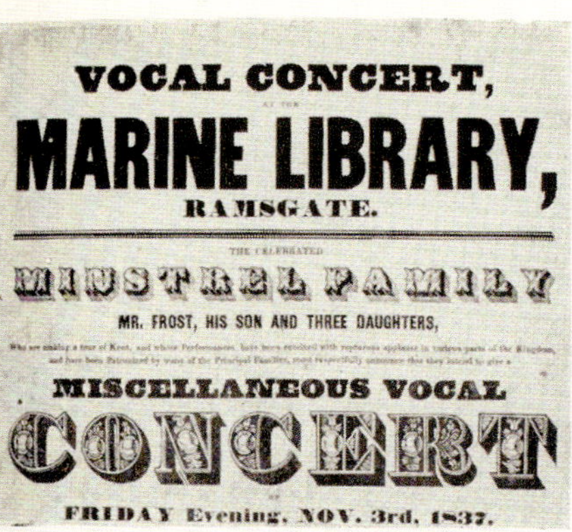

Heading of Concert Advertisement, 1837

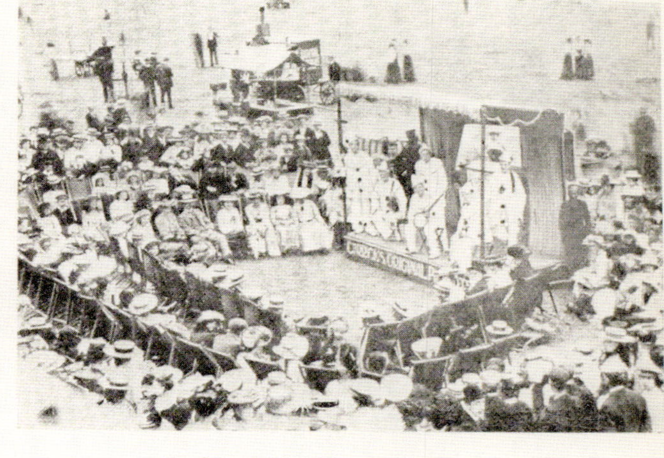

Carrick's Original Pierrots, Scarborough, *c.* 1900

The pleasures of the seaside are not confined to weeds and winkles; there is more to it than promenading and paddling. Though it may now cost three pennies to go on the pier, one penny will still produce the jerky terrors of the execution or the excitement of a fire, will predict your future or reveal the uncertainties of conjugal life. Though the seashell polka, together with black stockings and boaters, is a memory of the past, we are still entertained by carnival and pierrot as we sit nipped behind the knees by our deck chairs, sand between our toes, our critical faculties delightfully softened by the salt air and the pulse of the sea

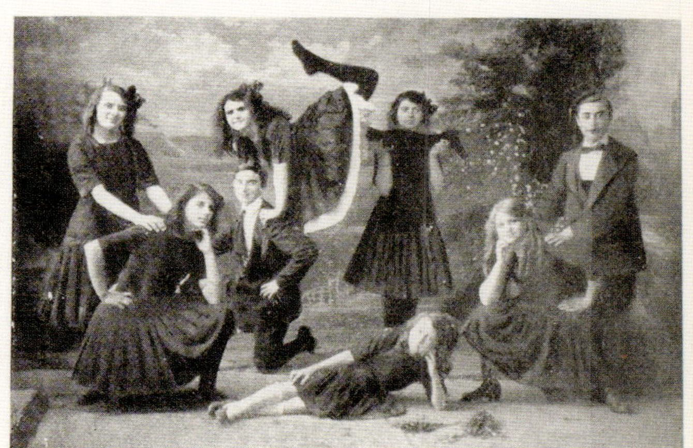

Riley's Revellers, Herne Bay, *c.* 1912

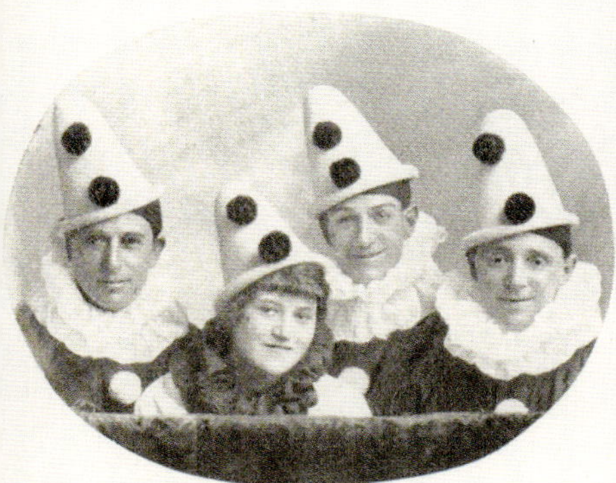

The Olympian Concert Party, Eastbourne, 1915. Harry Kemp, Winnie Tee, Jack Rickards and Ernest Pitt

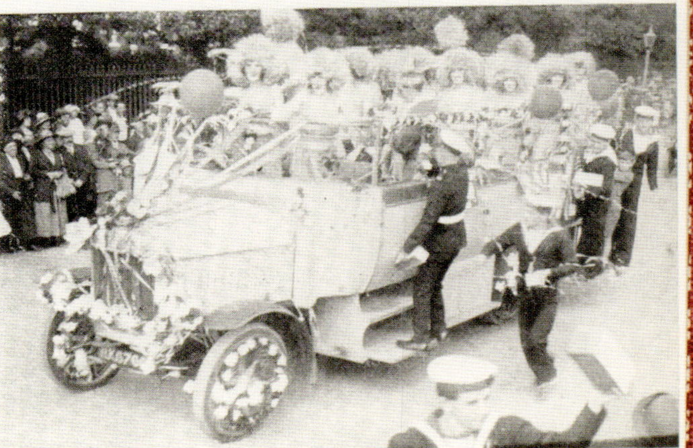

Southsea Carnival, 1923

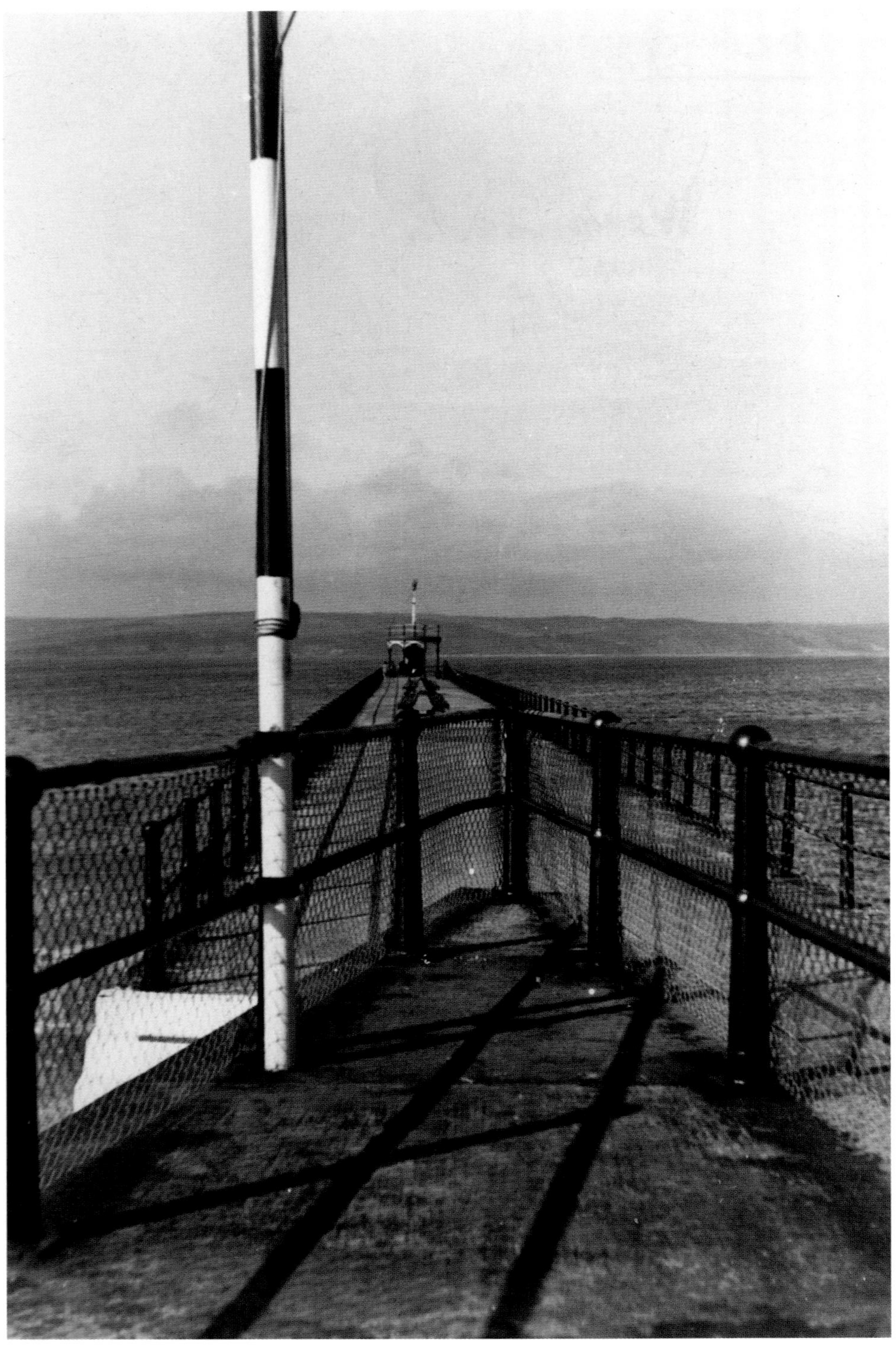

Stone Pier, Weymouth Harbour, 1937

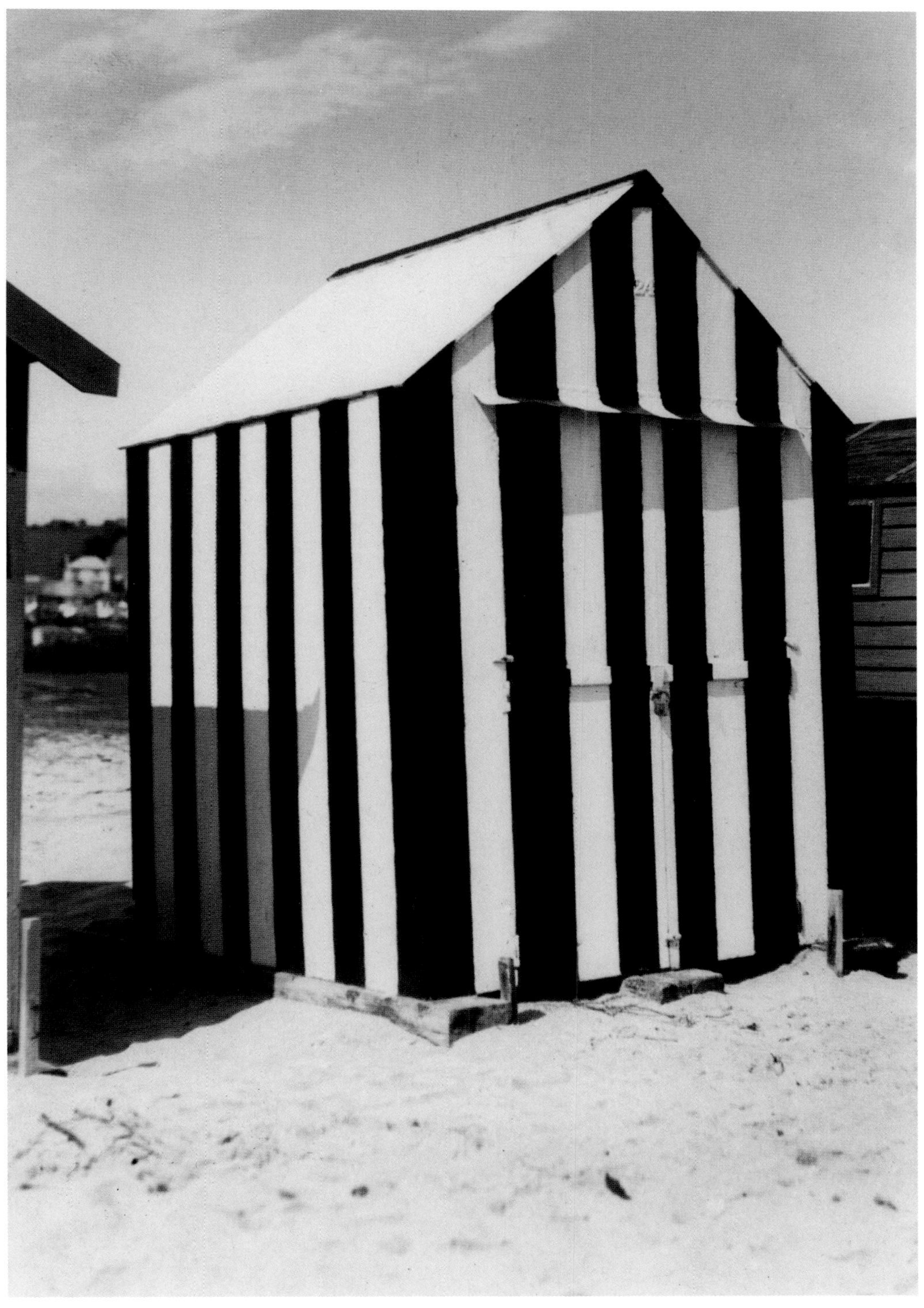

Striped Beach Hut, Par Sands, Cornwall, 1937

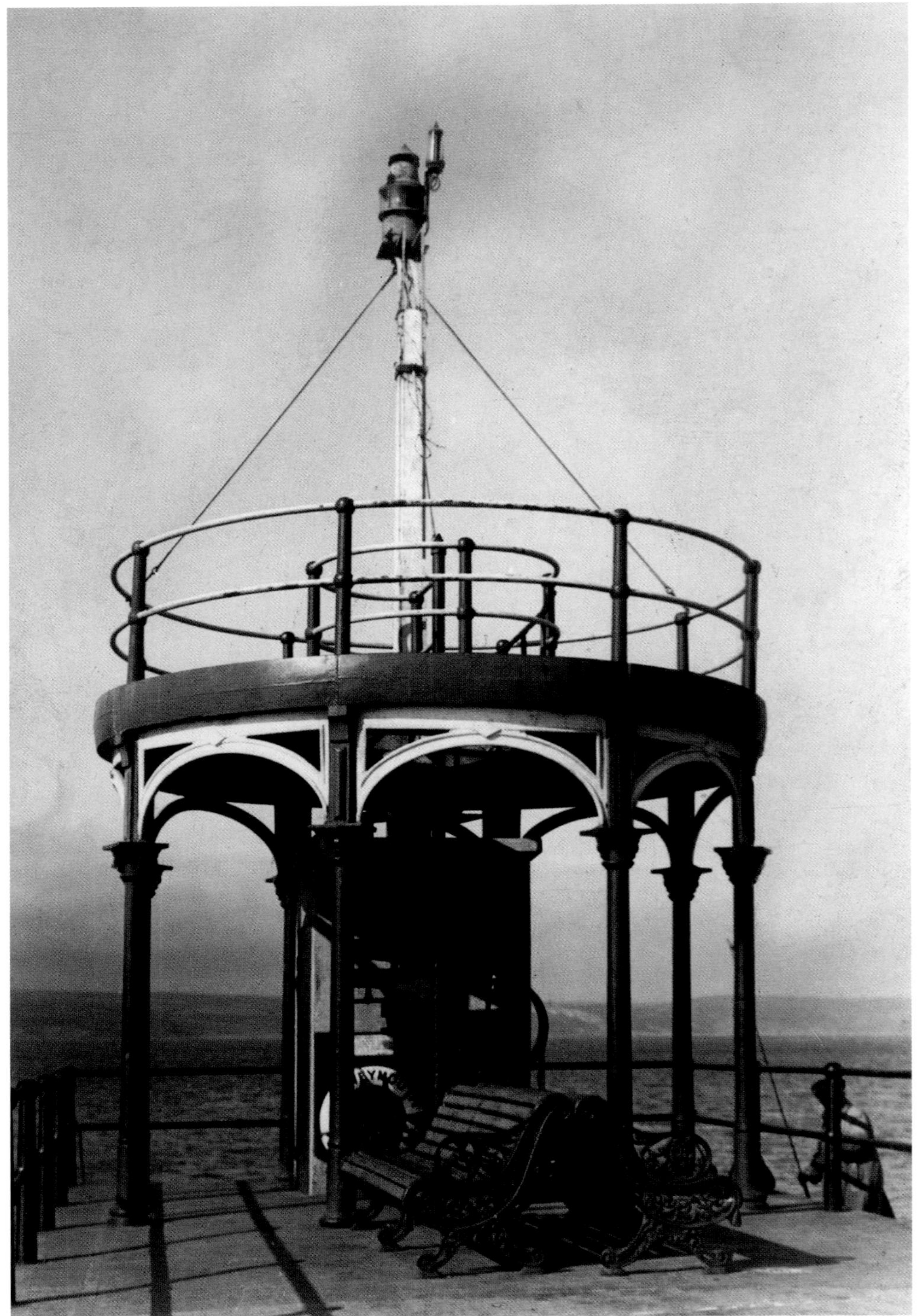

Stone Pier Light, Weymouth, 1937

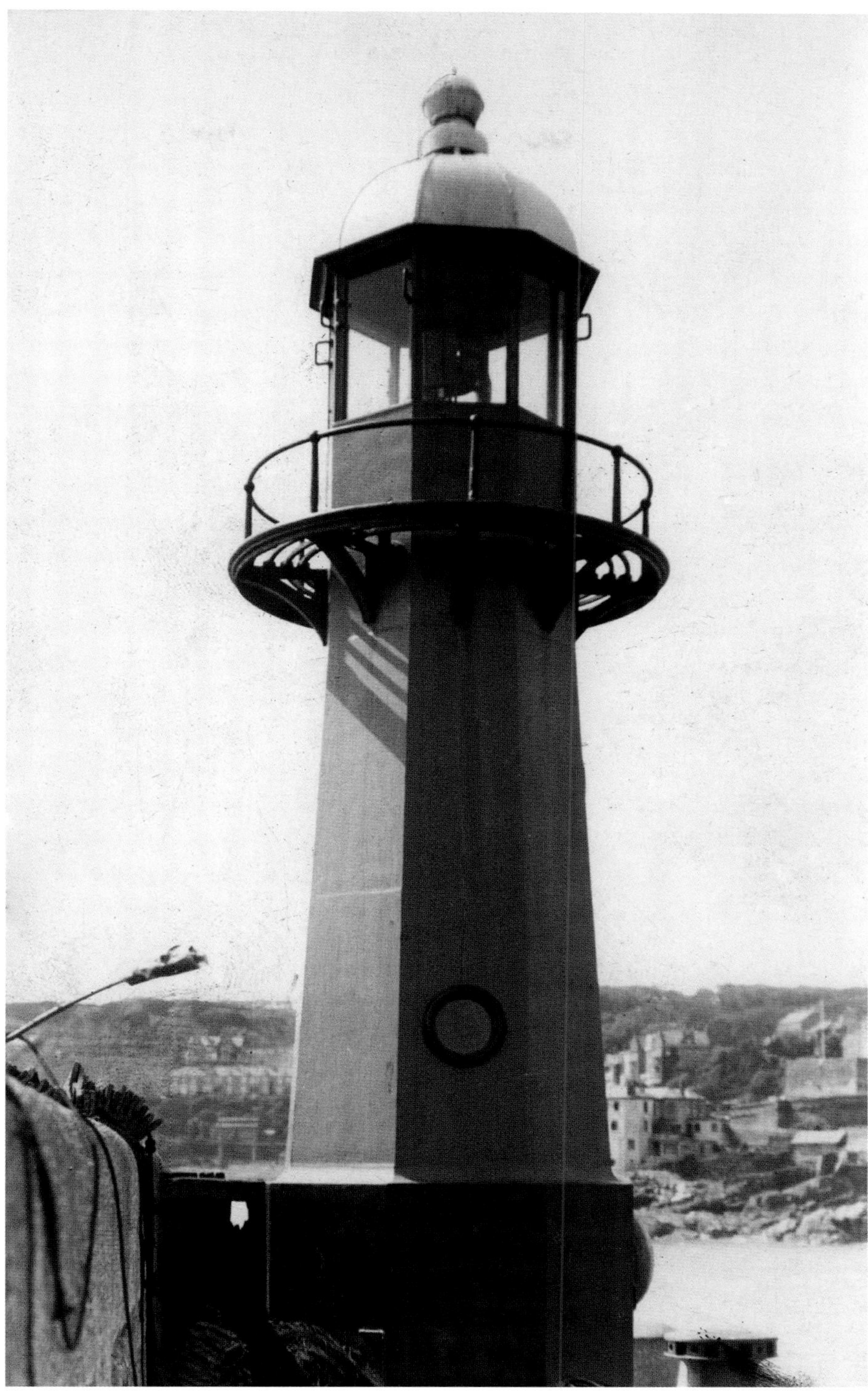

Pier Lighthouse, St Ives, Cornwall, 1937

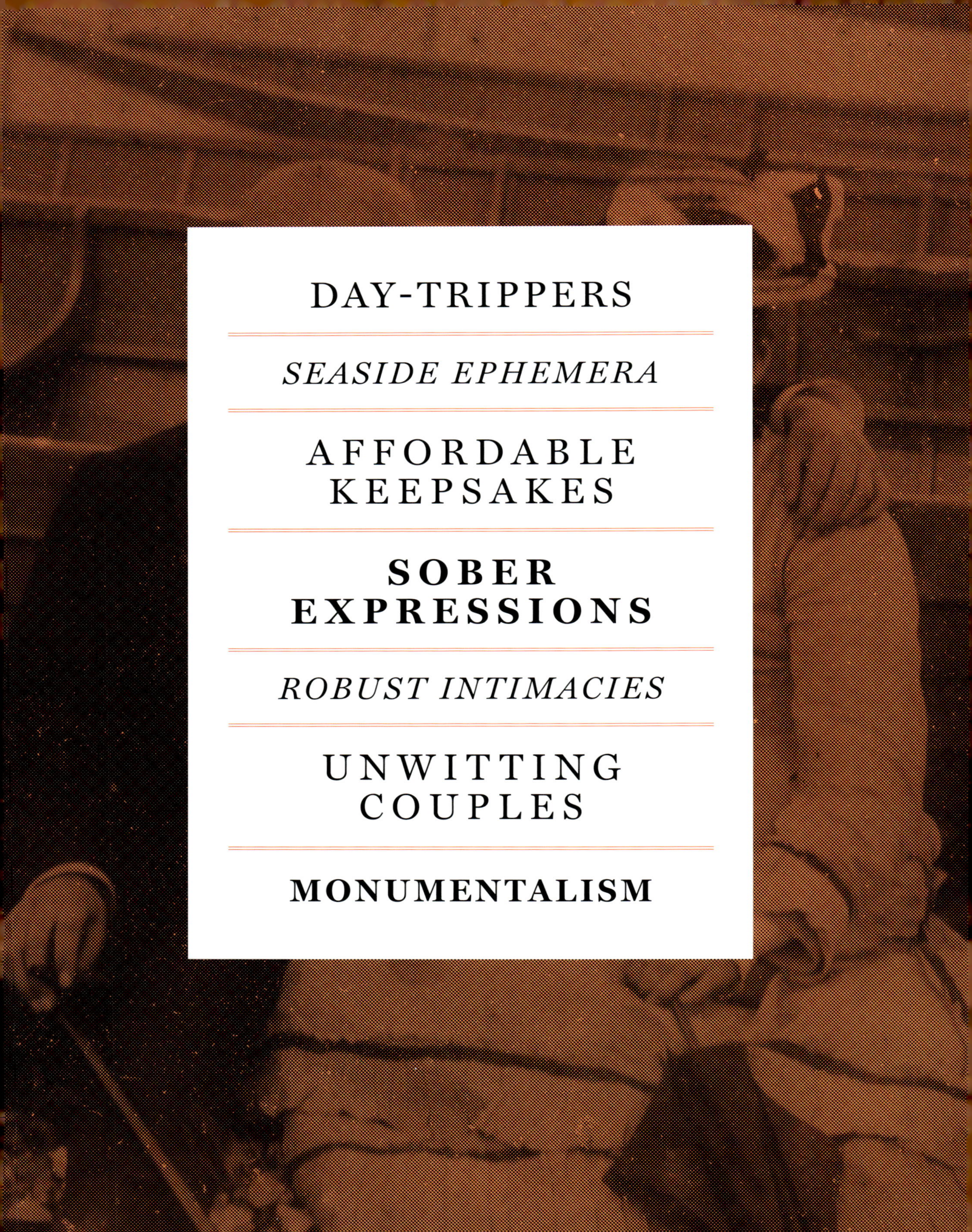

DAY-TRIPPERS
SEASIDE EPHEMERA
AFFORDABLE KEEPSAKES
SOBER EXPRESSIONS
ROBUST INTIMACIES
UNWITTING COUPLES
MONUMENTALISM

WAVES ON THE BEACH

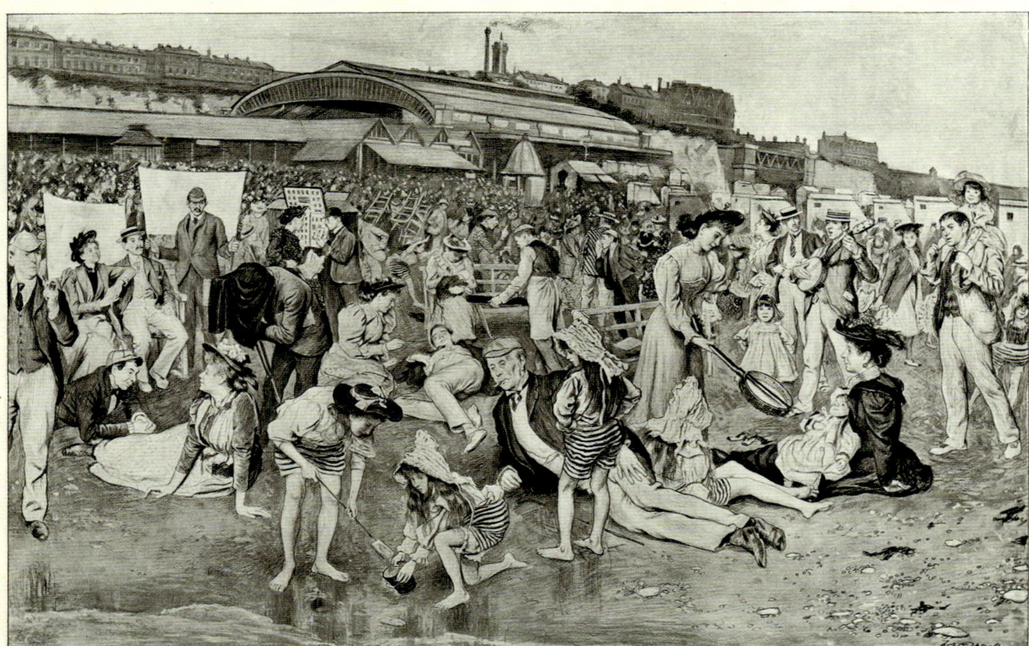

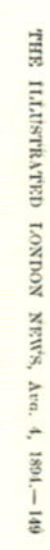

RAMSGATE SANDS.— BY W. W. RUSSELL.

Excitement is not a word customarily associated with Victorians. Yet a train's sheer speed, associated with a flashing landscape, and, on arrival at the seaside, the beach, with waves stretching to the horizon, must have caused even the most stalwart of Victorians' heart to skip a beat. Notions such as 'leisure' and 'free', when added to 'time', began to acquire an almost structured currency. Experiences and events so different, by contrast, from the quotidian were worth remembering and also, when it became technologically possible, visually recording. Consequently, the photographers hove into view.

The railway's effect in encouraging mass leisure-time migration to Britain's developing resorts in the mid-nineteenth century should not be underestimated. In the above *London Illustrated* graphic of Ramsgate's main sands,[1] we can see how conveniently the beach is serviced by the railway station, shown in the background with its large curved roof, bringing vast numbers of visitors directly to the seaside. A consequence of this increase in visitors, particularly day-trippers, was a proliferation, almost to epidemic proportions, of self-trained, itinerant photographers armed with camera, tripod and darkbox, vocally plying their trade in affordable seaside photography. This illustration also provides early insight into their practice. Among the crowd, the photographer makes his picture, an assistant holds a makeshift diffuser (necessary in the glaring beach light) and just beyond them is the darkcart, functioning as both mobile darkroom and advertising space.

Beach photographers such as these were ready to capitalize on the seasonal influx; these first mass producers of *plein-air* photographic portraits could number fifty or more on just a moderate-sized beach. So numerous and persistent were these enterprising men and

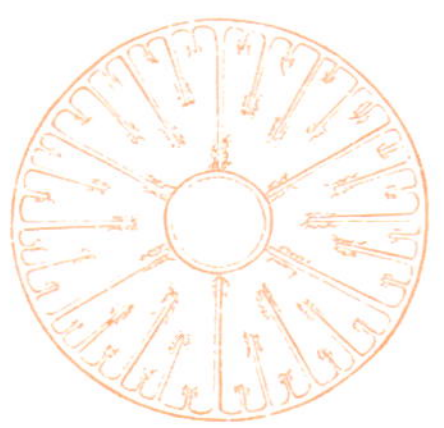

women that they drew derogatory epithets such as 'beach pest' and 'sand fly'. So prevalent were they that their equipment would frequently intrude on the picture-making of neighbouring photographers, as seen in the background of this seaside ferrotype (right) where two cameras on wide-spread tripods await another day's influx of sitters.

Despite contemporaneous criticism of these trading photographers, for the first time inexpensive while-you-wait photographic portraits, either as ambrotypes (glass-plate positives) or ferrotypes (direct positive images on enamelled iron) were being made not only *of* the working class but also *for* the working class. As the majority of seaside clients in this period were day-trippers' time was tight, and photographers needed to provide instantaneous pictures in order to secure a sale. Their rapidly produced images (normally taking around six minutes) were of course a vital feature of their trade and evoke a sense of the seaside as a site of instant gratification.

Over a century later, many of these humble ambrotype and later ferrotype beach portraits survive, often treasured by following generations, carefully located within family collections. Their survival suggests that at the point of purchase they were not perceived as mere cheap seaside ephemera, but rather affordable keepsakes. The medium of photography was, through this affordability, becoming increasingly democratized.

But how were these seaside visitors being represented? The early beach portraits from around 1860 are usually formal, with sitters largely rejecting the smile in favour of the sober expression more commonly associated with Victorian portraiture. If taken in isolation, such representations would suggest that the seaside was a place of rigid norms and formality. In fact, informality was present from the outset, just not routinely documented by the photographer. Within just a few seasons of the camera coming on to the sands, clients were increasingly willing to be photographed in relaxed poses, celebrating a day of leisure.

Photographers, particularly the more entrepreneurial ones working on beaches

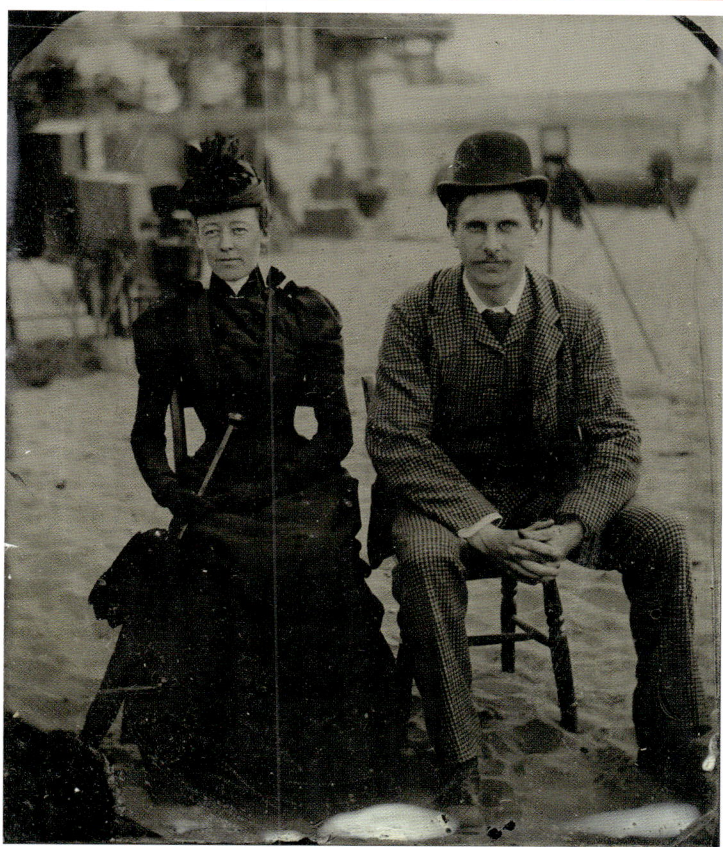

ANONYMOUS
Seaside ferrotype, *c.*1890

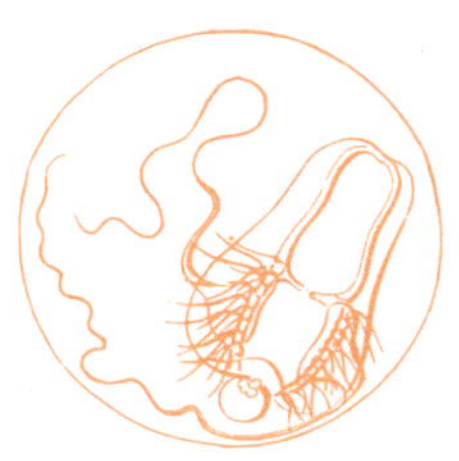

where there was often fierce and noisy competition, understood the value of novelty and differentiated their own pitches with gimmicks and props. This was taken still further by the numerous novelty seaside photographic studios who offered elaborately painted *trompe l'oeil* backcloths constructed as quasi-nautical worlds, in front of which clients would pose with beach paraphernalia – or, in the case of Charles Howell's slightly later Blackpool studio (p.2), sit astride motorcycles within an ever more ambitious and playful *mise en scène*. Such carefree activity, within or outwith the studio, was nevertheless bound by certain norms. To be snapped confidently reclining on the sands while smartly attired in blazer and beach cap would be one thing; to be surreptitiously photographed in an immodest sexual pose was another.

Yet Paul Martin's late nineteenth-century photographs of Yarmouth Sands offer a

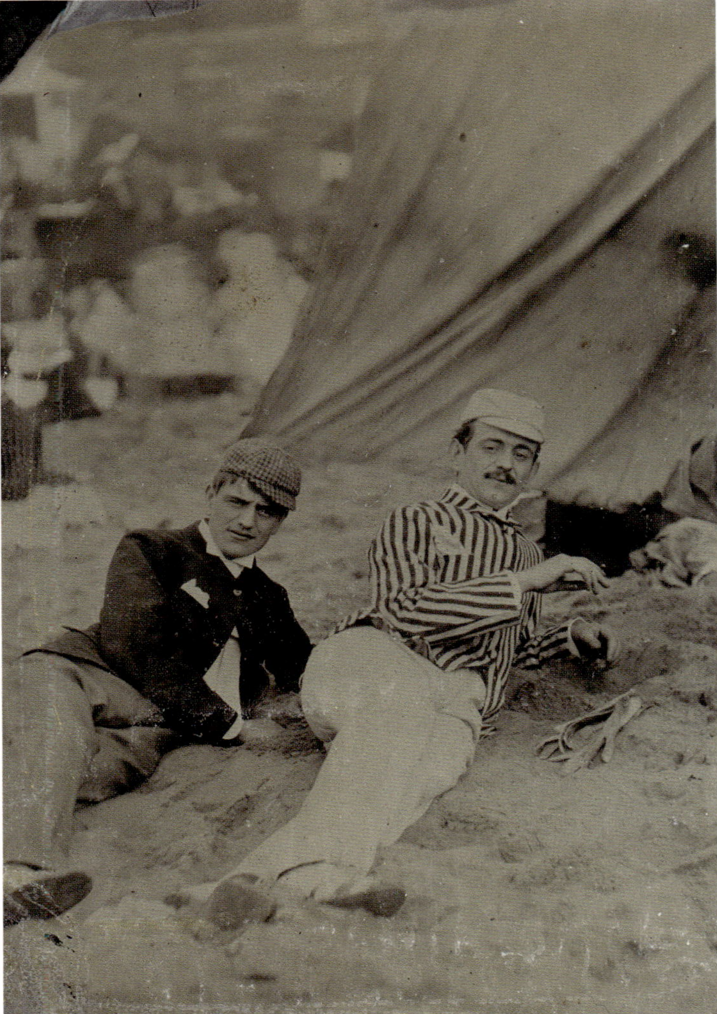

startlingly voyeuristic counter-perspective to the sanctioned decorous beach portrait. The unrestrained behaviours characterizing many of Martin's Yarmouth studies are astonishing. His surreptitious photographs, using an adapted Folio camera disguised as a brown paper parcel, capture robust intimacies on the beach with unwitting couples and groups shown relishing fervent physical embrace. One even goes so far as to show a man almost fully astride a woman (opposite).

Martin's capturing of such normally private behaviours suggests that, while it was rarely documented visually, the beach could be a site of transgression, where, within the public sphere of a coastal resort, social norms could be challenged and even suspended.

As many of the coastal towns' foreshores became a site of commerce, holiday pursuits and entertainments, a number of photographers consciously turned away from the social hubbub to signify – in individualized ways – the seaside as wild, elemental and idealized. Henry Peach Robinson, Nelson King Cherrill, Francis Mortimer and John Cimon Warburg utilized and established modern technologies and techniques to perpetuate photography's artistic capabilities, and by default proposed the photographer as artist.

Robinson's influential 1869 publication *Pictorial Effect in Photography* argued for the aesthetic capabilities of just such image-making, advocating the new medium's potential for moving beyond mere literal reproduction to creative expression. By the final quarter of the nineteenth century, pictorialism, as it came to be known, had an international compass, which would continue well into the twentieth century. As a movement, it was neither fixed nor defined; its amorphous and often argumentative core was perhaps best characterized as an approach rather than a prescribed style. But a common thread consisted in a challenge to objective photography, with pictorialists arguing that the medium's potency came not through a distancing objectivity, but through individual expression, manifested in creative interventions and crafted manipulations. Contemporaneous art movements, such as Impressionism, resonate in many of the pictorialist works, with this alignment to fine art being reiterated in the pictorialists' language. By repeatedly emulating and associating their photographic practice with established art forms, they established a 'painterly' discourse.

The influential editor of *Amateur Photographer*, Francis Mortimer, is a case in point. In many ways he typified a pictorialist approach, such that when discussing the challenges of making wild wave-studies, he used rhetorical devices to connect the photographic with the painterly and reveal the photographer *as* artist.

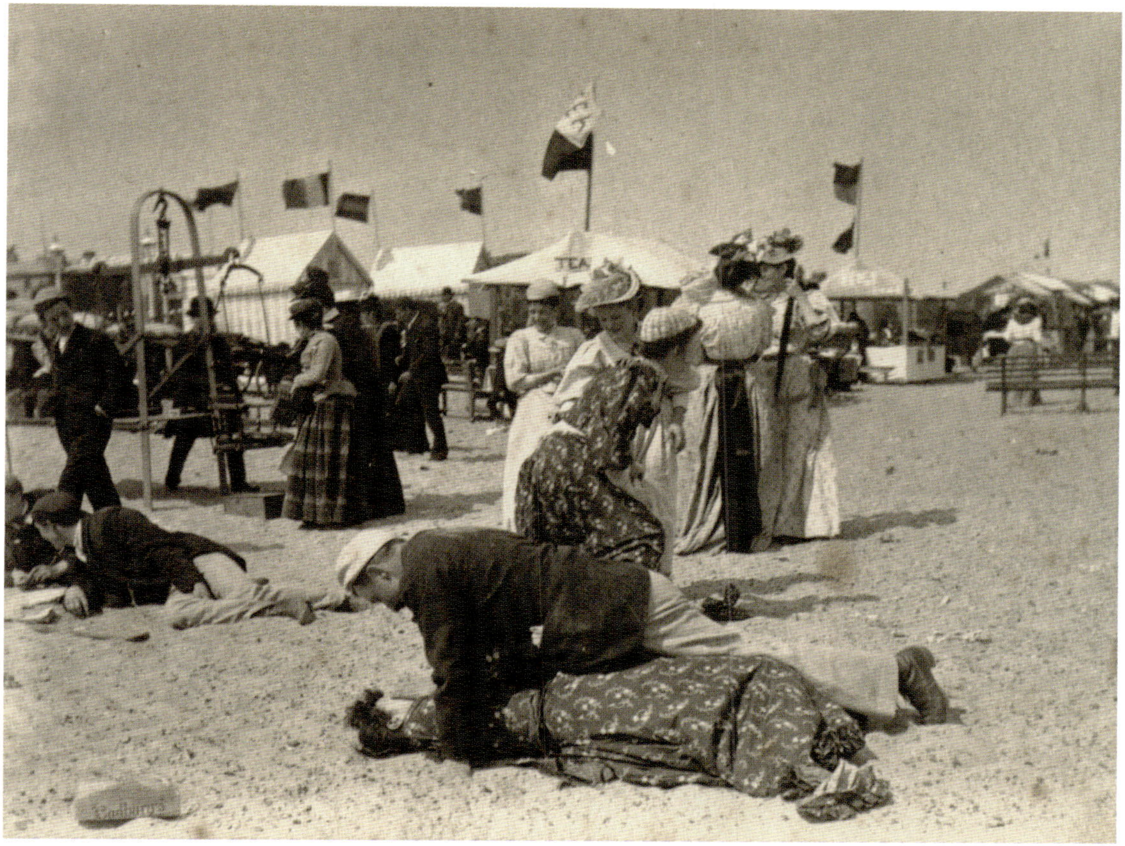

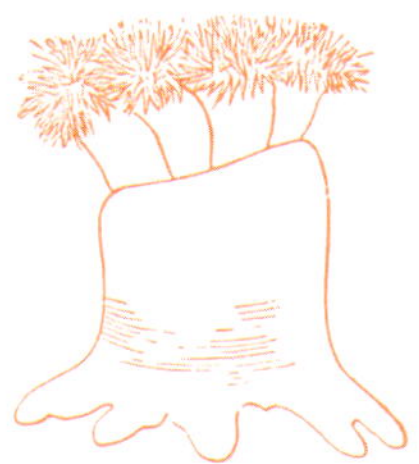

PAUL MARTIN
On Yarmouth Sands,
1895

Born in Portsmouth with a keen amateur photographer as a father, both the sea and photography were part of Mortimer's early socialization. He was an extraordinary innovator; although his work was at times suggestive of naturalism, he nevertheless rejected photography's potential for actuality, and instead promoted it as fine art. His enhancement of reality through 'after-treatments'[2] such as darkroom manipulations, elaborate oil and pigment printing processes and composite negatives challenged the contemporary boundaries of photography, placing him in the vanguard of those promoting the medium's capabilities beyond mechanical reproduction. But, as is the case with many creatives, Mortimer's assertions about capturing nature through the camera at times appear paradoxical. Here he seemingly argues against artistic intervention, proposing that the verbatim image should suffice:

... pictorial art is regarded by many as the idealization of Nature as seen through the temperament of the artist, surely Nature is beautiful enough at times to be reported verbatim.[3]

Perhaps such contradictory positioning should be viewed circumspectly. The photograph as two-dimensional object might make headway into showing what was seen by the artist, but not what was experienced. Mortimer's carefully applied darkroom after-treatments and combination plates, culminating in heightened chiaroscuro prints, are evidently not simplistic reflections of actuality, but rather refractions of his lived experience, a visual distillation of actuality into experience.

That experience for Mortimer was lived out in wild and inclement weather. He would go 'big wave' hunting, seeking an 'expression of nature and beauty', consequently needing to be tethered to the shoreline to counter the risk of being swept away. His writings go to great length to foreground the resultant perils. The character of what Mortimer refers to as the 'cameraist', who wishes to undertake such athletic seaside challenges, needs to embody a 'certain amount of recklessness' for, as he argues, bruises and broken apparatus are *de rigueur*. Recklessness, he asserts, needs to be accompanied by 'a companion with a stout rope'.

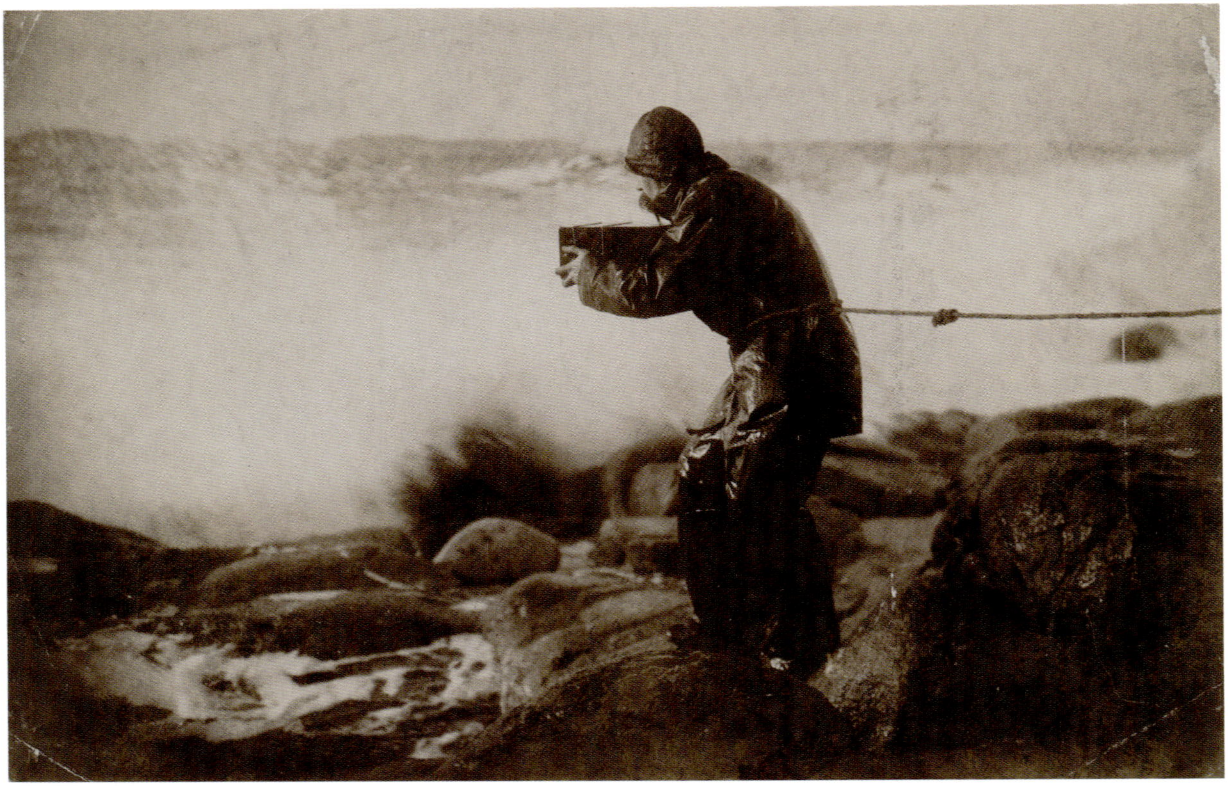

Mortimer's comments on the challenges of big-wave hunting are indicative of the romantic flourishes evident in his photographic prints. In the 1903 article 'On a Rocky Coast', he explores the technical difficulties, giving advice as to what to wear: oilskins and sou'wester with light flannel undergarments (preferably pyjamas) and avoidance of the mackintosh. Mortimer scathingly reports that the mackintosh will be 'found not only useless, but a positive hindrance'.[4]

GEORGE MORTIMER
Francis Mortimer
Big Wave Hunting,
Isles of Scilly, 1910s

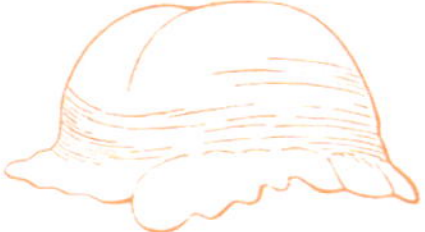

Accounts of big-wave hunting by Mortimer echo the probably apocryphal 'immersive' practices of J. M. W. Turner when, in the making of his 1842 *Snow Storm: Steam Boat off a Harbour's Mouth*, he is supposed to have been lashed to a ship's mast. In the first decade of the twentieth century, Mortimer produced dramatic photographic rough seas or 'wavescapes' by adopting a similar approach: tethering himself to a boat pitching off harbour or braced on a rocky outcrop at the hinterlands of seaside towns, his heavy camera optimally protected by the adaptation of oilcloth and Vaseline coverings. Saturated in the energy of nature and the power of the wave captured at close quarters, the resulting images are all the more thrilling and impressive for being hand- rather than tripod-held (as shown above, photographed by his nephew).

Mortimer was not alone as a pictorialist drawn to the shoreline, but not all chose to characterize the land's edge in such dramatic

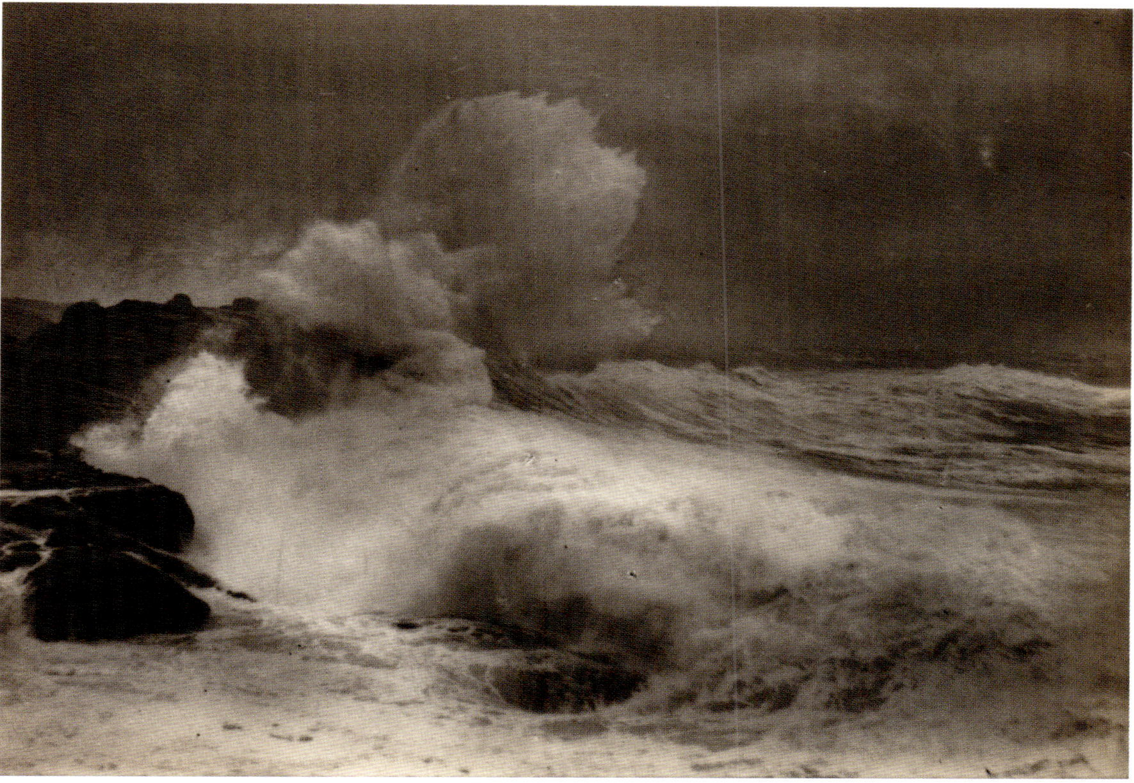

FRANCIS MORTIMER *Untitled*, seascape, *c.*1906

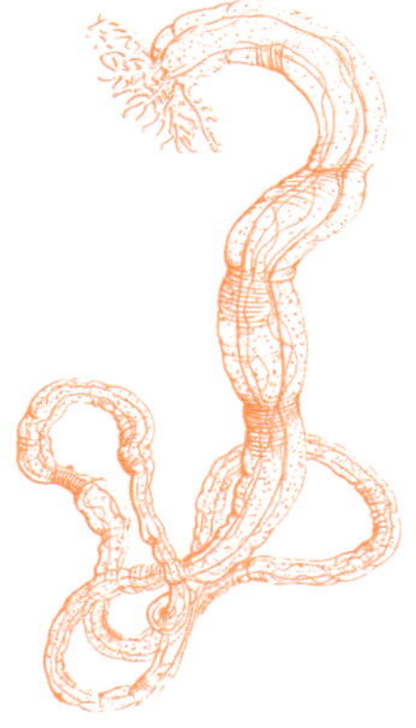

and muscular ways. Other British pictorialists such as Herbert Bairstow, Robinson and Cherrill sought to represent the environment as sublime in its tranquility and calm, focusing their cameras on unpopulated seashore, sand dunes and skies. In the same vein, John Cimon Warburg produced idealized seashores and through his very early use of colour – using autochrome glass plates – relocated more familiar scenes of the bucolic rural to the foreshore. Even when figures appear in Warburg's images they are placed at a distance and in their dress hark to an unspecified past time.

The pictorialists defiantly turned away from the seaside crowds and disassociated themselves from connotations of mass tourism. Many were dismayed by the modern visitor influx that threatened the very coastal tranquility and wildness that attracted them. They too were seaside visitors, but did not regard themselves as such and presented themselves as purposeful travellers rather than tourists – artists rather than technicians. Such a lofty stance was not ring-fenced to the pictorialists. T. Coan in 1892 and, two years later, the vociferous opponent to pictorialism P. H. Emerson both wrote critically of the seaside (specifically Yarmouth) spoilt by the invasion of day-trippers, their critique a thinly disguised thread of class tension.

Big waves were not of course exclusive to Mortimer; by the early twentieth-century, rough seas were also proving a popular and established theme for seaside postcards. Susan Hiller, in her 1972–6 conceptual work *Dedicated to the Unknown Artists*, creatively interrogates this phenomenon of the rough sea and pays homage to the anonymous postcard producers. In *Dedicated to the Unknown Artists*, Hiller collates maps, charts and 305 'rough seas' postcards into fourteen panels, which in scale and context (removed from the seaside postcard stand to the gallery wall) draw attention to the hitherto overlooked. A kind of monumentalism is created through

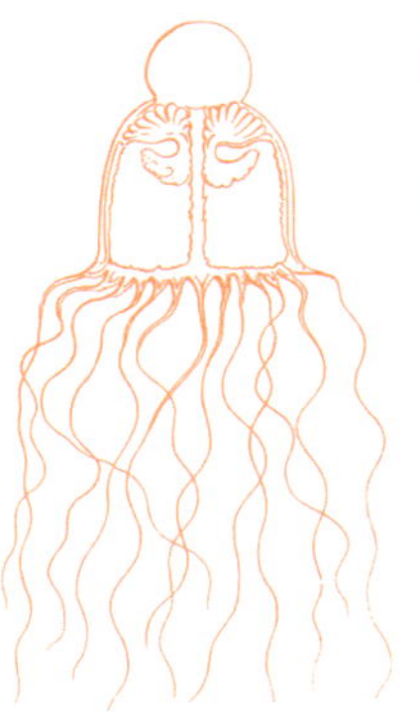

these modest cards, both individually and collectively. Hiller speaks of the excessive nature of such wild images and how she 'thought of the cards as miniature artworks',[5] focusing her and in turn our attention on the anonymous postcard photographers and post-production workers who imaginatively hand-tinted many of the images. Mortimer's aspiration to photography as art is thrillingly stretched to breaking point by Hiller's provocative use of the commercially prosaic postcard.

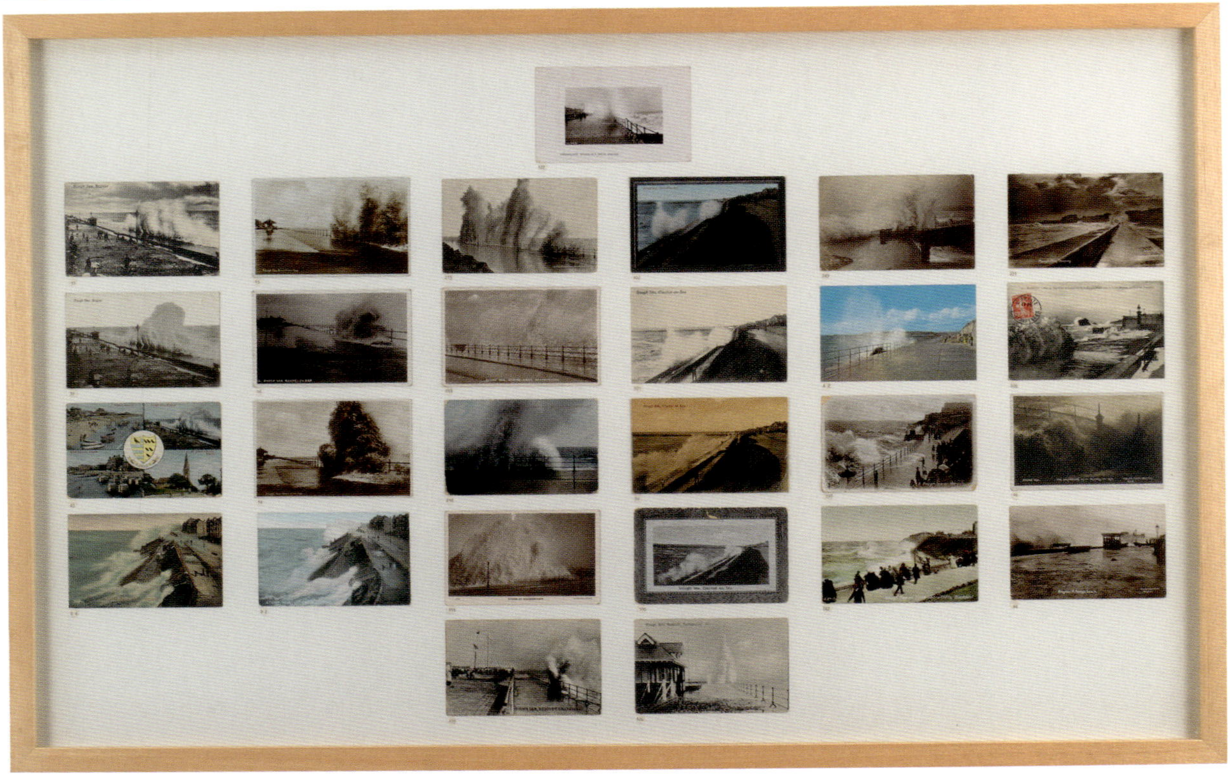

Some of the early pioneers' techniques might seem questionable in our post-atomic age, not least their use of uranium in the toning of photographic prints. Nineteenth-century experimentation using various chemical elements for printing and toning was commonplace, and as early as 1855 Charles Burnett was successfully printing with uranium.[6] Commercially produced uranium-printing paper was available until the turn of the twentieth century, and the four nineteenth-century prints opposite,

with their brown to red uranium tones, are characteristic of this process.

Here, William Crookes as photographer has dramatically fixed the sea's movement, and in using uranium has produced highly individualized images. Captured mechanically by the camera, the waves on this empty beach, through post-production methods of toning, are transformed into an artistic articulation of the depopulated seashore.

In our era of lightweight cameras and fast shutter speeds, the early photographs could easily be undervalued, regarded as romanticized to the point of whimsy. But these seaside images, along with those in this chapter's portfolio, are radical not only in their means of production but also in their makers' claim to achieve the status of art through mechanical reproduction. Taken at the edge of the land, these works signify, in deceptively complex ways, the edge of photography's own aesthetic and technical possibilities. [KS]

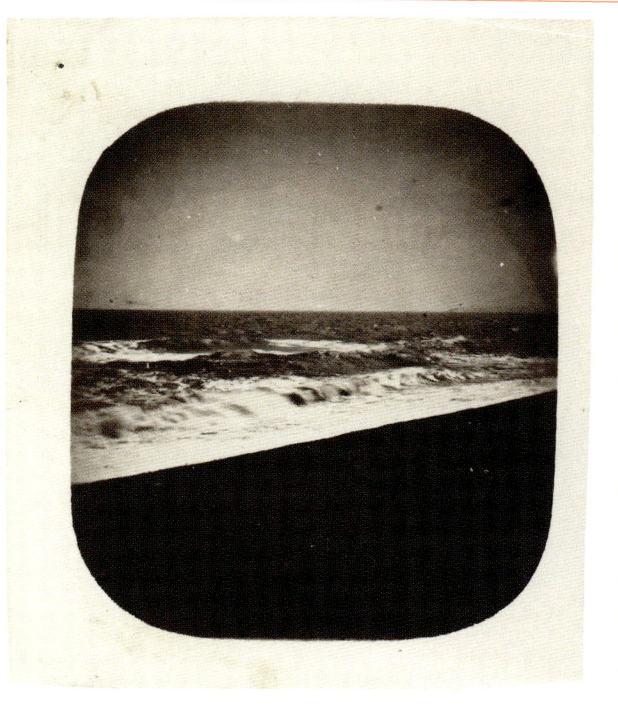

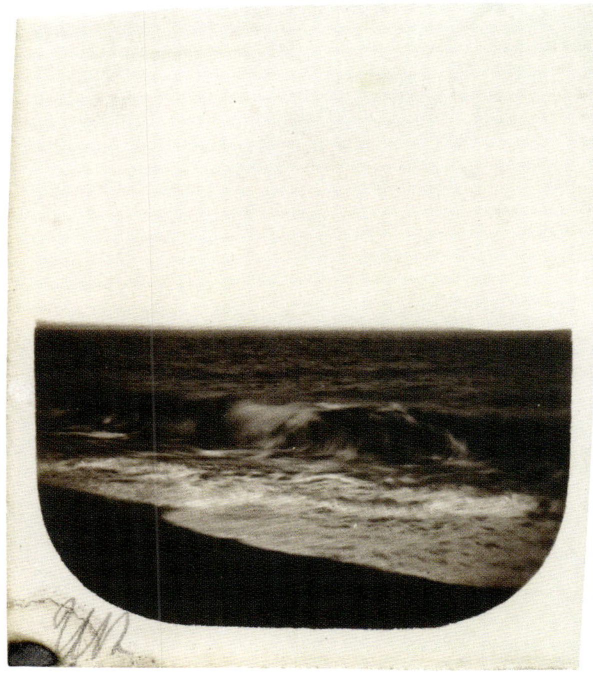

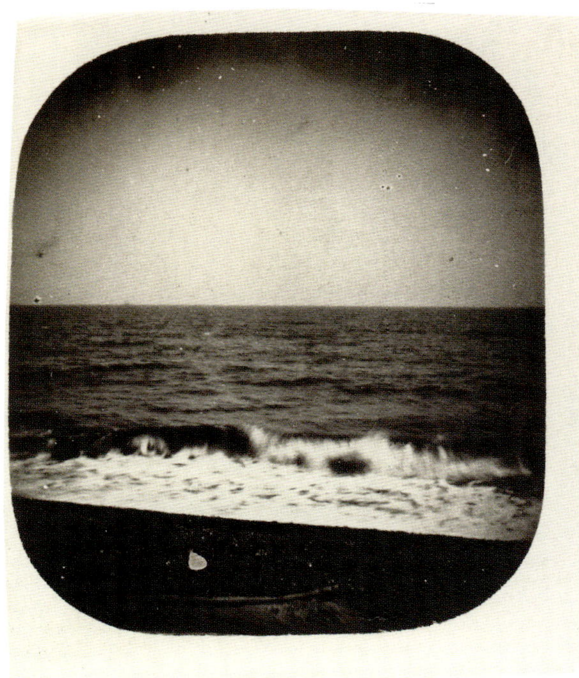

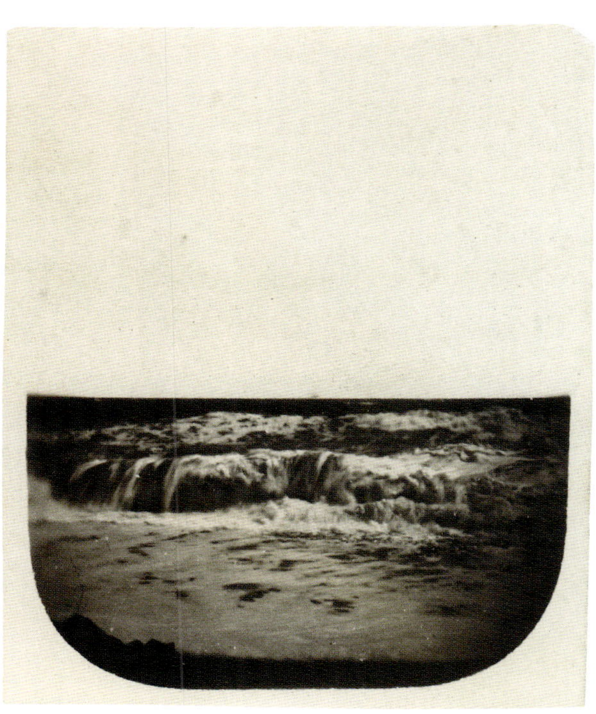

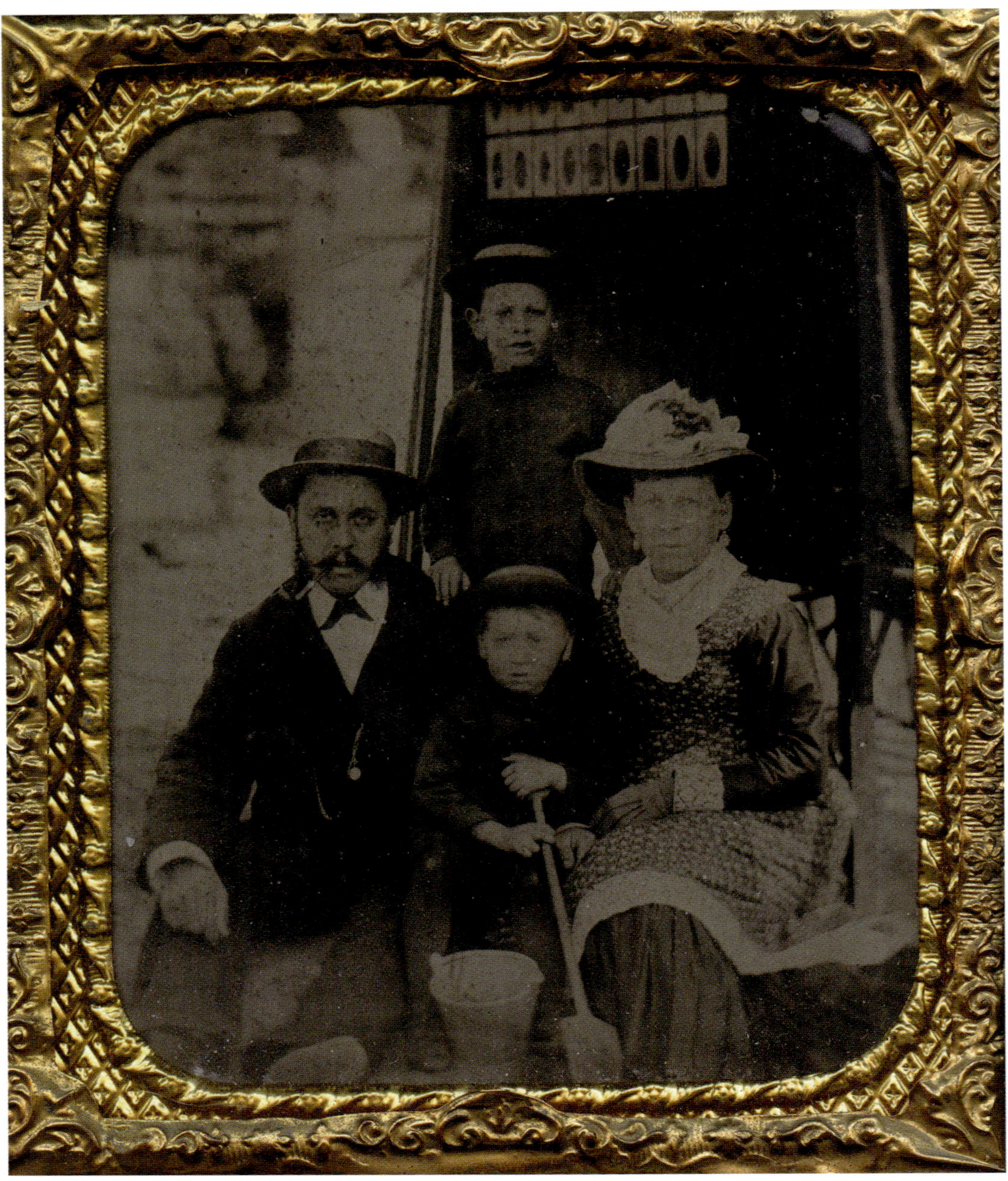

Cased ferrotype with photographer's darkcart also visible, *c.*1890

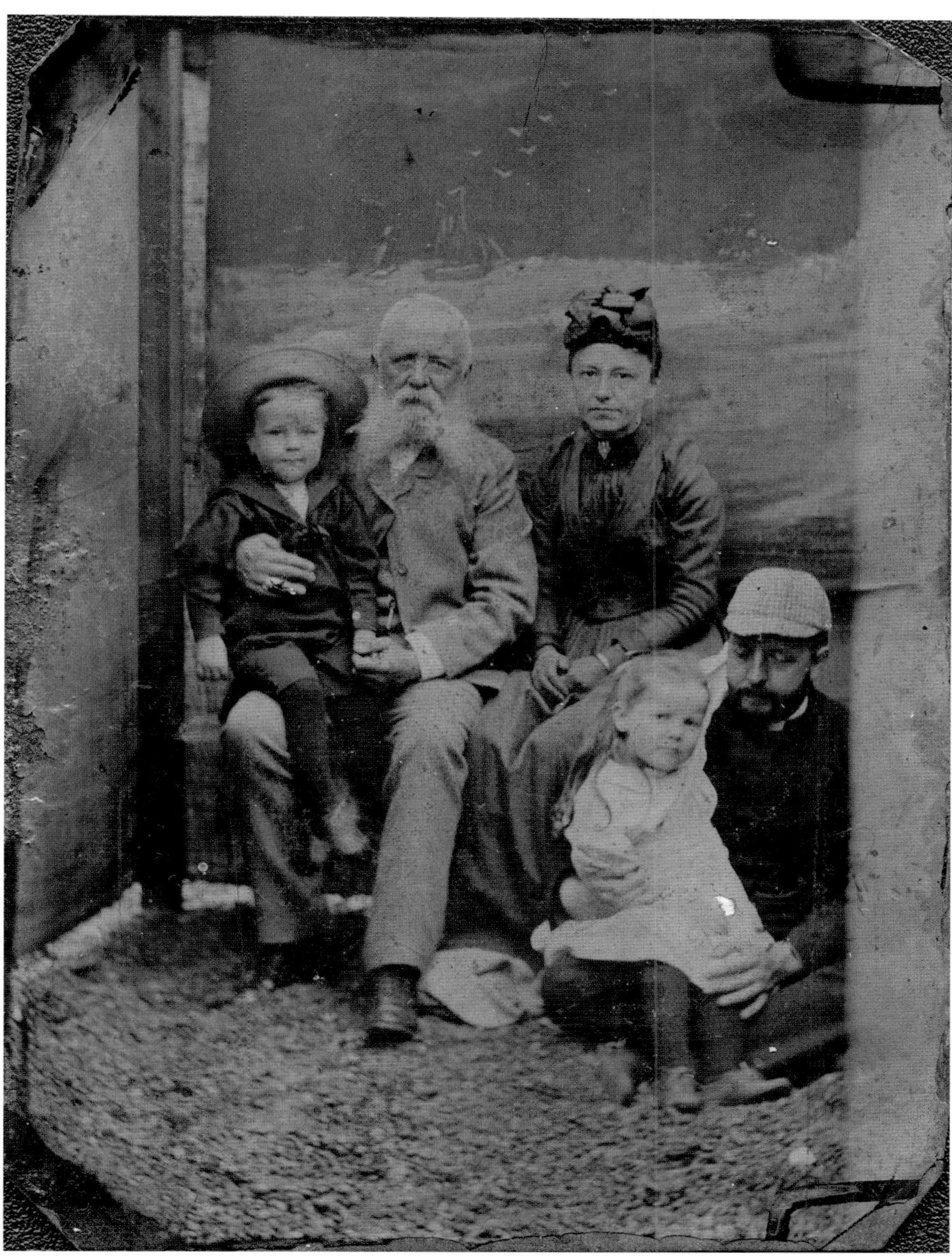

Ferrotype showing makeshift seaside-studio with hand-painted nautical backcloth, late 19th century

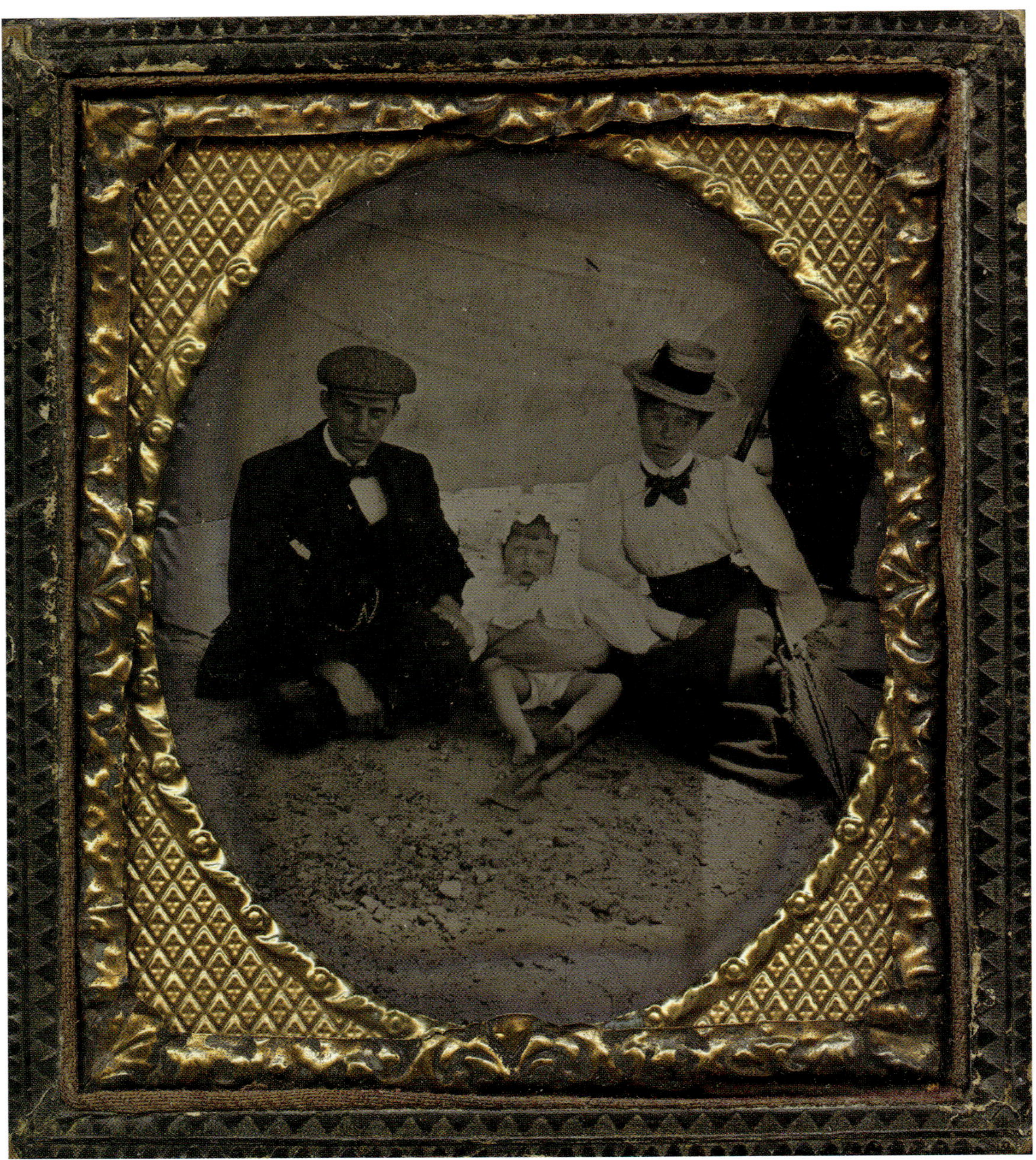

Cased ferrotype with photographer's assistant holding diffuser, *c.*1900

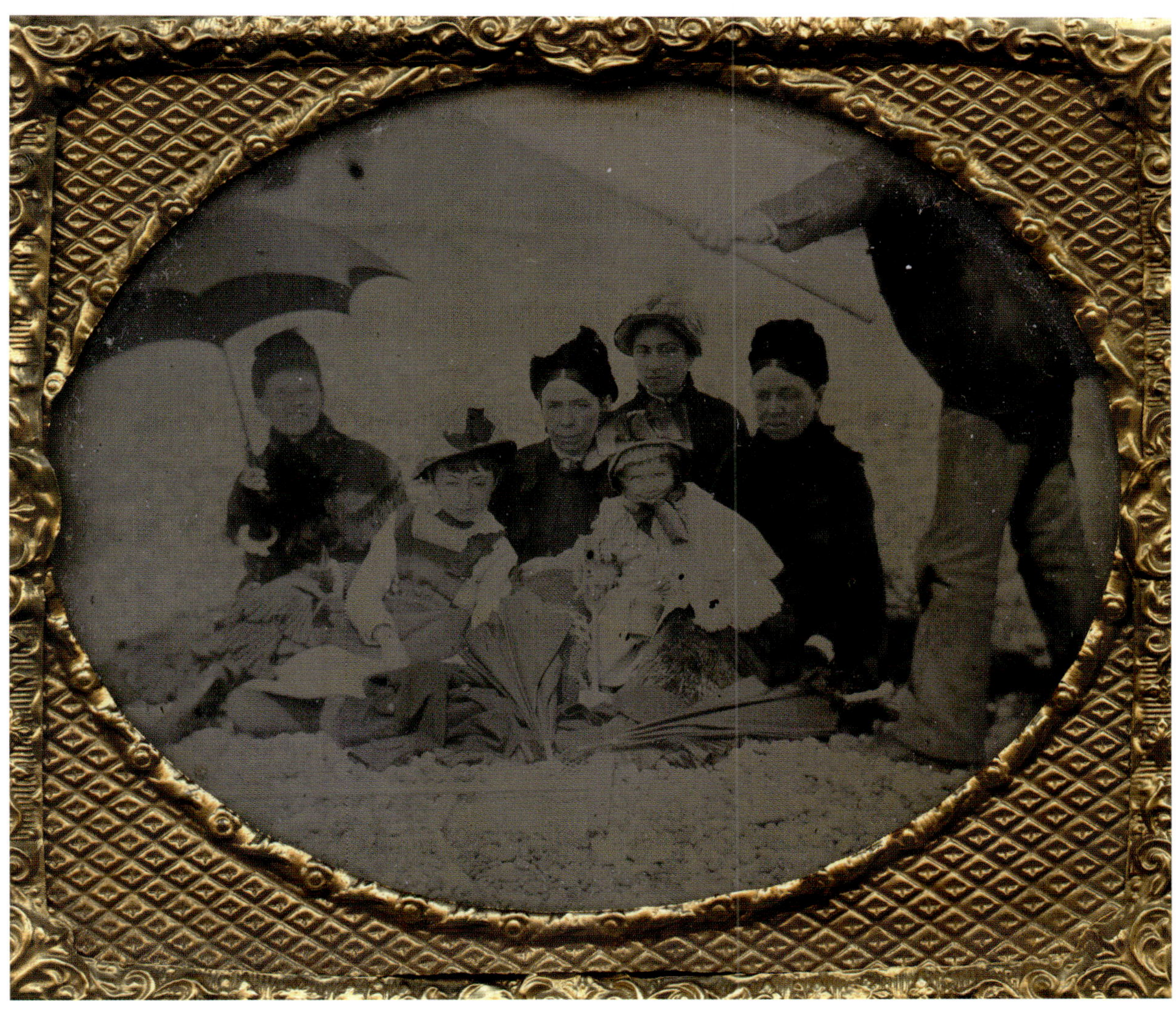

Part-cased ambrotype showing photographer's assistant with diffuser, *c.*1880–90

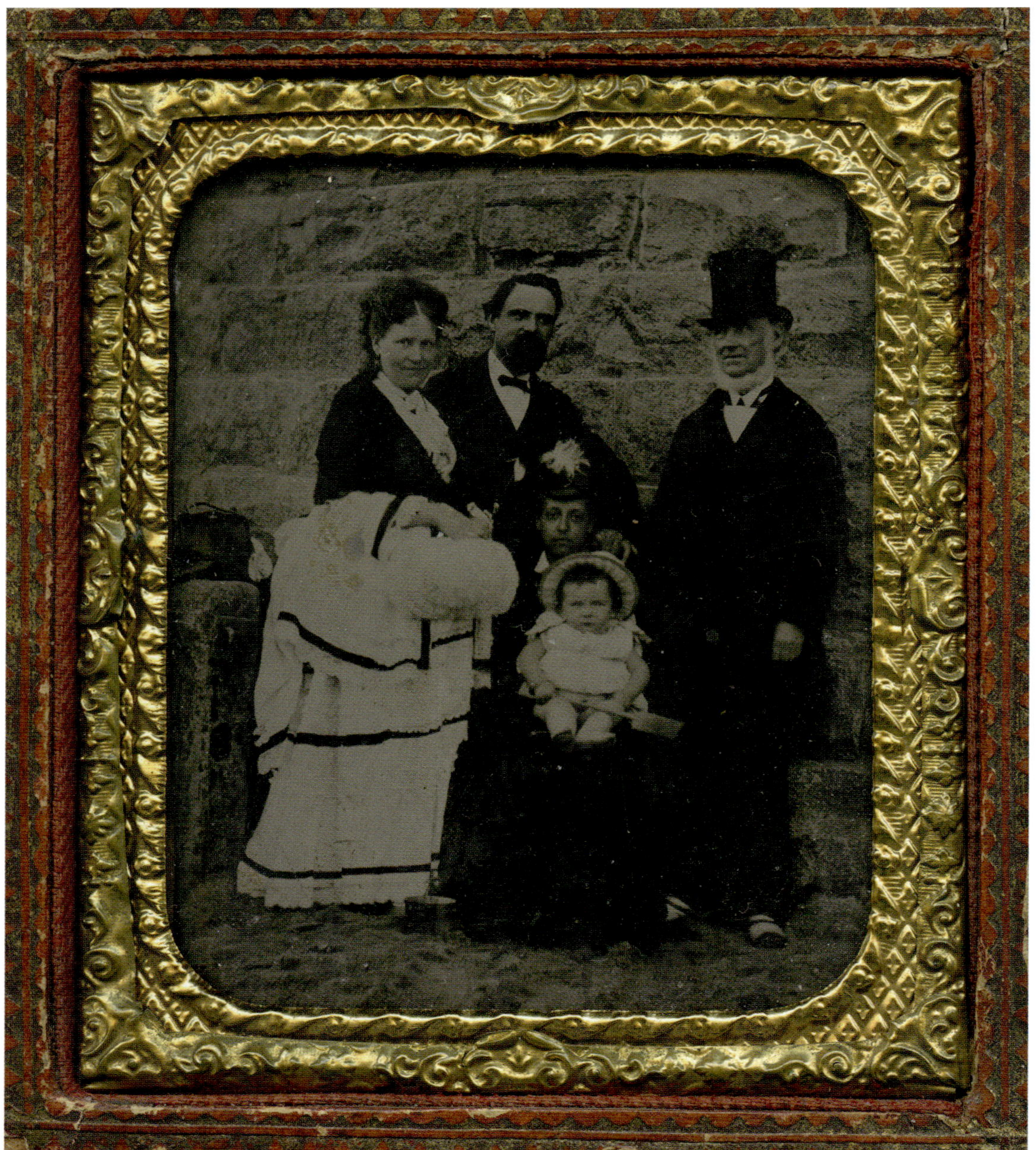

Cased ferrotype by Beach J. Price of Ramsgate Sands, *c.*1860

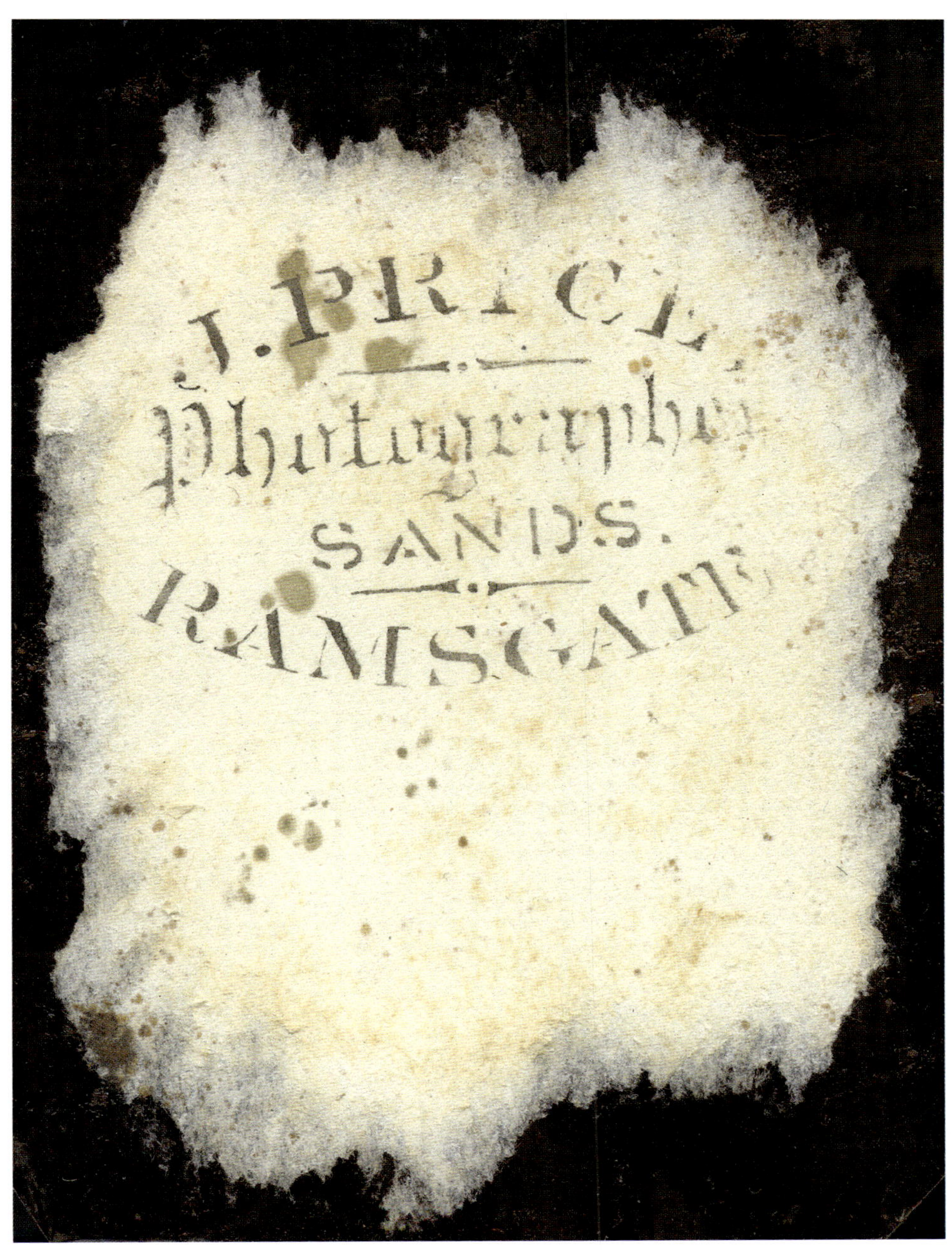

Reverse of cased ferrotype by Beach J. Price of Ramsgate Sands, *c.*1860

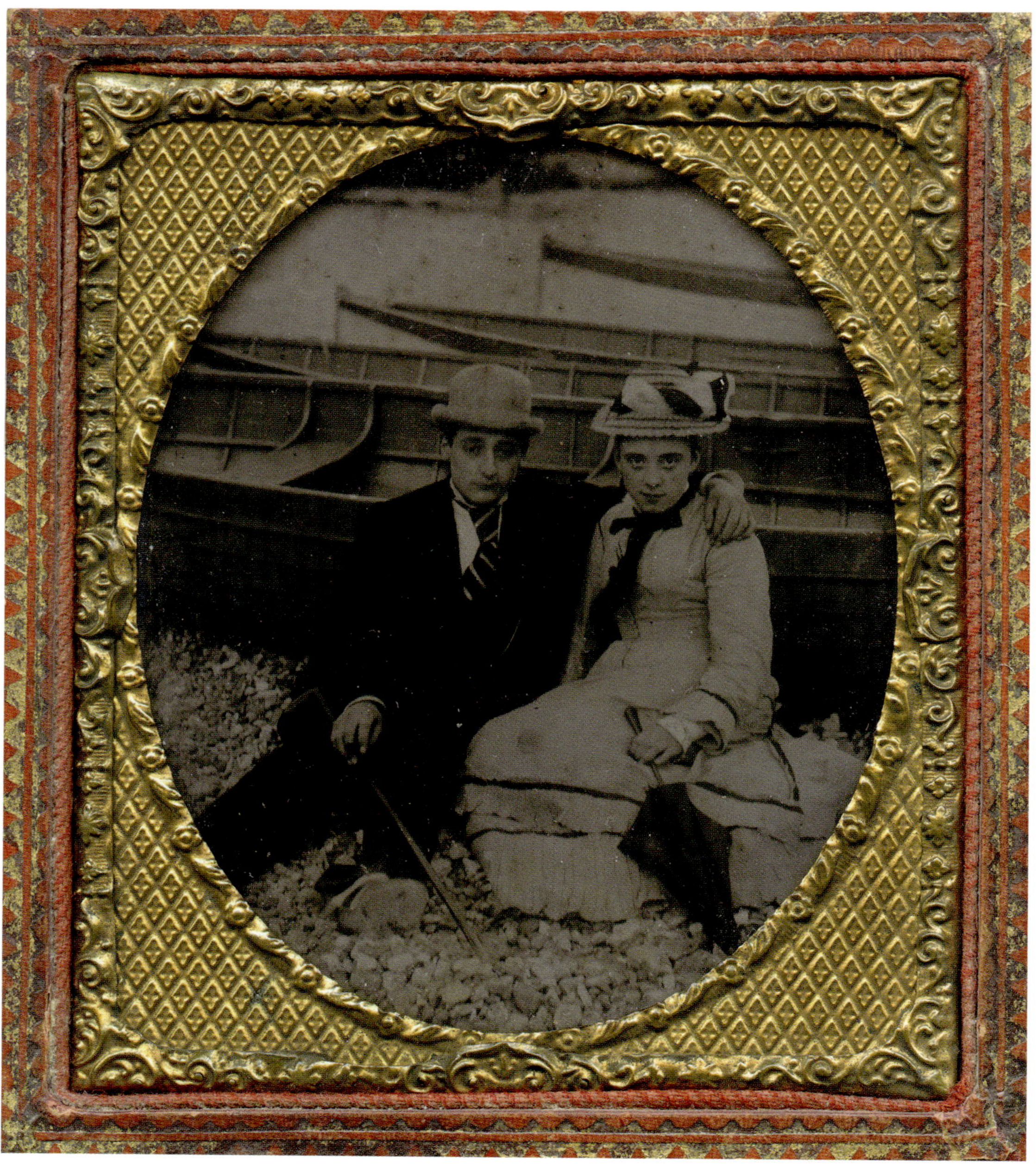

Cased ambrotype, possibly Hastings, *c.*1900

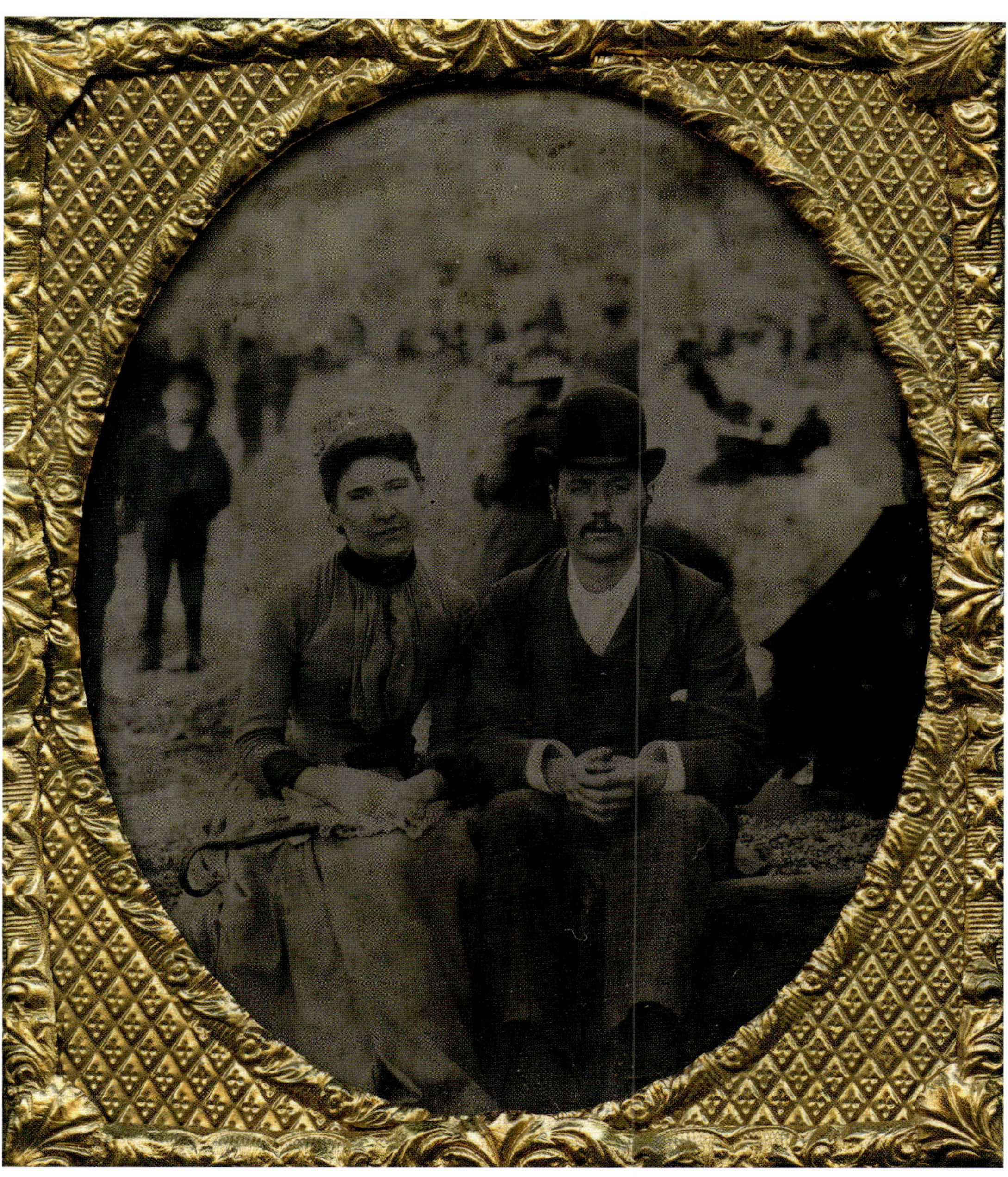

Part-cased ambrotype, *c.*1890

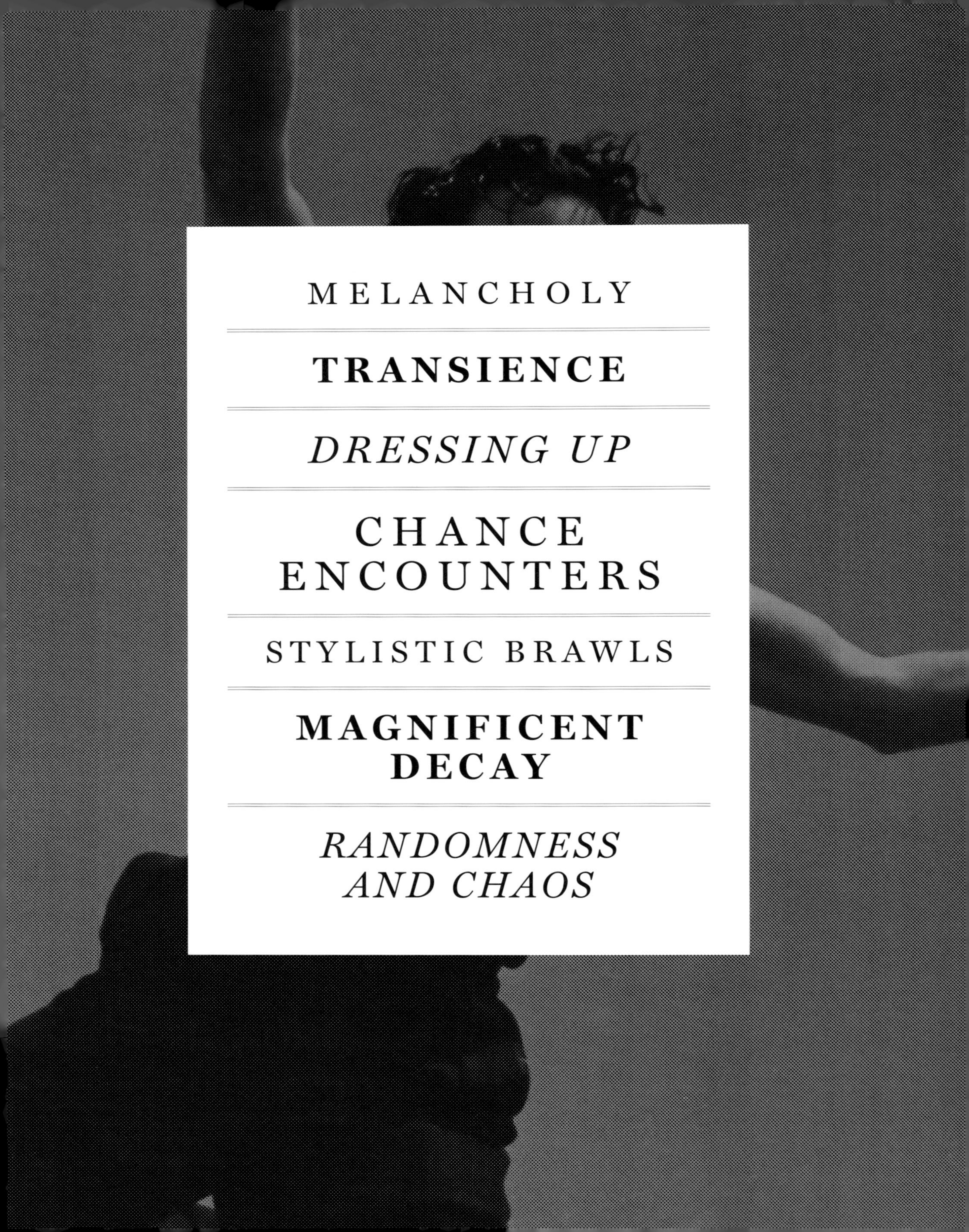

MELANCHOLY

TRANSIENCE

DRESSING UP

CHANCE
ENCOUNTERS

STYLISTIC BRAWLS

**MAGNIFICENT
DECAY**

*RANDOMNESS
AND CHAOS*

SEASIDE BOHEMIAS

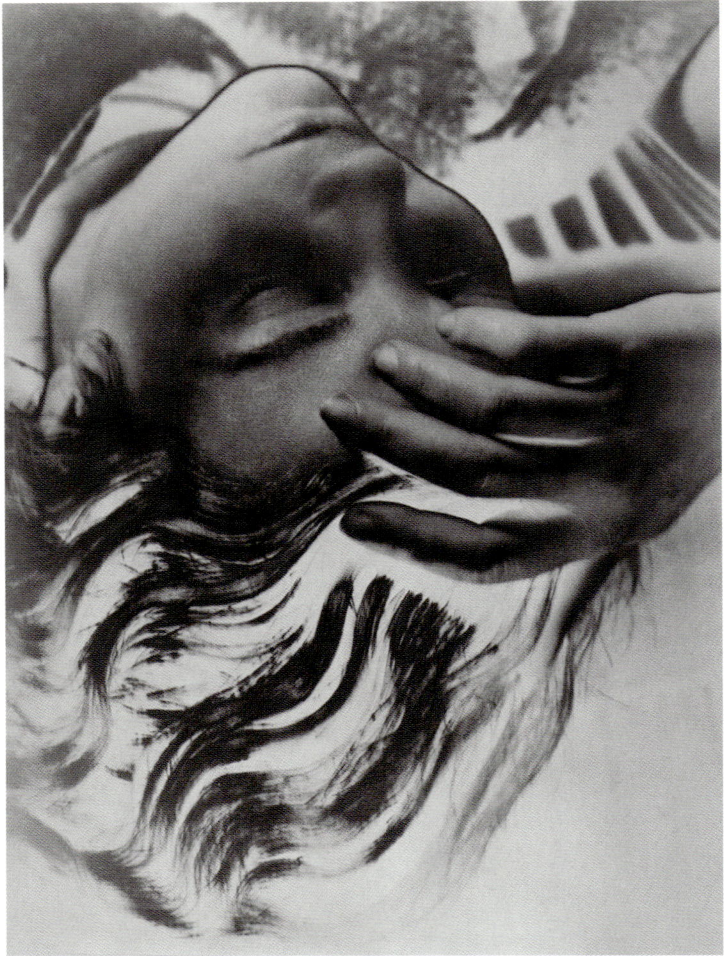

In April 1928, twenty-year-old Helen Muspratt opened a photographic portrait studio in the seaside town of Swanage in Dorset. Young, enthusiastic and highly innovative, Muspratt, over and above the day-to-day portraiture at which she excelled, produced a set of portraits of the Purbeck avant-garde (see above) that are an invaluable part of the history of seaside bohemia.[1]

Sometimes for recreation, sometimes for work, the seaside was hugely influential on artistic life in England, and bohemia found a niche there. Best known, and much documented, is the artists' colony at St Ives in Cornwall, established in the late 1930s. The photographer Roger Mayne, most notable today for his London street photography,

HELEN MUSPRATT
Portrait of Eileen Agar,
solarized photograph,
1935

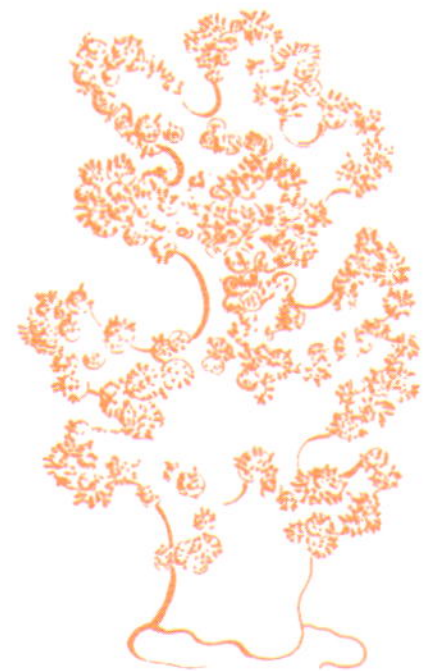

made a comprehensive documentary of St Ives artists and their works in the 1950s. As well as photographing artists in their studios, Mayne made informal group photographs that describe life among the artists in this most important of British art colonies. There is a 1965 photograph of the poet W. S. Graham and painters Karl Weschke and Bryan Wynter in a Zennor kitchen – beer bottles on the table, washing hanging above the stove – that captures a world of young men, opinionated, passionate, among whom Mayne would have felt entirely at home.

Dressing up was a prerequisite of bohemia: travelling theatre companies and Pierrots spent summer seasons at the seaside and were a popular part of holiday entertainment up until the end of the 1950s. Pierrots were anarchic; they dressed in the costumes of the *commedia dell'arte*, with their roots in Europe and as itinerants were attractive to English bohemians. Unlike the music hall *artistes* (who also had their followers among the avant-garde), Pierrots were wistful and melancholic. Their romance and their transience added to the sense that at the seaside, true bohemia was attainable. Pierrot troupes were not only photogenic: competition between them was stiff and they needed photography to popularize themselves, via the picture postcard and the studio portrait (see opposite).

Muspratt was born in Bangalore, India, and moved with her parents to Swanage in 1921. After studying photography in London, she returned to Swanage to set up a portrait studio and to see what cultural life on the Isle of Purbeck had to offer. She was not disappointed. From the beginning, Muspratt was determined to be much more than a local studio photographer. Her photographic interests were wide-ranging and not confined to the bread-and-butter work of studio portraits of children, engaged couples and family groups.

Muspratt's introduction to the Purbeck bohemians came through Francis Newbery, former head of Glasgow School of Art, where he had taught the architect and designer Charles Rennie Mackintosh. Although

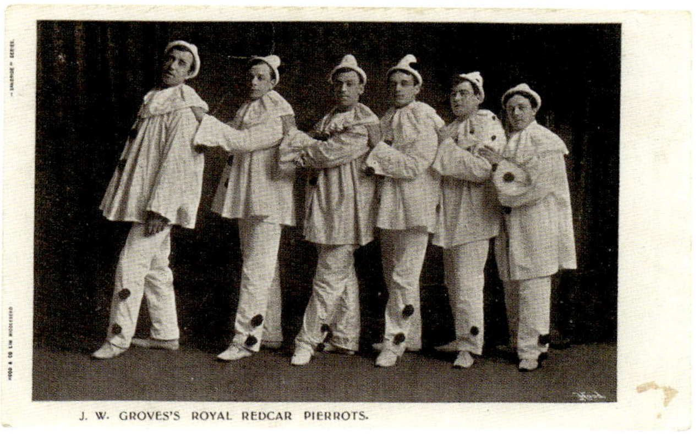

HOOD & CO., MIDDLESBOROUGH
J. W. Groves's Royal Redcar Pierrots, early 20th century

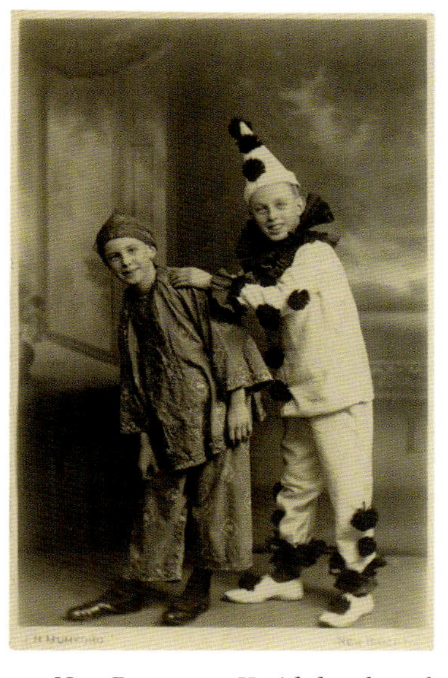

H. MUMFORD, NEW BRIGHTON, *Untitled*, early 20th century

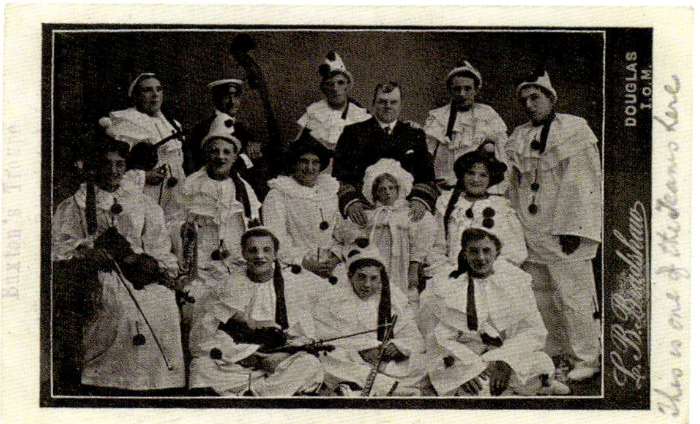

L. B. BRADSHAW, ISLE OF WIGHT
Buxton Troupe, early 20th century

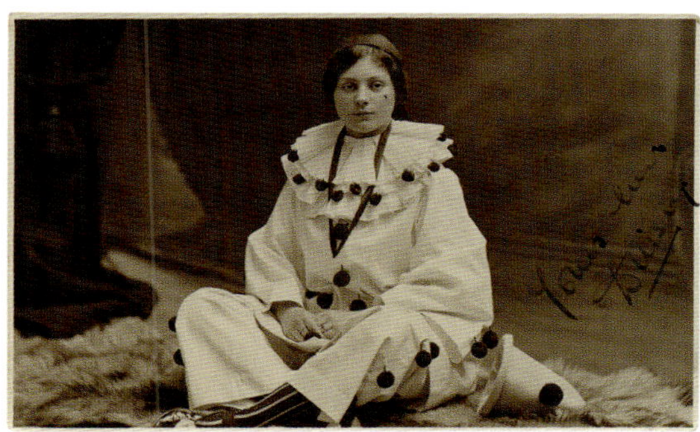

HOUGHTON PHOTO, MARGATE, *Untitled*, early 20th century

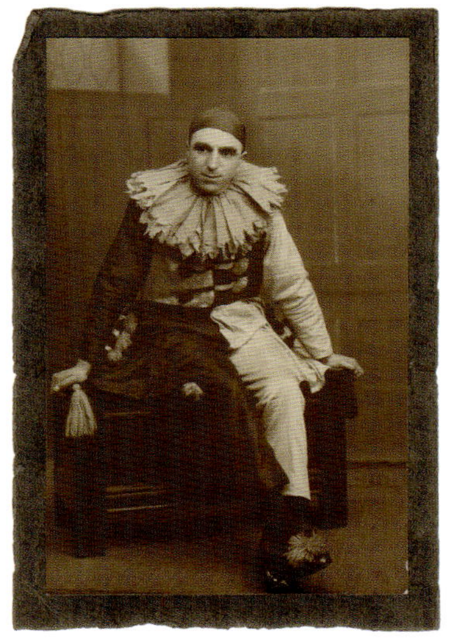

PHOTOGRAPHER UNKNOWN, *Untitled*
Cabinet Card, early 20th century

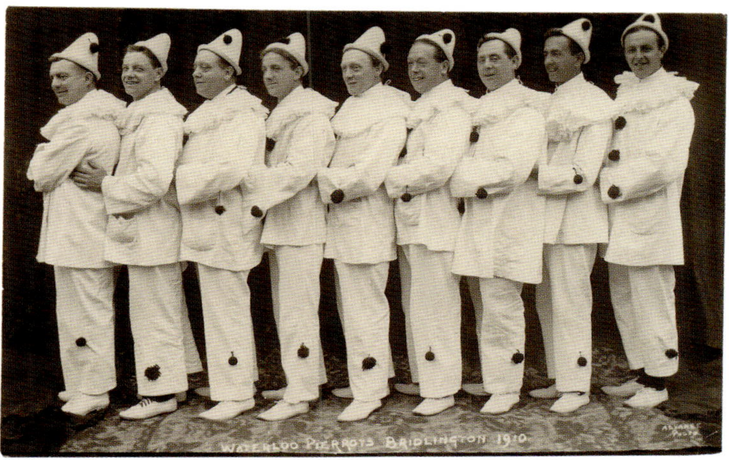

PHOTOGRAPHER UNKNOWN, *Waterloo Pierrots, Bridlington*, 1910

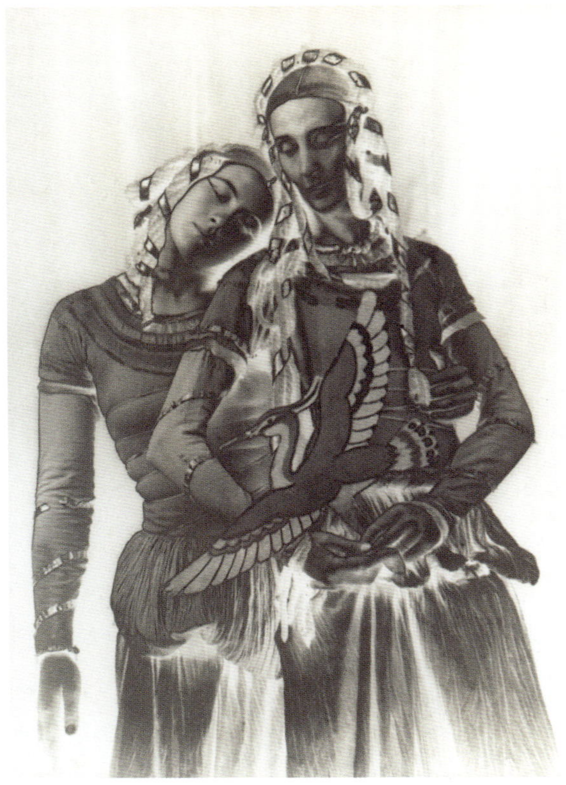

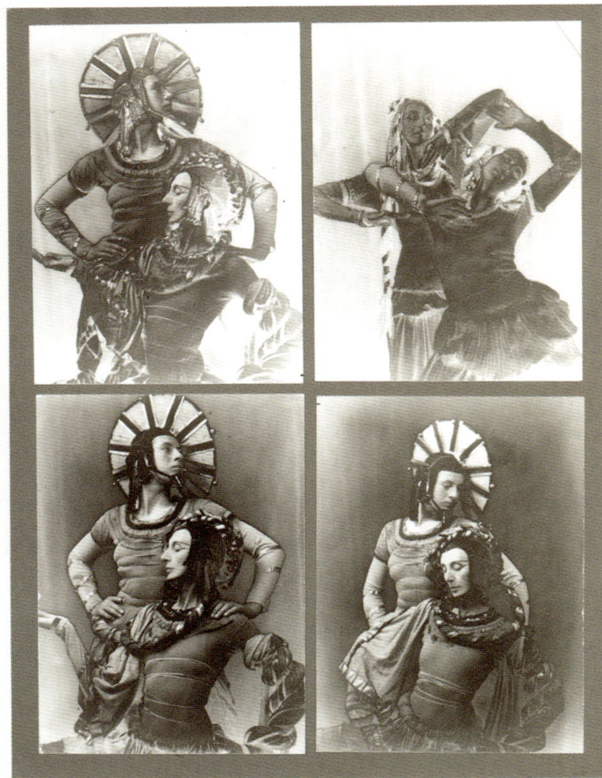

Muspratt set up her legendary partnership in Cambridge with fellow photographer Lettice Ramsey in the early 1930s, the Muspratt studio continued to prosper in Swanage, with the help of Helen's sister Joan.

Muspratt might have become one of hundreds of women photographers running portrait studios in a small town. But the partnership with Lettice Ramsey brought new richness to Muspratt's life and work as both women explored European photography, in particular the work of Man Ray, who introduced the technique of solarization to British photographers. Solarization, with its elegant silvering and its ethereal surface, was perfectly suited to portraying the bohemian group with whom Muspratt began to work in Swanage in the 1930s. What was learnt and perfected in Cambridge was brought to Swanage, and she began to photograph the remarkable Spencer Watson mother and daughter, Hilda and Mary (above). Her series *Hilda and Mary Spencer Watson Performing*

ABOVE LEFT AND RIGHT

HELEN MUSPRATT
Hilda and Mary Spencer Watson Performing Jacob and Esau, solarized photographs, *c.*1932

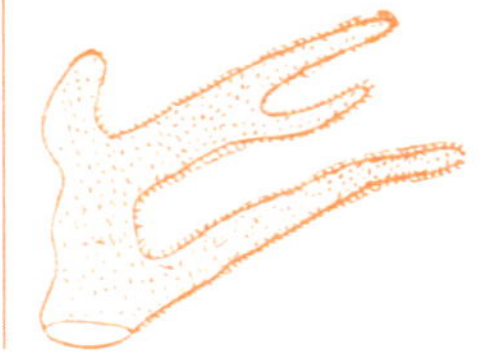

*Jacob and Esau, c.*1932, is solarized, and is remarkable in its innovation and power as the Spencer Watsons adopt stylized poses in their rich costumes. English bohemia had never been so well portrayed – this was fine studio photography, preserving the memory of a particular moment in English cultural history. Hilda and Mary ran their own theatre at their home, Dunshay Manor, where Muspratt photographed performances.

Purbeck was popular with the avant-garde. In his 2015 book *Purbeck Arcadia*, Ilay Cooper lists Duncan Grant, Vanessa Bell, Lytton Strachey, Mark Gertler, Clive Bell and Virginia Woolf as regular visitors. Vanessa Bell took photographs at Studland, as did others in the group, and both she and Grant painted there. Other artists came in and out – Augustus John was a visitor, as was the writer Robert Graves, and one particularly adventurous family lived in a caravan.[2]

Hilda Spencer Watson performed often with her ensemble at the Mowlem Hall in

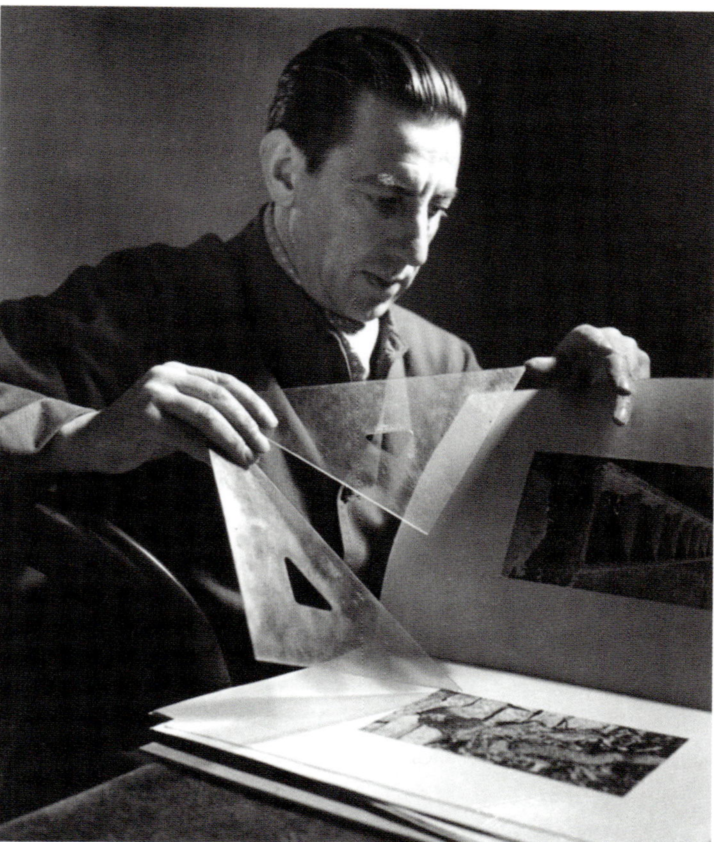

Swanage, and later at her own theatre at Dunshay Manor. She also had a London studio theatre and toured with her troupe. Muspratt recorded the Swanage performances, and through the Spencer Watsons she was also able to photograph the singers Norman Notley and David Brynley, making a solarized portrait of them in the 1930s.[3] Muspratt remained Hilda Spencer Watson's favourite photographer.

Throughout England in the 1930s, small bohemias existed, many by or near the sea. Most of them have not been recorded, apart from the odd snapshot here and there. Muspratt's modernity, her curiosity and her position as a photographic innovator means that this moment in time, and these remarkable women who performed with such vigor and elegance, have been immortalized.

Two other important visitors to Swanage in the mid-1930s were the painters Eileen Agar and Paul Nash. Nash came to Swanage for his health, and also to photograph, write and edit the Shell Guide to Dorset. Nash was already known as a painter and skilled photographer by the time he arrived in Swanage with his wife Margaret, and his welcome from the Purbeck bohemians was a warm one. In Muspratt he would have found a kindred spirit who took photography seriously and who was keen to experiment. Muspratt photographed Nash and Agar in 1935. Her portrait of Nash is sombre and plain, suiting his gravity (left), but her solarized photograph of Agar is highly charged – Agar leans backwards and her solarized hair is like a metal waterfall (p.64). *Portrait of Eileen Agar* has become Muspratt's best known and most admired photograph, and was shown in the Tate Britain exhibition 'How We Are', in 2007.

From time to time, interest in seaside bohemias is revived. In 1990 the filmmaker Jonathan Meades made *In Search of Bohemia* as part of the series 'Abroad in Britain'. 'The exotic', Meades declares at the beginning, 'begins at home'. Later in the episode, Meades visits Hastings and its suburb of Bohemia. For Meades, Hastings encapsulated bohemia: 'Do the people fit the name? The place certainly does.' Standing behind Meades as he strode across the pebbly fishing beach in Hastings was Laetitia Yhap, a painter who left London in the 1980s and who has lived in Hastings ever since.

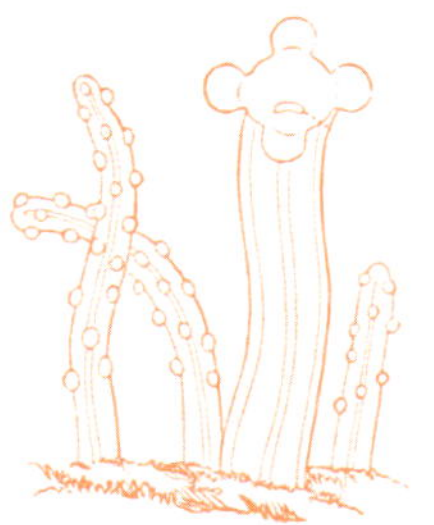

> The entire town of Hastings should be called bohemia … it possesses the randomness, the chaos, the juxtapositions of the sublime and the pathetic that inform bohemian lives. … overripe, blowsy, it has a bruised amiability that only the fallen can ever achieve Any urban organism is a work of perpetual progress, but this is different, it's a series of abandoned works which attempt to occupy the same canvas … chance encounters, stylistic brawls … This is a town whose buildings lack any sort of consensus. They all, as is still said here, do their own thing.

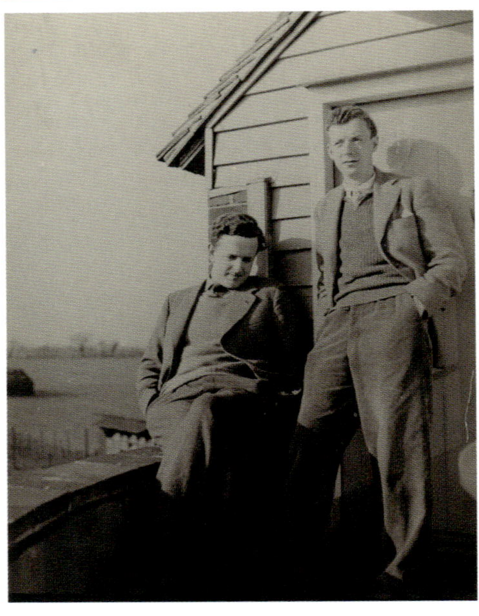

Meades interviewed artists Gus Cummins and Angie Braven and also attended an impromptu performance by Fiona Pitt-Kethley in a magnificent decayed house in St Leonards-on-Sea, Sussex. Some years before, at the beginning of his trip around the British coast, travel writer and novelist Paul Theroux had also visited the artists' community in Hastings, spending time with the well-known painter John Bratby, who was at the centre of this particular seaside bohemia. The idea of the outsider bohemian artist, a vehicle for popular comedy, gained particular traction after the end of the Second World War with Tony Hancock's *The Rebel* in 1960 and also as Gulley Jimson, played by Alec Guinness, in *The Horse's Mouth*.

For many artists and writers, bohemia was an unsatisfactory but necessary state, brought on by poverty. If theirs was not to be a life of drudgery, bohemians required servants. For those without, like the writer Katherine Mansfield, who spent a time living in a primitive cottage, housework overwhelmed everything. Penelope Fitzgerald's family lived in a leaking houseboat from the 1960s after moving away from the Suffolk coast, where Fitzgerald had set *The Bookshop*, her novel about small-town rivalry in the arts. She

UNKNOWN
PHOTOGRAPHER
Britten standing and
Pears sitting outside
the Mill, *c*.1943

UNKNOWN
PHOTOGRAPHER
Britten and Pears
standing with drinks
in the garden, *c*.1954

became friendly with the bohemian Fiennes family while in Suffolk, with the Freuds, and with Iris Birtwistle, poet and gallery owner.[4] Though photographs from the Fitzgeralds are fairly ordinary domestic fare, Mark Fiennes became a photographer and made many portraits of his large family, including actors Ralph and Joseph.

The seaside will often try to recreate its bohemias; an artists' community is usually the first indication that regeneration will follow. But in the 1930s, bohemias were almost accidental, coincidental. Paul and Margaret Nash came to Purbeck in search of better air for Paul's damaged lungs. Muspratt set up her studio in Swanage because that was home. When European travel became an impossibility in wartime, artists sought out Cornwall. The curiosity of photographers and filmmakers has given us these records of seaside bohemia – Mayne's photographs in St Ives, Muspratt's in Swanage and the work of Vanessa Bell and Virginia Woolfe at Studland.

Benjamin Britten and Peter Pears lived on the Suffolk coast for many years from 1942. In their first Aldeburgh house on the seafront (where their neighbour was the *Picture Post* photographer Kurt Hutton), Britten and Pears recorded their lives as composer and singer, and founders of the Aldeburgh Festival. The photographs are snapshots, which tell a remarkable story of lives lived in creativity on the bleak east coast of England. Young men pose on the beach in sports jackets

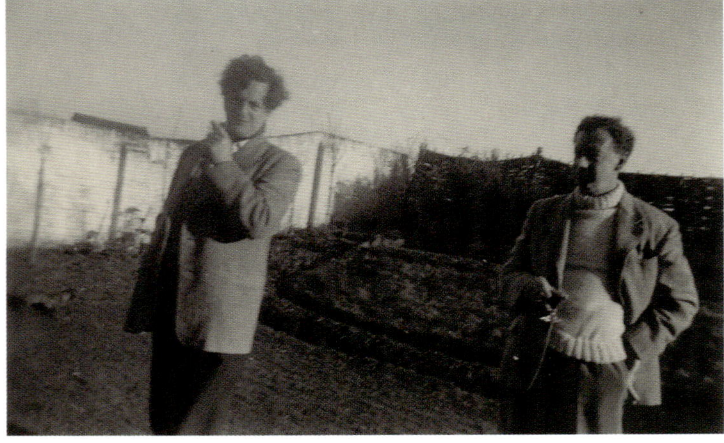

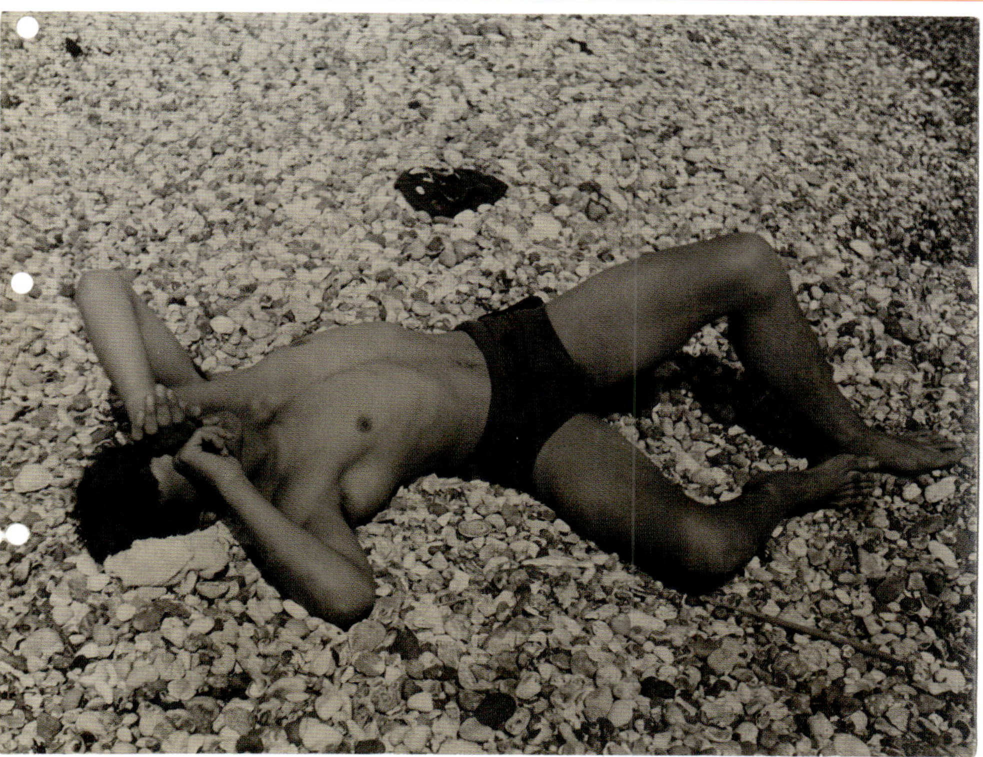

KEITH VAUGHAN
Pagham, 1939,
from *Dick's Book
of Photographs*

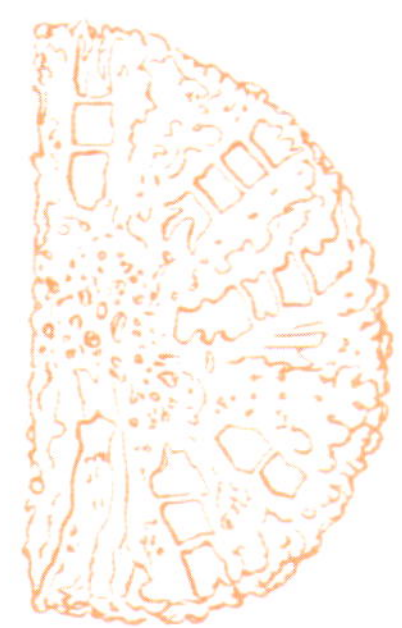

and woolly jumpers, and there is excitement – new work, new frontiers. For Britten and Pears and their friends, the beach was important (their first house looked directly on to it); it was the playground where friendships grew and ideas were born.

Elsewhere on the east coast, in Happisburgh in Norfolk, another group of artists had created a seaside haven. Ben Nicholson, Barbara Hepworth and Henry Moore had a longstanding connection with the east coast and recommended Happisburgh to Hepworth. As marriages dissolved and new friendships burgeoned, the two summers at Happisburgh in the early 1930s were documented in photographs. Though the focus for the group would later shift to Cornwall, memories of this Norfolk bohemia remain.

The artist and theatre designer Keith Vaughan was also a skilled and prolific photographer. Vaughan was interested in the photographs in numerous body-building magazines, and at some time after 1939, he made *Dick's Book of Photographs*, which documents a series of sun-filled days at the seaside at Pagham in Sussex (above and pp.72–5). Photography was important to Vaughan in other ways – like many of his generation of artists, he used photography to record information for later artworks. For Vaughan, gazing through the camera at a nude male subject made the act seem less like peeping and more a part in the creative process. The camera freed Vaughan from some of his inhibitions and fears about his homosexuality.

Vaughan first visited Pagham in 1935, and spent the next three summers there.[5] He stayed in an old railway carriage with his lover Harold Colebrook and began to take photographs:

The Pagham period was already underway by the time Stan appeared. [Vaughan had photographed Stan at Highgate Ponds in London, and described him as a blond-haired Apollo.] Most weekends throughout the summer Harold and I would go down to the hut. Sometimes with others but often alone. All day we would walk over the deserted beaches, talk and bathe in the sea. It suited our fantasies to behave like pagans. The summer of those years seemed to have been uninterrupted sunshine. I exposed hundreds of feet of Leica film. I am certainly glad I did because in the end images are better than memories and the results of those summers still exist and reveal the simple innocent face of the complicated pagan eroticism.[6]

Most of the photographs Vaughan made in these summers before the outbreak of the Second World War were lost, and even when his effects were sorted after his death in 1972, few emerged. The subject of this chapter's portfolio section, *Dick's Book of Photographs* was made by Vaughan for his brother Richard, as the Second World War broke out. Richard was killed in 1940, but this extraordinary compilation survived, discovered after Vaughan's death. It detailed not only the bodies of the young men who Vaughan came to know during the Pagham summers, but also landscapes, details of the beach and its flora. *Dick's Book of Photographs* is a record of those summers in Pagham, where, briefly, a queer bohemia flourished. Elsewhere in Vaughan's photography, there are glimpses of freedom and abandonment – in Vaughan's cottage in Essex, at Highgate Ponds – but nowhere else does the freedom and carefreeness of Pagham exist.

The 1920s and 1930s in Britain saw the creation of a range of seaside bohemias – from photographer Lee Miller's and artist and poet Roland Penrose's Farley Farm in Sussex, where visitors were often taken off to Brighton for the day – to the temporary arcadia of Vaughan's Pagham. Bohemianism was an inevitable part of breaking from the inhibiting rules of the upper middle class and going back to nature. Being at the seaside perhaps gave permission to act differently, to break the rules – Agar and Nash's passionate friendship was formed in the otherwise quite prim resort of Swanage; Britten and Pears were able to retreat to the flat seascapes of Suffolk. Seaside holidays could be liminal spaces, where structures could be relaxed and anything could happen. Seaside bohemias were created both in resorts and out-of-the-way places. The carnivalesque spirit of the seaside was always present, and the working-class seaside holiday, with its Pierrots and procession, was looked at with fascination mixed with horror. [vw]

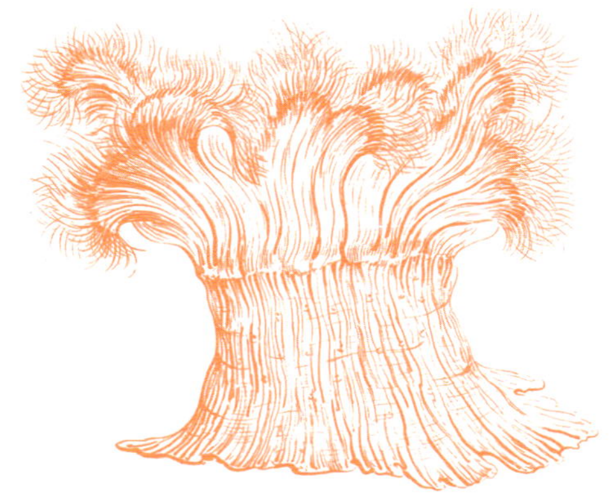

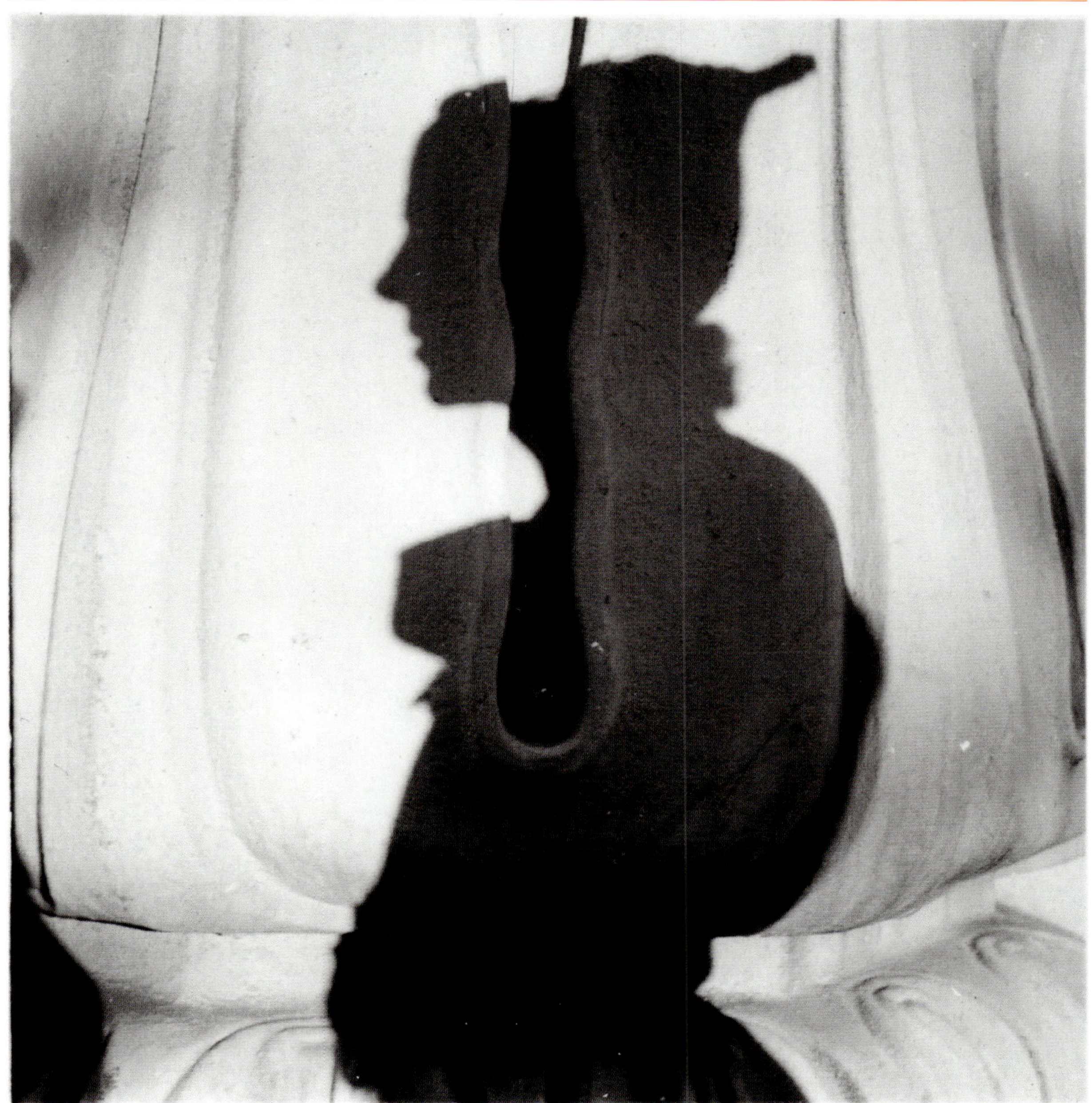

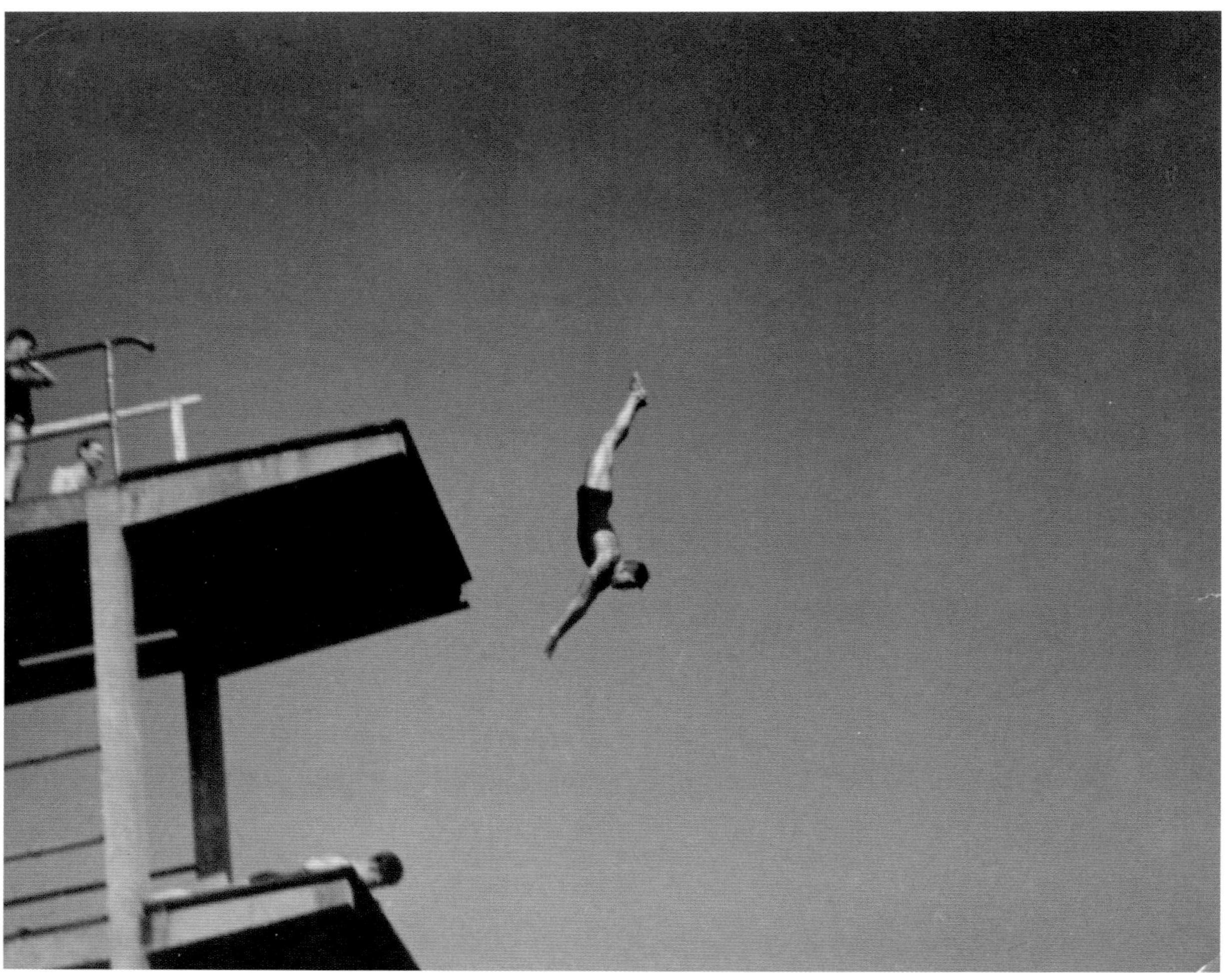

Young Men Diving, late 1930s

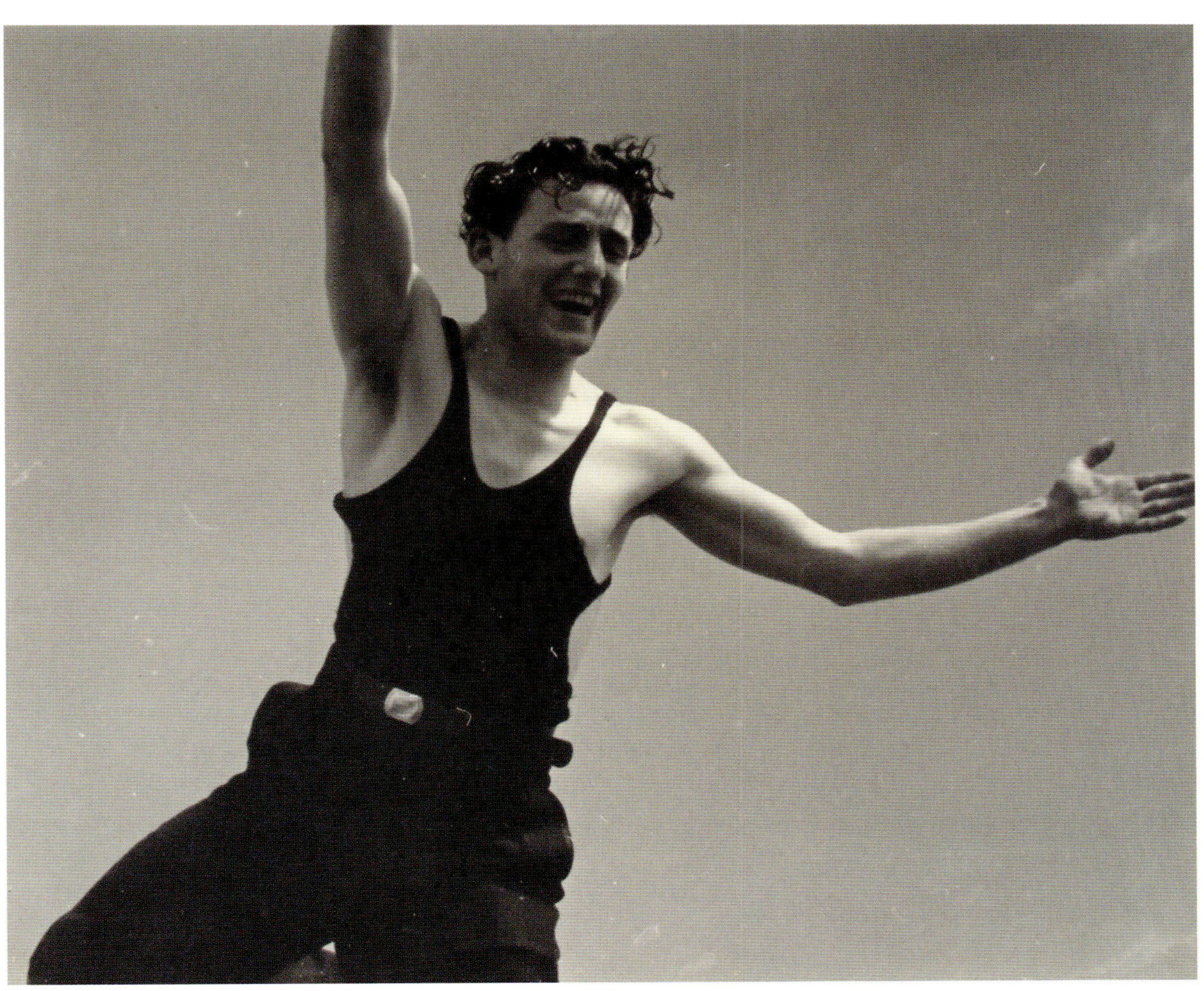

A Young Man Leaping, late 1930s

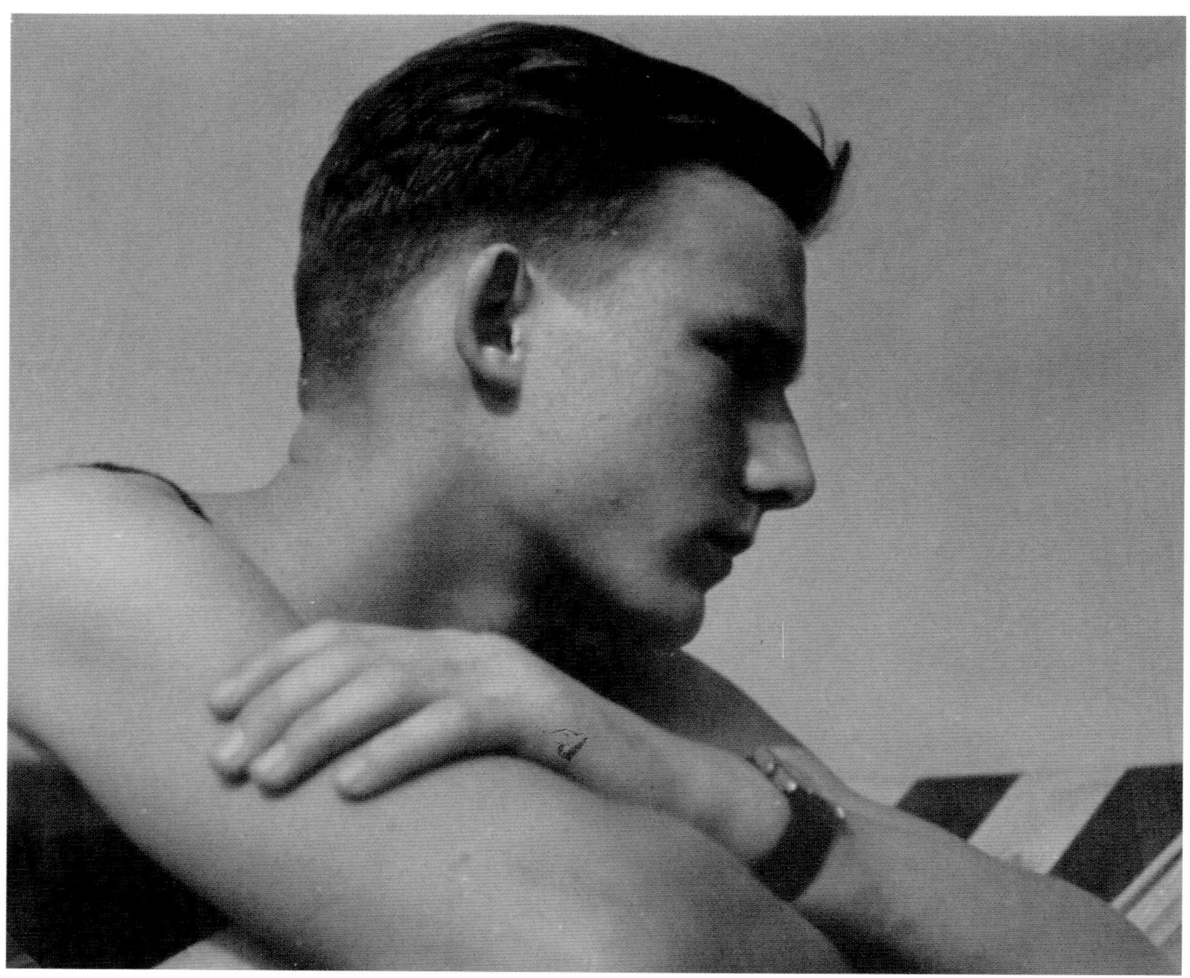

Ulli, late 1930s

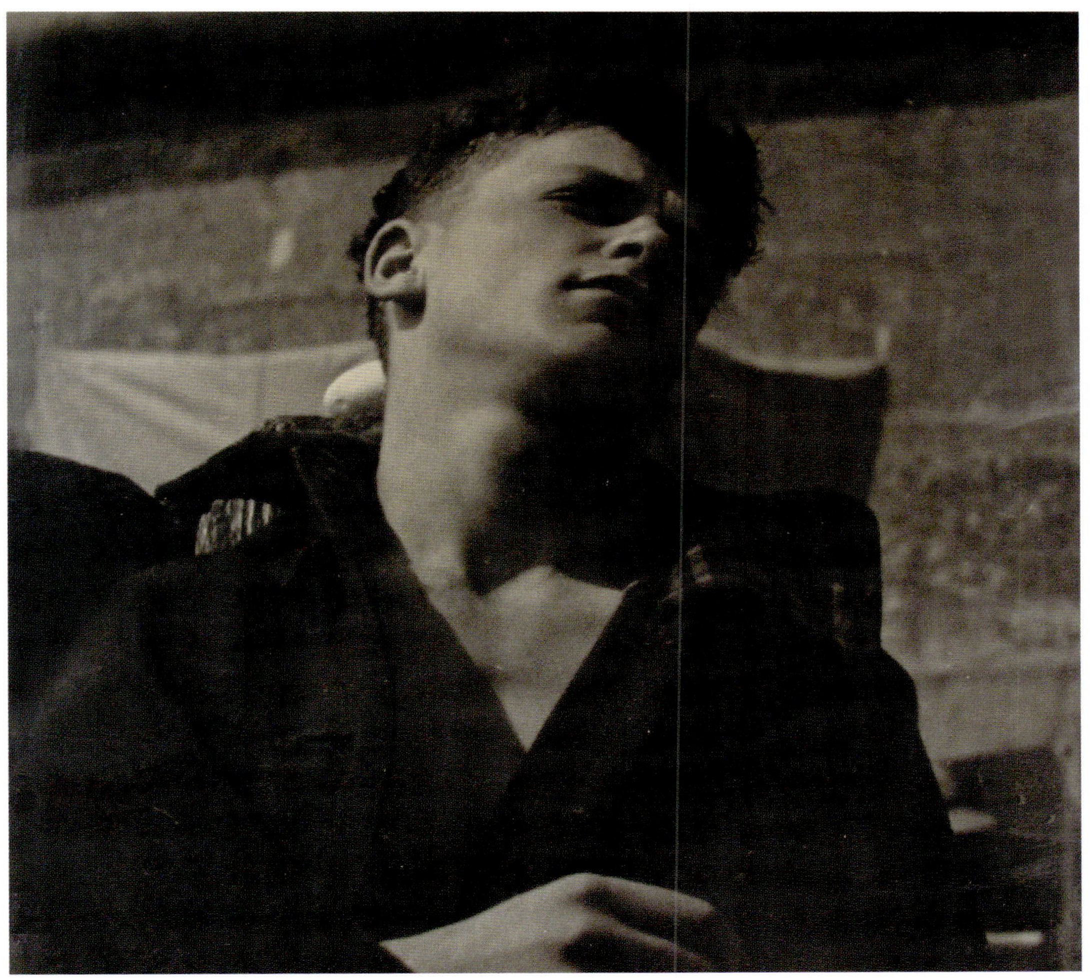

House Captain, late 1930s

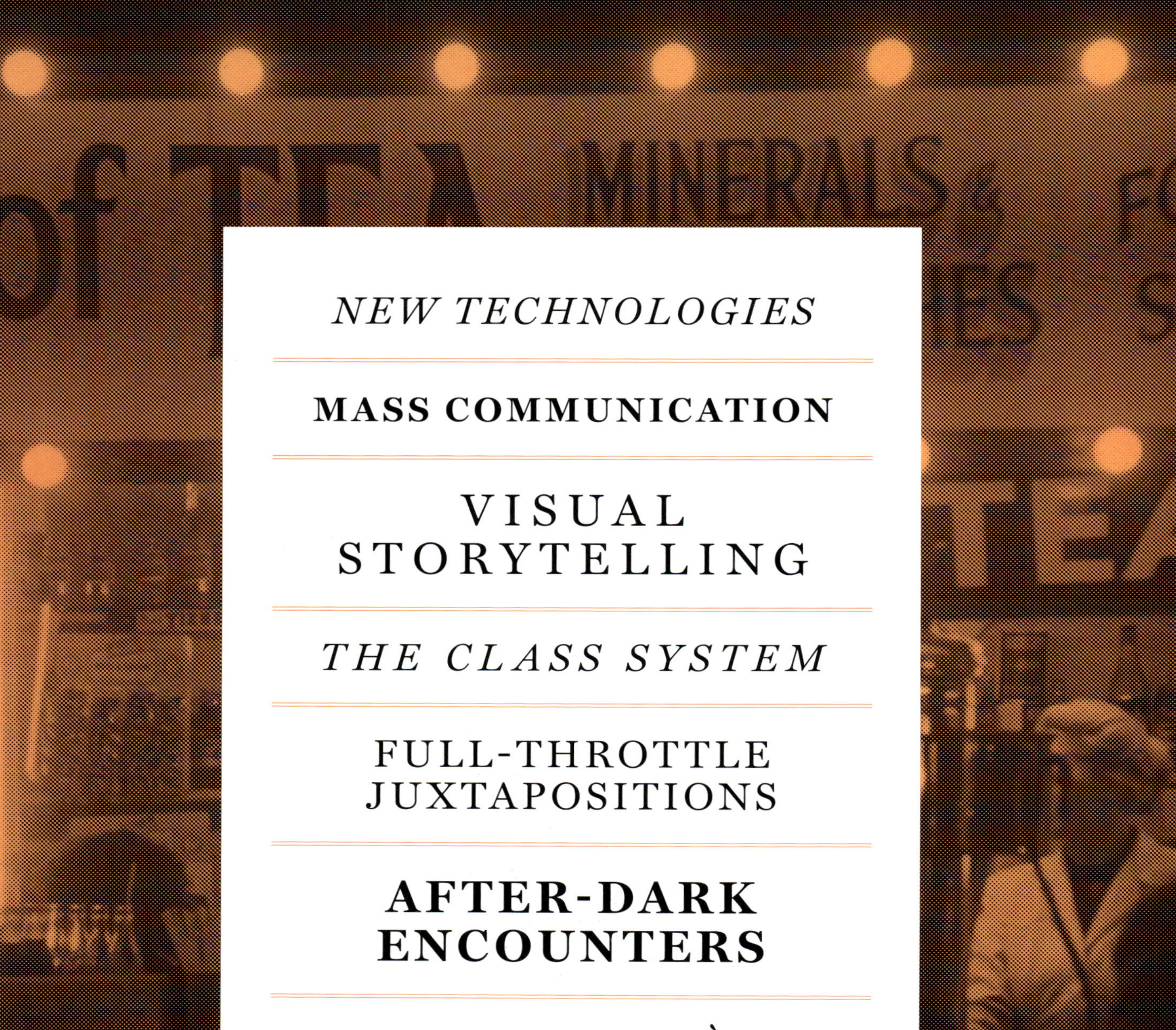

NEW TECHNOLOGIES
MASS COMMUNICATION
VISUAL STORYTELLING
THE CLASS SYSTEM
FULL-THROTTLE JUXTAPOSITIONS
AFTER-DARK ENCOUNTERS
MISE-EN-SCÈNE

REPORTING BACK

PICTURES FROM THE EDGE

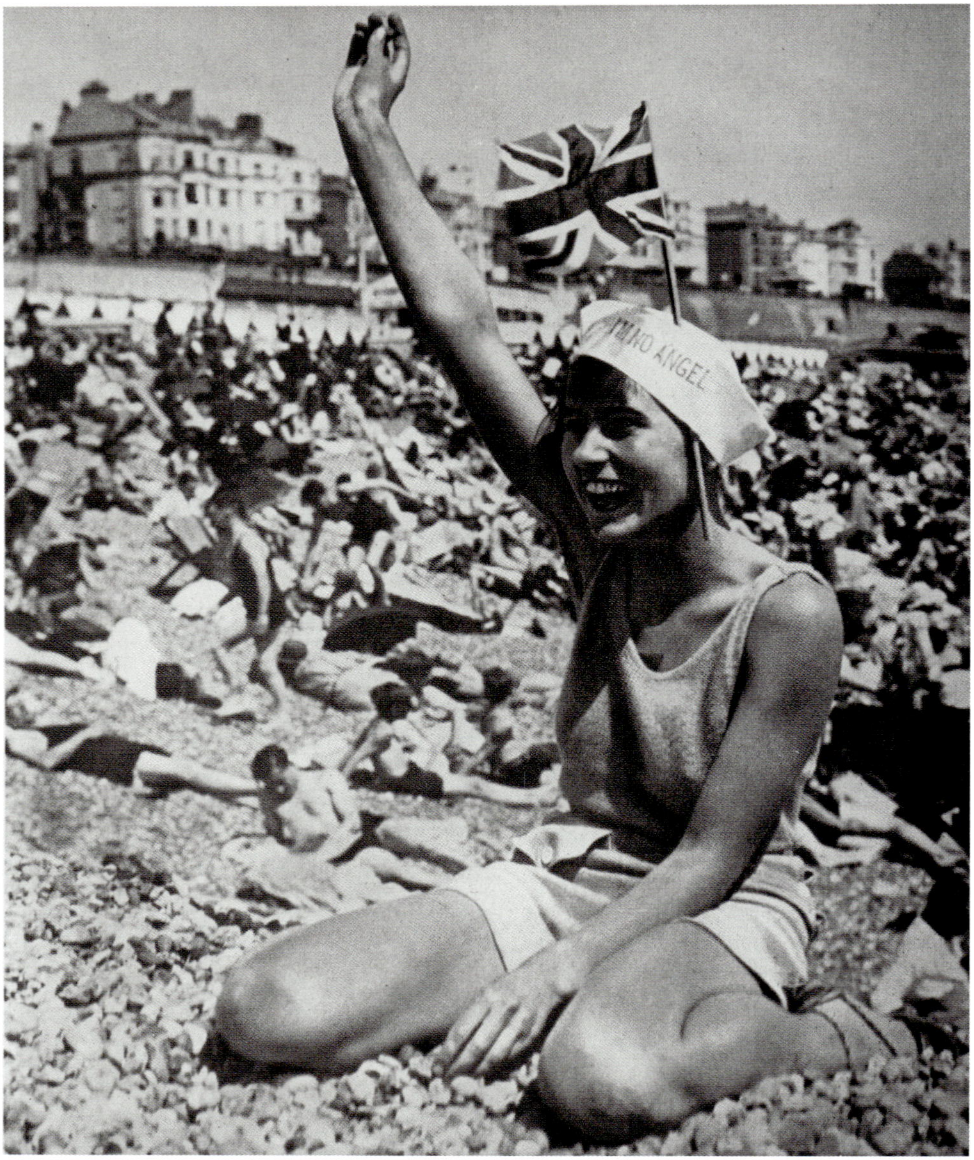

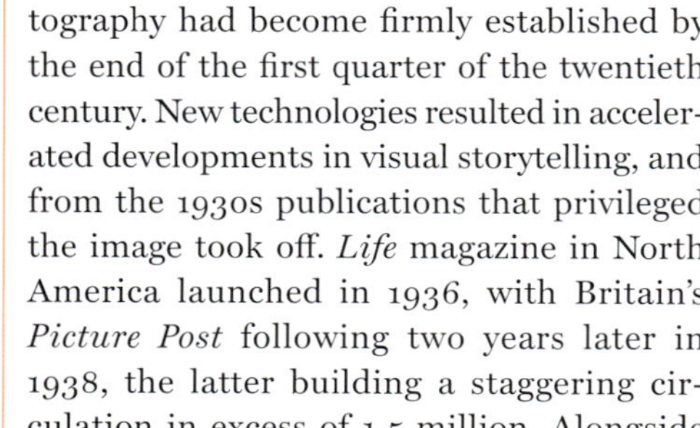

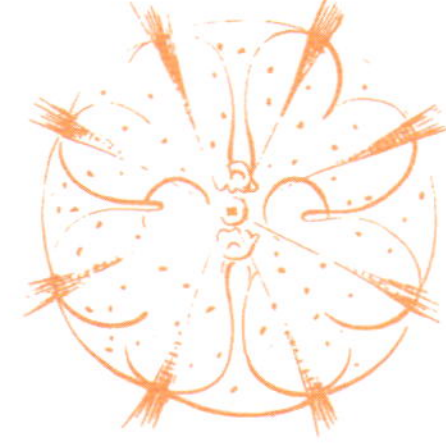

As a means of mass communication, photography had become firmly established by the end of the first quarter of the twentieth century. New technologies resulted in accelerated developments in visual storytelling, and from the 1930s publications that privileged the image took off. *Life* magazine in North America launched in 1936, with Britain's *Picture Post* following two years later in 1938, the latter building a staggering circulation in excess of 1.5 million. Alongside these picture staples, publications such as *Weekly Illustrated* and *Lilliput* also achieved impressive sales. With mass circulation, the market for reportage and photojournalism rose exponentially. The context for photography had up to this point been limited; art galleries were yet to recognize the medium as worthy of exhibiting or purchasing, and there was equally little appetite for private collectors to invest in photographers in the way we see today. Thus, the 1930s can be seen as a pivotal moment when photojournalists and documentary artists would benefit from a new climate, which saw the currency of the image inflating, and opportunities for photographic authorship developing.

Bill Brandt contributed to a number of the emerging picture publications, including *Lilliput*, *Picture Post* and *Weekly Illustrated*. Predating these photographic commissions, Brandt's monographs from the mid-1930s evidence his authorial impulse in storytelling visually and his early interest in reportage. *The English at Home* (1936), his first photobook, is an indicator of intent. German-born Brandt, who had moved to Britain from Vienna in 1934, surveyed his newly adopted country with the incisive eyes of an outsider.

The sixty-three photographs in *The English at Home* generate a collision of imagery, where the British class system is at times portrayed as almost caste-like and in places the full-throttle juxtapositions feel akin to visual gamesmanship. The image pairings by Brandt of *Travels for the Highest* #53 and *Rest for the Lowest* #54 or *East End Playground* #57 and *Kensington Children's Party* #58 prove particularly didactic. Writer Raymond Mortimer's introduction to the book endorses this, proclaiming that many 'children are less well nourished than our dogs and worse housed than our pigs'.[1] Yet to categorize *The English at Home* wholly as class bifurcation would be an over-simplification. With the benefit of placing *The English at Home* within Brandt's entire *oeuvre*, a more nuanced interpretation can be made. At a more fundamental level, he is developing creative strategies that move his development towards being an artist of individual works, rather than a photographer producing photo-stories. If this requires 'constructing' reality, then so be it.

Dominated by urban scenes, *The English at Home* shows the seaside surprisingly infrequently. Of the sixty-three photographs only three are explicitly taken at the coast, and these include the penultimate image *The Brighton Belle (I'm No Angel*; opposite). Though presented by the publisher – B. T. Batsford – within the genre of documentary photography, *The Brighton Belle (I'm No Angel)* is not actually a happenstance beach encounter by Brandt. This photograph can be regarded as the 'creative treatment of actuality'.[2] It might appear to epitomize the English or – perhaps with the vigorous fluttering of the Union flag – the British at the seaside, but this seemingly joyful modern young woman in search of a fast time (*I'm No Angel*) is not British. She is Danish émigré Ester (née Bonnesen) – Brandt's sister-in-law. Ester Brandt dominates this picture: at once divorced from and imposed on the crowded Brighton beach background with its distant populous mass.

In *The English at Home* Brandt shocks us in showing a country of great privilege and poverty, yet *The Brighton Belle (I'm No Angel)* resists class allocation. The very placement of Ester at the seaside in beachwear transcends categorization. Her gesture and costume locate her neither with Brandt's other worn-out working women nor with the formal dress codes associated with the privileged class. In seeking a subject's 'atmosphere', Brandt willingly directed and constructed photographs, harnessing friends, family and props to fabricate a potent appearance of *mise-en-scène* as actuality. As Paul Delaney observed, 'if the friends he used were not, in reality, English – well, who was to know?'[3] Rather than any slight of hand by Brandt, this connotes his working as artist and auteur, using everything in his aesthetic armoury to construct his envisioned image.

Unlike Brandt, many photographers were reporting back not as auteurs, but as press photographers. As such, and in the interest of production efficiency, division of labour was necessary as they delivered the picture, they relinquished editorial control and copyright. Newspapers were stabling increasing numbers of staff photographers and, through expanding demands for images, would also be drawing on the growing number of national and international photographic agencies such as Keystone, Topical, Planet, Report, Central Press and INP for content.

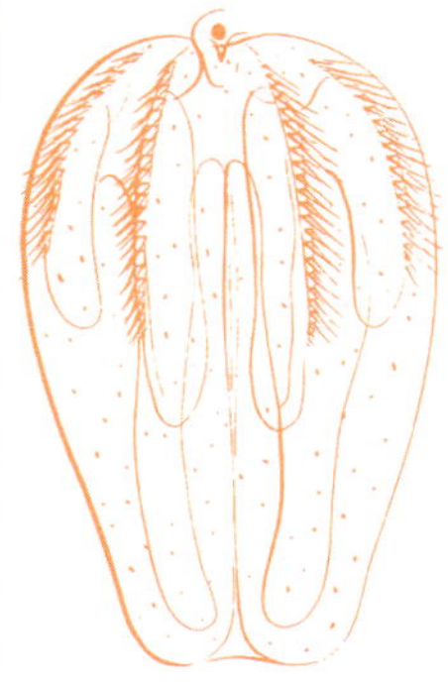

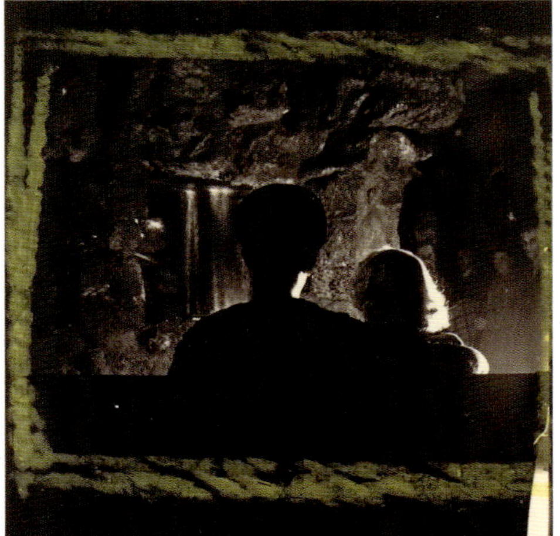

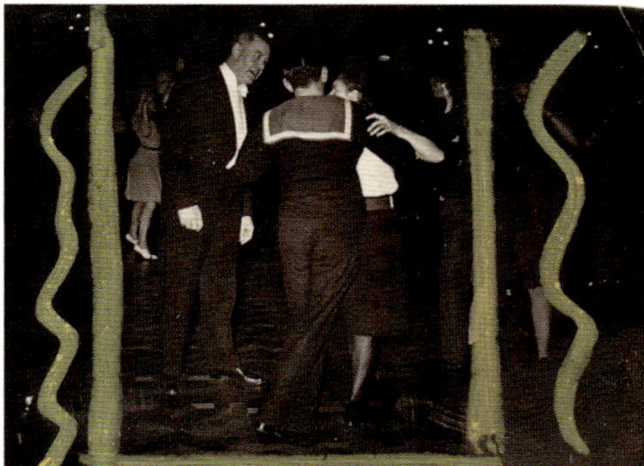

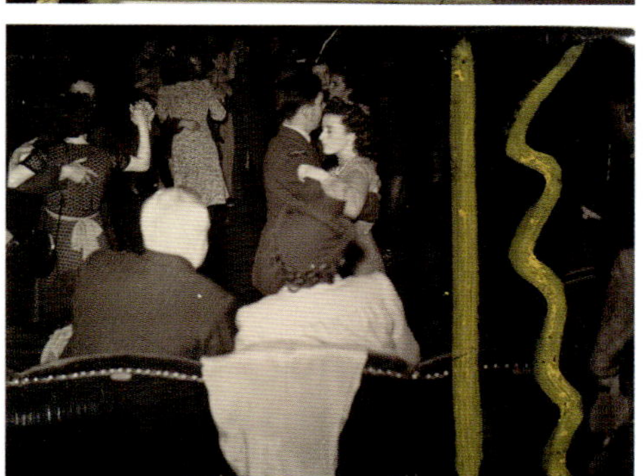

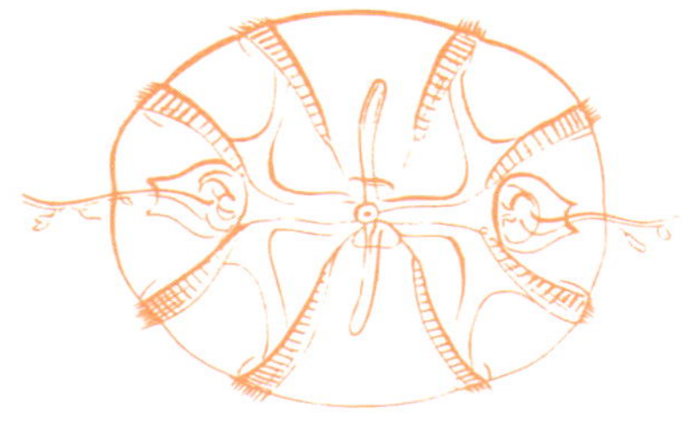

So while photographs had become a significant and expected part of contemporary reporting, photographers frequently published anonymously, and even those publications that privileged the image showed a similar pattern of anonymity. In the late 1930s, *Weekly Illustrated* had neither photographers nor journalists credited, and the innovative *Lilliput* consistently credited photographers inconsistently. For example, in *Lilliput*'s September 1946 issue Brandt's British composer portraits are clearly credited to him, as too are individual images by Ladislav Sitenský, Willy Ronis and Ferenc Berko, but numerous other photographs are simply bylined to picture agencies.

Newspapers such as the very popular *Daily Herald* employed many staff photographers. George Roper, F. Greaves, A. Tanner, Terry Fincher and the Saidman brothers (Reuben and Barnet) all contributed (often anonymously) to the visual reporting in the *Daily Herald*. Seaside stories were inevitably a seasonal staple and consisted of typical tropes: British stoicism in the face of bad weather; perennial family pleasures on crowded beaches with paddling at the water's edge; guest-house landladies keeping order and adult fun at various seaside fairgrounds, theatres and ballrooms. Yet despite such predictability, *Daily Herald* photographers proved more than capable of circumnavigating the cliché, providing visual surprises and often strangeness.

The Saidman brothers are a case in point. From the *Daily Herald*'s vast archive, it is impossible to verify fully which brother was responsible for which image, their pictures being simply stamped on the reverse as 'Saidman'. But these night scenes at Blackpool (above, left) can most likely be attributed to Reuben, whose love of nocturnal shoots was well documented, including the lengthy feature 'Black as Night' in the North American *Popular Photography* magazine.[4]

Saidman's 1943 wartime contact prints of Blackpool's famous Tower Ballroom (above, left) show the repeated use of a 'backseat' viewpoint, which coupled with

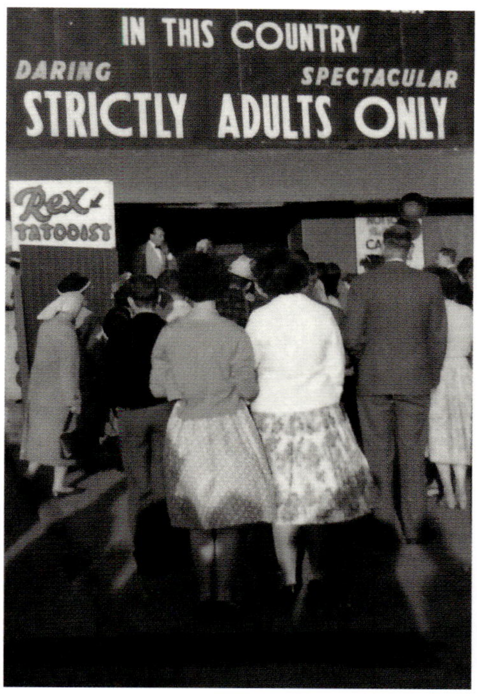

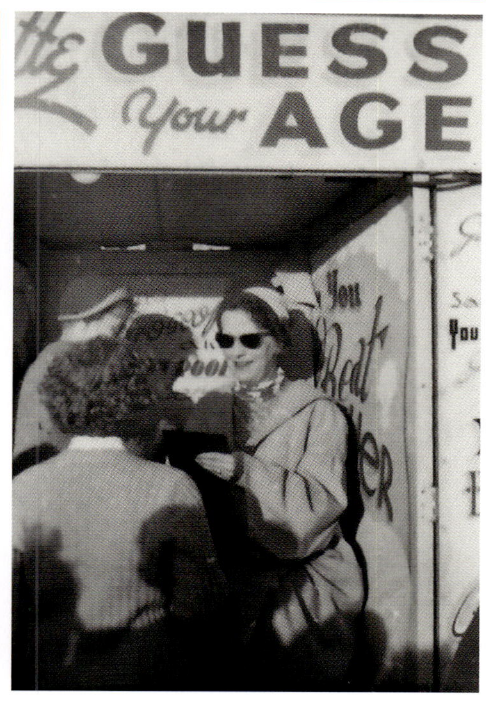

an expressionist chiaroscuro, creates an unsettling and claustrophobic intimacy in these after-dark encounters. The yellow Chinagraph mark-ups, probably made by the picture editor, add further constraints, heightening the sense of bodies bound within darkened spaces.

Our attention, or perhaps fixation in the post-war years, on adult seaside pleasure is maintained in Terry Fincher's photographs of Blackpool (above). Better known for his documentation of many global conflicts and recognized as an outstanding press photographer, Fincher joined the *Daily Herald* from Keystone Photo Agency in 1957. His reactive abilities, undoubtedly honed in conflict situations, were put to a different purpose in 1958, when Fincher cruised Blackpool's arcades at twilight finding seaside stories of adult fun and letting loose.

The *Daily Herald's* summer season issues usually also involved light-hearted reporting on British seaside resorts, and frequently returned to the nation's preoccupation with the weather. Roper in Brighton, Greaves in Margate and Tanner in Southend all had

picture-stories on this theme, each offering fresh takes on the family enduring rather than enjoying the seaside.

Greaves's photograph is particularly striking. Published as part of the *Daily Herald's* August 1949 'Holiday Story', Greaves shows an impressive capability in elevating the most prosaic scene into something visually akin to the biblical (p.82). The shrouding of these Margate figures, with their darkened drapery, contrasts starkly with the nakedness of the small child held protectively in his mother's arms, and Greaves, at the press of a shutter, absurdly harks back to Renaissance depictions of the Holy Family.

Unlike the *Daily Herald's* feature journalists, photographers were not routinely credited within the publication, and identification is now often only achieved through examining archived records and annotated contact sheets. Such enquiry has discovered or rediscovered these press photographers transcending expectations in their inventive interpretations of well-worn subject matter.

Crediting the photographer was a prevalent practice in a number of illustrated

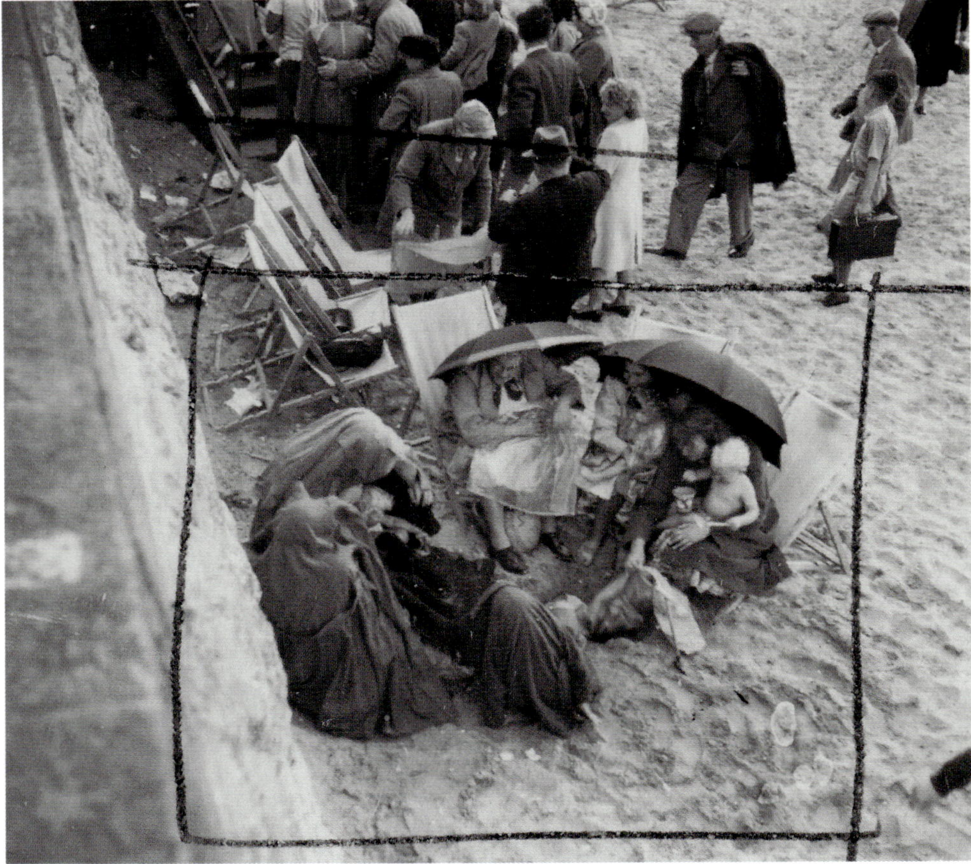

publications including *Picture Post*, whose staff photographers, such as Burt Hardy, Kurt Hutton, John Chillingworth and Haywood Magee, would usually be collectively listed within each issue and then individually credited with a picture-story. *Picture Post*, established in 1938 as a photojournalist magazine in Britain, rapidly gained in popularity and enjoyed mass circulation. With its emphasis on the photograph as a means of communication, it provided fresh opportunities not only for photographers stabled at the magazine, but also for freelancers such as Brandt and, later, Grace Robertson.

Issues from the summer 1954 *Picture Post* show the rise of the photographer's brand as currency and also the continuing appeal of the British seaside as subject matter. Chillingworth's *Blackpool Nightlife* (July; opposite, above) and Robertson's

Mother's Day Off (25 September; p.84) both foreground the role of the photographer. In the former, Chillingworth's photograph captures the demotic (and for the most part commodified) pleasures of high-season Blackpool in lavish colour. *Blackpool Nightlife* is accompanied by effusive writing by John Raison and champions both Chillingworth as photographer and all the joys that 1950s Blackpool could provide the visitor by day or by night.

The night shots in particular, including this image of the tea bar that didn't make it into the final picture-story, are a visual spectacle, but evoke little of the demi-illicit atmosphere of the earlier *Tower Ballroom* by Saidman (p.80) or the pacy street photographs by Terry Fincher from Blackpool's amusement arcades. For Chillingworth, the seaside resort at night is a site of rather more sanitized pleasures –

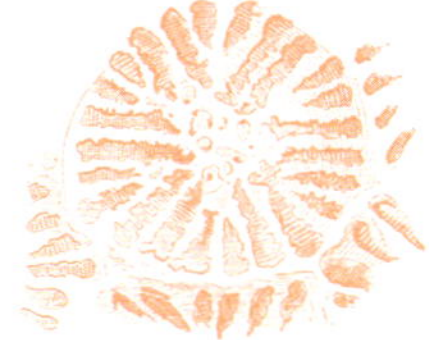

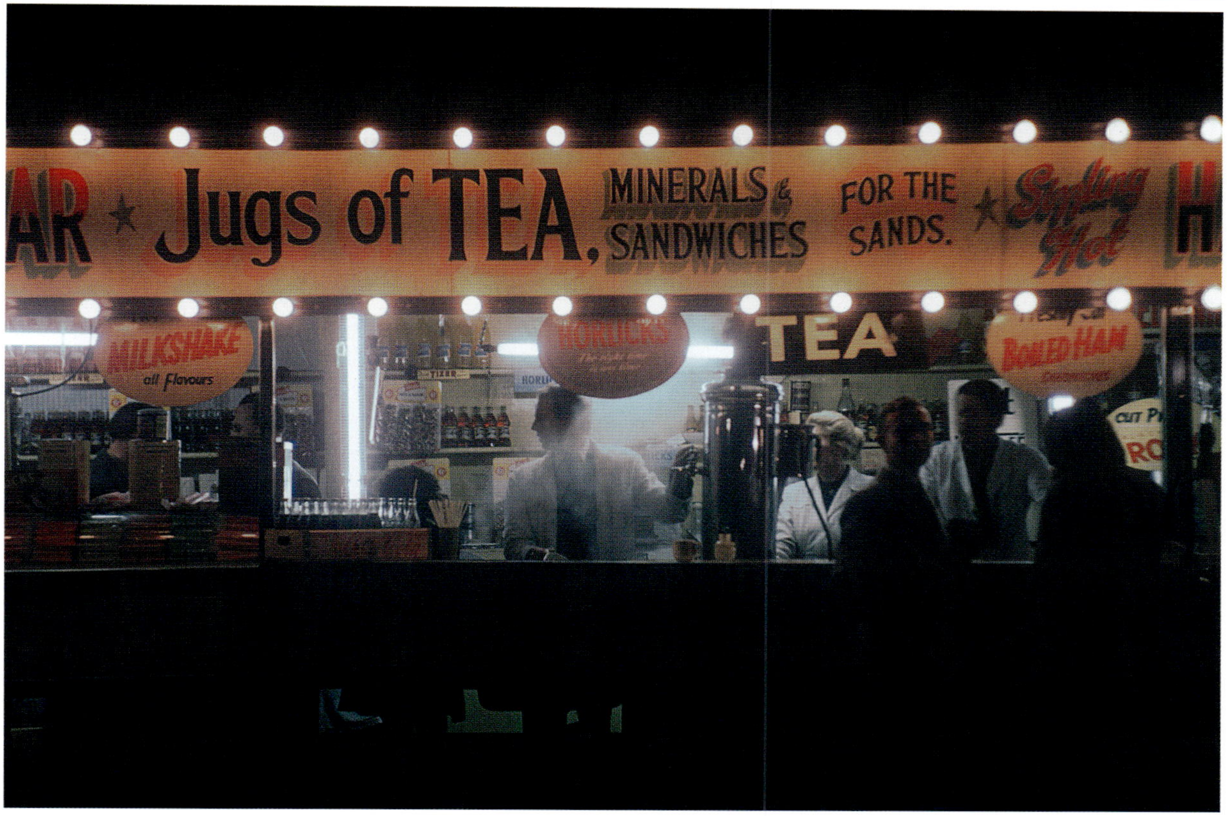

a cup of tea at any hour. Interestingly, among the ten published photographs, one is given a subtle and easily overlooked credit to Barnet Saidman. This suggests that while the photographer had become a vital and respected contributor to the illustrated magazine, some names were still better known than others.

In contrast to the contemporaneity of Chillingworth's colour interpretation of 1954 Blackpool, the black-and-white images of Robertson's *Mother's Day Off* (p.84), published less than two months later, could readily be taken as from an earlier era. In the 1950s Robertson was still one of very few female photojournalists and was recognized as highly adept at photographing other women's lives. In an interview, she revealed how she 'found it interesting to find out what made my own sex tick'.[5]

Illustrating this motivation, *Mother's Day Off* documents a female pub group on their annual knees-up outing from Bermondsey to Margate. Emphasis is placed on the deep working-class culture and the community in which these women are rooted. In the same interview, Robertson stressed how these 'women were so confident in their sense of themselves. They were survivors. They were very supportive of each other, and it gave them a terrific cohesion'.

The group of full-bodied women are uninhibited by Robertson's presence and camera, and despite the inherent still and mute characteristics of photography a raucous energy is nevertheless communicated. This female vitality is amplified further by brief captions written in the register of the women's own voices: 'We danced and danced till our bloomers showed. And nobody cared a rap.'[6] Ironically, Margate – as a preferred seaside town for working-class trippers from London – seems of the least significance here. In any recognizable sense it remains unseen, as Robertson focuses her camera not on the

JOHN CHILLINGWORTH
Blackpool Nightlife,
July 1954, from the
series *Bank Holiday
in Blackpool*

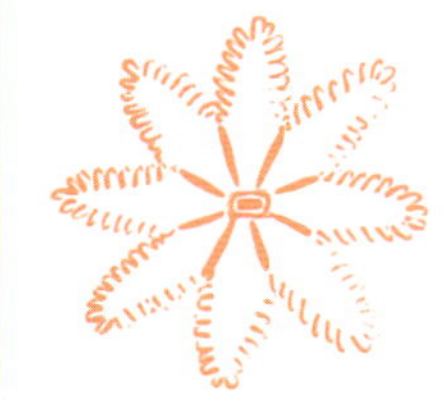

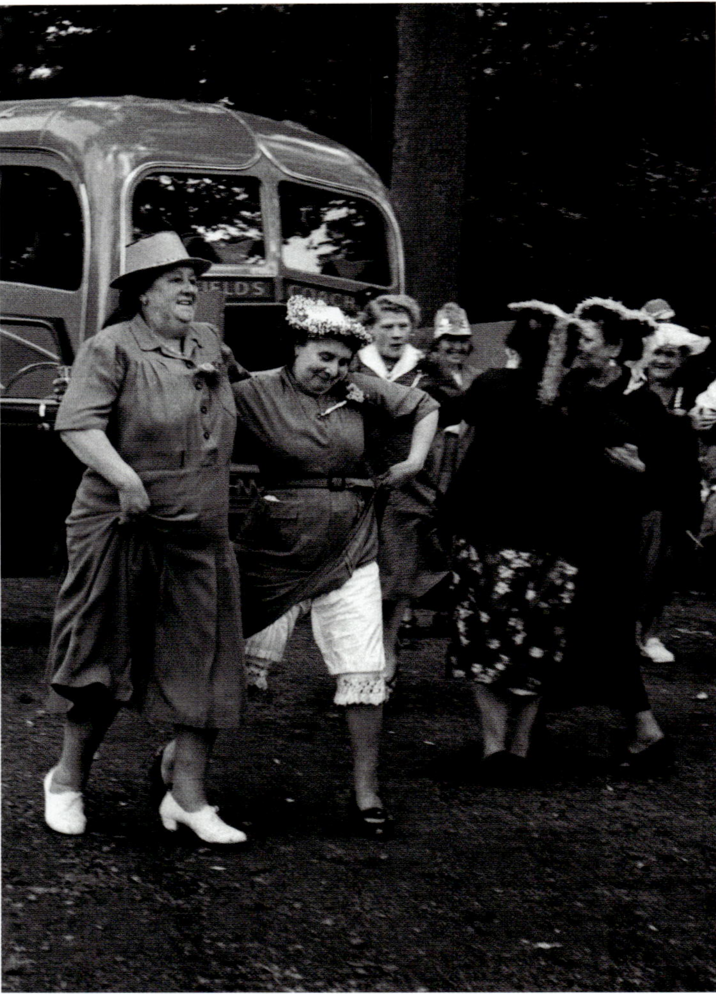

GRACE ROBERTSON
Mother's Day Off,
25 September 1954

had been very much their day, and it was certainly one I was never to forget.[7]

This gendered narrative and Robertson's visual way of telling evidently proved attractive, as just two years later she revisited this theme for a *Life* magazine commission, travelling with a similar women's group, this time from Clapham, and publishing under a lightly modified title: *Mothers' Pub Outing* (1956).

The reward for a freelance photojournalist such as Grace Robertson was a degree of autonomy, but with that too came a dimension of insecurity. Alternatively, to be a staff photographer brought security but inevitably reduced levels of autonomy. One way the photographer could benefit from both greater freedom and representation would be within a photo agency, and from the 1930s agencies proliferated. The increasing global demand for photographs required servicing via an organized structure for delivery, and photo agencies proved a profitable solution throughout the 'golden era' of photojournalism.

The most legendary agency remains Magnum Photos, established in 1947 by Henri Cartier-Bresson, Robert Capa, George Rodger and David 'Chim' Seymour, and structured atypically as an international cooperative run by the photographers themselves. Within this cooperative, the photographer maintains copyright and Magnum facilitates image use and distribution to multiple publishers throughout the world. Characteristically, these photographers possess uncompromising visions, and within Magnum the position of auteur is confidently held.

Countless Magnum photographers have unsurprisingly ventured to Britain's edges to document the seaside, including Cartier-Bresson. For the omnipresent, globetrotting Cartier-Bresson, who worked across every continent, Britain was a very near neighbour, and his archive contains numerous seaside images from the 1950s onwards. Compared to global stories covered throughout Cartier-Bresson's career, the British seaside must have appeared uneventful, offering him little more than respite. But through this lack of

trip's destination, but the women's camaraderie and experience. It is not only her camera that fixes the exuberance and timbre of these Bermondsey women, but Robertson's writing too, she later reflected that:

> I became one of them. As they formed conga lines and kicked their legs, they tried to grasp me, draw me into their enjoyment: 'Come on, luv,' they pleaded, 'have some fun!' I was having fun alright, trying to keep up with them. They were certainly showing a young woman from a rather different background what stamina and frank, unaffected enjoyment could mean. It

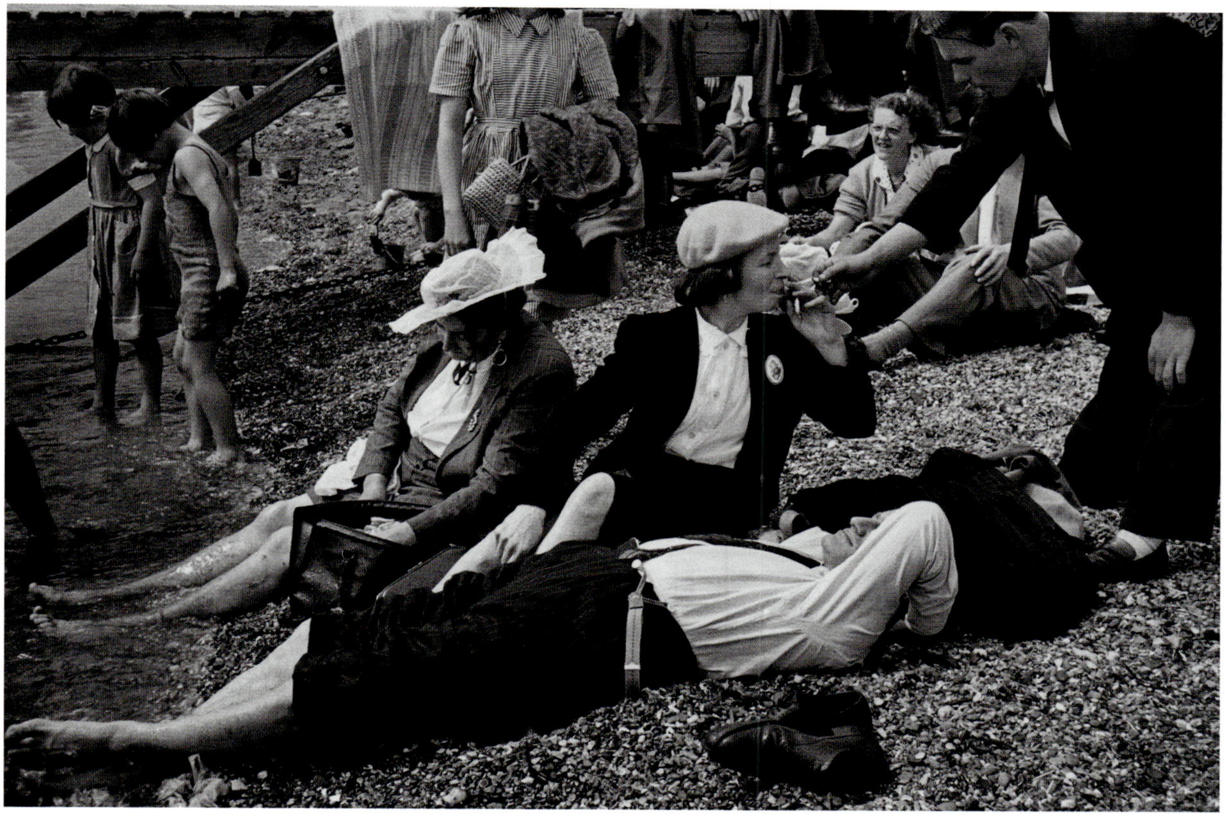

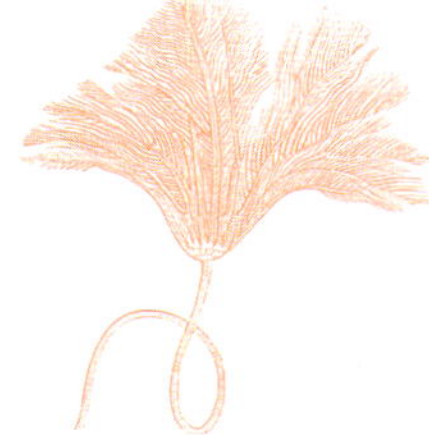

incident we can fully appreciate the quiet precision within his work – whether that is in the reportage of Blackpool or Brighton in the 1950s or 1960s, or the more melancholic individual images from the 1970s, as shown in this chapter's portfolio section (pp.88–93).

Visits from Magnum members were often just fleeting dashes in rapid response to an editorial commission or to gain a story with publication appeal. Through the Magnum lens, everyday seaside scenes are often estranged, not least because of the cooperative's international membership; the images produced originate from the acute eye of the outsider.

Marc Riboud, travelling from France in 1954, is just one example of that keen Magnum outsider's eye. The photograph made by Riboud in Southend-on-Sea typifies this (above). The structure of the image glides the viewer across and simultaneously into the photograph – and what a puzzling image it

is! The two women holding the central space seem incongruous alongside the increasingly modern beachgoers who surround them. Located right at the water's edge, the older woman, with a hat ornate enough to adorn one of Robertson's mothers on their day off, cools her legs in the shallows. Her curious semi-somnambulist action of rooting in her handbag piques our interest. But it is the central female figure that demands the viewer's attention; paradoxically, she appears wholly out of place and yet utterly composed – simultaneously enigmatic, witty and eccentric.

Brandt's *Brighton Belle (I'm no Angel)* (p.78), made almost twenty years earlier, seems by far the more modern beachscape, while Riboud's *Southend-on-Sea* – with its anomalous female protagonists – lingers at a seaside past. Riboud is not alone in such interpretation; Magnum's Bruce Davidson similarly presents the British seaside as

MARC RIBOUD
Southend-on-Sea,
1954

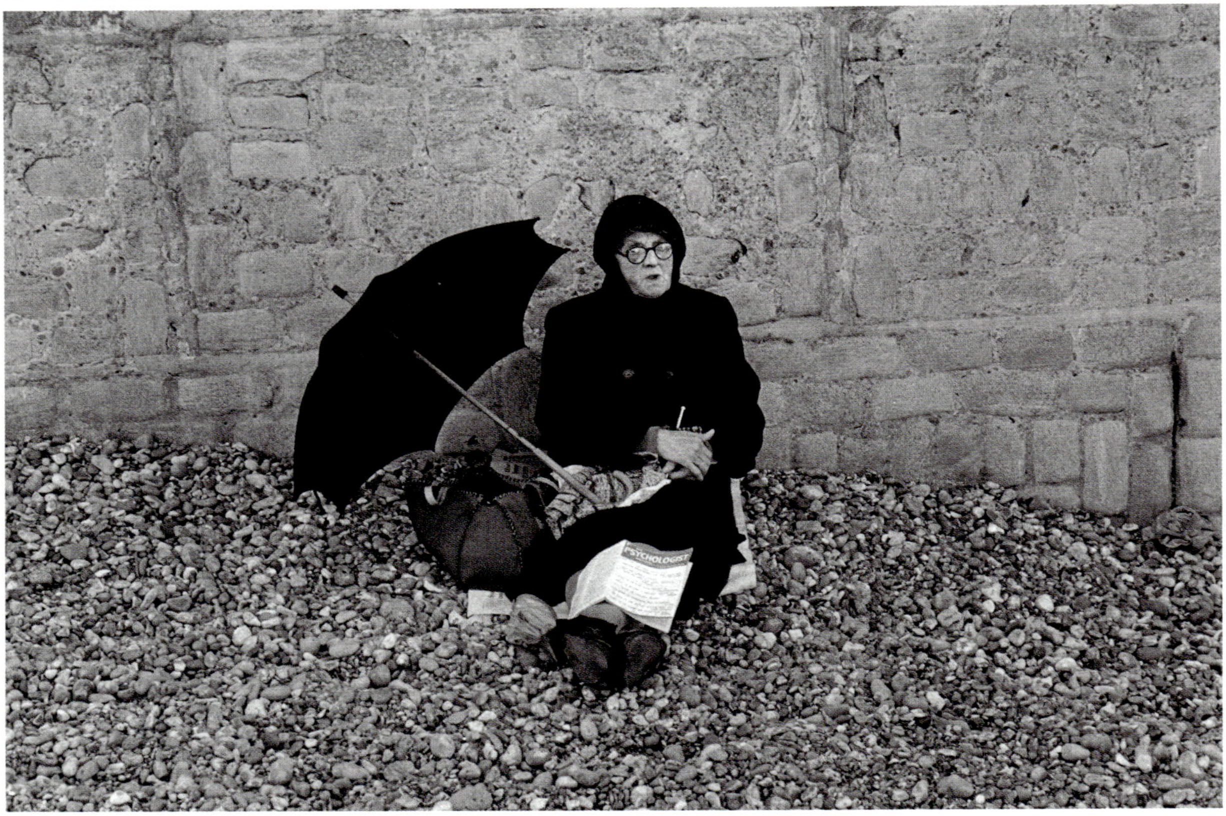

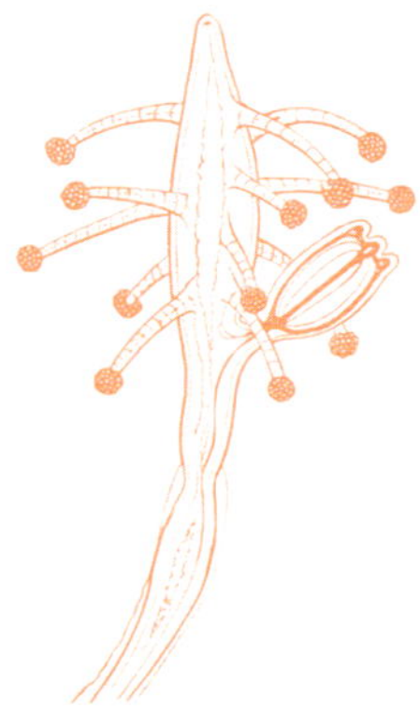

a 'last remnant' of a country on the verge of – but not yet – modernizing.[8] Davidson's 1960s commission *Seeing Ourselves as an American Sees Us: A Picture Essay on Britain* for *Queen* magazine in April 1961 (which ran to a comprehensive twenty-two pages) suggests that while Britain might have been heading towards the Swinging Sixties, not much seemed to be swinging at the British seaside. Davidson's *Woman in Black on a Stone Beach* (above), taken in Brighton for the feature, evokes the Victorian rather than the modern. This formidable woman defiantly returns our scrutiny and yet rewards our attention. If taken at a glance she is unhesitatingly typecast – a remnant of times past – but for the observant, her reading matter, the thoroughly modern *The Psychologist* magazine, delightfully undercuts any lax supposition. Davidson, like Riboud, has an eye for the eccentric, and the visual twist here is fine-tuned.

BRUCE DAVIDSON
Woman in Black on a Stone Beach, Brighton,
1960

Magnum member David Hurn has been a committed photographer of the seaside since the early 1960s, and his repeated returns provide one of the most detailed and lyrical visual chronicles of British resort cultures. When Hurn was interviewed about the practice of picture-making at the seaside for the book *On Being a Photographer* (2007), he stated:

> There is usually no point in just rambling around a beach looking for pictures in general, because the visual overload precludes seeing anything. So the first essential is to know, in some specific way, what you are looking for.[9]

Unlike Davidson, Riboud and Cartier-Bresson, the seaside for Hurn is familiar turf, forming a significant part of his own narrative history. Here he is the insider, whose documentation of this familiar place and people

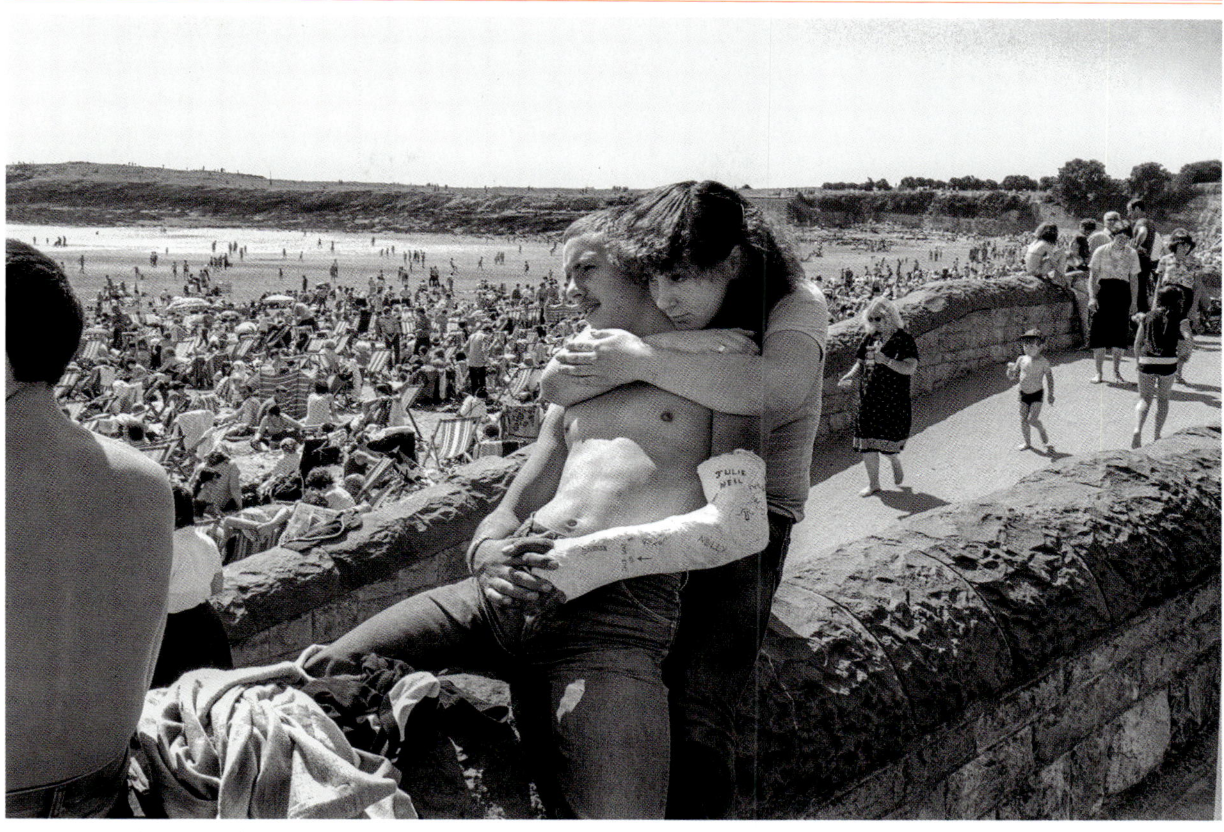

David Hurn
Barry Island, Wales,
1981

transforms mundane moments into timeless, intimate, humane narratives. By the 1980s, with this embracing couple at Barry Island, Hurn was creating layers of visual meaning; they seem to be engrossed in one more distant scene, while simultaneously creating another. Their hands are mirrored, while his plaster-cast arm surely implies that her grip on him needs to be just that little bit tighter.

In the topsy-turvy era of the twenty-first century, one is more likely to encounter the photographers discussed here in the gallery, archive or photobook than on the newsstand. Since the 1950s and the introduction of television news reporting, other media have fiercely competed for the audience's attention. It is not entirely a pessimistic environment; print publications that value reportage remain, particularly within the weekend broadsheets, but traditional outlet opportunities have contracted at the very time the population of photographers has increased. Digital and web-based reportage offer exciting and evolving platforms, but their sustainability remains contentious for those photographers requiring a living from their work. For Cartier-Bresson, photographic reportage, or, as he referred to it, a picture-story 'involves a joint operation of the brain, the eye and the heart'.[10] While this is metaphorically true, it also requires an audience and channels of distribution. [KS]

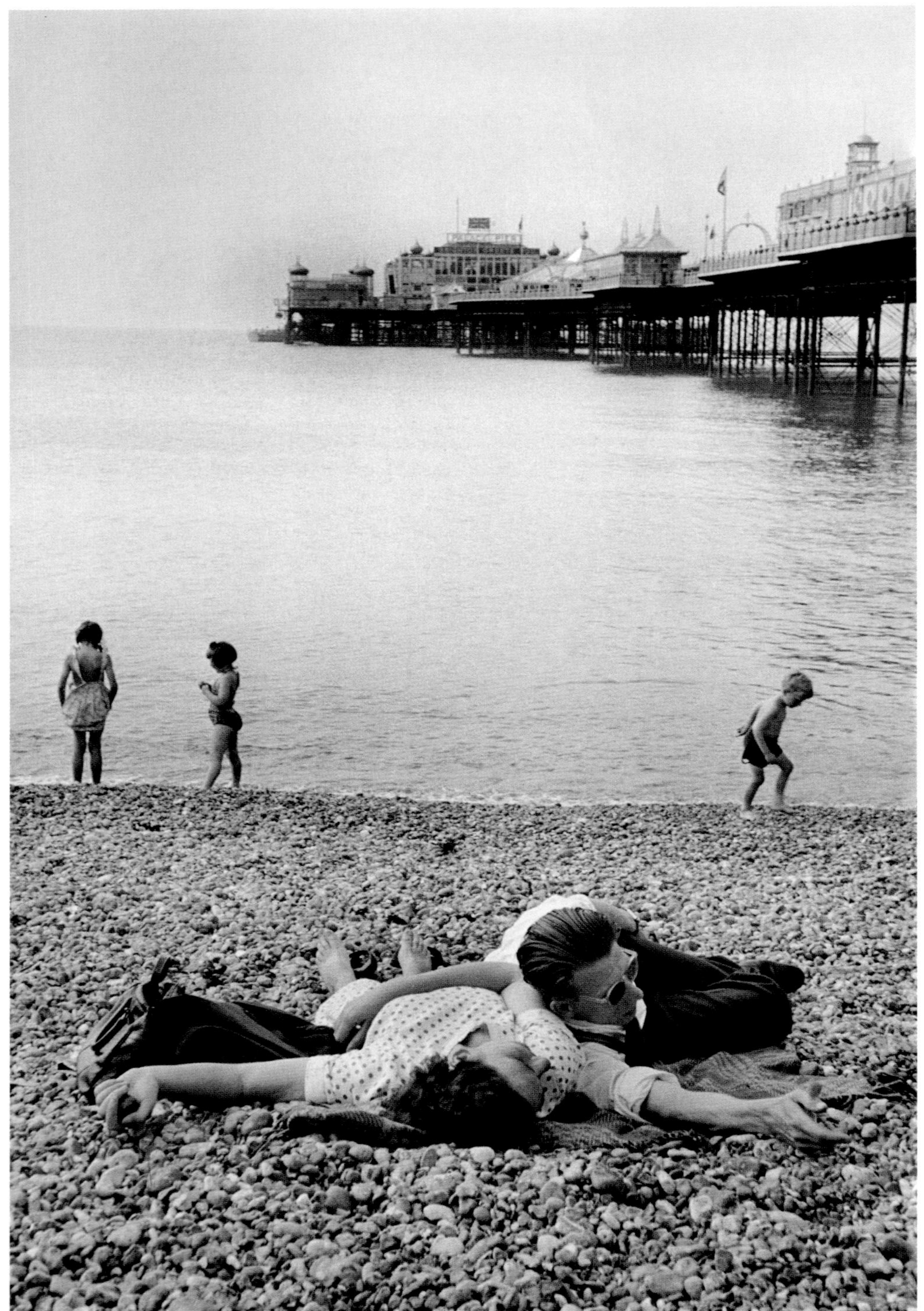

England, 1978

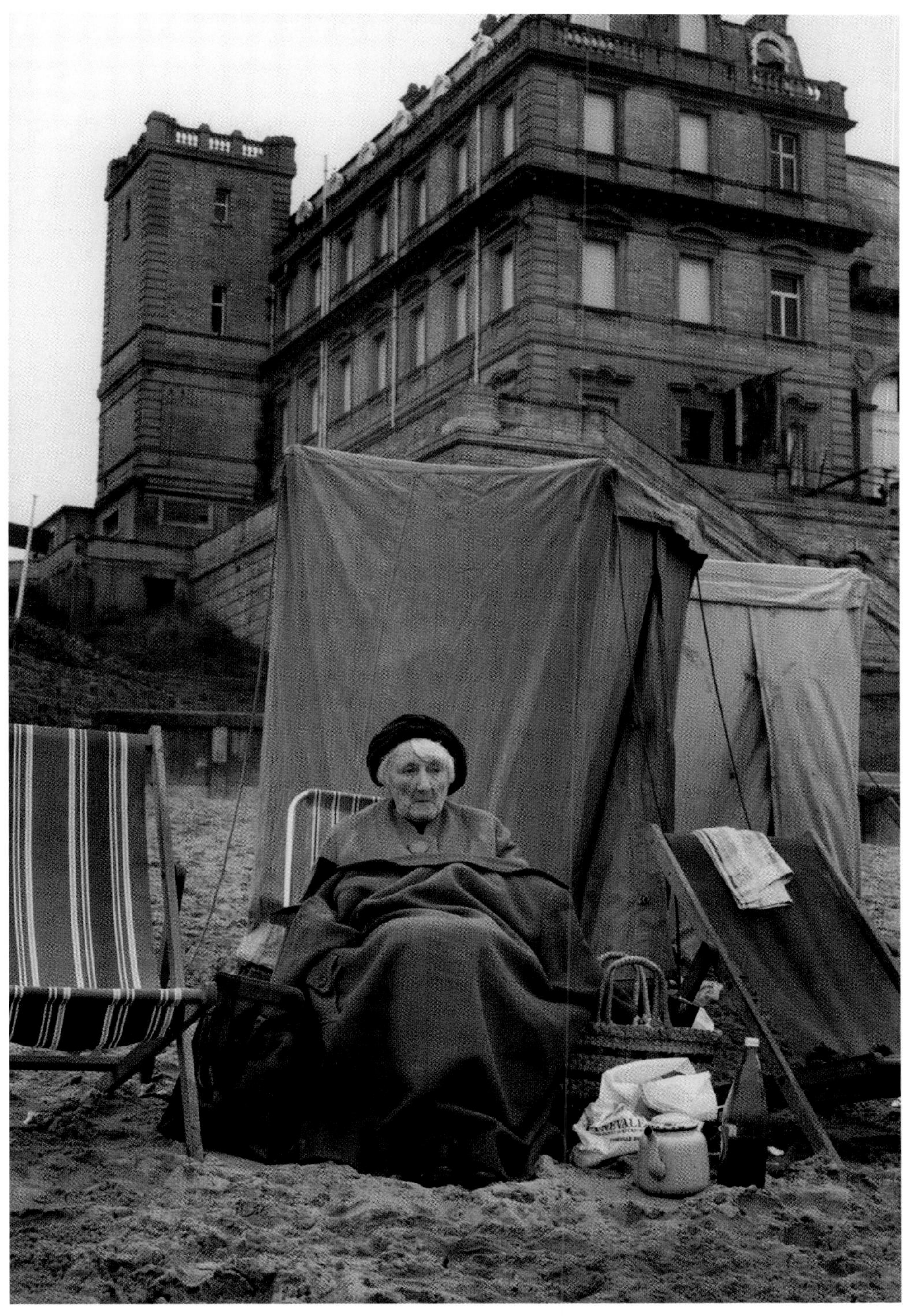

Brighton, 1953

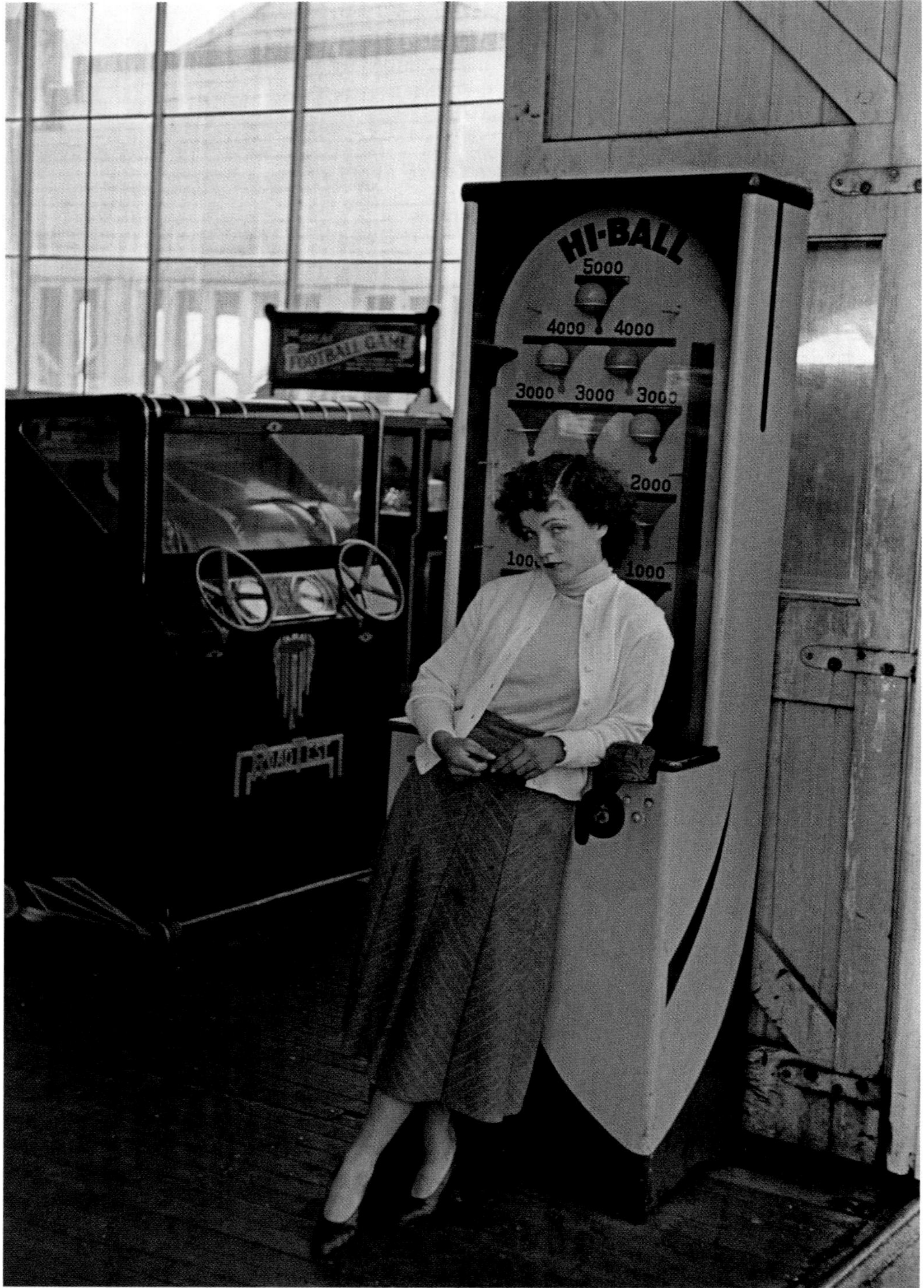

Brighton, 1953

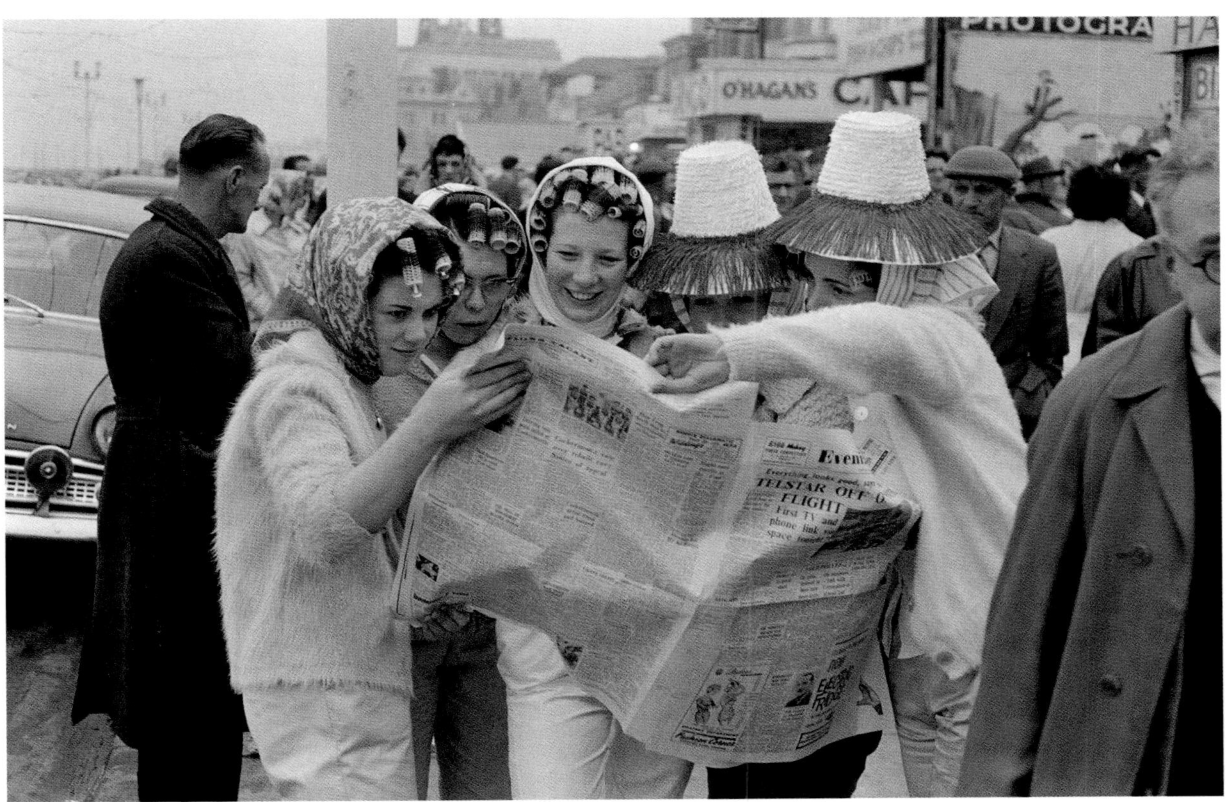

ABOVE AND OVERLEAF · Blackpool, 1962

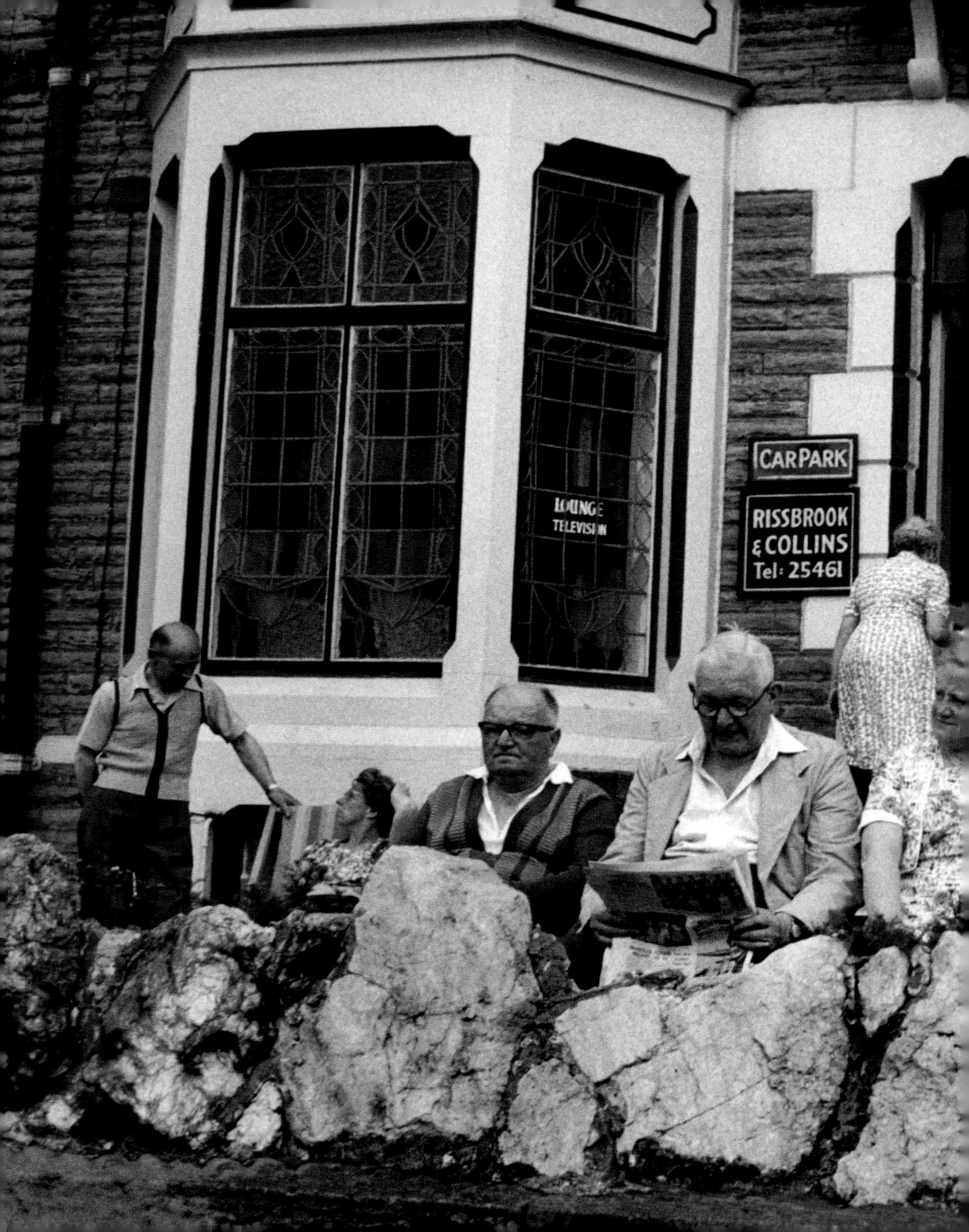
LOUNGE
TELEVISION
CAR PARK
RISSBROOK
& COLLINS
Tel: 25461

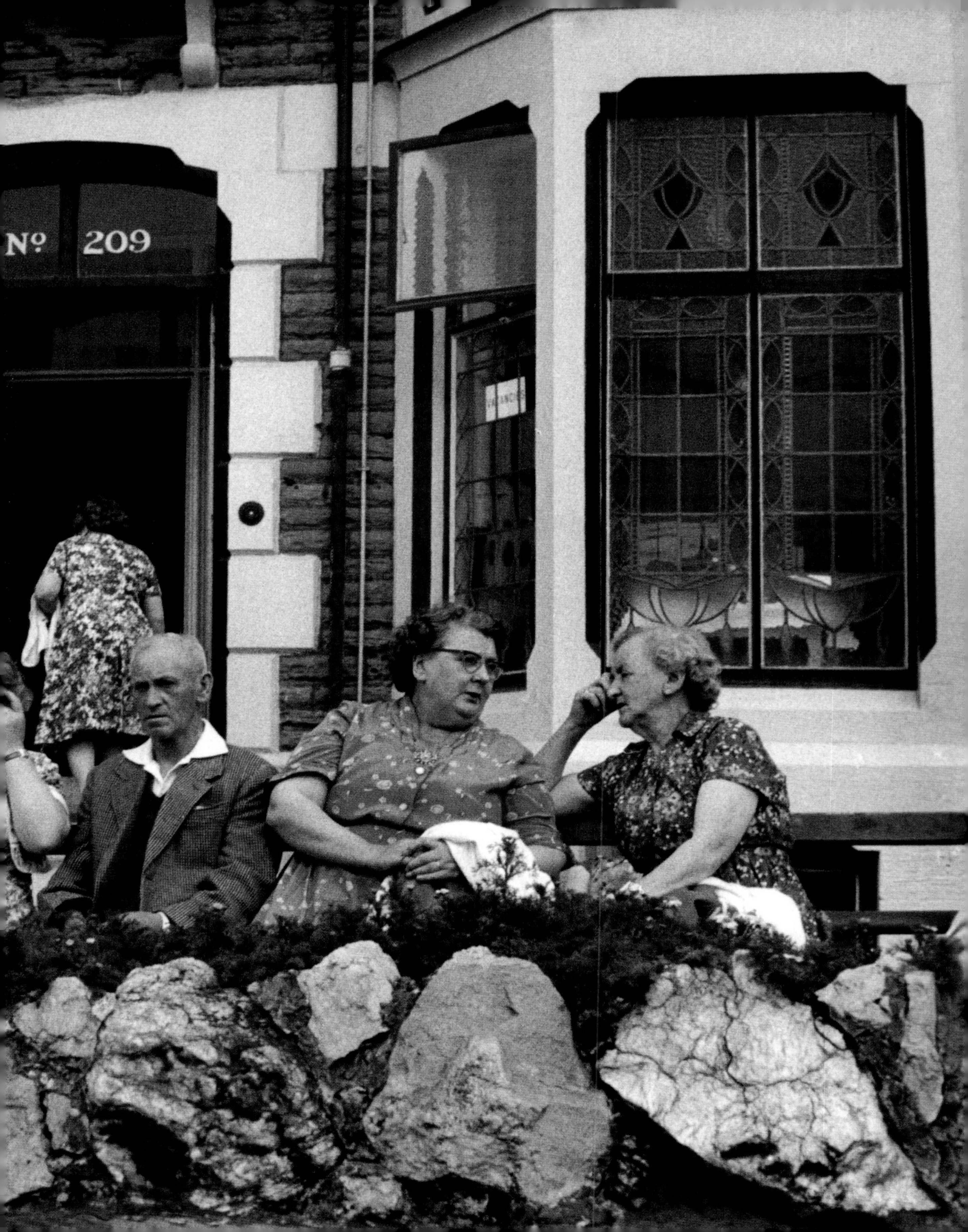

N.º 209

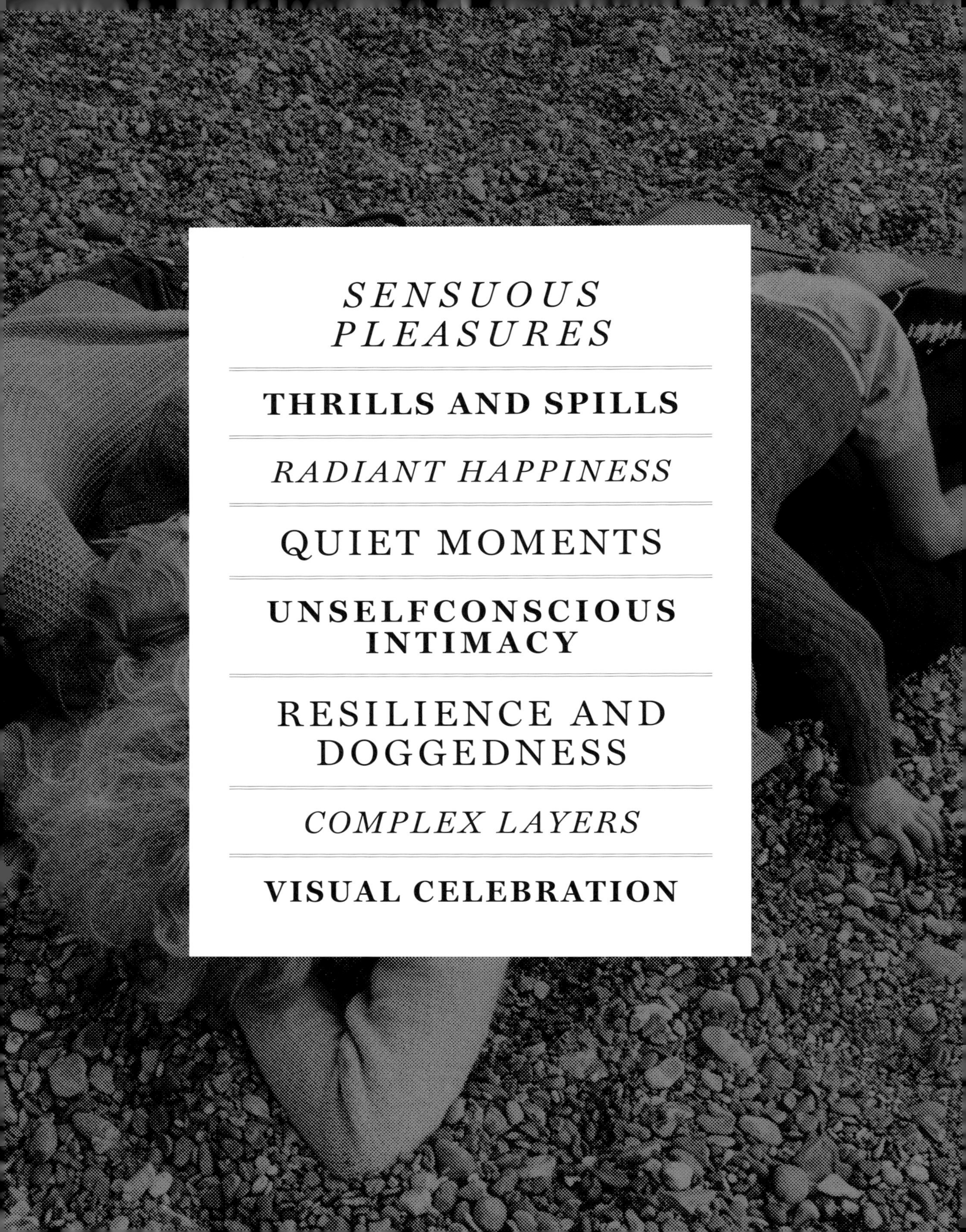

SENSUOUS PLEASURES

THRILLS AND SPILLS

RADIANT HAPPINESS

QUIET MOMENTS

UNSELFCONSCIOUS INTIMACY

RESILIENCE AND DOGGEDNESS

COMPLEX LAYERS

VISUAL CELEBRATION

HALCYON DAYS

SUN, SAND AND SENSUALITY

August Bank Holiday – a tune on an ice-cream cornet. A slap of sea and a tickle of sand. A fanfare of sunshades opening. A wince and whinny of bathers dancing into deceptive water. A tuck of dresses. A rolling of trousers. A compromise of paddlers. A sunburn of girls and a lark of boys …[1]

Dylan Thomas's 1946 radio broadcast 'Holiday Memory' rhythmically captures the exciting, noisy and sensuous pleasures of being at the seaside. In his paean to the seaside, a single day's excursion offers welcome escape from hard-working lives, capturing a shoreline of thrills, spills, play and rare respite from mundanity. R. C. Sherriff's earlier and gentler *The Fortnight in September* (1931) similarly transports the reader to the interwar years as we accompany the suburban Stevens family on their annual seaside holiday. Sherriff's novel is consciously provincial, the first hundred or so pages given over to the minutiae of the highly anticipated journey from the family's terraced home in Dulwich to Bognor and their modest seaside boarding house – Seaview. Overflowing with the routines and rituals of the Stevenses' lives, Sherriff quietly creates seaside vignettes and brings to the fore: 'a spirit of joyful, unrestrained freedom … no servants – no masters: no clerks – no managers – just men and women whose common profession was Holidaymaker.'[2]

From experience, we empathize when told of how the novel's gentle and unassuming patriarch felt:

radiantly happy: as young and as light as a schoolboy. Everything around him was so unutterably fresh and clean: bronzed faces – open shirts – bare legs – blue sky … Mr. Stevens took a deep draught of the air – pressing out his lower ribs to let the ozone penetrate to the lowest part of his lungs: these were the moments that justified every pain in life – every disappointment – every humiliation.[3]

Sherriff creates the feeling of sheer liberation that seaside resorts provided, while avoiding slipping into seductive nostalgia by juxtaposing these fleeting halcyon days with the broader context of lives lived beyond the vacation. He reminds us that such joyous times were heavily counterbalanced by contained and constrained existences in mid-twentieth-century Britain.

As with literature, photography has made its own contribution to the nation's narrative of the seaside as a place of 'radiant happiness'. We have seen elsewhere that, almost from the beginning, the beach attracted photographers seeking to fix the seaside visually as a site of perennial pleasure, and that since the 1850s the seaside, with its huge numbers of pleasure-seeking visitors has provided rich visual terrain for photographers.

Jane Bown's 1954 *Southend-on-Sea*, powerfully evokes just such leisure time (opposite). It also characterizes the early work of Bown: black-and-white, square-format photographs using a medium-format Rolleiflex and rejecting even the minor encumbrance of a light meter (thus requiring her to gauge exposure by light falling on the back of her hand). Bown's self-deprecation as photographer is well documented; on more than one occasion she asserted she was no more than a hack. Notwithstanding, she was a highly respected photojournalist working at the *Observer* from 1949, and it is hard to reconcile the pejorative and mercenary elements associated with 'hack', with the sensitivity, immediacy and integrity of Bown's *oeuvre*. *Southend-on-Sea* is a case in point. It is a sensuous photograph; perhaps a double-portrait? An early image by Bown, it characterizes a visual trait of hers at the time – to photograph the back of people. As Germaine Greer noted in her analysis of Bown: 'she has photographed some of the most expressive behinds in photography.'[4]

The rejection of the face, whether due to aesthetic decision-making or perhaps Bown's inherent shyness, removes nothing from the final image. It is characteristically precise and contains scant information: the connection between the picture's two subjects

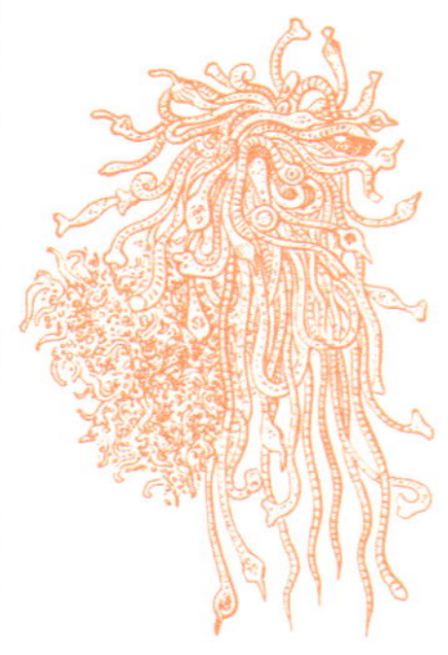

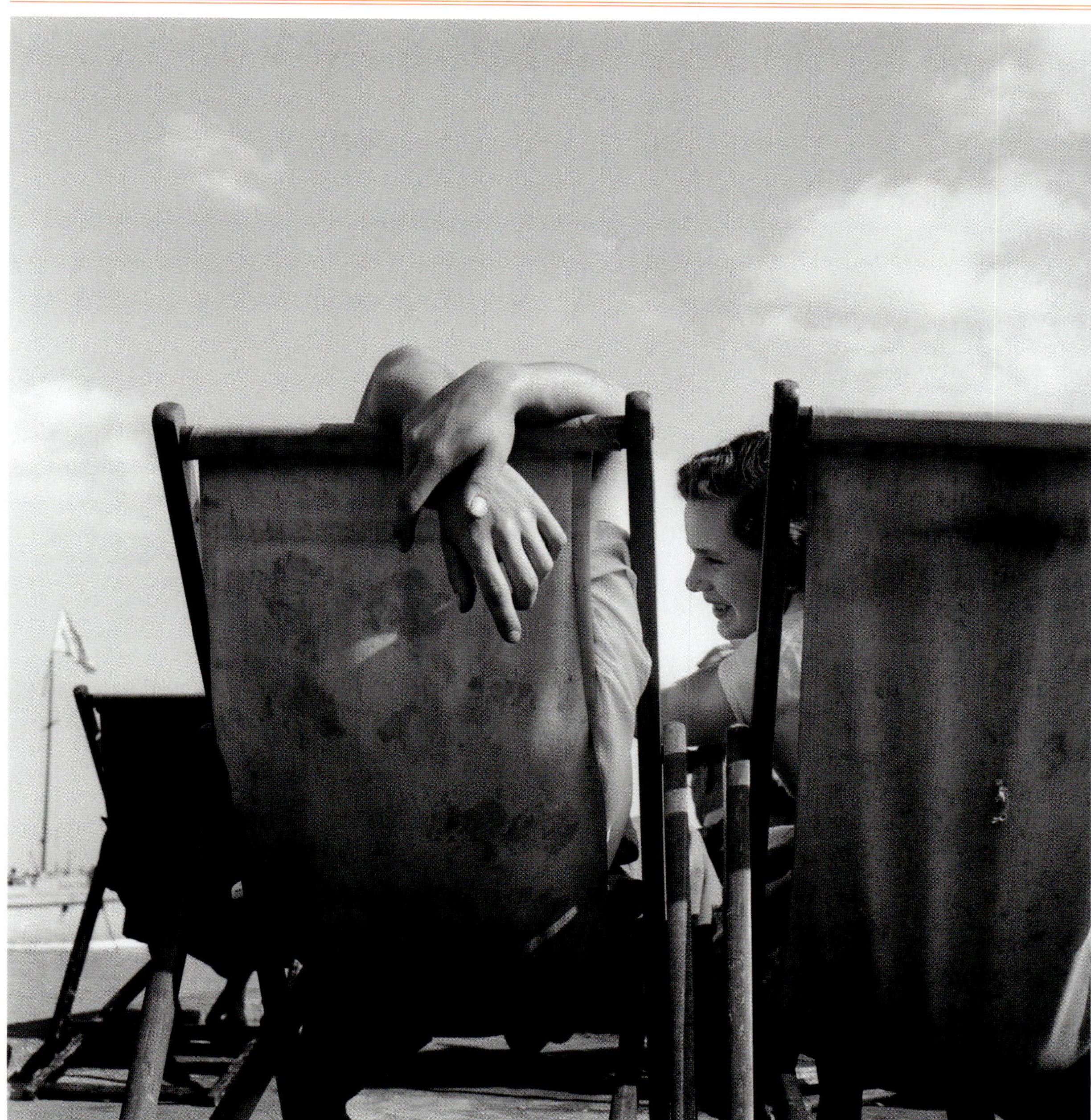

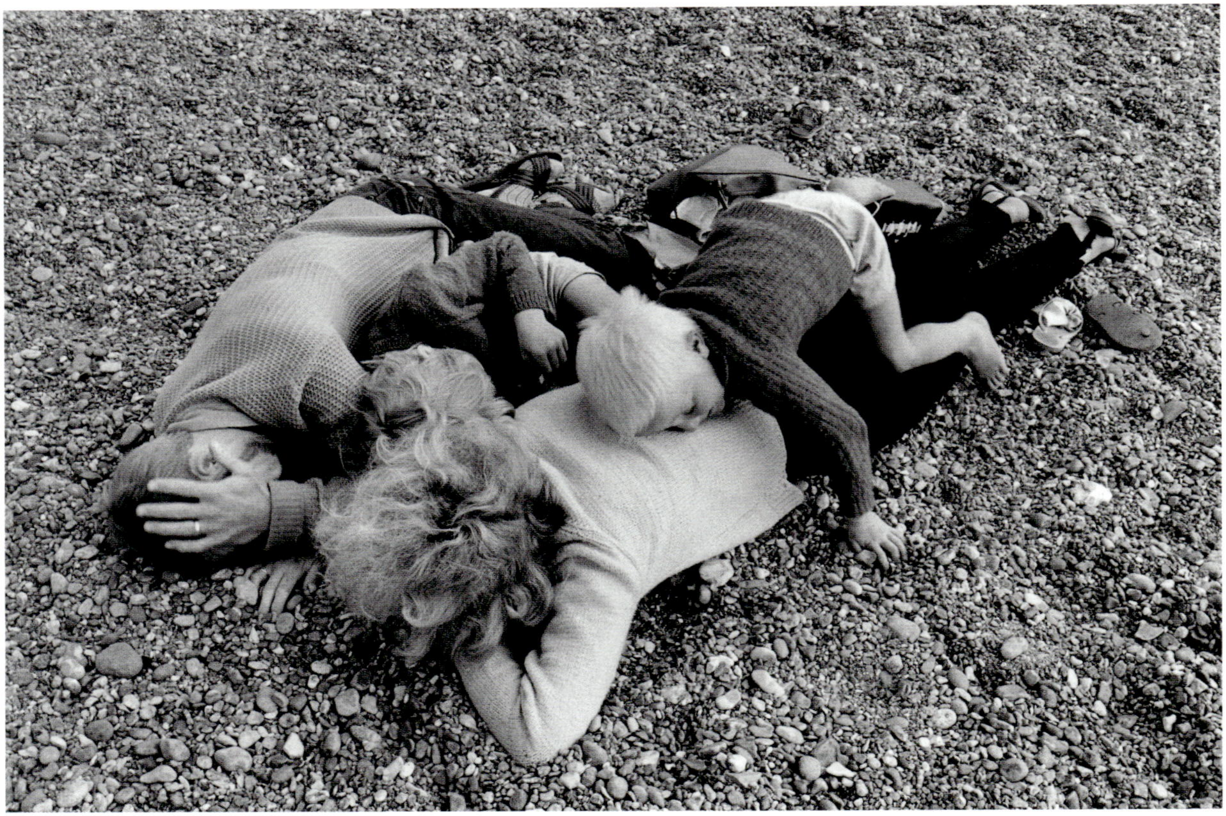

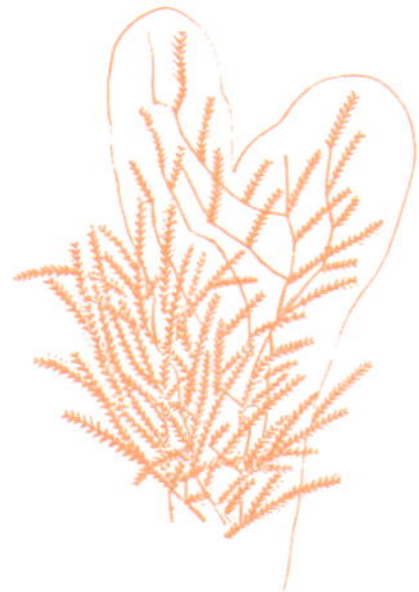

is apparent. Here, as well as a back, we, of course, see a young woman's smiling face in profile, as she leans forward, seemingly delighting in her unseen male companion. Of him, we are shown the hands, evocative of confidence. In their leisure they indicate an assured masculinity, endorsed by the sense of weight in the deckchair, his muscular form filling the canvas and providing a contrast to the light shaping of the woman's seat. They are a couple at the seaside, separated physically yet connected by glance and emotion.

Southend-on-Sea is unapologetically romantic; unsurprisingly, Bown aligned her own practice, what she referred to as the 'finding' of the picture, to that of love: 'for that moment when I look through the lens, when absolutely everything is exactly right, love is the only way to describe what I feel.'[5]

Uncluttered, intimate and immediate, *Southend-on-Sea* is quintessentially Bown and in its theme of seaside leisure embodies

ANNE BRAYBON
Sweater Weather,
Brighton, 1969

and perpetuates mythic qualities of 'devil-may-care' and licence, laced with an air of insouciant sexuality to accompany the sun and sea.

Over a decade later another reticent female photographer, Anne Braybon, was producing her own seaside images, this time in Brighton. Braybon's work from the late 1960s was surreptitious in its making – observing beach life at a distance. At the time she was an art student employed as a seasonal worker making seaside photographs of Brighton's numerous day-trippers, which the visitors would then buy as souvenirs. Braybon (now best known as a creative director, photo historian and photography commissioner) noted in interview that while she had a certain presence – she was youthful and attractive – as a consequence of her diffidence she would often 'grab' the image.

But cheap seaside mementos were not her only photographs. Braybon also talks of the

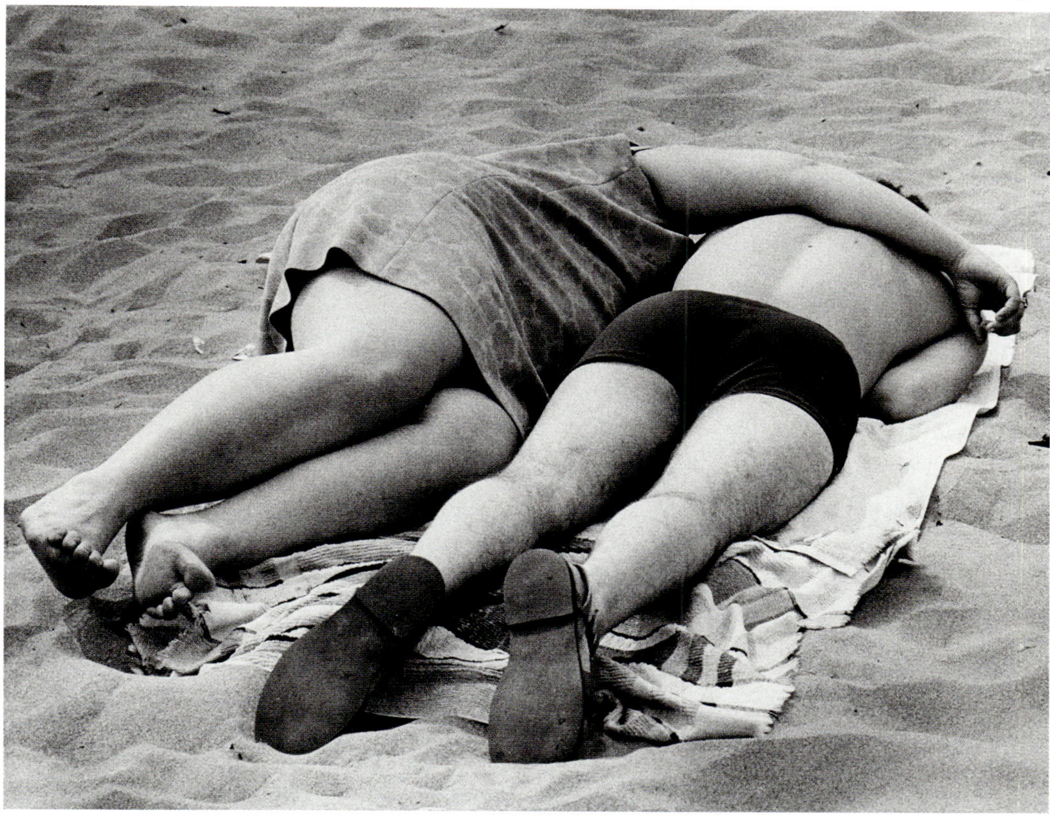

pictures 'I made in-between', where her own photography found voice and image. Taken during quieter moments of the day, these photographs were frequently produced by Braybon leaning over Brighton's promenade railings, observing the beach below.

This kind of practice is perhaps indicative of her unwillingness, even inability, to go on to the beach and mix with the beachgoers. Nevertheless, through this distancing Braybon manages to capture unselfconscious intimacy. A family 'bundle' – their fully clothed bodies interwoven with one another, with a child so folded between his parents as to be almost lost from view – are all oblivious to Braybon's camera (opposite, above). They unwittingly demonstrate British resilience and doggedness when faced with seaside pleasures: the day appears cold; they lie on pebbles rather than sand. Yet the family appear completely at ease with each other's touch and weight.

Shirley Baker
Love on the Beach,
Abersoch, Wales, 1968

As Braybon was working in Brighton, Shirley Baker was taking occasional trips away from her usual urban environment in the north-west to photograph working-class day-trippers in Abersoch, Wales. Baker was as much a visitor as those she photographed, and the incisive insight into street life she had achieved on the terraced streets of Salford and Hulme in Manchester was smoothly redeployed on her own trips to the coast.

The shoreline environment might have been new terrain, but the working-class communities she photographed were familiar subjects. Baker's humanistic documentary approach is apparent in *Love on the Beach* (1968; above), which predates her better known and extensive 1970 beach series from Blackpool and the south of France. Nothing unsympathetic invades Baker's photography; she might photograph the heft of a body at the seaside, but never resorts to simplistic stereotyping or caricaturing her subjects.

As with Bown's *Southend-on-Sea* and Braybon's Brighton work, Baker's *Love on the Beach* unexpectedly denies access to the face. Yet it is the body and that weighty embrace that gives this image its visual force. The bodies become landscapes in the sand, undulating and monumental, with the visceral pleasure of lying in the sun becoming tangible and physical in a caress unlikely to be enacted in those days anywhere in public other than on the beach.

While at the seaside the couple are fleetingly freed from adult responsibilities, momentarily appearing as new lovers delighting and absorbed only in the company of each other. There is something domestic and familiar in the embrace; the crumpled towel beneath the couple echoing the mattress at home, the woman's trunk of an arm pinning the man to the towel but also holding him to her.

This couple, abstracted from the broader beach scene by Baker's careful framing, are highlighted by their immersion in one another – like Braybon's family, they seem mutually at ease. But these works were never intended as innocuous or idealized nostalgia; photography as nostalgia was abhorrent to Baker, who worked tirelessly to document real lives, believing that while the camera was 'capable of great things',[6] this could only be achieved through disciplined observation and scrutiny. Placed into the wider context of Baker's work, one is struck by how fleeting are these days in the sun.

In common with Baker, a deep commitment to place and space characterizes the practice of Finnish-born Sirkka-Liisa Konttinen. From 1969 Konttinen relocated to Britain's north-east, and *Writing in the Sand* is not only testament to the place but also to the time that she took over two decades to complete a project that not only celebrates the seaside, but shows the shoreline as vital demotic space for working-class people to gather.

As a founding member of the film and photography collective Amber in Newcastle upon Tyne, Konttinen has operated within the workshop model of production since the late 1960s, championing Amber's underpinning principle of celebrating working-class culture. Konttinen, despite her outsider status, successfully documented the traditional working-class communities, providing her own fresh-eyed observations into the terraced homes and lives of the Byker community, in contrast to those halcyon days when day-trips to the nearby bays of Whitley and Cullercoats were organized.

Whitley Bay (June 1989; opposite) is an example of conditions the seaside presents for the photographer. Konttinen's coastal work benefits from the bright light, where shutter speeds can be fast, action frozen and a terrific sense of motion communicated. The barefoot youth, taut, powerful and balletic, volleys the ball to unseen teammates. Its barely contained exuberance and energy against a background of uninterrupted space suggests the body and mind freed, let loose for expansive and noisy play.

Movement is amplified still further in a forty-five-minute film *Writing in the Sand* made by Konttinen in collaboration with partner Peter Roberts. Made at Amber in 1991, the film visually pans, scans and jump-cuts over 400 of Konttinen's seaside photographs, while complex layers of beach sounds and regional voices create a diegetic seaside backdrop. Through the use of camera movement across the static image, the viewer is taken on a celebratory and extended seaside journey where, rather than observing the beach, they experience the communities eking out each moment of the day.

Collectively, the seaside photographs by Konttinen, Baker, Braybon and Bown demonstrate how the beach offered a welcome opportunity to shake off adult responsibilities and return to the earlier, carefree, pleasures of childhood, with space and time to find or rekindle affection. They can be seen as a visual celebration of the seaside and those who enjoy it, but also a celebration that is tempered by the knowledge that such times are all too fleeting.

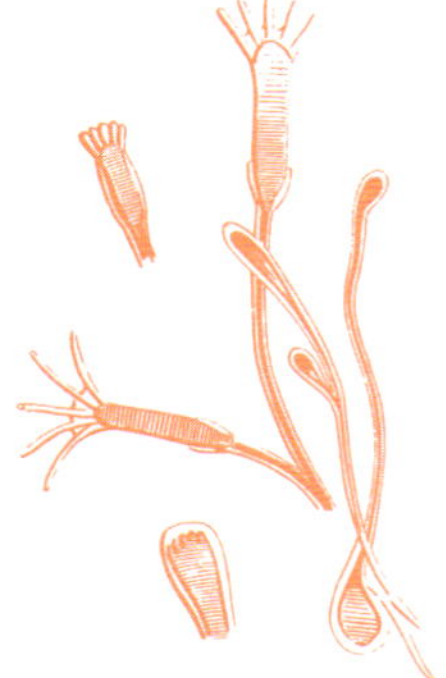

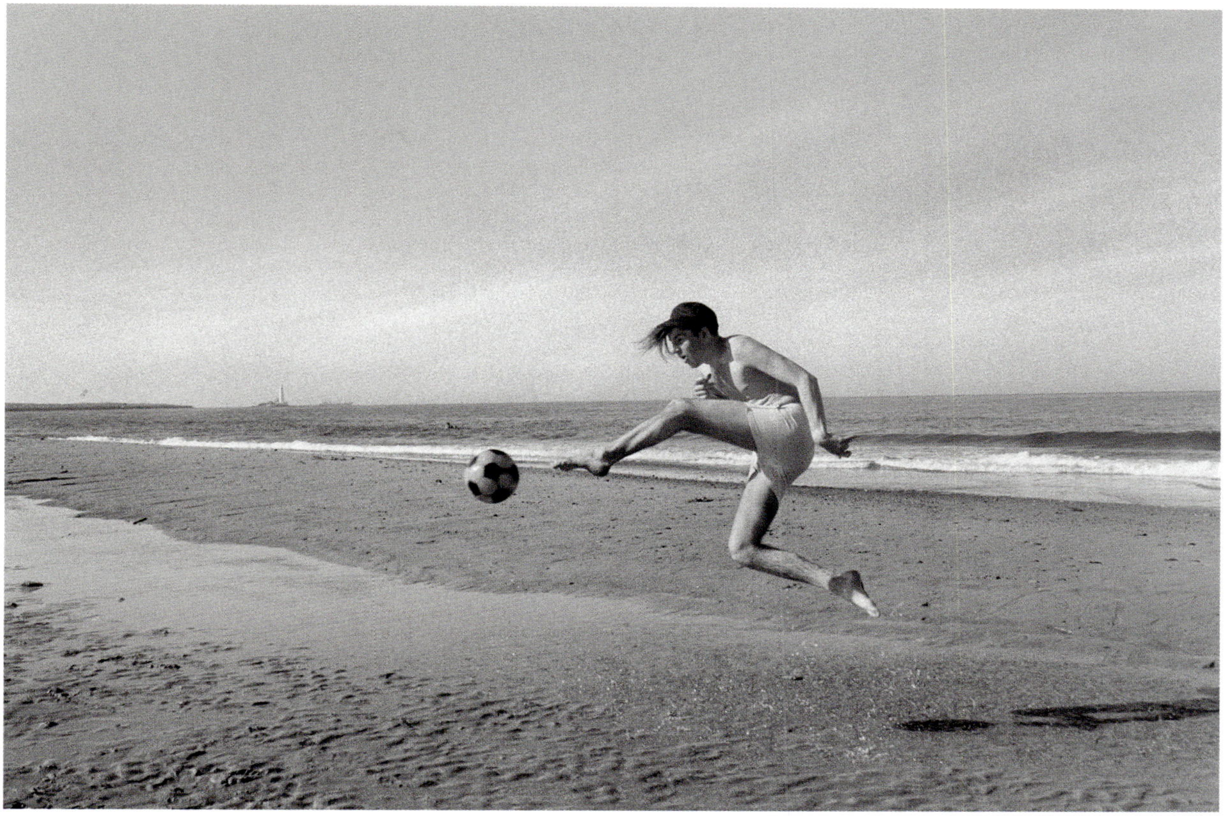

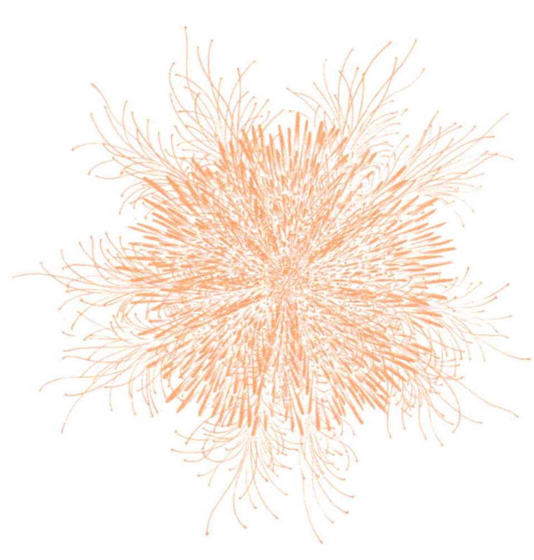

As Dylan Thomas's prose alerts us: 'fathers, in the once-a-year sun, took fifty winks.' Leisure in the sun for the working classes in mid-century Britain was not only hard-earned but brief:

If it could only just, if it could only just,' your lips said again and again as you scooped, in the hob-hot sand ... 'If it could only just be like this for ever and ever amen.[7]

[KS]

Sirkka-Liisa Konttinen
Whitley Bay, June 1989, from the series
Writing in the Sand

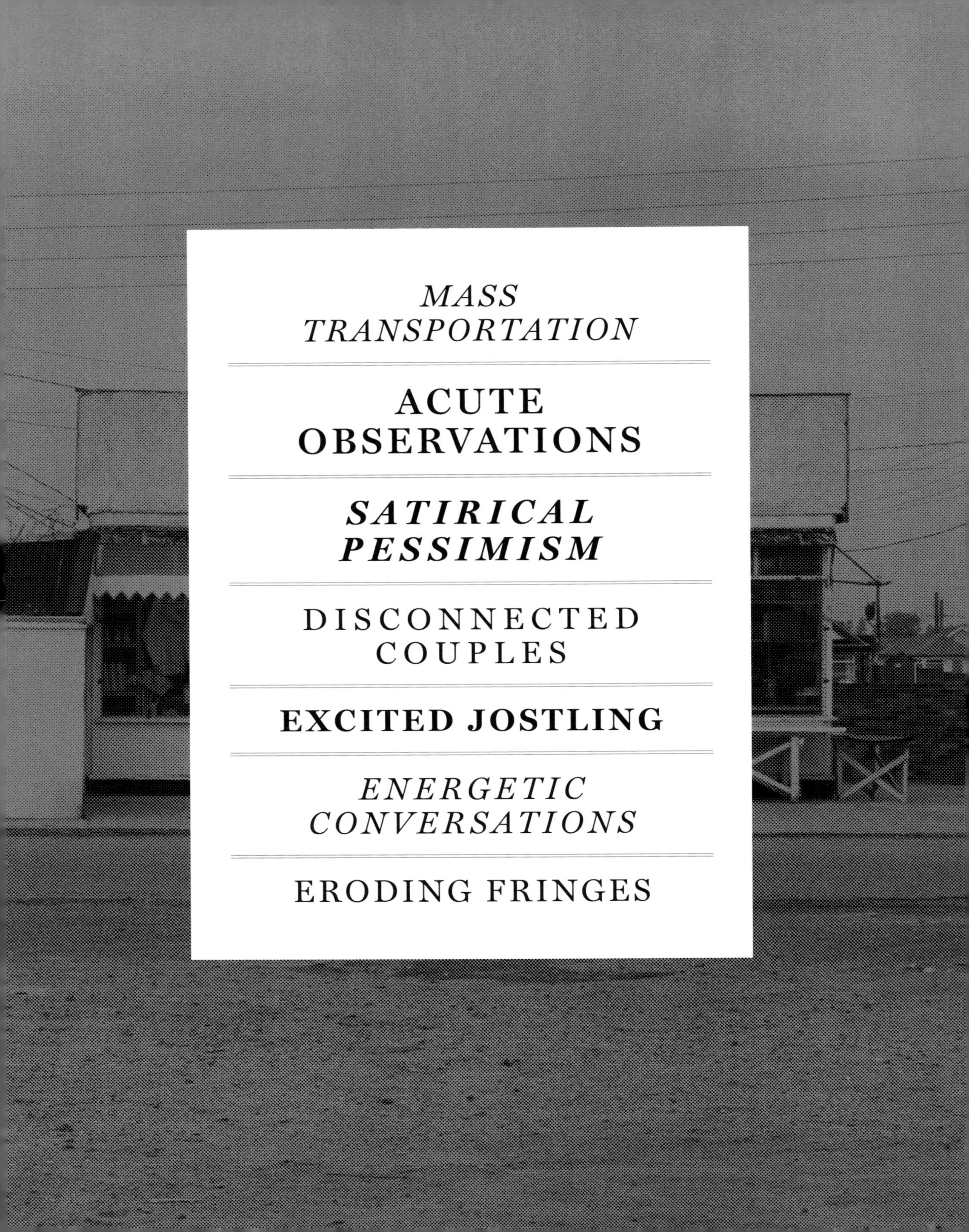

MASS TRANSPORTATION

ACUTE OBSERVATIONS

SATIRICAL PESSIMISM

DISCONNECTED COUPLES

EXCITED JOSTLING

ENERGETIC CONVERSATIONS

ERODING FRINGES

ROAD TRIPS

PHOTOGRAPHY ON THE MOVE

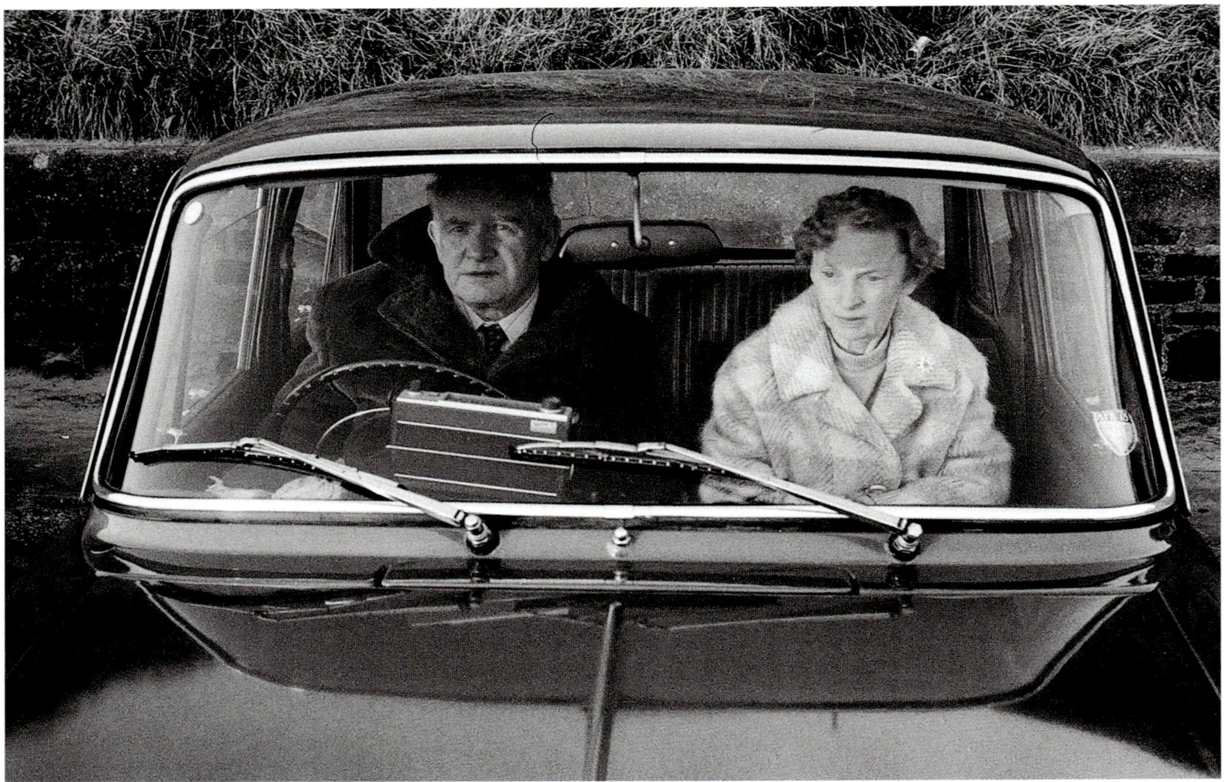

From the mid-nineteenth century, mass transportation through the development of the railway network, including lines directly servicing the seaside towns; regular steamboat services from cities to coastal resorts; and from the 1920s charabancs, coaches and, increasingly, motorcars, all brought the tourist to the coast. On an island as modest in scale as Britain, those determined to get to the seaside normally could, and, for all but the poorest, from the early twentieth century there were opportunities to experience the seashore, even if just for a single day.[1]

As the tourists headed coastward, so too did the photographers. From the middle of the nineteenth century Francis Frith systematically photographed seaside towns for commercial purposes and, though undertaking much of the photography himself, so vast was the enterprise that he deployed other travelling photographers to take pictures too. Towards the end of the century, Sir Benjamin Stone, though motivated by culture

Iain McKell
Untitled, from the series
Sea View, 1976

rather than commerce, nevertheless used a similar method to Frith, creating a national photographic record 'for the benefit of future generations [of] the manners and customs, the festivals and pageants, the historic buildings and places of our times'.[2] Such ambitions naturally necessitated ever-improving transport infrastructures.

The late nineteenth century enabled individual photographers such as Paul Martin to visit seaside resorts serviced by the railways, and by the twentieth century an increasing number of personal photographic projects would encompass the British seaside. Tony Ray-Jones's *A Day Off* (which originally began as the book dummy entitled *England by the Sea*)[3] is an obvious example: his handwritten notes from 1966 alphabetically list over twenty resorts to be documented while travelling the country in his Dormobile.

David Hurn recently reflected on this ease of access to the seaside: 'when I first started in photography, it was in London … at the

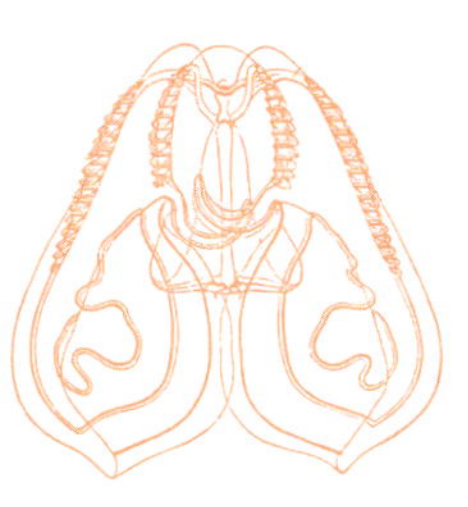

weekends, I could get away from current affairs, I could go down to Herne Bay on the train ... it was very close.'[4] Colin Thomas talks of the repeated pull of the seaside, enticing him to return time and again. Thomas, like many of the photographers discussed here, was by then a car owner. The car provided individualized, fast, easy access to rich photographic terrain, facilitating a rapid dipping in and out of coastal towns, and in common with the seaside newcomers, photographers might be characterized by the pejorative moniker 'blow-ins'.

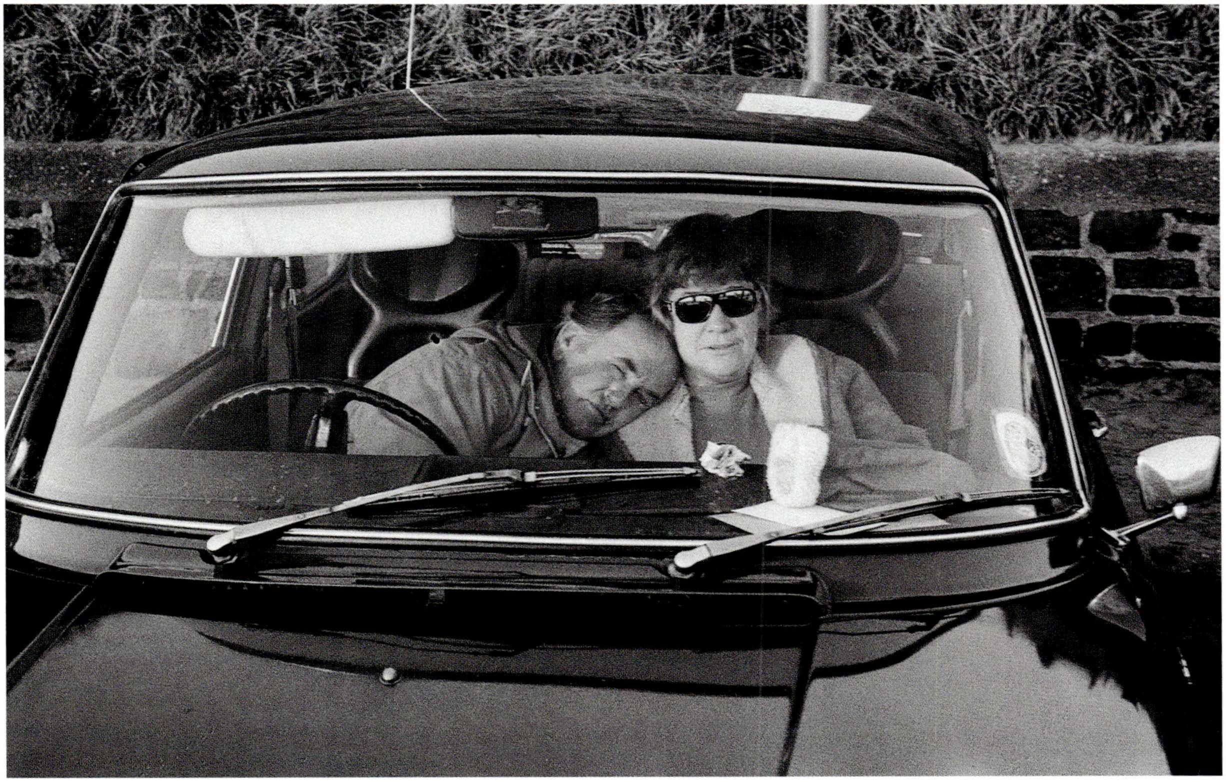

But Iain McKell diverges from this model. McKell was no blow-in; he was a Weymouth local growing up at the seaside, with parents working as hoteliers. For the McKells tourism was integral to family life. Weymouth repeatedly figures in McKell's photography (see pp.16–23), yet from adolescence he sought to escape seaside parochialism, moving away in search of the life of an artist. His working life has combined the highly successful career

Iain McKell
Untitled, from the series
Sea View, 1976

of fashion photographer with acclaimed personal documentary projects. His numerous seaside series from 1970 onwards consistently show an understanding of the characteristics of small seaside towns. His *Sea View* series (above and opposite) is indicative of this with McKell's characters sitting in their cars within a self-imposed, constraining space.

These photographs are a mournful return to the seaside: communicating unadventurous lives, which unwittingly provided a visual precursor to Paul Theroux's literary observations of the British at the seaside:

They sat in their cars and stared out at the sea. They were on every beach road ... I saw them everywhere, eating sandwiches, drinking tea out of the plastic cups, reading the paper, looking fuddled. They always faced the water. They were old couples mostly, but they never seemed to be holding conversations ... they did not seem to

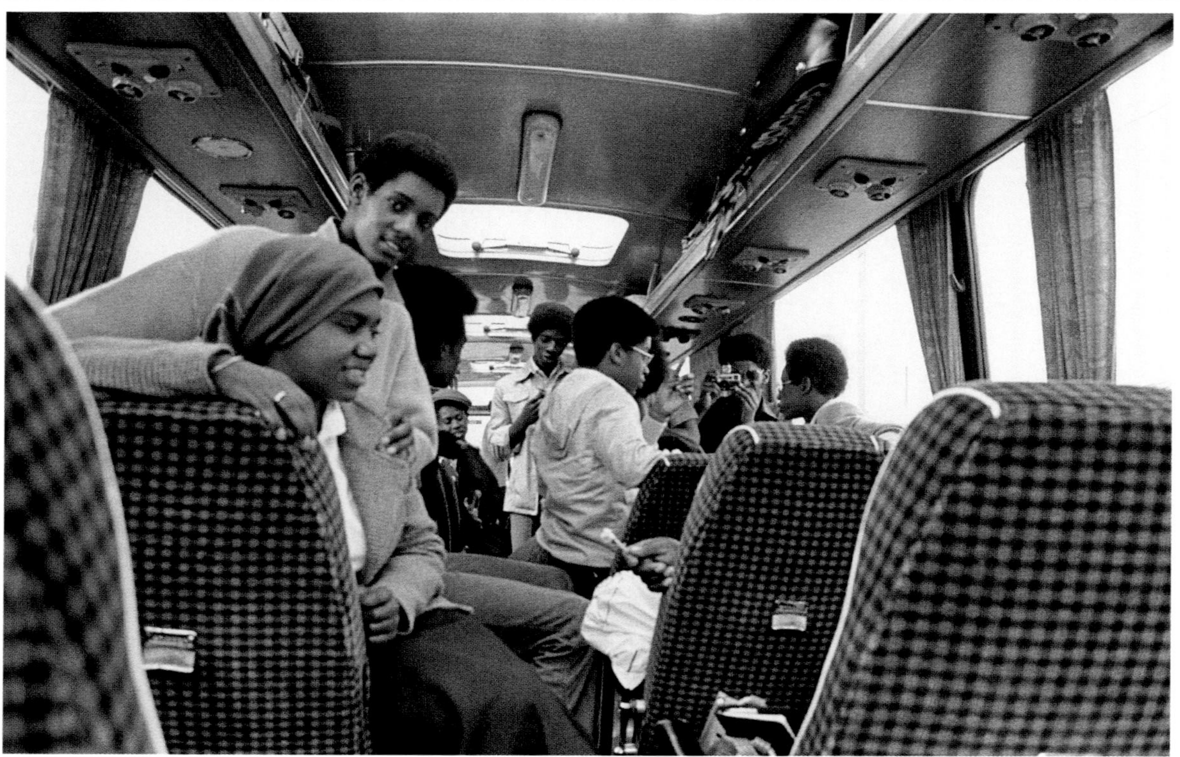

be looking at anything in particular. Their expressions were a little sad and empty, as if they were expecting to see something beyond the horizon or under the surface of the waves.[5]

McKell's *Sea View* series documents that perennial feature of the British seaside: car owners almost doggedly sitting out by the seaside, removed from onshore winds playing havoc with hair and from the perceived slightly alien nature of the social life of the beach and promenade.

As with McKell, Michael Bennett's extraordinary *Seaside in Summer and Winter* (1980) inflects acute visual observations with satirical pessimism. This series – with many of its photographs included in this chapter's portfolio (pp.114–23) – was commissioned by Llandudno's Mostyn Gallery, briefing Bennett to document the town in winter for an exhibition in the following year. The then progressive gallery director Hugh Adams actively encouraged a melancholic picturing of the

North Wales seaside town. But at the point of delivery Adams had gone and the passive desperation captured by the photographer was not quite what was anticipated by the incoming director. To salvage the gallery's position, Bennett was asked to return and record what was assumed would be a more optimistic summertime view. Contrary to the commissioner's expectations, Llandudno in summer appeared in Bennett's photographs as austere and alienating as in wintertime. The submitted work was ill received, with the new gallery director Clive Adams openly loathing the work and the regional press printing numerous critiques.

Partisan locals' bewilderment is understandable. Bennett's work is utterly uncompromising, with one photograph exclaiming in uppercase: 'YOU HAVE BEEN WARNED' (p.114) – warned of what? It reads as a 'scare' sign, alerting us to the dangers of a visit. Nevertheless, his work foreshadowed the huge decline in visitors in the 1980s, thereby providing a robust visual antidote to any

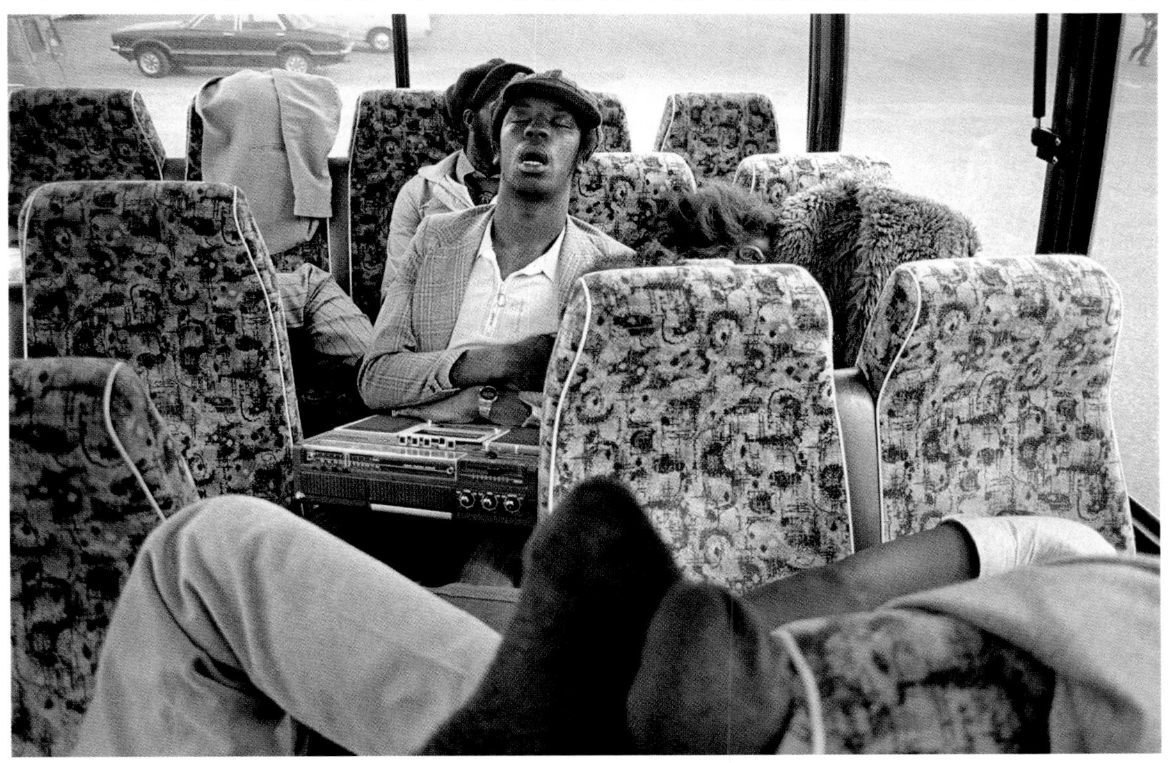

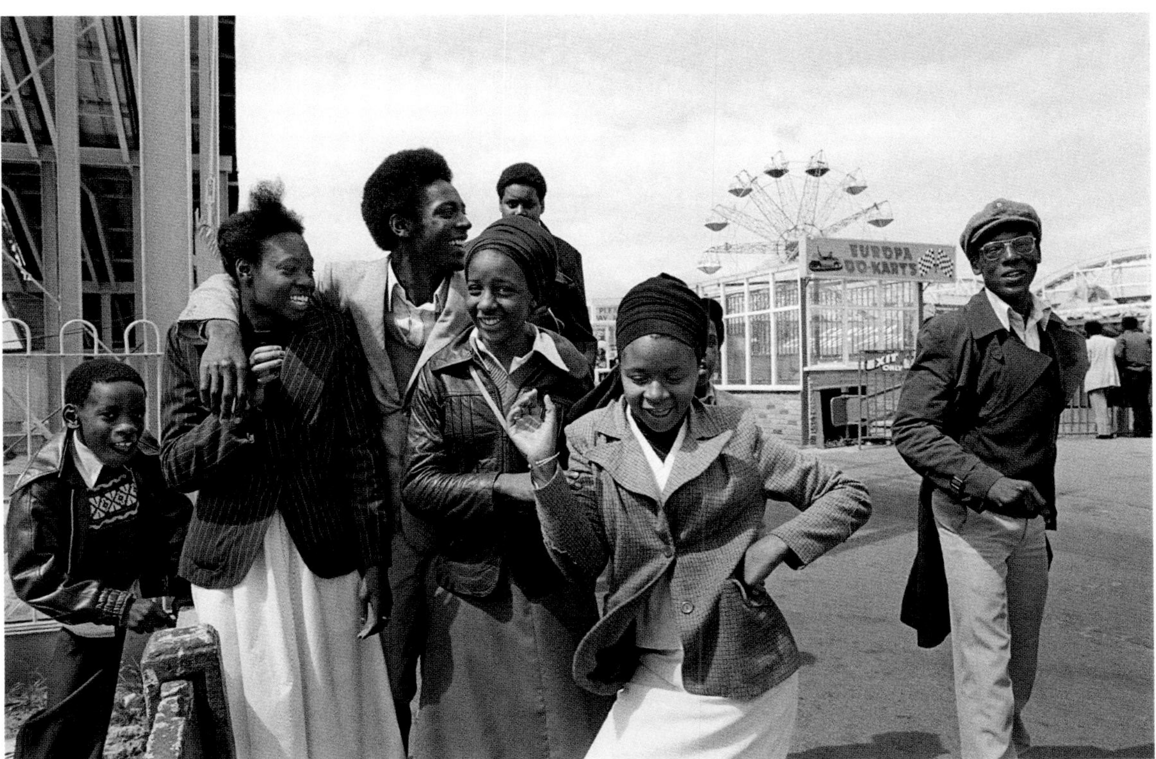

EUROPA
GO-KARTS

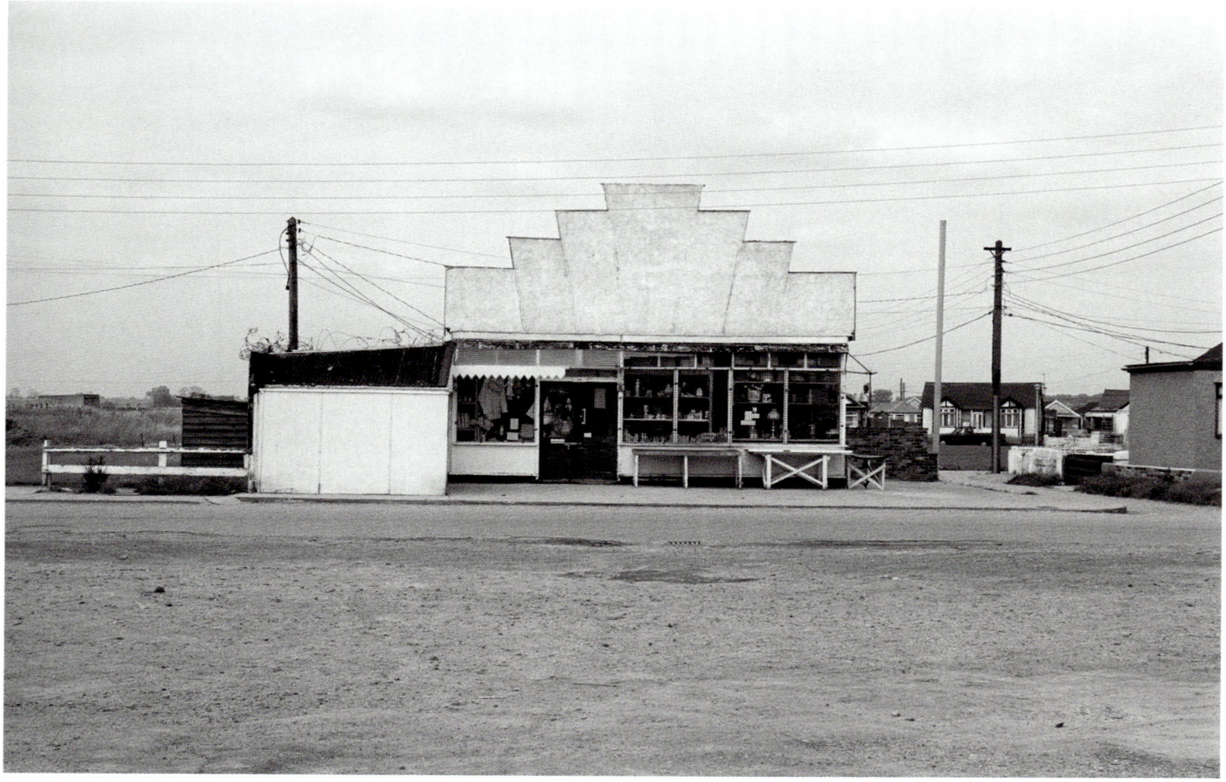

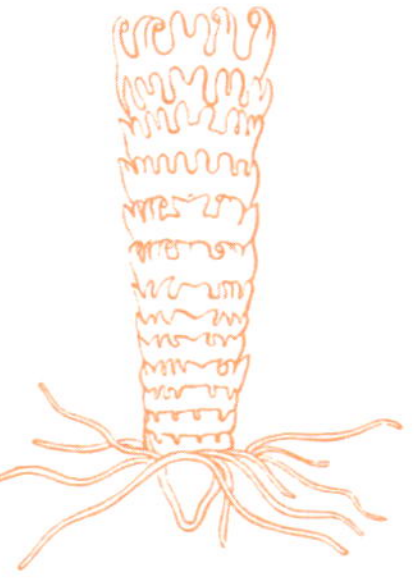

STEVE FERRIER
Jaywick, 1989

rose-tinted assumptions about the British seaside.

Seaside in Summer and Winter presents Llandudno as a place of disconnected couples staring blankly, bored not only with one another, but perhaps also with life itself. Listless groups look vacantly to Bennett's camera and a woman absentmindedly picks at her teeth as she awaits customers at a snack kiosk. His documentation of a seaside town in decline is both unedifying and unappetizing.

Vanley Burke's extraordinary documentation of 1970s seaside day-trips by the Jamaican population of Handsworth provides an optimistic counter-voice to the melancholy of Bennett. As ever, Burke's focus is his own community, creating fidelity to experience, what Stuart Hall described as 'insider's portraits' of an 'indigenous black space'.[6] The seaside trips organized by Burke's father, documented in these photographs, seem to be as much about the journey as the destination. Burke frames the coach as a space of anticipation where excited jostling for seats, energetic conversations and day's-end exhausted open-mouthed sleep are all accompanied by sounds from the boombox.

Once at the destination, community rather than place dominates Burke's frame. The day-trippers not only fill the shot, but also overspill it, confidently excluding everything and everyone beyond the community group. Such insider documentation – what Burke refers to as *histograph* – privileges this visiting community. Burke photographs from within rather than outwith the community; he is as intrinsic a part of the group as those whom he documents. As Bennett's work sirens 'YOU HAVE BEEN WARNED', Burke's sings 'WE ARE HERE', with the seaside location playing but a minor role. Although the images are made within the context of Thatcher's individualized Britain, Burke forcefully champions collective, community experience.

The documenting of seaside hinterlands in Thatcher's Britain of the 1980s proved popular

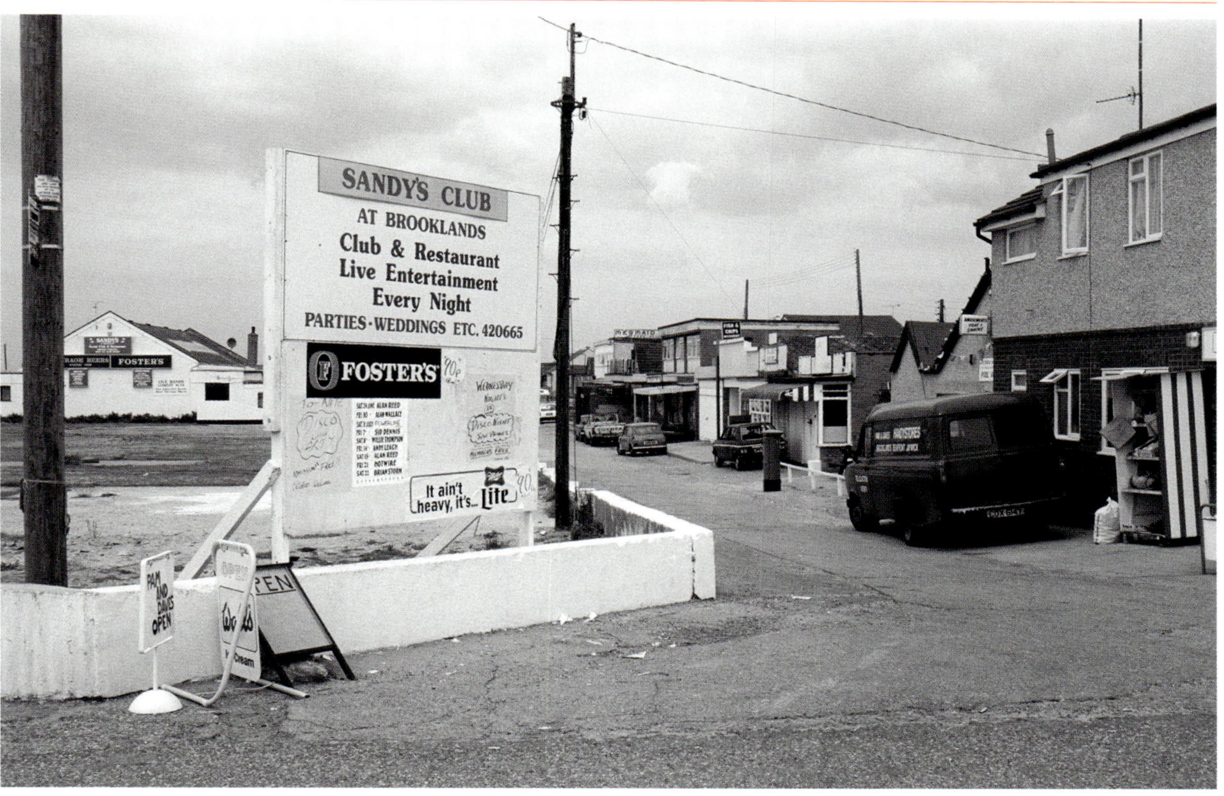

to a number of photographers, including Steve Ferrier and Anna Fox. Increased car ownership provided not only access to the coast, but also an ability to cruise around and find unsettling, eroding fringes. Their photographs frequently go beyond merely showing: they also acerbically comment on the state of the seaside and, indirectly, perhaps, the state of the nation. Ferrier's three-year observation of the transient development of seaside outer suburbs in the late 1980s takes us to Essex, and specifically Jaywick (opposite and above). The work made by Ferrier suggests pessimism and transience: the prosaic architecture, street furniture and depopulated streets signify what Ferrier refers to as a 'detachment from the rest of the country'.[7]

Yet Jaywick had been heralded as an exemplar of the British self-made, unplanned seaside resort. For the architecture critic Sutherland Lyall it stands as 'not shanty town jerry building but an indigenous British paradigm'.[8] Nevertheless, due to general

STEVE FERRIER
Sandy's Club, Jaywick,
1989

economic recession and the local authority's overt policy of blocking both development and the provision of services, Jaywick fell into a decline in the 1990s and beyond, far worse than shown in Ferrier's photographs, such that, according to the Government Indices of Multiple Deprivation (2015), it stands at the top of the list.

Anna Fox, only recently graduated from Farnham, produced images that similarly grate on the eyes with *Hayling Island* (1986; overleaf). Under the tutelage of Martin Parr and Paul Graham, as a student Fox had found the excitement and power of colour photography compelling. This was, after all, the period in which Parr was bringing to completion the seminal *Last Resort* series, and to which Graham's *Beyond Caring* belonged. The challenge to the documentary photography orthodoxy made by these new British colourists profoundly influenced Fox. She could see for herself how amplified colour and flash could play a significant part

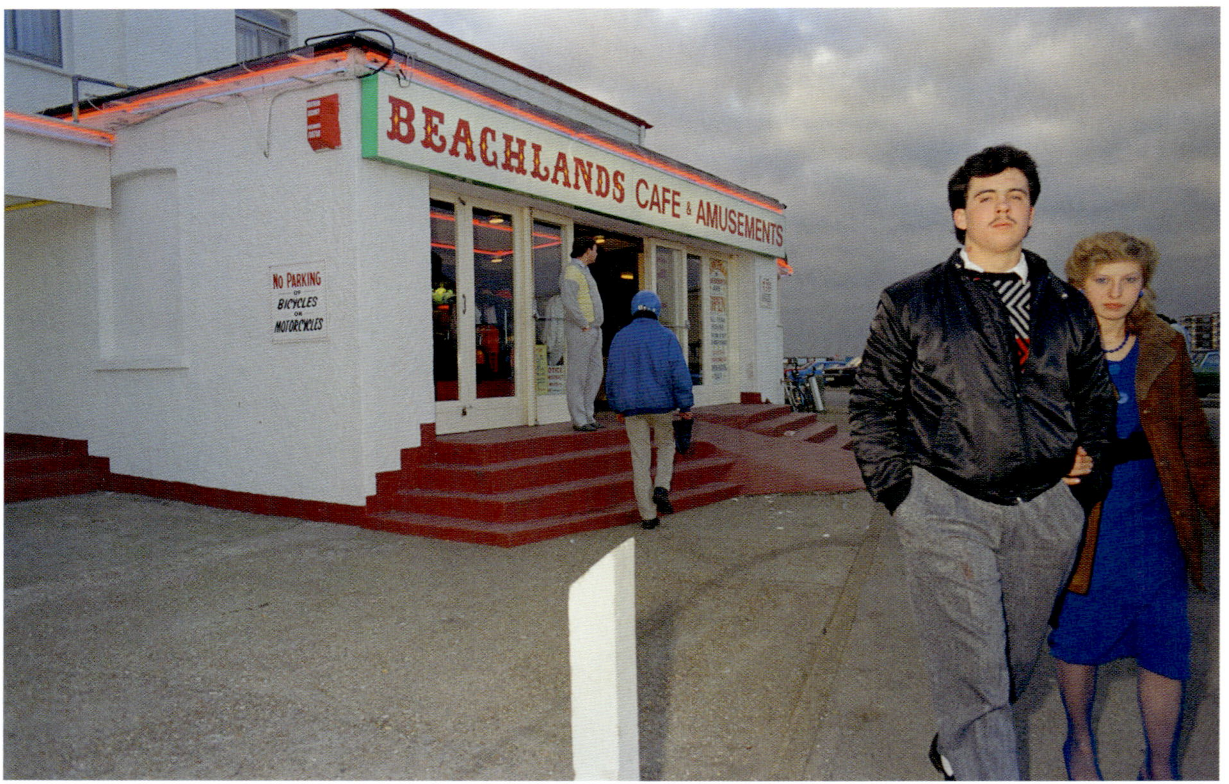

ANNA FOX
Hayling Island, 1986

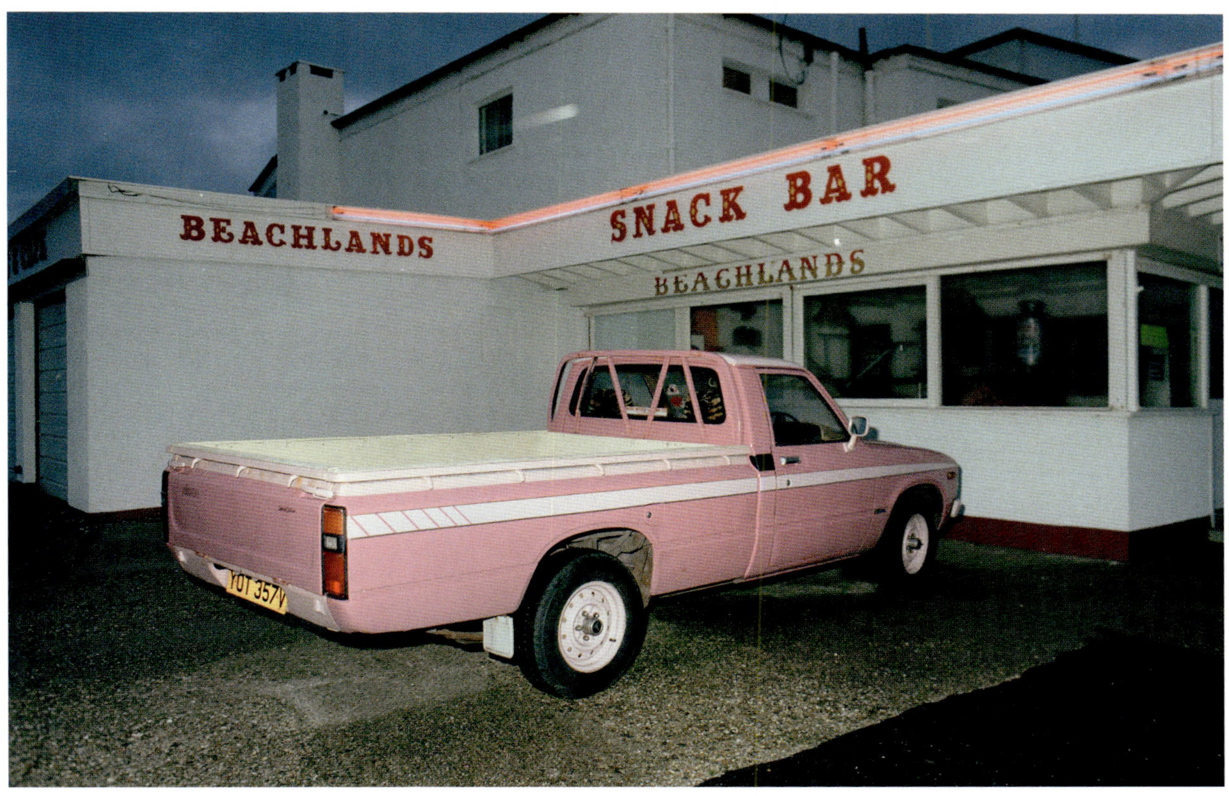

ANNA FOX
Hayling Island, 1986

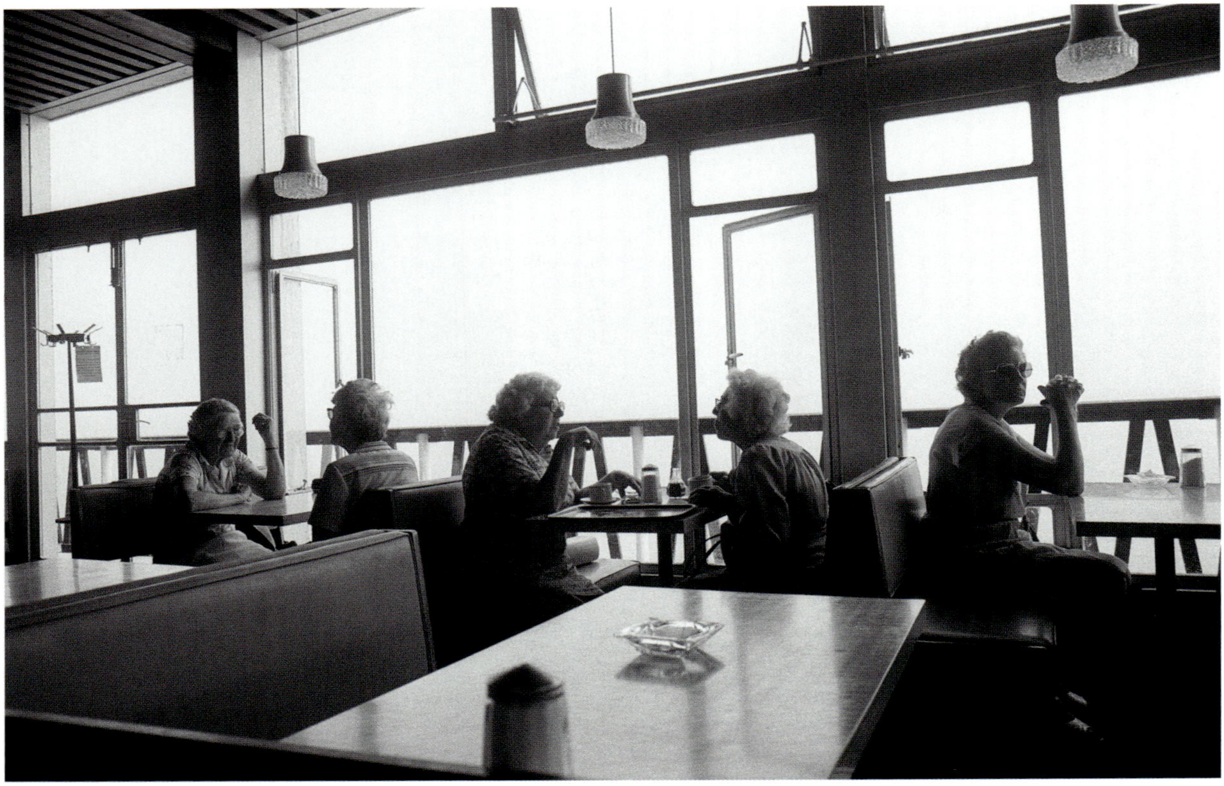

in communicating meaning photographically. Photography could convey anger and be distasteful, not only in *what* but *how* it showed.

Fox's seaside is man-made and hostile, a synthetic assembly of concrete, brick and steel. The environment's (un)natural bleakness is heightened by the glare of her camera's flash and the acidity of her colour palette. It is wintertime in Hayling Island, specifically Christmas, but the yuletide festivities seem to have passed by the Beachland's café featured in the series. Fox constructs a land of the suffocatingly mundane, simultaneously a threat to and alienated from the natural environment of the seashore.

Rather than focusing on the decline, desperation or alienation that understandably characterizes much 1980s seaside photography, Colin Curwood takes a very different approach. Despite a period of national recession, mass unemployment and depressing decline in British manufacturing, Curwood's seaside is a place of determined

Colin Curwood
Eastbourne, 1983

optimism and commonality of experience, where friends or family groupings are relaxed and at ease with one another. His couplets of older women, grouped in an Eastbourne café, are a keen example of his tenderness (above). The women, extraordinary in their similarity of gesture, dress, spectacles and 'shampoo and set' hairdos, hark back to more familiar and more certain times. It reassures us that the so-called 'commonplace' is a rich seam still to be mined in British life and culture.

As with Curwood, Colin Thomas's photography has a lightness and optimism that defies the era of its production. Thomas's 1980s road trips necessitated highly domesticated expeditions, conflating photography with family holidays to static caravan parks on the Welsh coast. With individualism being recognized as a key characteristic of the decade, these provided not only affordable breaks but were regarded as (slightly) more individualistic than neighbouring holiday camps. The peeking baby cocooned by the

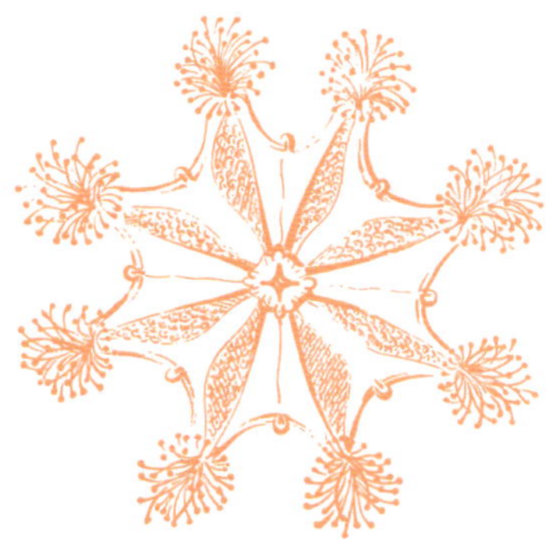

carrycot in Thomas's *Brynowen Caravan Park* (1986; above) is his son Gareth. Redolent of the democratization of travel, the carrycot was designed specifically for easy transportation in the car.

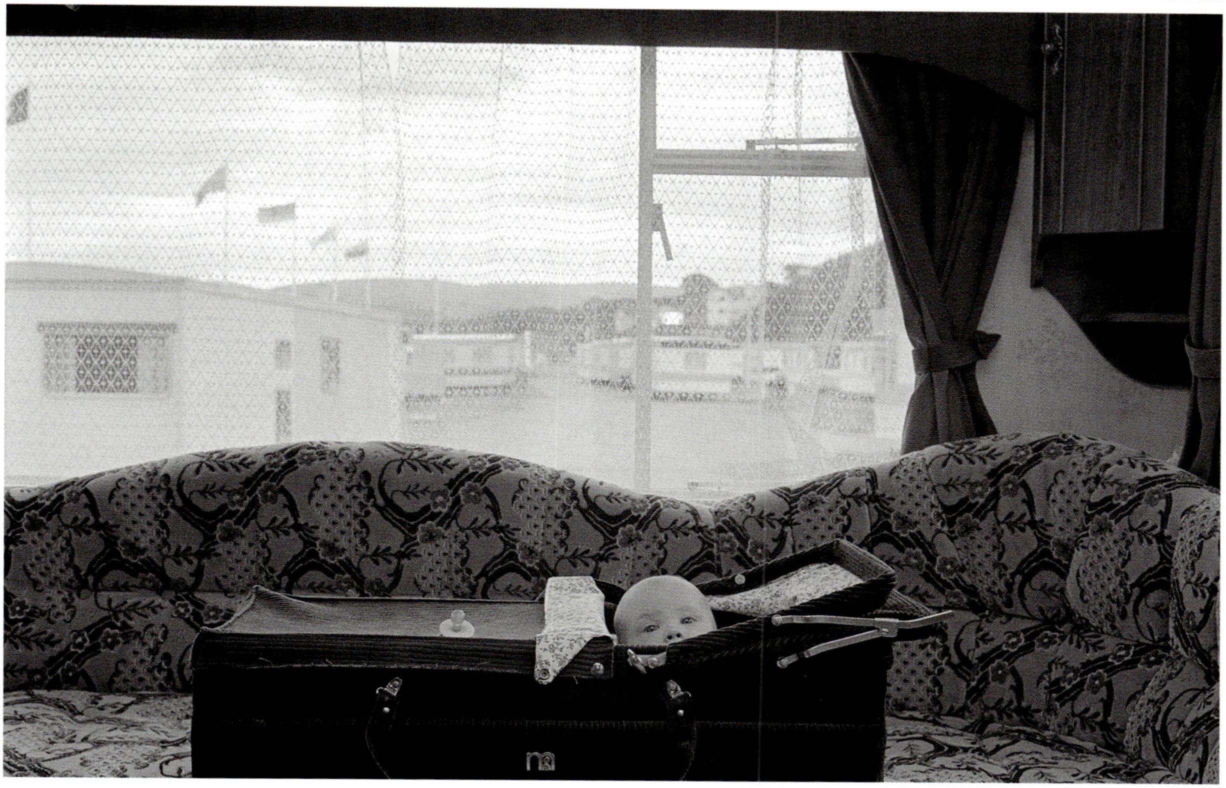

Nevertheless, this photograph, as its title shows, is not only of an endearing baby; beyond, and framed by the net-curtained window, the regimented caravan park stretches into the distance. It is difficult to see this location as idealized, but these were for Thomas trips 'home', the caravan site a mere five miles from his birthplace of Aberystwyth. In this return, we see Thomas, as father, repeat routines and rituals of seaside visits from his past, transmitting them to the next generation. Some thirty years later, despite, he says, the risk of being 'hit by seagull shit', he is still returning.

To survey British seaside photography is to come to regard most photographers as blow-ins: arriving, making work and then, tide-like, receding from the coast at day's end.

COLIN THOMAS
*Brynowen Caravan
Park*, 1986

This might be a point of criticism: the connotation of the photographer hijacking the sands for a quick photo opportunity. But this would be mistaken, for there is a keenness in newcomers' fresh eyes and focus. They can make strange the often over-familiar. This is acutely exemplified in Bennett's Llandudno series *Summer and Winter*, with its revelation of truths that were difficult to face. [KS]

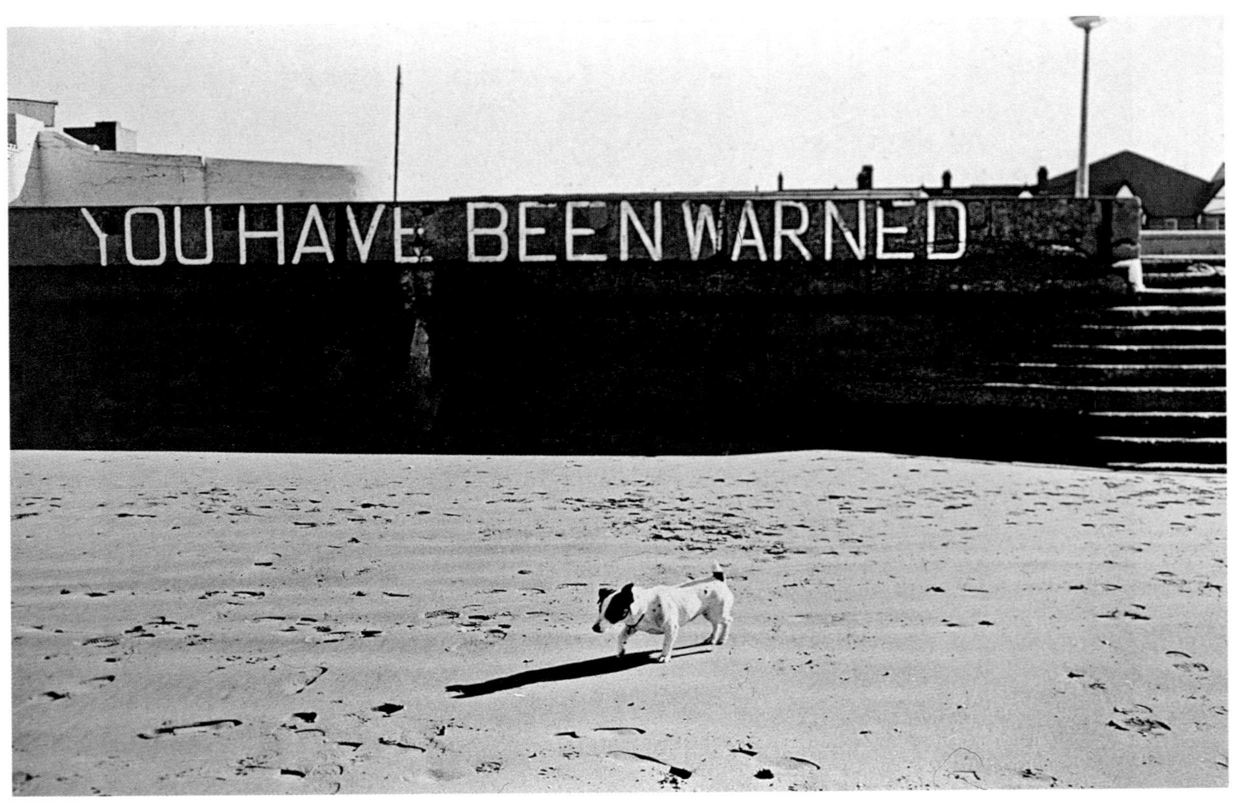

Seaside in Summer and Winter, 1980

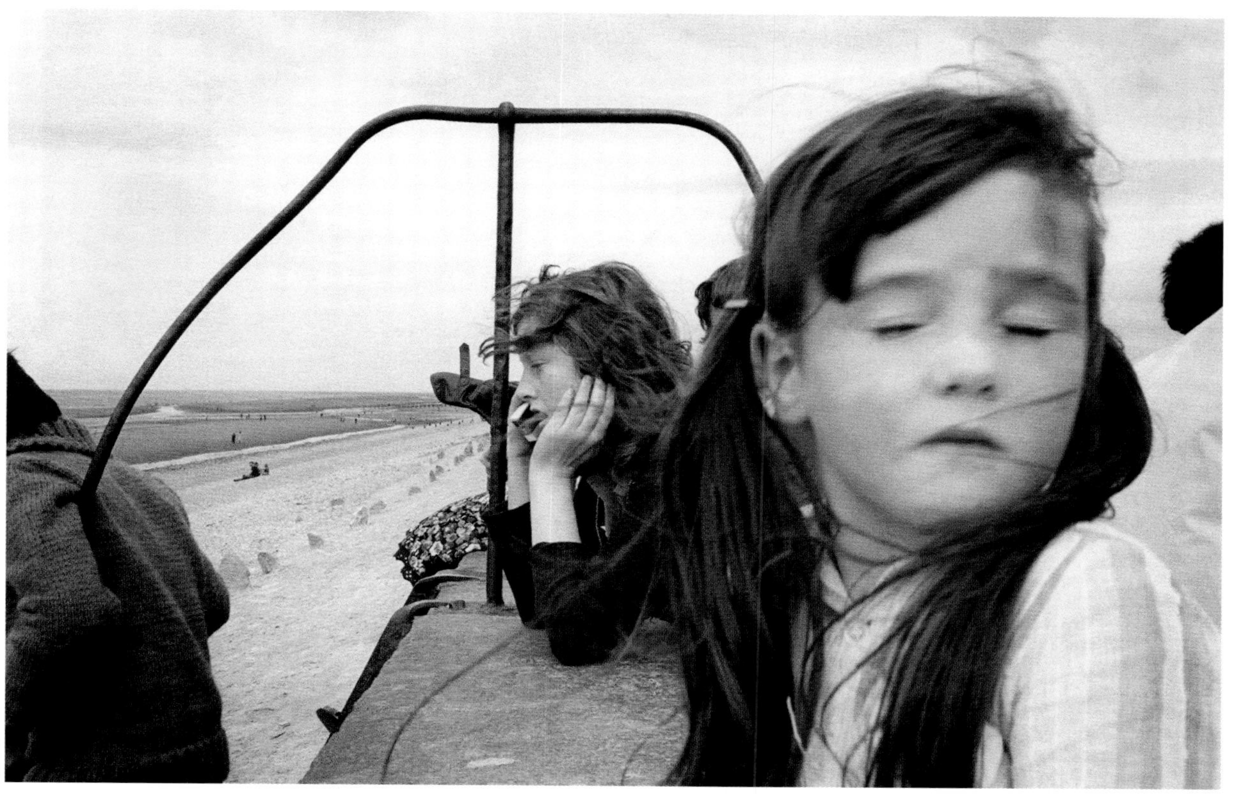

The Beach, Towyn, 1979

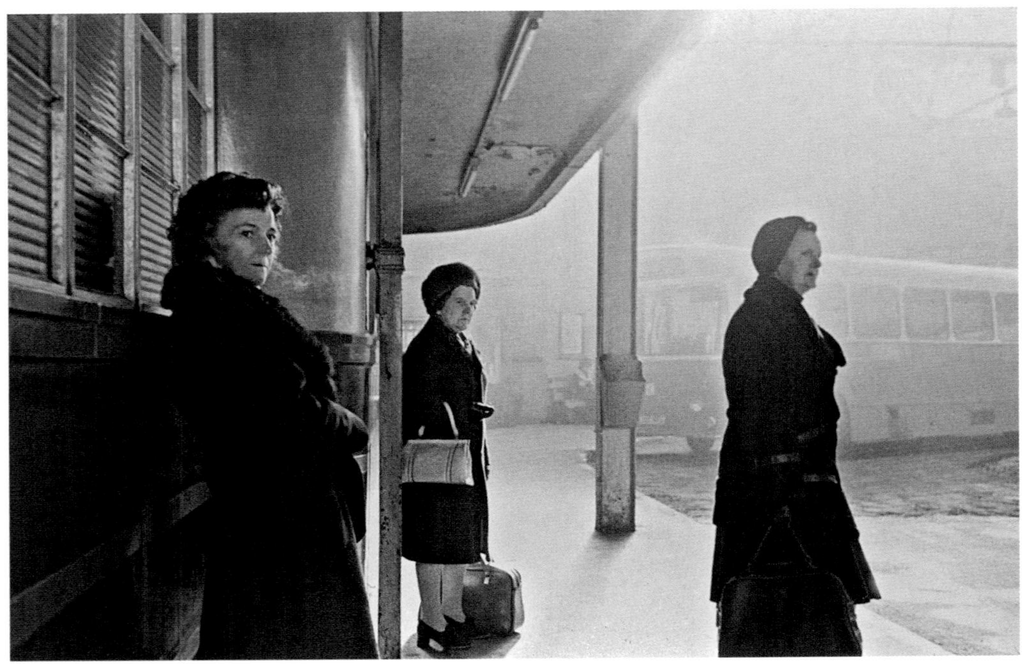

Untitled, 1979

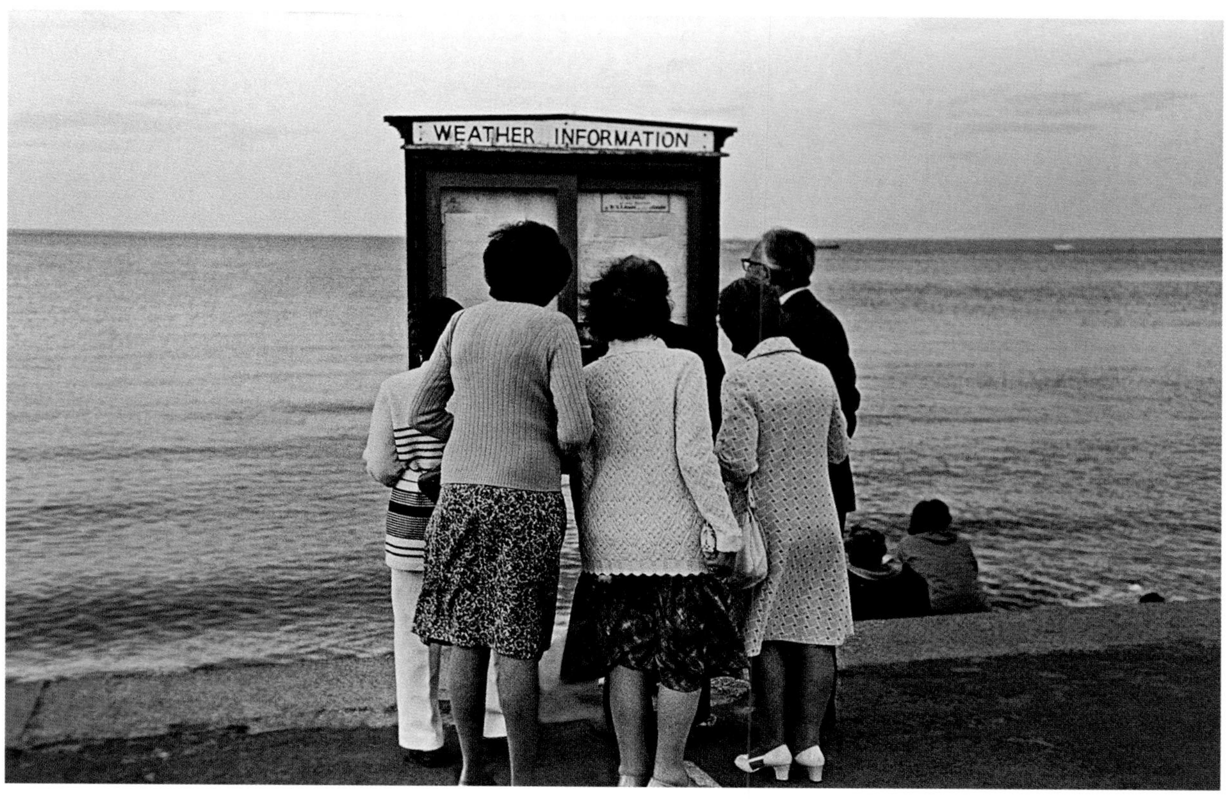

Weather Information, 1979

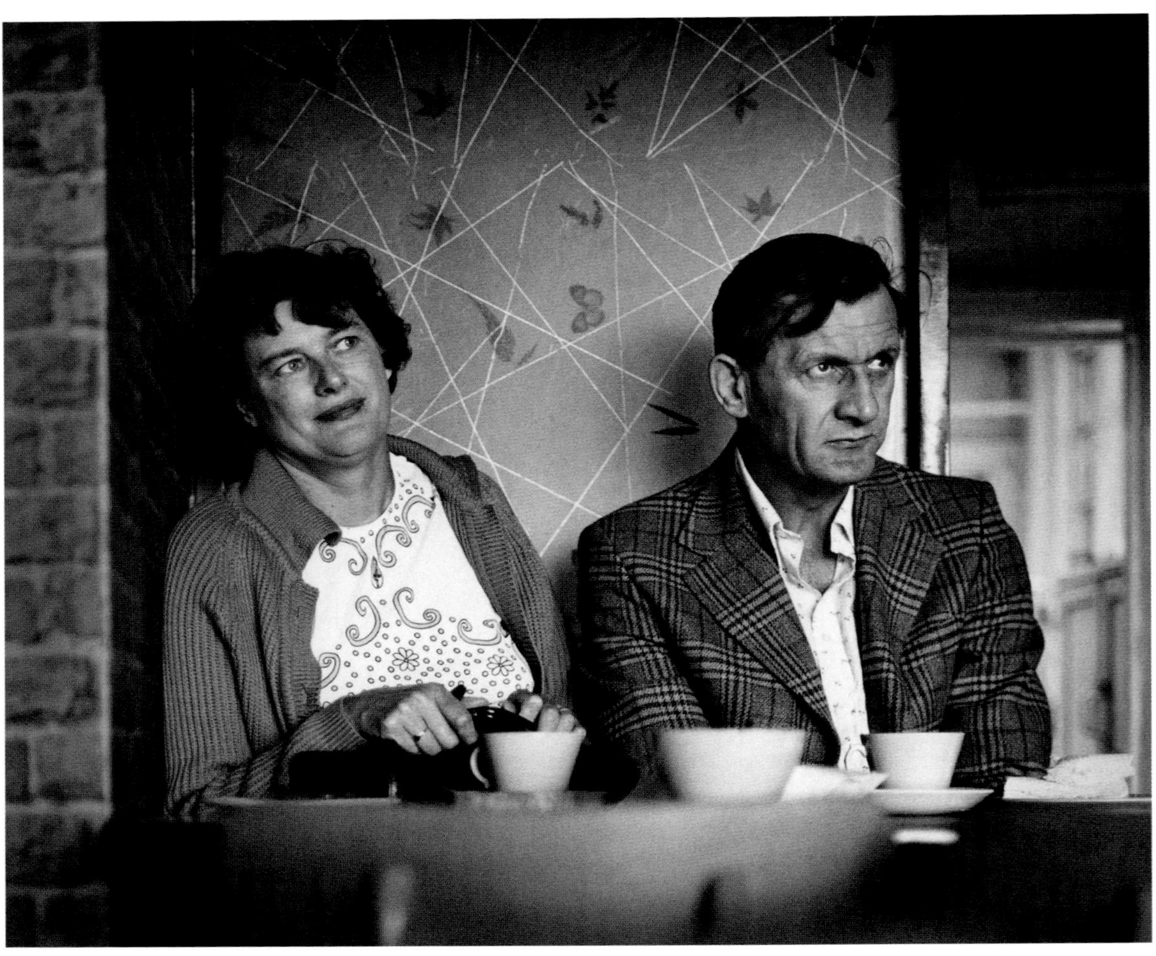

About to Order a Cheese Sandwich, St Leonards-on-Sea, 1977

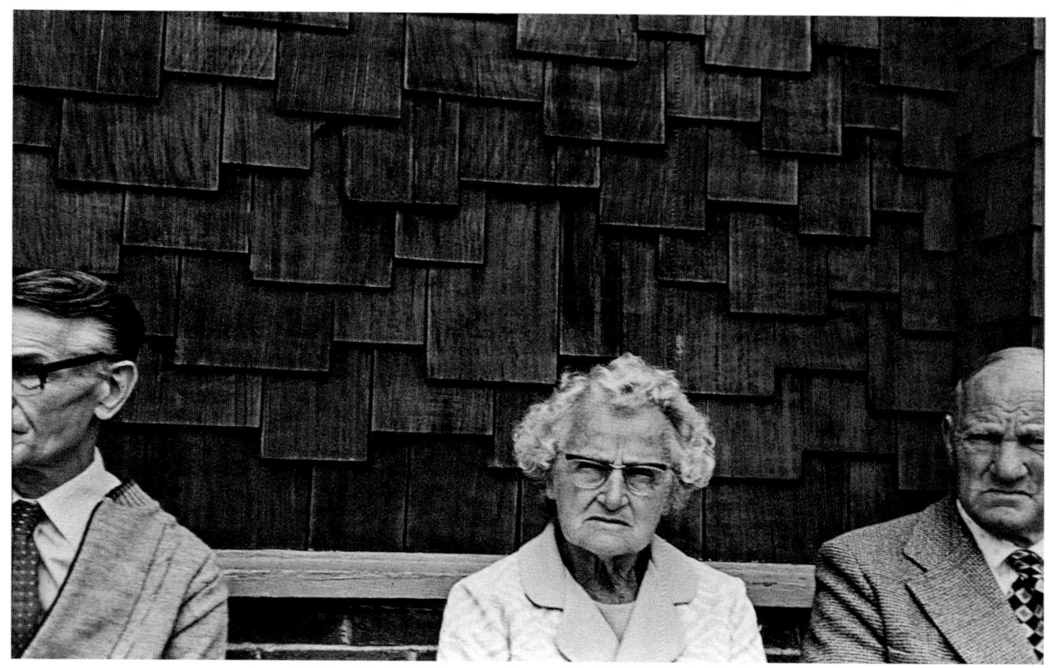

Untitled, 1979

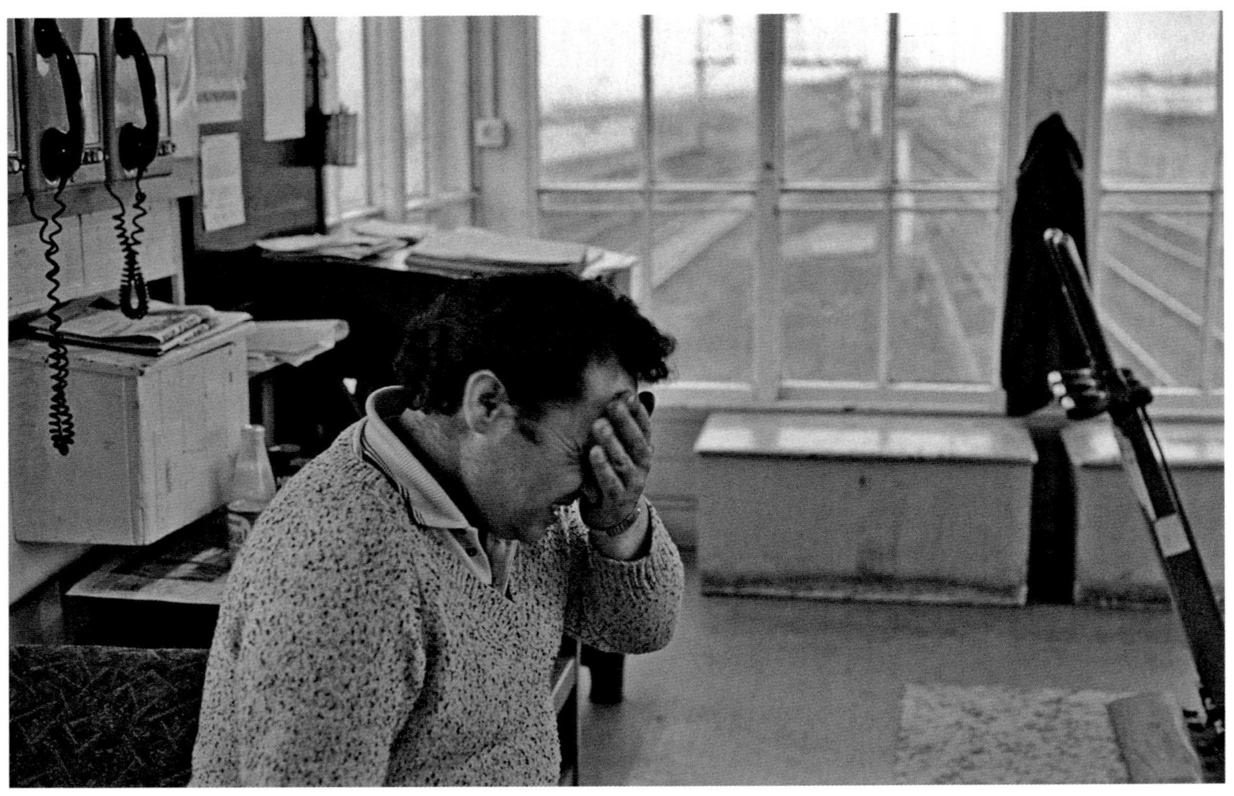

Signalman, Abergele, 1979

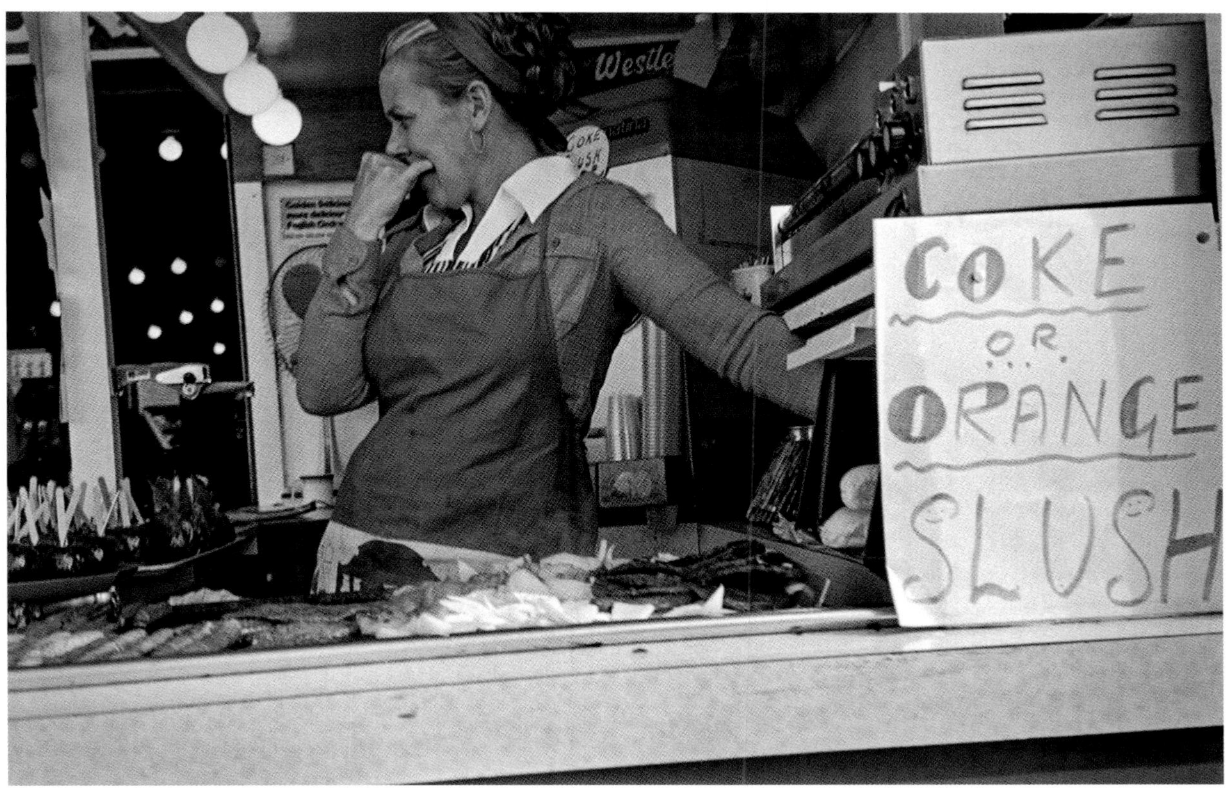

Kiosk, Rhyl, 1979

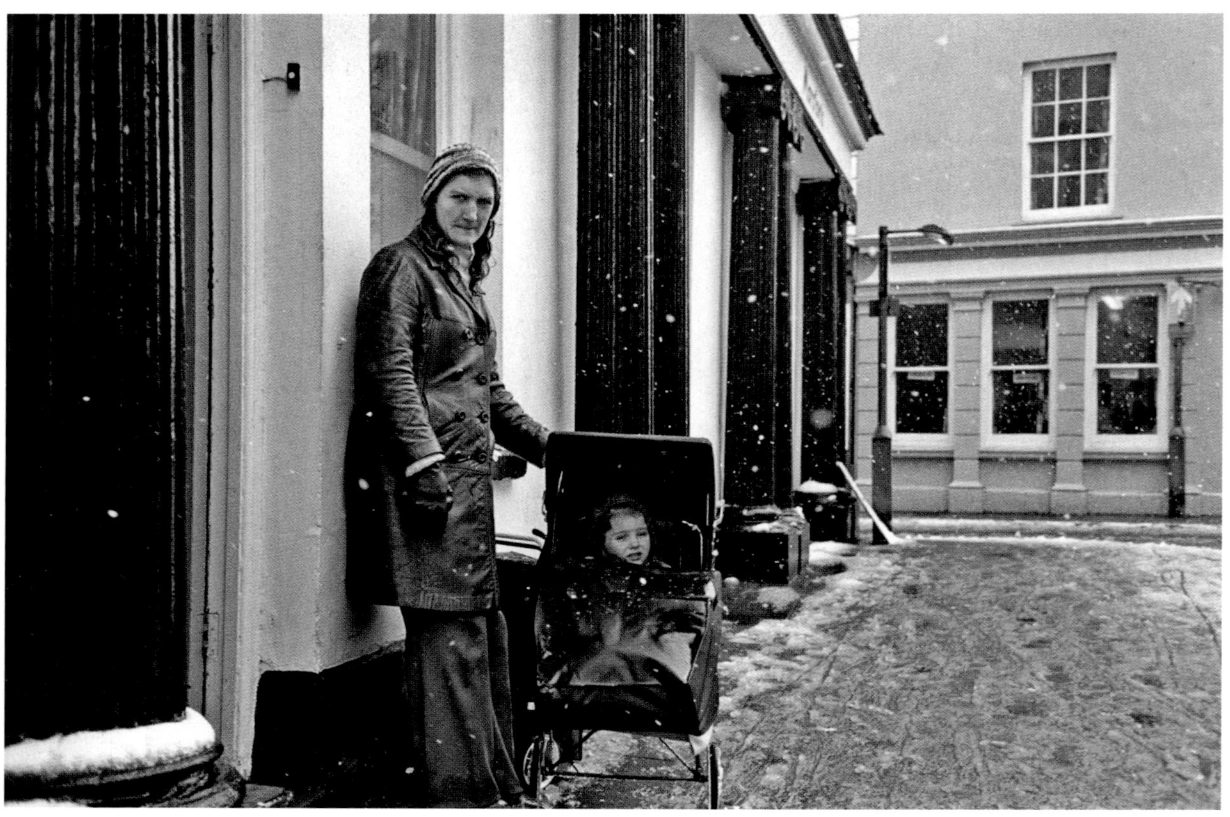

Winter, Conwy, 1979

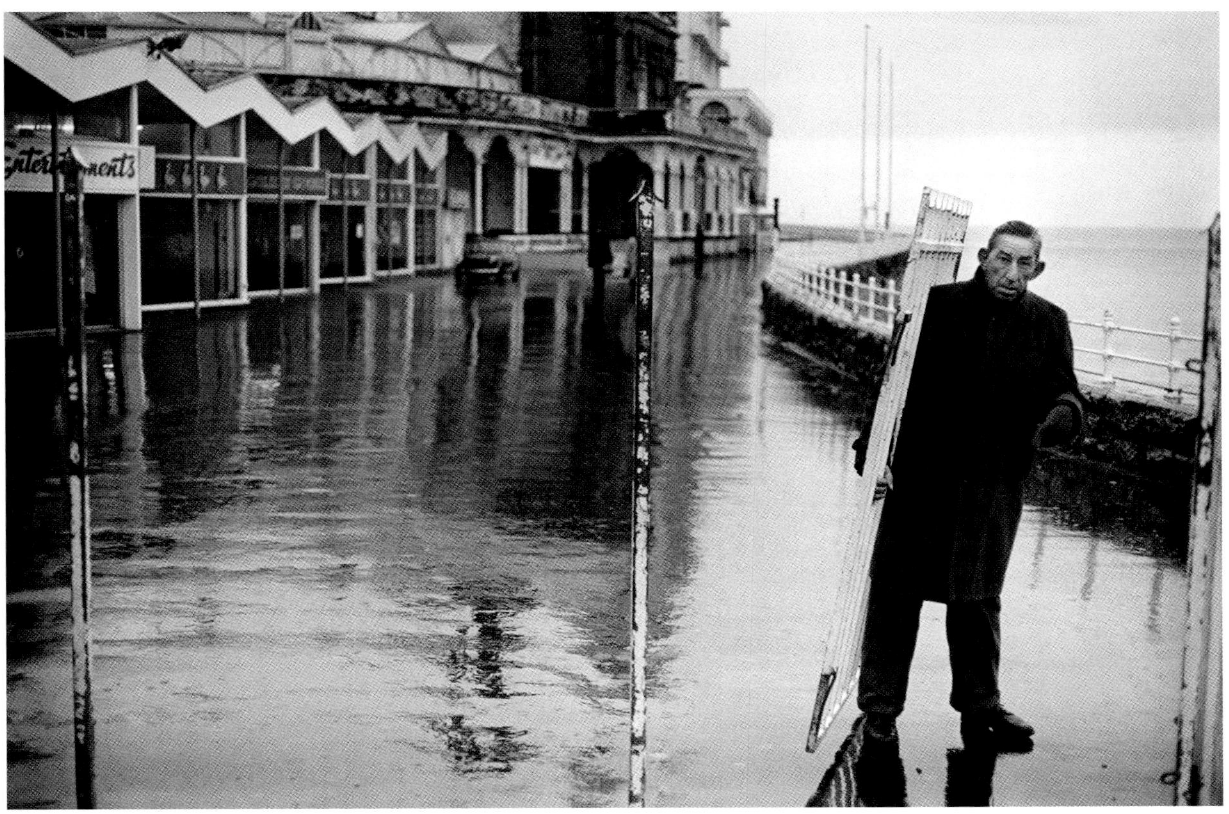

Pier Closing Time, Llandudno, 1979

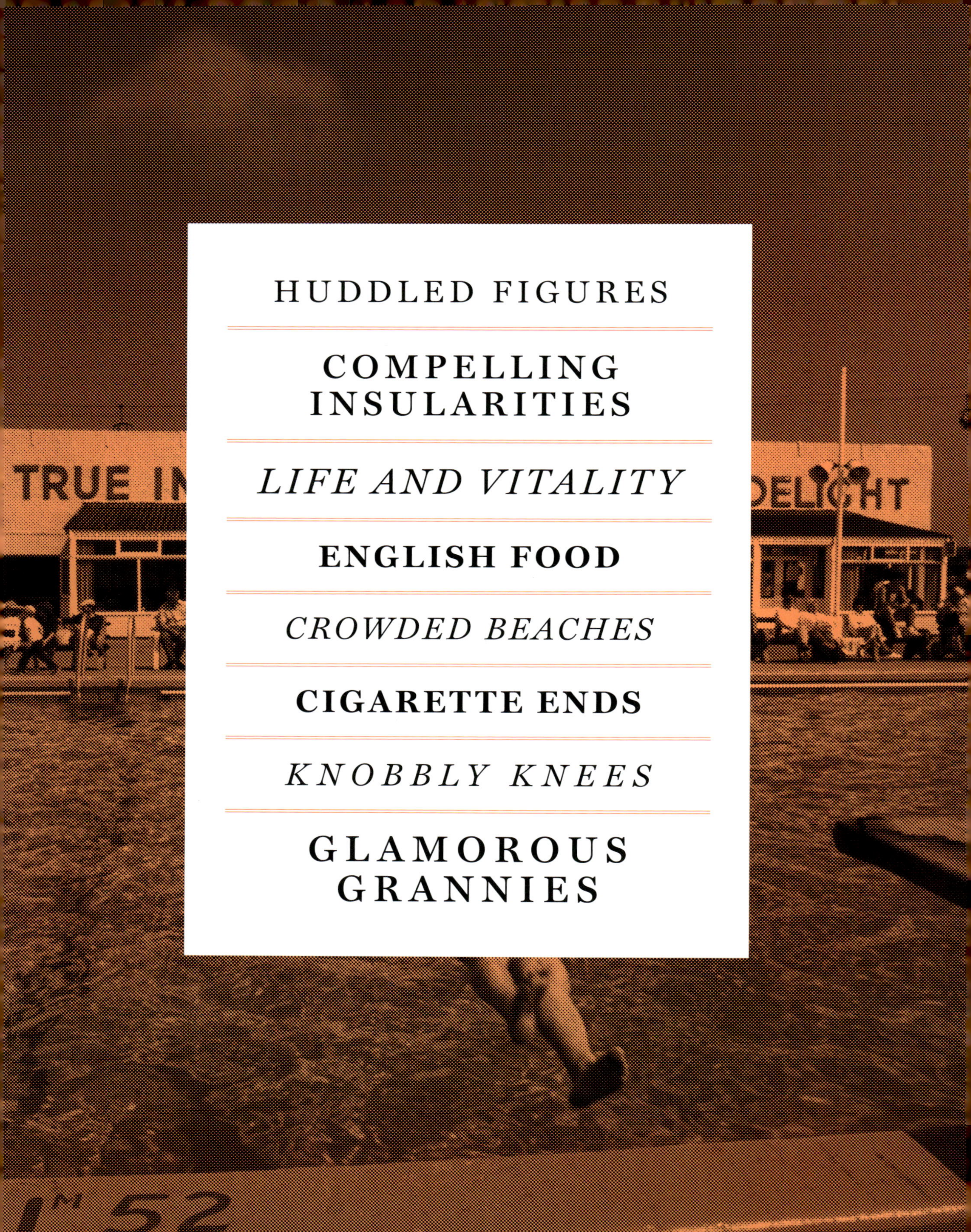

HUDDLED FIGURES

COMPELLING
INSULARITIES

LIFE AND VITALITY

ENGLISH FOOD

CROWDED BEACHES

CIGARETTE ENDS

KNOBBLY KNEES

GLAMOROUS
GRANNIES

TRUE IN

DELIGHT

Iᴺ 52

WHO'S LOOKING AT THE FAMILY?

SEASIDE CHRONICLES

FROM THEN UNTIL NOW

In 2016 the curators of *Seaside Photographed* put out a call to photographers and custodians of archives to send in work that was relevant to the theme. The photographers could be amateurs or professionals, or somewhere in between – they could be still practising or may have stopped taking photographs altogether. Some held archives of their own work that had not been seen for decades; others had inherited or acquired collections of photographs. The response was enormous, and contained a number of archives of family photographs.

Family photographs made at the British seaside during this period could be said to be generic – they share certain characteristics; they are usually taken outside and locations are, more often than not, a beach, a hotel or an amusement park. Photographs were taken with cameras using film, not digitally, and it was impossible to see what the photographs would look like until they were collected from the processor; photographing on holiday was a leap of faith. Family photographers tended to take photographs of family members – there are not so many preserved records of amateur documentation of buildings, or unknown people, or even of the sea. Views, of the harbour or the bay, of fishing boats and crowds, were easily available as postcards, professionally made and printed in large quantities. These were sent to friends and relatives – photographs of the family were more private, for home consumption, for the preservation of memories. They were an integral part of most British vacations – a holiday unrecorded in photographs was a holiday that had not quite existed. The photographs were proof that not only could a family afford to go away, but also that they were united in each other's company: a demonstration of their shared domestic values.

In the popular 1970s television comedy series 'Sykes', Hattie Jacques and Eric Sykes played a twin brother and sister, living in suburbia. Holidays were an important location for the theatre of the absurd, which formed the core of 'Sykes'. In the episode *Squatters*, Eric and Hattie arrive home from holiday to find their home has been occupied by tramps, while in *Holiday Camp* (1975) Eric is exhausted by the constant round of entertainment; the hall of mirrors, false noses, the ghost train, the sack race, knobbly knees and the rain. *Caravan* shows Hattie and Eric taking a holiday in the middle of a thunderstorm. *Stay at Home Holiday* (1979) is a nightmare of locked doors, lost keys, forgotten passports, missed planes and humiliation, while in *Holiday in Bogsea* (1974) again set in the pouring rain, Eric and Hattie stay in a boarding house run by a martinet landlady and Eric sets himself the task of identifying a newspaper reporter for a prize. The setting is dour, the plot has traces of *Brighton Rock* and at one point Eric attacks his hotel room: 'I hate this wall, I hate these pictures, I hate this view.' Popular entertainment during these years did not show the British seaside holiday in a positive light. Everything was decaying, it rained all the time and the entertainment was unsophisticated. Holiday camps had morphed from the high-minded middle class outdoor life of the 1920s and 1930s and had become cheap, gaudy and regimented outlets for the working class in Britain. Eric, a mildly eccentric absurdist, repeatedly signals his frustration with the typical British family at the seaside.

Likewise, that champion of the abject and the absurd Tony Hancock and his writers created a number of episodes of his 1950s BBC series around holidays; tales of misfortune and misunderstanding – a trip to Southend ends up in Paris (*A Holiday in France*, 1955); a job for Hancock in rascally Sid James's holiday camp venture lands him in in the middle of a live artillery range (*The Holiday Camp*, 1955); and in *Back from a Terrible Holiday* (1956), Hancock discovers that Sid has rented his home out.

The message from these post-war years was that seaside holidays were traumatic; the British had returned uneasily to a coast that had been out of bounds during the Second World War and symbolic not of safety and pleasure, but of the first line of invasion. Bad things happened when the British went

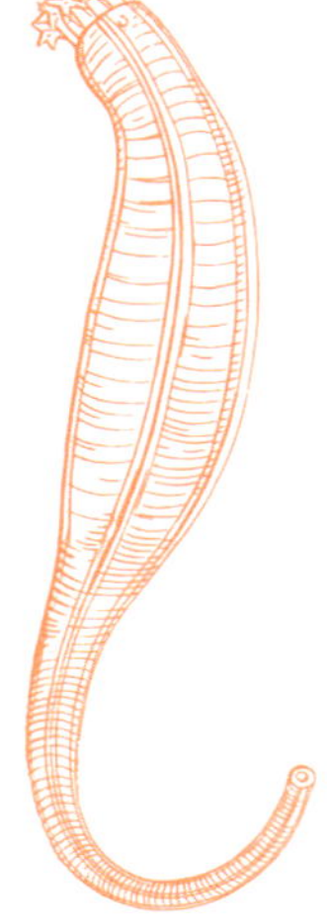

ABOVE AND BELOW

MARTIN PARR
New Brighton, England,
from the series
The Last Resort, 1983–5

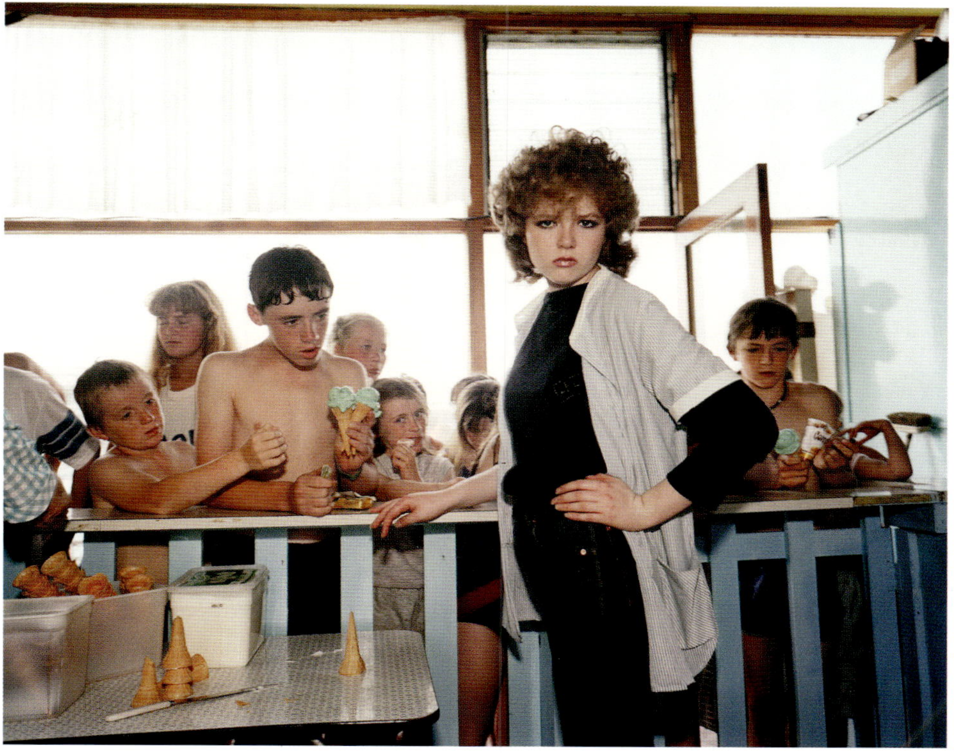

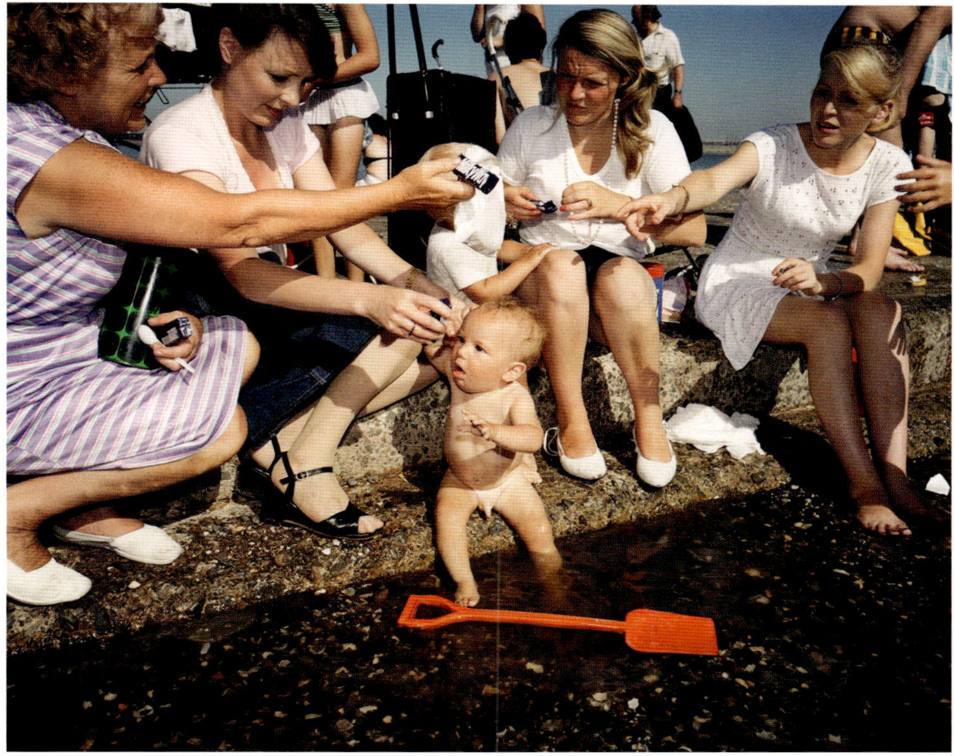

on holiday – misunderstandings on a grand scale, loss, discomfort and rage.

Fast-forward to the 1980s and Paul Theroux's *Kingdom by the Sea* (1983) – the American author's account of his tour around the British coast. Beginning in Margate, Theroux is intrigued by the coldness and joylessness of the British seaside resort – reporting on the huddled figures who crouch fully clothed on the beach – the constant talk of war in the Falklands, and the compelling insularities of the British. Walking around the same area in Kent where Paul Nash had made photographs in the 1930s, some fifty years earlier, Theroux, already disenchanted with the English coastline, wrote:

> I walked to Greatstone on the bungalow strip and then to Lydd on the same strip ... crazy paving, gnomes, a birdbath, a rectangle of cruelly pruned rosebushes ...[1]

At around the same time as Theroux was touring the British coast, staying in one damp guesthouse after another, documentary photographer Martin Parr was making his colour chronicle of New Brighton in north-west England (previous page), departing from the black-and-white work that had made him so much part of the new independent photography of 1970s Britain. Theroux had called in at New Brighton in 1983, recording that he

> saw British people lying stiffly on the beach like dead insects, or huddled against the canvas windbreaks they hammered into the sand with rented mallets, or standing on cliffs and kicking stones roly poly into the sea – and I thought: they are symbolically leaving the country.[2]

Parr's photographs of New Brighton, self-published as *The Last Resort* in 1986, were in bright colour, and documented the fading, scruffy resort and its visitors in a way that was new to British photography. *The Last Resort* sparks with life and vitality,

as crowds of women gather around a baby, children sunbath on concrete and a young woman serving in a chip shop stares at the photographer in disbelief (previous page).

Parr documented the seaside in film as well as photography, often using the tight shell of the family as a motif. In *Think of England* (1999), a middle-aged couple in the beige dining room of a Weymouth boarding house eating a roast dinner confided to Parr: 'We've never been abroad ... everything we want is here ... Good old English food that don't upset your stomach.'

Seaside attractions – funfairs, mini-golf, organized games and competitions – form the centre of much of the absurdism of comedy in film, photography and broadcast media from the mid-1950s onwards. Take, for example, the farce and physical theatre of John Cleese's and Connie Booth's 1970s TV series 'Fawlty Towers', where a seaside hotel and its eccentric proprietor become a focus of cultural and social misunderstanding, where guests are to be both feared and humiliated and management is a series of bizarre misadventures. Tales of loss, of exasperation, but above all of disappointment, dog these narratives and establish the tourist as the Fool in sprawling comedies of manners. It is the disaster dream of lost passports, missed connections and unfulfilled expectations.

In Tom Jackson's 2017 publication *Postcard from the Past*, Jackson juxtaposes postcards with the message written on the back. From Mousehole in Cornwall, one holidaymaker wrote: 'Water is freezing. Weather uninteresting. Hope you are the same. On no account reply to my last letter.'[3] From an unidentified destination: 'This is the horrid beach.'[4] From Weymouth, just one word: 'Murder'[5] and from St Mawes: 'Have ended up in Cornwall instead of Ibiza – it's a long story.'[6] From Woollacombe, Devon: 'Yesterday I caught 3 of my fingers in the car door.'[7]

A logical and timely social media codicil to Parr's *Boring Postcards*, to 'Fawlty Towers' and Sykes's and Hancock's holiday traumas, *Postcard from the Past* emerged from a Twitter account and holds up a distorted

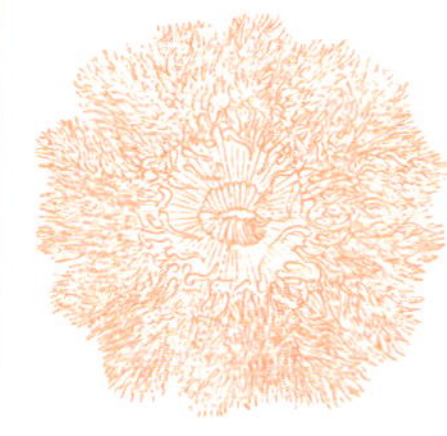

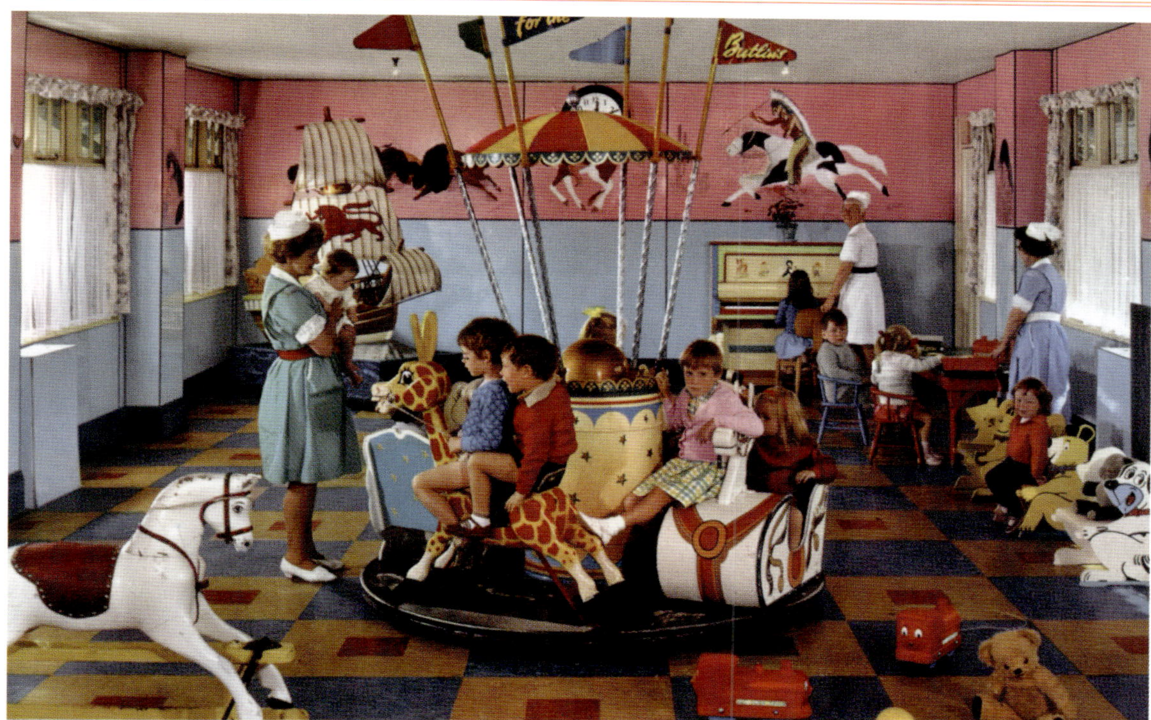

BUTLIN'S FILEY—*The Nursery*

Photo : E. Nägele, John Hinde Studios.

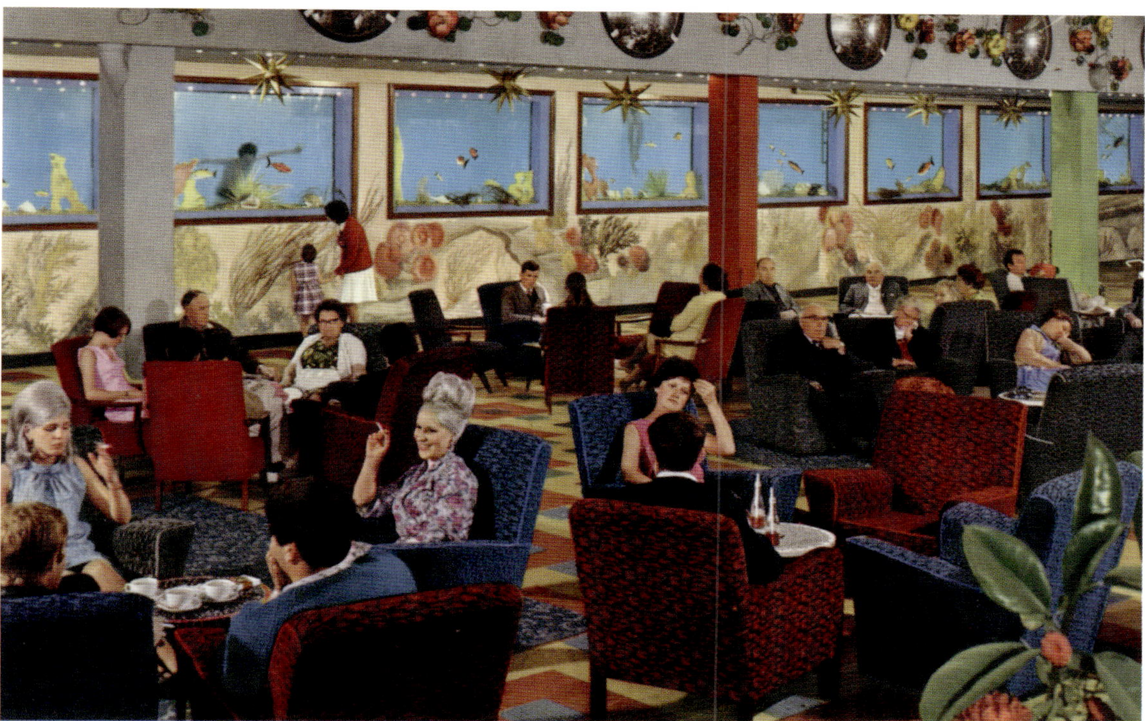

BUTLIN'S BOGNOR REGIS—*Lounge Adjoining Indoor Heated Pool*

Photo : E. Nägele, John Hinde Studios.

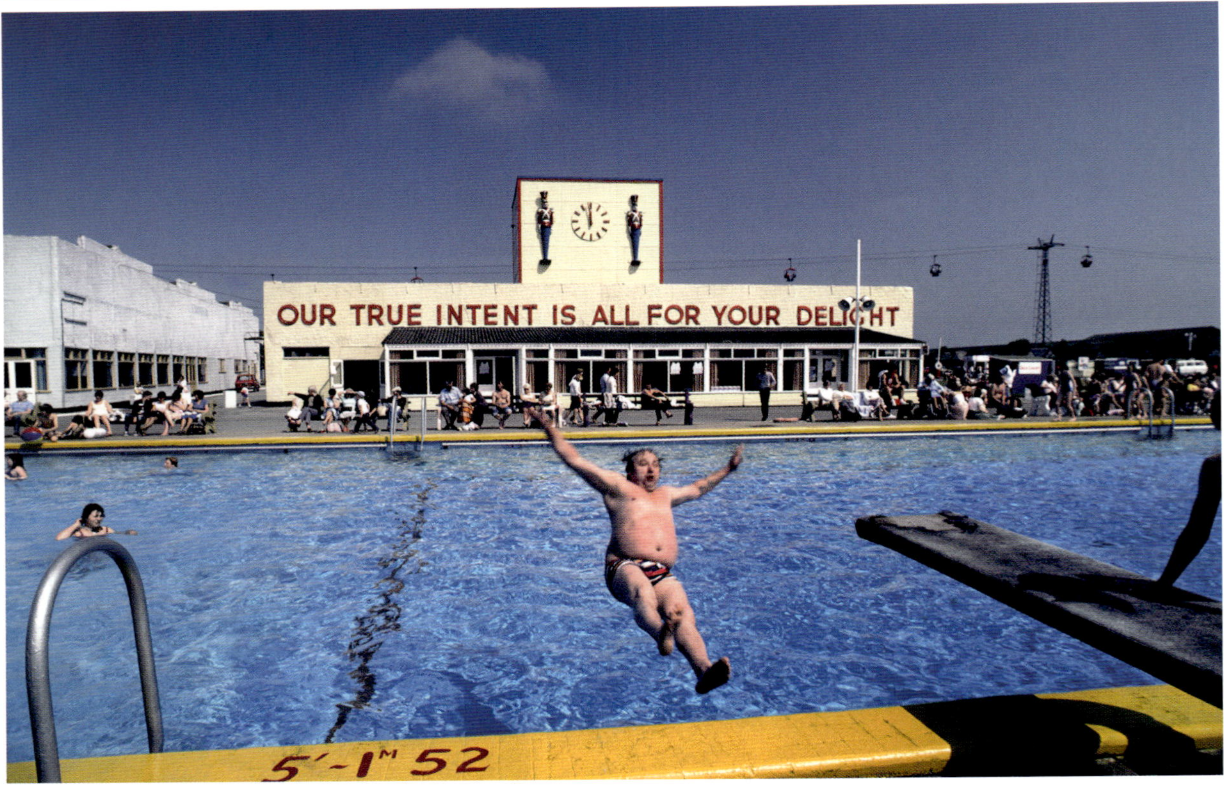

mirror to ourselves and our holiday histories – small accidents, bad thoughts and
mysterious requests.

Parr, who is an inveterate postcard
collector, is an admirer of the work of the
John Hinde postcard company, established
in 1956 by the veteran colour photographer
John Hinde and his team of photographers –
Edmund Nägele, David Noble, Joan Willis,
Elmar Ludwig and Hinde himself (see p.129).
Like many postcard producers, John Hinde
employed highly skilled photographers with
considerable aesthetic and technical range –
Hinde himself was a photographer with a significant reputation, with a number of publications and outstanding abilities as commercial
photographer, and, through his work in the
Second World War, a skilled propagandist.
Hinde and his team were accomplished in
the creation of tableaux from real life using
models and props, and gave the British
family holiday the edge of glamour needed to
compete against the emerging destinations of

southern Europe. British seaside attractions
emerged, through the lens of the John Hinde
photographic team, as marvels of structure
and light. In Hinde's extended series of postcards for Butlin's holiday camps, models were
beautifully dressed and decorous and very different to how they would appear in the later
documentaries of Butlin's made by Dafydd
Jones, Parr, Daniel Meadows and Barry
Lewis in the 1970s and 1980s. For Meadows
(overleaf), who was employed as a Butlin's
'walkie' with fellow Manchester Polytechnic
student Parr, Butlin's was a threatening place:

As a theatre and cinema goer with an
excitable imagination, my head was
full of the many recent class satires I'd
seen or read that were based in holiday
or military camps and by the seaside:
Arnold Wesker's *Chips with Everything*
(1962), Joe Orton's *The Erpingham
Camp* (1966), Richard Attenborough's
Oh! What A Lovely War (1969) and

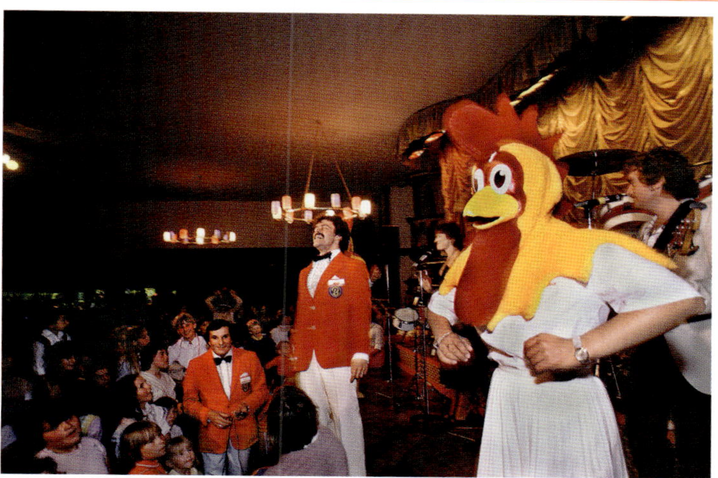

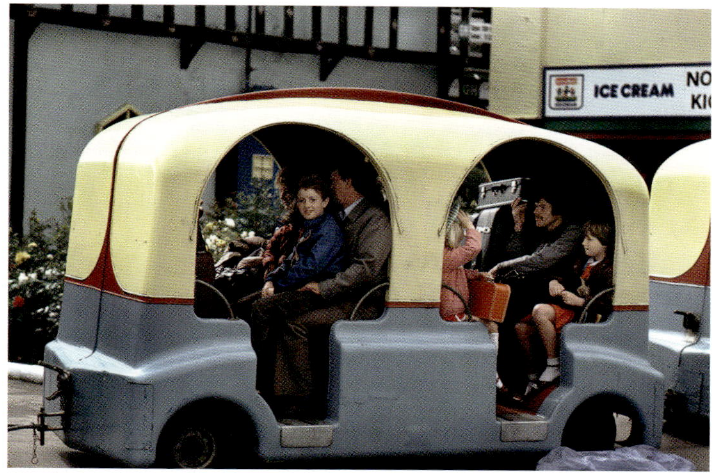

ICE CREAM

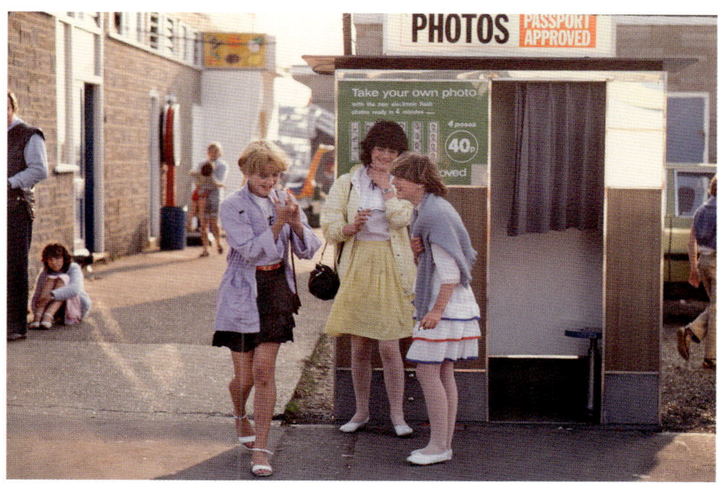

PHOTOS
PASSPORT
APPROVED
Take your own photo
4 poses
40p

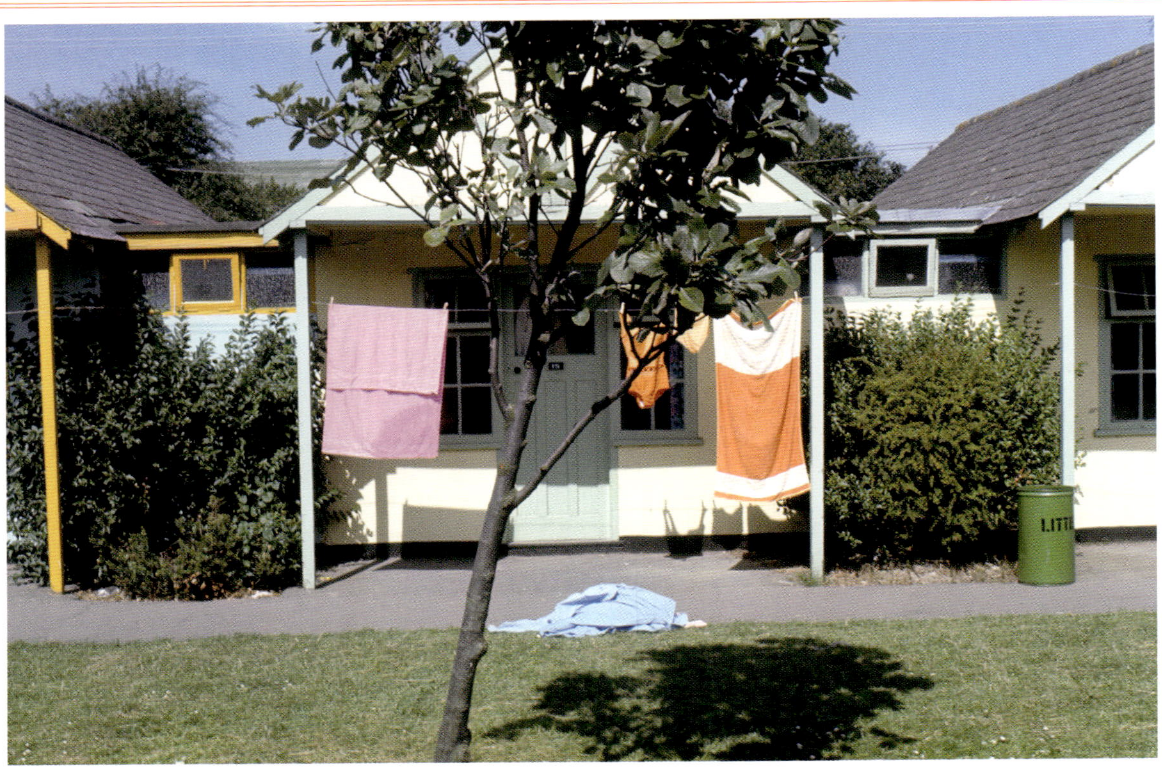

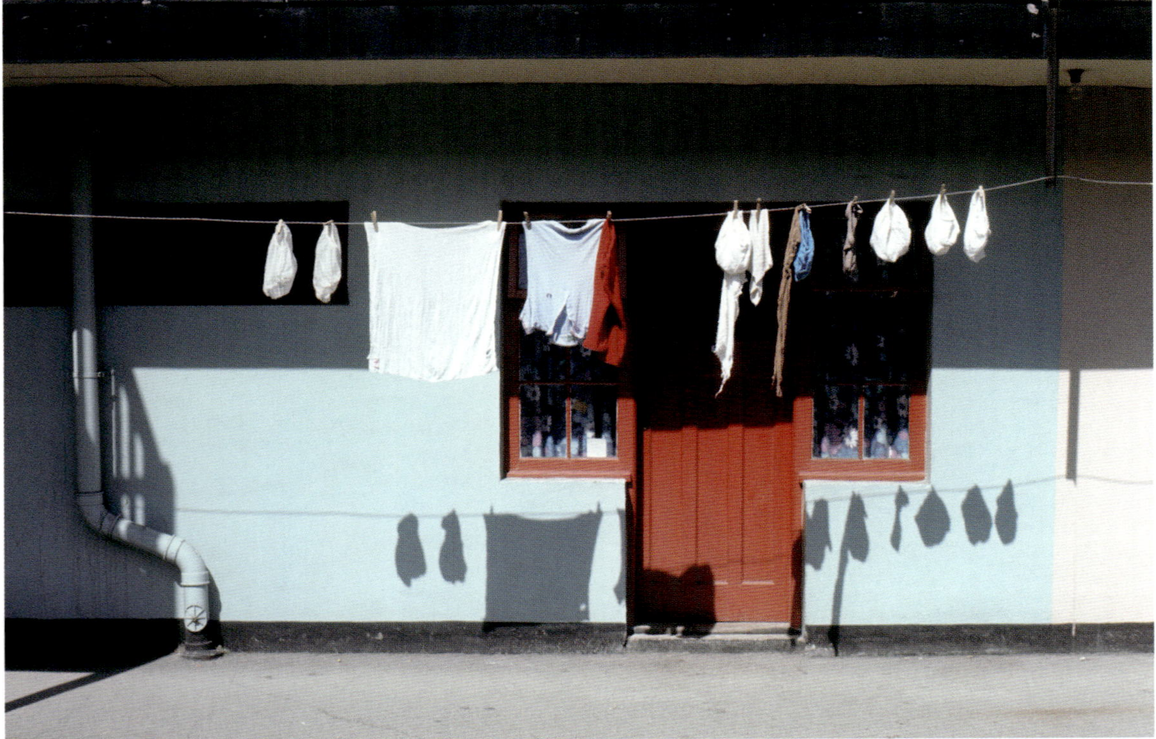

Sydney Pollack's *They Shoot Horses Don't They?* (1969). Fact or fiction, Butlin's had me spooked.[8]

Barry Lewis, a contemporary of Parr and Meadows, and part of the emerging British independent photography grouping, photographed Butlin's some ten years later (pp.130–1):

In 1982 Network [photo agency] had just started and I was ... on the *Observer* magazine ... I suggested the story to photograph Skegness, where Billy Butlin started it all in 1937. Perhaps it was a return to my childhood ... but more likely I recognised it as a strong light story as Thatcher was thrusting us into a war over the Falklands. I worked with the writer Ian Walker and we had amazing access to the madhouse (Butlin's thought it would be another puff piece and good exposure). We spent 2 weeks in the camp and returned several weeks later when the Royal Marines were doing a week's full display, parachuting in, combat, the whole nine yards including pushing recruitment ... the war needed cannon fodder. Twenty years later I was making a 2-day puff piece on the rebranded camp ... the journalist mistakenly mentioned my *Observer* piece ... the room went icy and the press person said it took years to recover from what they saw as a publicity disaster![9]

For Dafydd Jones (overleaf and pp.136–7), who had trained as a painter, photography had become increasingly attractive and, keen to gain experience, he responded to an advertisement in the *British Journal of Photography* in the late 1970s for a 'colour-walkie photographer', and soon reported for the start of the season at Butlin's holiday camp in Minehead.

I nervously made my way there from Oxford. I was issued with camera equipment and a uniform. A tiny shared chalet was going to be my home for the next few months. I met Chris and Phil, fellow photographers from Derbyshire who filled me in on what the work was going to be like. We would work on commission. Taking pictures in bars, fairground rides, the dining halls and around the camp. The job involved selling and collecting cash as well as taking pictures.

The first picture on each film would have a number on it and was a free picture which would usually be done of the other employees at the camp. We'd give away these pictures.

... Most of the holiday-makers hardly left the camp. It was an eccentric, peculiarly English place. Early in the season the camp was quieter and the holiday-makers were older. As we entered summer we moved into the peak season. Everywhere was busier. Although they had more cash the holiday-makers seemed unhappier. There was a weariness and sometimes everyone seemed a bit exploited. I wanted to show this in the pictures.

Although I had a degree in Fine Art I hadn't been really been trained in photography. At the beginning of the season we were given basic instruction on taking posed pictures with flash. I now had the time, a subject and access to practice. I was doing my personal pictures in a kind of documentary style along with a bit of art school aesthetic. One of my duties at the camp was to dress up as one of a pair of figures from outer-space called Toot and Ploot and pose for pictures. I wanted to capture the looks everyone gave us ... without spoiling the moment. Vicki in the photo dept. solved the problem by lending me her Olympus trip camera. The small camera looked the part with my spaceman outfit.

I travelled up to London on my day off to buy a bulk roll of black-and-white

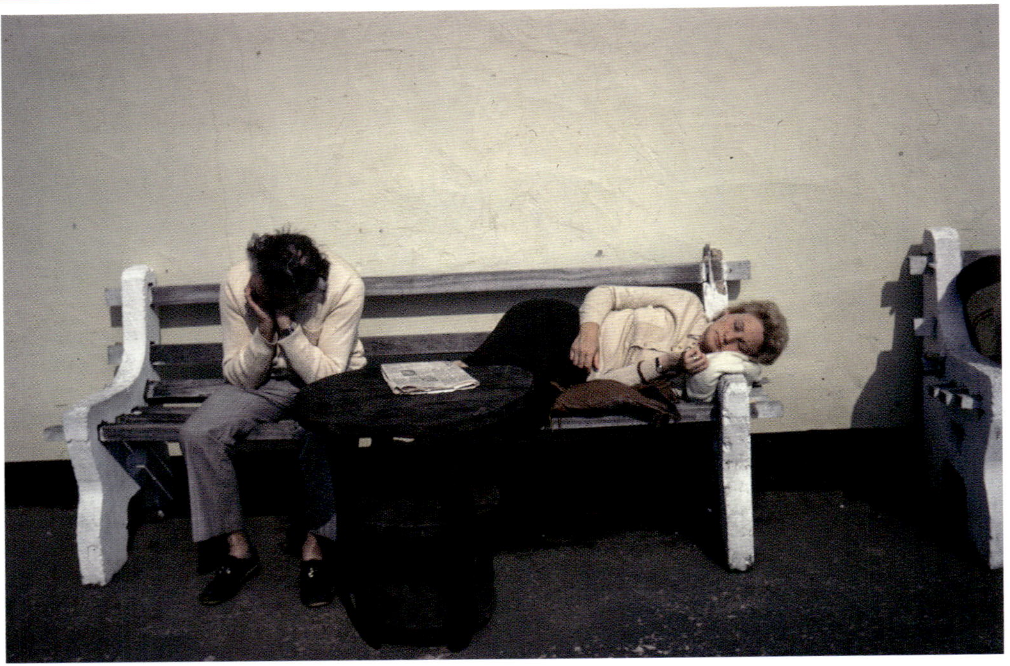

DAFYDD JONES · Resting just outside Butlin's Holiday Camp,
Minehead, 1979, from the series *Butlin Land*

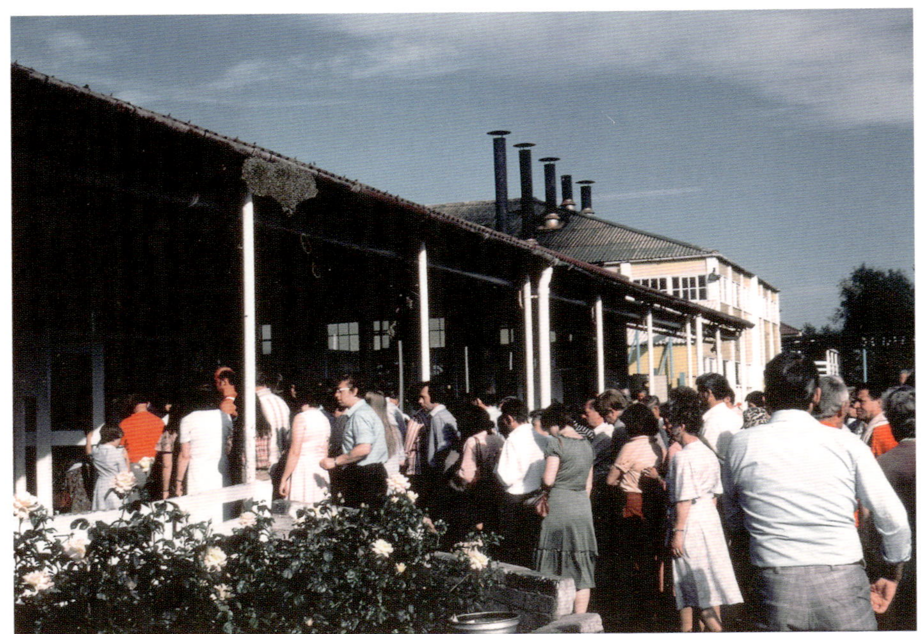

DAFYDD JONES · Queue to enter the dining room,
Butlin's Holiday Camp, Minehead, 1979, from the series *Butlin Land*

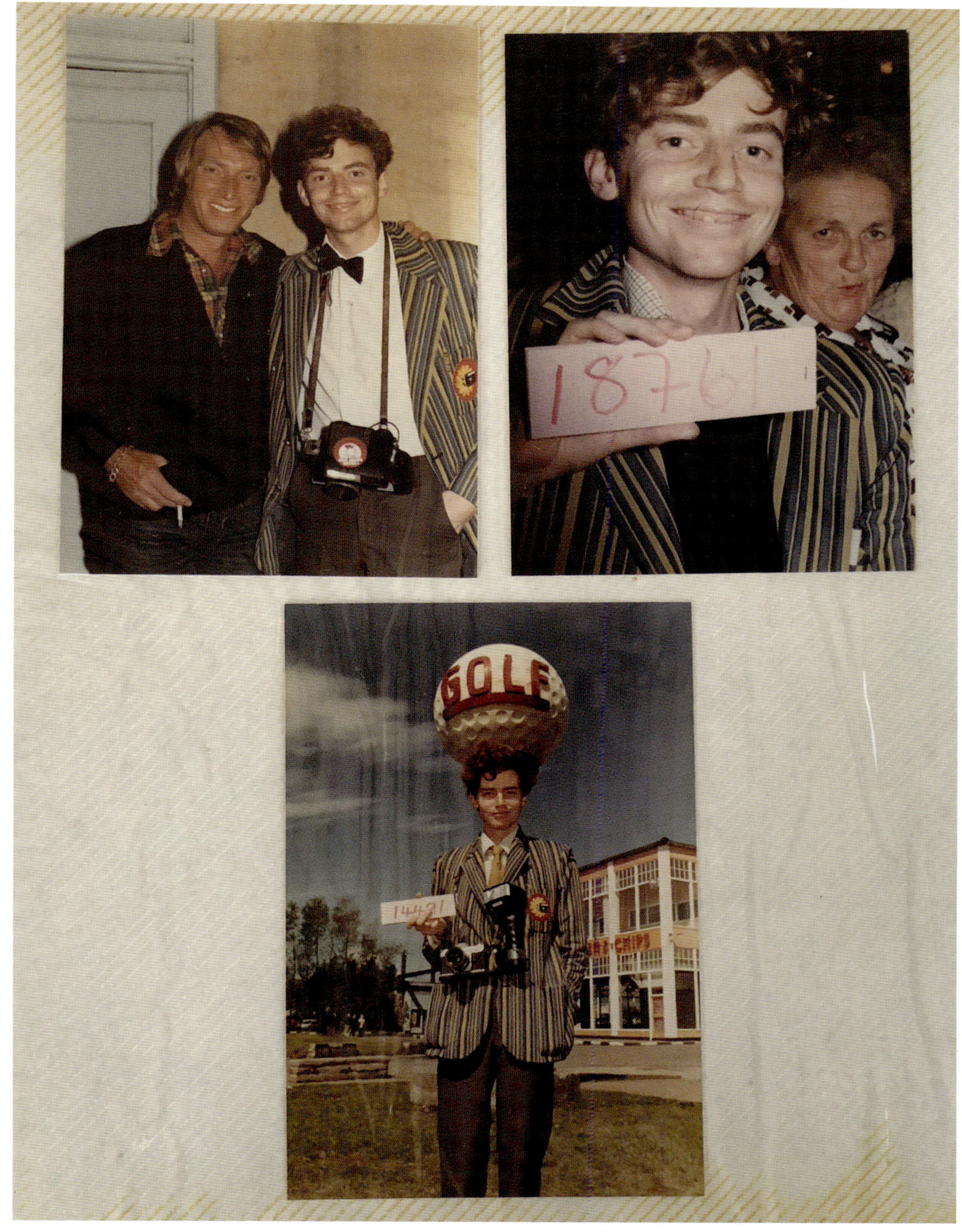

DAFYDD JONES · Page from Dafydd Jones's Butlin's album;
(top left) Jones with Frank Ifield at the Beachcomber Bar,
Butlin's Holiday Camp, Minehead, 1979, from the series *Butlin Land*

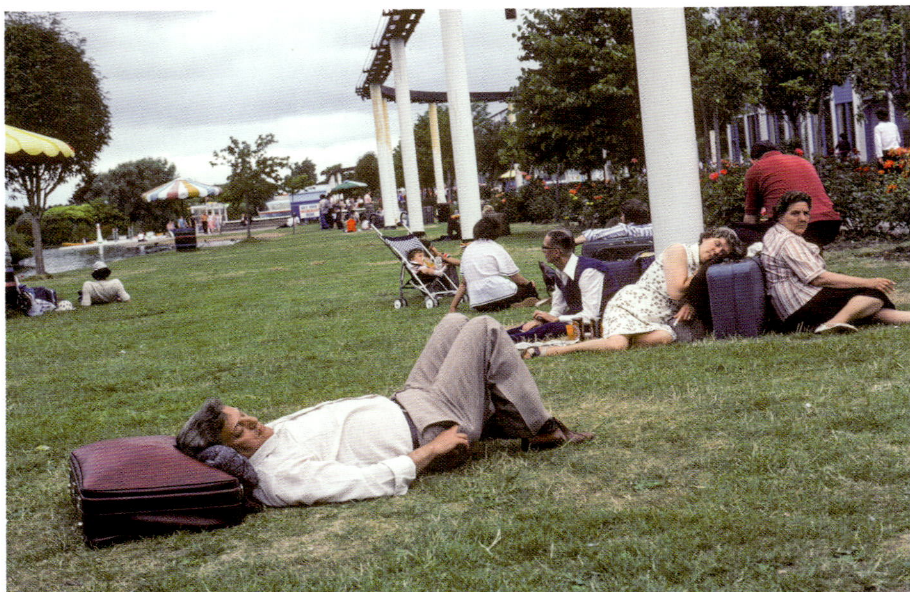

DAFYDD JONES
New arrivals waiting for their chalet at Butlin's Holiday Camp, Minehead, 1979, from the series *Butlin Land*

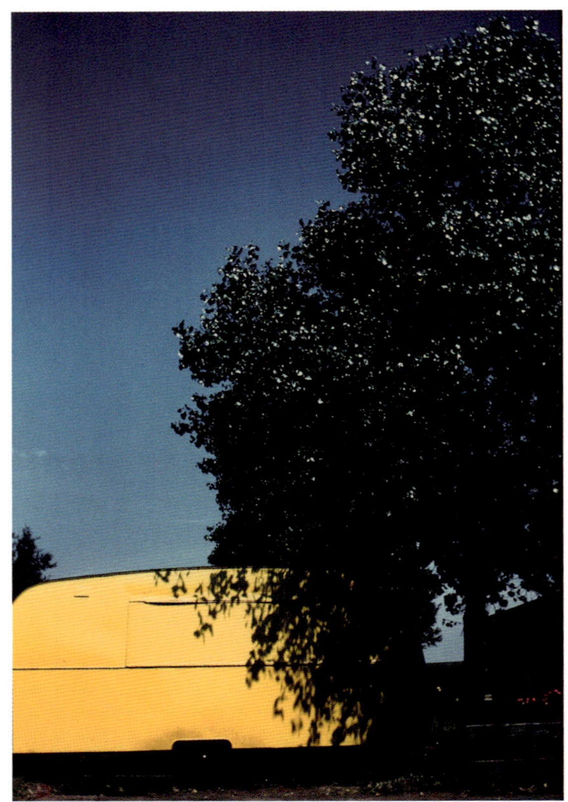

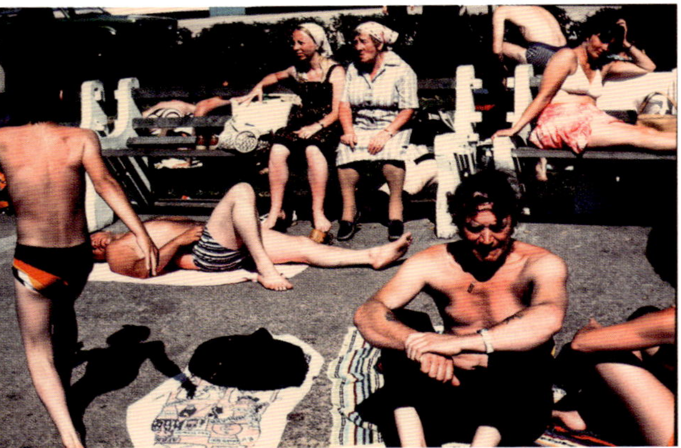

DAFYDD JONES
Butlin's Holiday Camp, Minehead, Summer 1979, from the series *Butlin Land*

DAFYDD JONES · Yellow caravans in red camp at Butlin's Holiday Camp, Minehead, 1979, from the series *Butlin Land*

film and more colour film. The colour pictures were taken on Kodachrome slide film 64 which would come back to me a week or so after processing. I wouldn't see the black and white pictures until 6 months later when I developed the film.[10]

The photographs produced, in black-and-white and colour, by these young photographers are inevitably comic. Post-war British holiday camps were essentially performative arenas in which highly organized (and sometimes humiliating) games and competitions were played out by working-class families on a once-yearly holiday. Set against the background of stylish themed bars and works canteen-like dining rooms, Butlin's camps were puzzling, fascinating and sometimes dark places, particularly for the young photographers who worked there. For these aspiring documentarists, Butlin's was immensely formative and their work there formed the basis of a significant series of critical documentaries. It was at the seaside that these emerging photographers learned to work quickly and critically, and to engage with their subjects. Like the writers of 'Sykes', Hancock's 'Half Hour' and 'Fawlty Towers', they saw the seaside holiday as performed comedy of the absurd. Knobbly Knees, Glamorous Grannies, Redcoats, chalets, luxury hotel style reformed and recycled for mass consumption – the stuff that documentary dreams are made of.

In between and around these critical documentaries and posed tableaux are the 'real' family photographs, carefully kept over the years or sometimes discovered in the bulging boxes of boot sales and fleamarkets. We attach much sentiment to these photographs, comparing them perhaps to the set-ups and stiffness of the holiday postcard, or to the sly wit of the documentarists. These photographs are seen to be agenda-less, innocent, but when was photography ever so?

In an August 2017 edition of the *Guardian* magazine, writer Yvonne Singh describes a family excursion to Southend-on-Sea on the Essex coast in the 1970s:

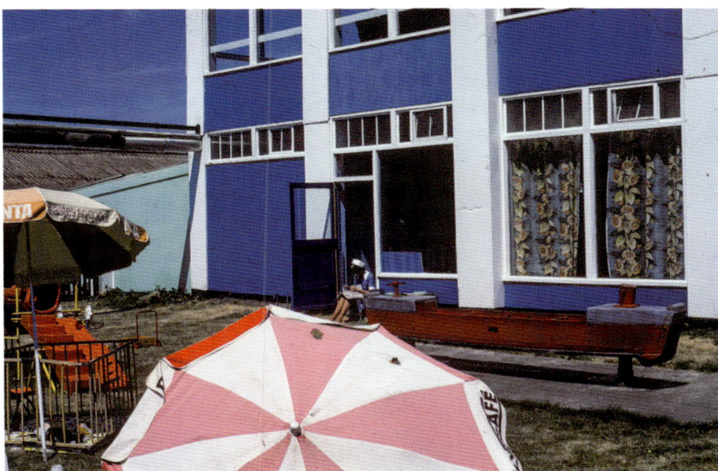

Grey concrete was the bulwark of my childhood: concrete subways, concrete fountains, concrete flats. With the concrete came the graffiti: 'Keep Britain white'; 'Paks [sic] out'; 'NF'. Even the Dolphin swimming pool … was a huge grey edifice in the middle of a roundabout … There's a photograph I treasure of my late mother and me at Southend. We are both ankle-deep in moss-coloured water … Mum and I are both smiling. And so my love affair with the British seaside began.

Artist Lucy Bentham has acquired a large archive of one family's photographs (overleaf). Existing only as negatives, and anonymous, one section documents a summer family holiday at the seaside. They were made in the late 1950s, in an unknown location. Central to the story of these photographs are a woman, two boys and two girls. Looking at them is like trying to fit together a frustratingly complex jigsaw, with many of the pieces missing. Are those two boys brothers? Who is the commanding and statuesque woman in the striking black-and-white swimming costume, stiff and stretched across her torso, white swimming cap clutched in her hand? The charm of these photographs is in their mystery. We are shut out from this family by their anonymity and their self-sufficiency; and there is a painful sense of loss. There is

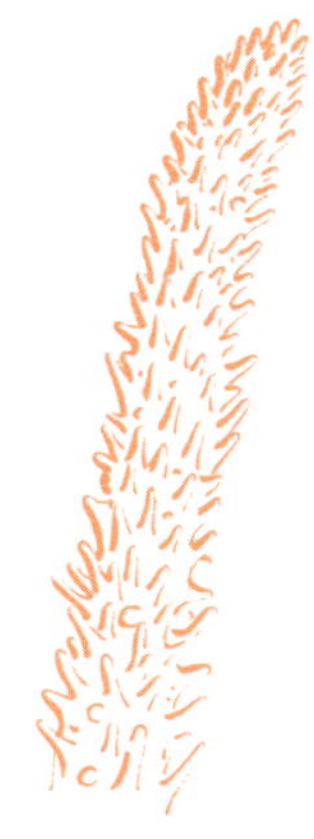

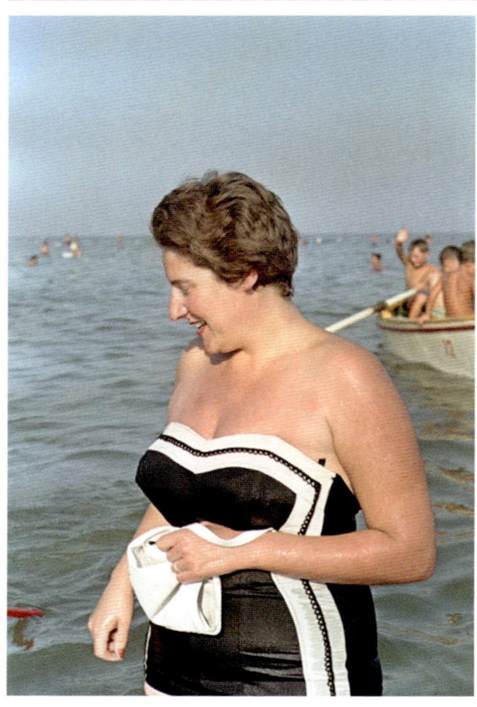

They portray family and friends relax-
ing at the beach. Ray loved to capture
moments of the everyday for posterity
and loved nothing better than snapping
these moments at the seaside, which,
conveniently, was right on his doorstep.
His mother-in-law owned a beach hut
close by to the shingle bank known
locally as The Street which jutted out
into the sea. Living in Whitstable, the
seaside was part of Ray's life for over 40
years and was always appreciated for
its diverse ways, from swimming in it
every summer to its freezing over in the
winter of 1962/3.[11]

Lawson's seaside photographs are about
familiarity, with people and place. The stony
Tankerton beach is by no means a white-
sands paradise – it looks uncomfortable and
chilly. But the Lawson family, stylishly attired
in colourful prints and winged sunglasses,
seem entirely at ease, passing teacups, eating
ice lollies and selecting biscuits. Lawson was
adept at capturing a moment, of joy, absorp-
tion or laughter.

Reginald Slader's images of family on the
Isle of Wight, though taken in the mid-1960s,
are like photographs of a much earlier time
(pp.140–1). Slader's father, photographed
in July 1965, snoozes on a deckchair, fully
muffled up in overcoat, waistcoat, cap and
heavy shoes; in another image his Uncle Tom

something so wholesome about this family
group, as they swim, play in the wet sand, eat
breakfasts and picnics. They are characters
in a partial narrative with a fragmented plot.

The family in Raymond Conrad Lawson's
1950s photographs are stylish and joyful
(opposite); they fill the frame of each of
the photographs, which Lawson's nephew
Nick Cordès has printed from the original
transparencies. Born in Canada, Lawson
returned with his family to London as a
five-year-old in the early 1930s. Largely self-
taught, Lawson studied for a while under the
society photographer Baron de Meyer. He
photographed at both the London Olympics
in 1948 and at the Festival of Britain in 1951,
using Rolleiflex and Pentax cameras. Lawson
and his wife Alma settled in the seaside town
of Whitstable in Kent, where they brought
up five sons and became pillars of the local
Catholic community. Lawson became parish
photographer, photographing communions
and making class photographs at the Catholic
primary school. The photographs opposite
were all taken on the beach at Tankerton in
the summer of 1959. Cordès remembers:

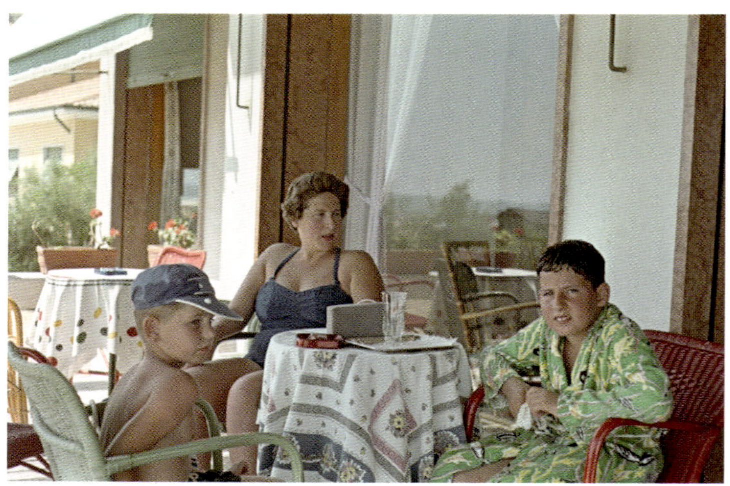

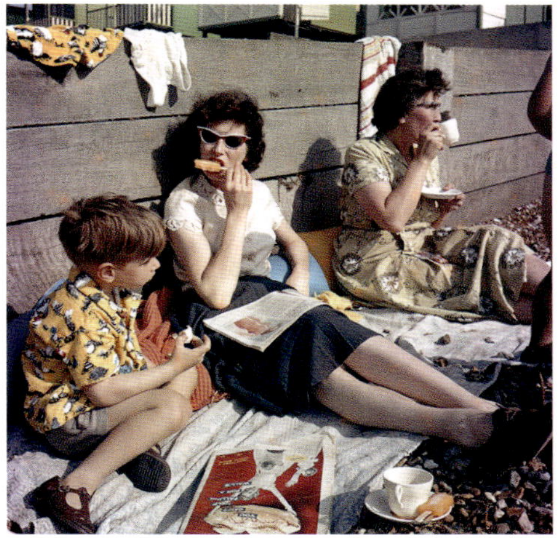

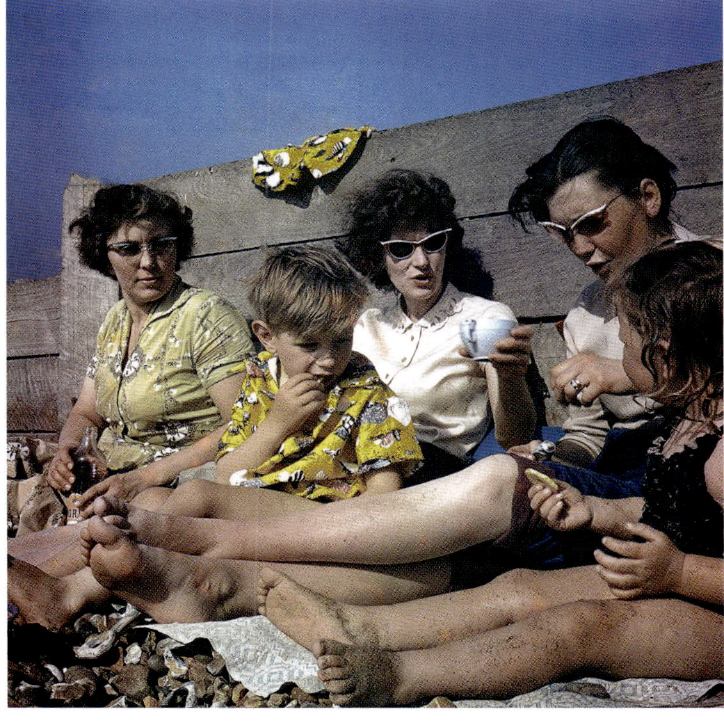

RAYMOND CONRAD LAWSON
Left to right: *David Wood,*
Sheila Wood and Alma Lawson, 1959

RAYMOND CONRAD LAWSON
Left to right: *Alma Lawson, David Wood,*
Sheila Wood, Margaret Cordès and
Karen Peters, 1959

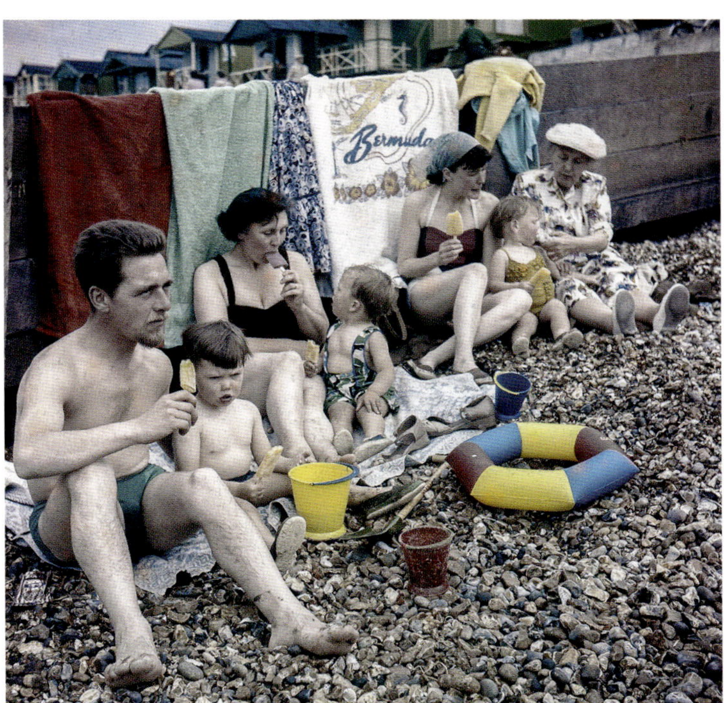

RAYMOND CONRAD LAWSON · Left to right: *Wally Cordès, Mark Lawson,*
Alma Lawson, Bernard Lawson, Margaret Cordès and Amy Smithers, 1959

poses with his son, wearing a thick black suit and a trilby, with a cigarette, all set against the background of ramshackle seaside buildings and family huddles. Three years later, in 1968, the Isle of Wight would host the first of its now legendary music festivals and Italian photographer Enzo Ragazzini would make a record of events in a series of remarkable photographs depicting the rise of festival culture and the anarchy of early music entrepreneurship (pp.198–205). That such different worlds could exist in the same seaside sphere is not surprising – that narrow strip between the physical coast and the sea is liminal, all things to all people, a departure from everyday life.

Slader was a civil servant and keen amateur photographer with a love of adventure and an interest in the English coast. As his son Tim recalls: 'he always felt the British Isles had so much to offer he would never see it all. He particularly enjoyed the coast because of its extreme diversity: from the wild seas around Cornwall to the Jurassic cliffs of Devon, from the holiday beaches of Kent to

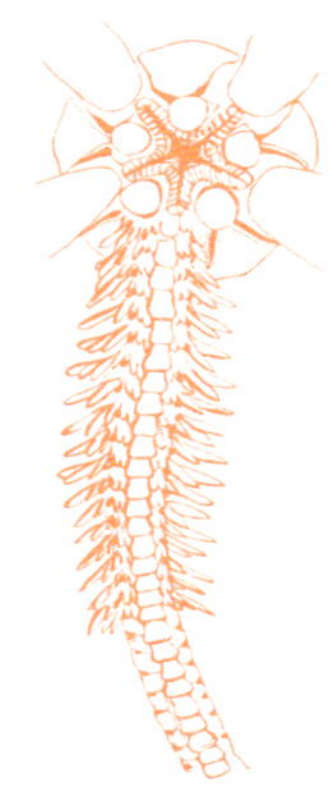

the wind-swept sands of Northumberland. He always took his camera with him looking for patterns and character.'[12]

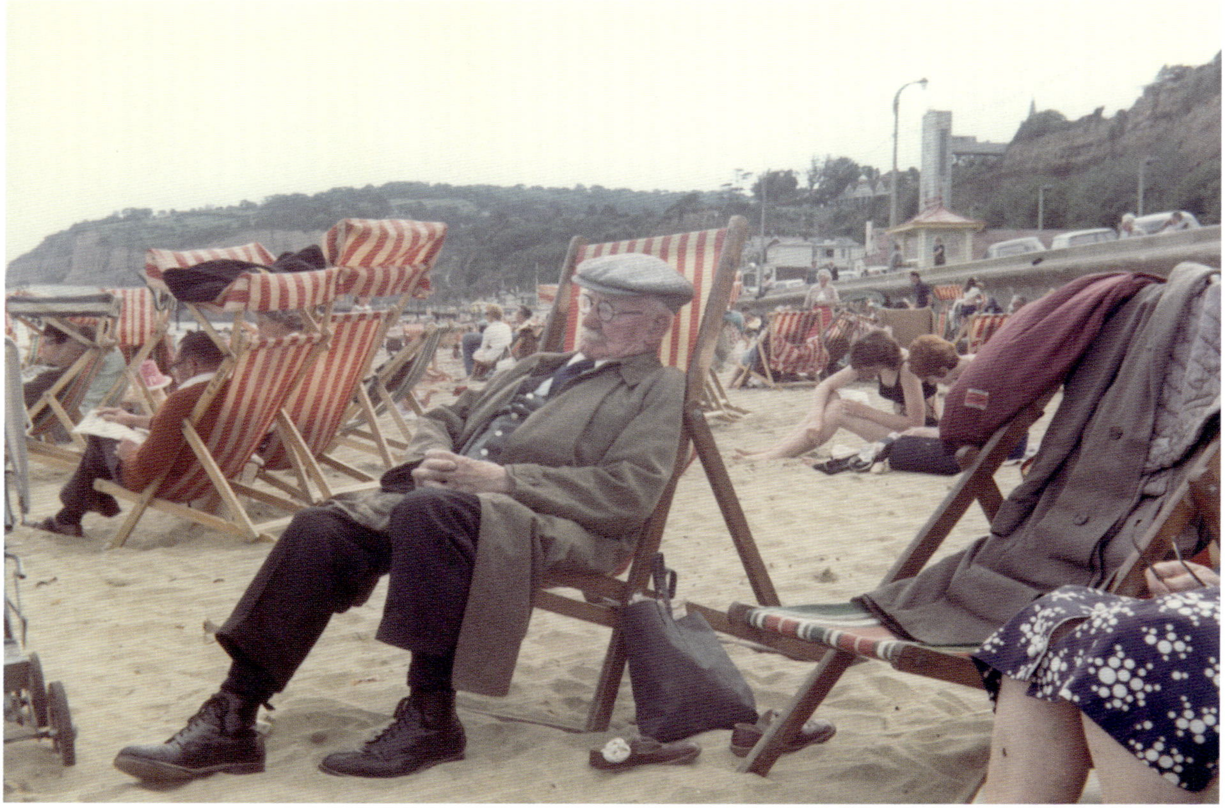

A fitting corollary, perhaps, to the seaside chronicles of the early 1970s, documentarists and their *éminence grise*, English photojournalist Tony Ray-Jones, is the archive of family photographs by Pat Gwynne, made from the mid-1960s to the early 1970s. When Ray-Jones was making his seminal trip around Britain, published posthumously as *A Day Off* in 1974, he established a set of tropes that many of the emerging photographers of the 1970s would follow in their own explorations of the British seaside. Domestic and amateur photographers remained untouched by this sea change in photographic tastes.

Gwynne, along with the many thousands of skilled amateur photographers operating around Britain in the 1960s and 1970s, produced a far more intimate portrait (p.143). One of twin brothers, Gwynne was brought

REGINALD SLADER
*Isle of Wight,
Shanklin Beach,*
July 1965

up in a Dublin orphanage and moved to a Barnardos children's home in London in the late 1920s. After training to be a printer, Gwynne moved to the predominantly Catholic artistic community at Ditchling in East Sussex, where he worked with Hilary Pepler, who had been a founder of the Hampshire House Workshops, aimed at providing enhanced opportunities for working men, before moving to Ditchling in 1913. Here Pepler set up the Saint Dominic's Press and joined the Guild of St Joseph and St Dominic at Ditchling after converting to Catholicism. As a Catholic, Gwynne was eligible to work at the press in Ditchling, and he continued as a printer, setting up his own press later in Sussex.

All photographs have authors, and in the 1950s and 1960s many thousands of those authors were largely anonymous, except to family, friends and fellow members of Camera Clubs. While the seaside was not the only location for family photographs, it was certainly the most intense. Amateur photography attracted (or was available to) more men than women, and Camera Clubs were dominated by men and arranged around competitions, complex rules and glamour sessions. Many of the photographers who photographed their families in the 1950s and 1960s were amateurs only in the sense that photography was not their main occupation. Gwynne was a printer; Slader was a civil servant with a passion for photography; Lawson, in his capacity as 'parish photographer', was semi-professional.

The largely undiscovered history of British amateurs, which has been obscured both by the low status of the 'snapshot' and by attempts to vernacularize, or to make nonprofessional photography quirky, or ironic, fitting a contemporary agenda. The story is more complex. Slader, Gwynne and Lawson, in their documentation of family holidays, used photography not only to memorialize moments, but also to see what it could do when presented with the complex notion of the family holiday. Most of the work in these archives is about the beach, about the peculiar English weather, which has families either in swimming costumes or macs. It is about those fantastical scenes that photographs throw up all the time – four bodies framed by the oblongs of towels, as four women absorb the sun with legs not long released from the chafe of stockings in Gwynne's *Ruth and Co.* (1967; p.143), formal wear on the beach in Slader's *Isle of Wight* (1965; opposite) and the symphony of winged sunglasses in Lawson's 'Tankerton' series (p.139). These family archives have been preserved by the photographers' families, or, in Lucy Bentham's case, by an artist–curator, in the knowledge that they have importance beyond the social, and a shared conviction that these are concentrated, and informed, artistic practice – not accidental or casual.

Archives are slippery, and context is all. Photographer Natasha Caruana found a photograph album that documented the stag party of her husband from a previous marriage in the seaside resort of Brighton: 'I saved

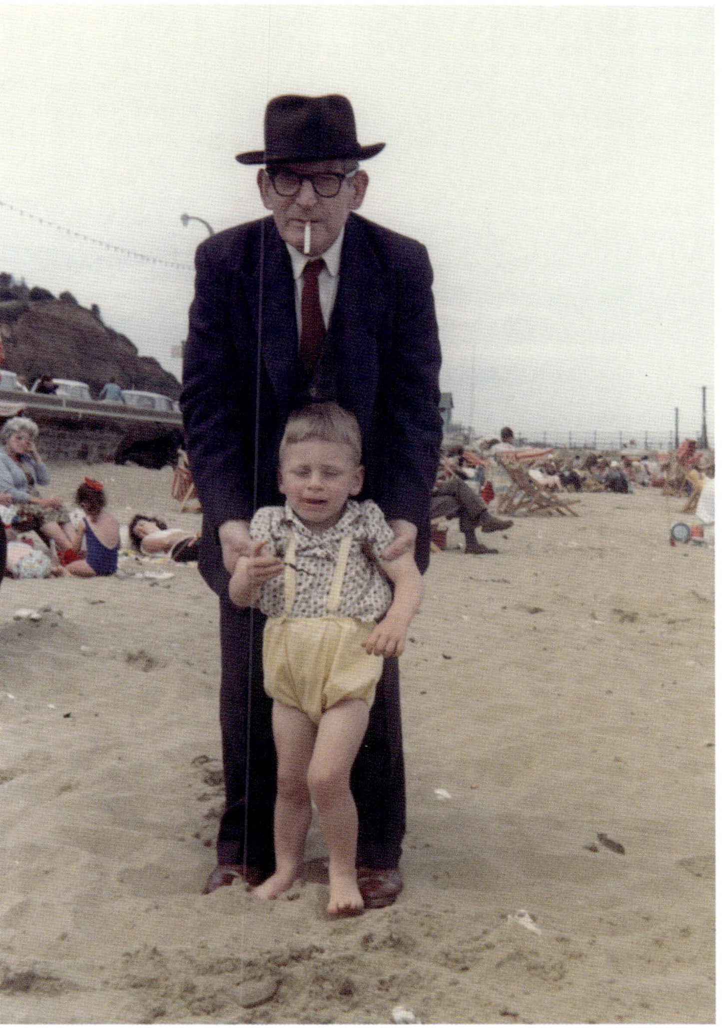

REGINALD SLADER
*David with Uncle Tom,
Shanklin Beach,*
July 1965

the album from being thrown away in 2015. As I literally picked this out of a black sack I see the item as a found object – which is part of a larger archive I now own.' Caruana gave the album, shown in this chapter's portfolio, a title: *Ritual Humiliation* (pp.144–9). This object – its finding, titling and remodelling as a part of the artist's practice – throws up many questions. It is an intimate object, slightly battered and fading, and originally consigned to the rubbish dump – an unwanted part of the past as the marriage ended.

Brighton, seen for so long as a magnet for the illicit, the alternative, the fun-seeking, the criminals, has, since the interwar years, been a magnet for photographers, artists, writers and poets. John Piper was fascinated by it and took many photographs there, as did almost every documentary photographer of the 1950s, 1960s and 1970s. Photographer Lee Miller took artist friends on day trips to Brighton and Bill Brandt produced a story for *Lilliput* magazine. Paul Theroux wrote about it disapprovingly in *The Kingdom by the Sea* (1983): 'I saw only bums and day-trippers.'[13] And for author Graham Greene in his novel *Brighton Rock* (1938), there was only sadness, cruelty and despair. For many lesbian, gay, bisexual, transgender and queer (LGBTQ) people in the 1950s and 1960s, Brighton was, however, a safer place than many. The South Coast Branch of the Minorities Research Group, founded in London in 1963, was in Brighton, and many men and women were drawn to a town where prejudice and persecution was much less severe.[14]

In *Ritual Humiliation* Brighton is the destination for a group of young men celebrating Simon Sweetman's impending marriage in 1997. The album is laid out as a narrative, and uses as its frontispiece the Stag Night invitation, which invites friends to Sweetman's 'ritual humiliation'. The photographs in the album (taken by the best man and others) are interspersed with various handwritten notes.

Pictures of bad meals and slightly embarrassed women, plus an excursion to the fairground, morph into something more sinister as the daylight fades. First Sweetman strips, and then, naked, he is wrapped in clingfilm around a lamppost. 'Simon pisses himself with fear' reads one of the bantering notes. The photography is poor and indistinct – blurry, unformed snapshots – and uses the seaside resort as a permissive location for this strangely demasculinized sexual romping. *Ritual Humiliation* was destined for the rubbish, part of a past to be negated, but instead its new, more public life will extend and change both its narrative and its cultural position. For Natasha Caruana:

I had a mix of emotions. On the one hand, it was an incredible piece of

photo history (the handwritten notes, the clothes, the decor) particularly because the album was created by men. However, it was difficult to see Simon being bullied and for it to be recorded for prosterity in this way. I can't imagine what it would've been like to be stripped naked, tied to a lamppost, thrown water over and then left on the sea front. AND for the whole ordeal to be presented to you on your wedding day like a holiday album.[15]

Photography that happens at the seaside – family life on public display. Only every so often in the raw – perhaps with Martin Parr in *The Last Resort* though his gaze is habitually restrained, certainly with Caruana's *Ritual Humiliation* album. The writing on the seaside postcards that Tom Jackson has collected is bittersweet, tiny messages of banality, mystery and indignation. Lucy Bentham's anonymous archive is like a magic spell, where we spin into make-believe, Raymond Lawson's a fantastical collection of colours, patterns and surfaces. Reginald Slader's are like photographs from another time, but in fact from the mid-1960s, Pat Gwynne's not as casual as they seem. The postcards produced by John Hinde photographers are of models acting being families – they are unsullied and perfect. The 'real' Butlin's families portrayed by Dafydd Jones, Daniel Meadows and Barry Lewis are more disarrayed, unused to spectacle and performance, cheap suitcases, poor clothes and the inequity of a week's holiday in a ruthlessly class-dominated Britain. Like Hinde, Jackson, Slader, Lawson, Gwynne, Parr and Sweetman's friends, all these storytellers have a plot in mind – something that they want us to believe.

The mystique of the seaside crowds into all of these photographs – a place where we undress and lie in the sun, where we celebrate rituals, where we can feel that we are someone else in another place. 'That's me in the picture', we shout, until we can no longer recognize ourselves. [vw]

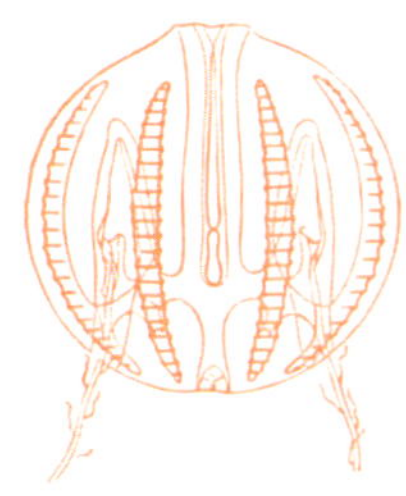

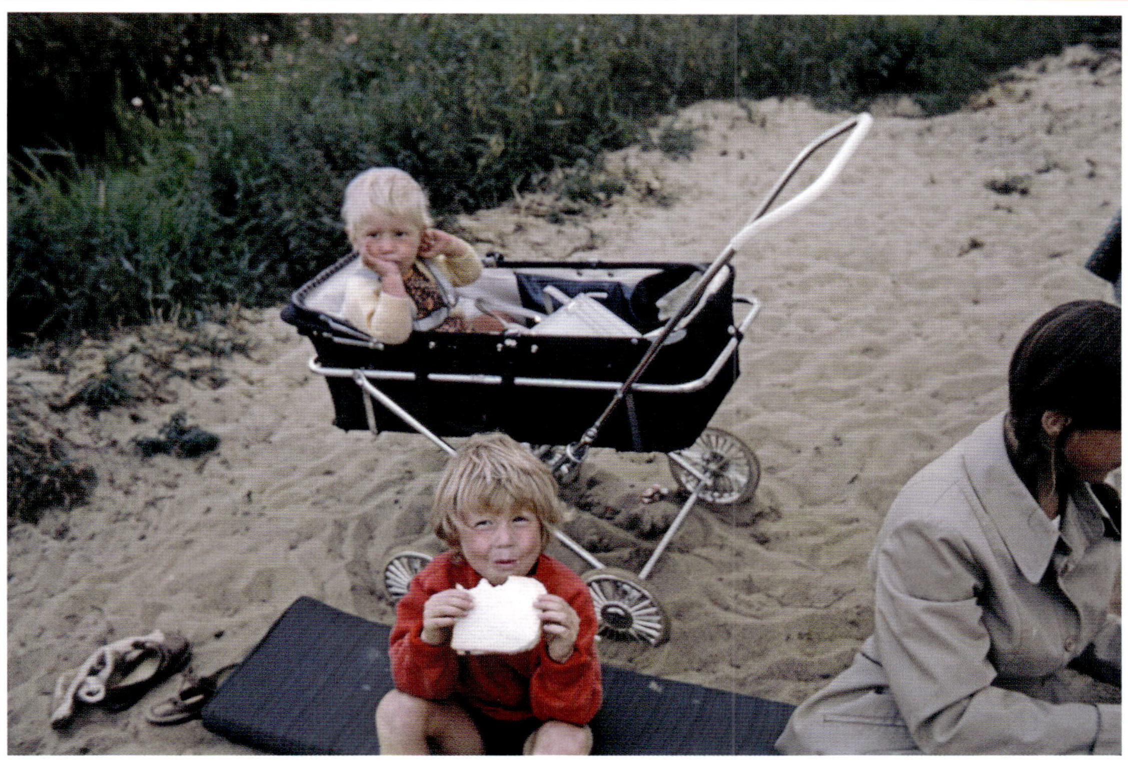

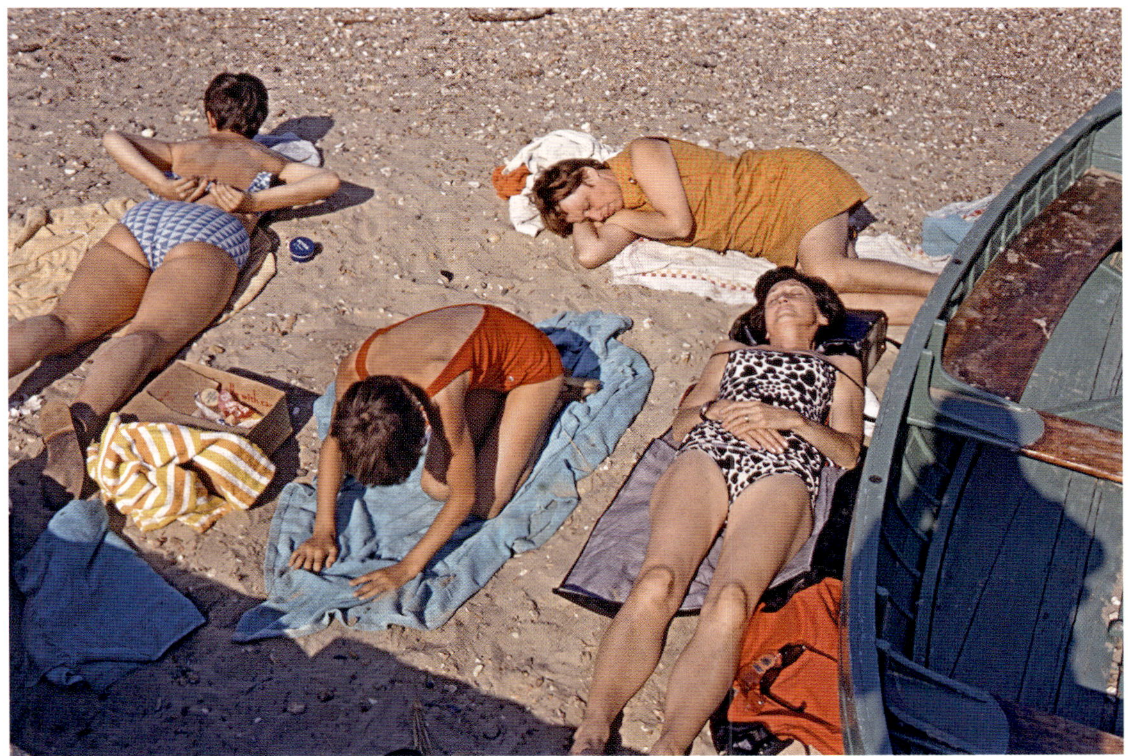

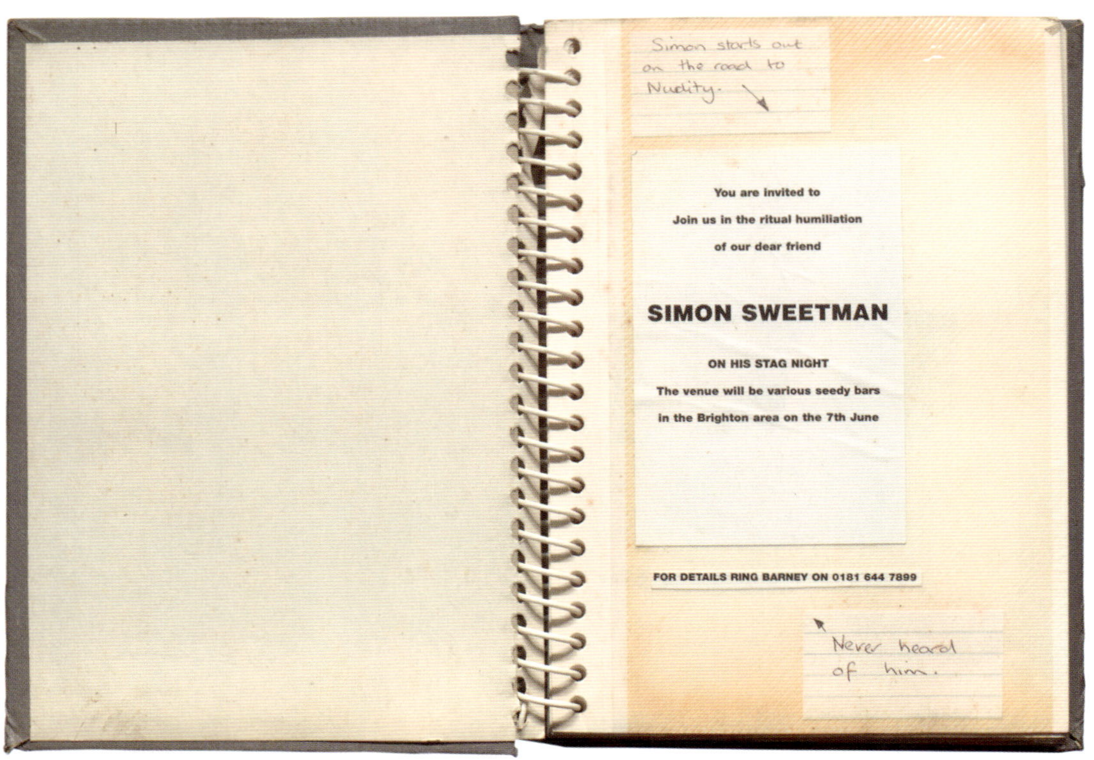
Simon starts out
on the road to
Nudity.

You are invited to
Join us in the ritual humiliation
of our dear friend

SIMON SWEETMAN

ON HIS STAG NIGHT
The venue will be various seedy bars
in the Brighton area on the 7th June

FOR DETAILS RING BARNEY ON 0181 644 7899

Never heard
of him.

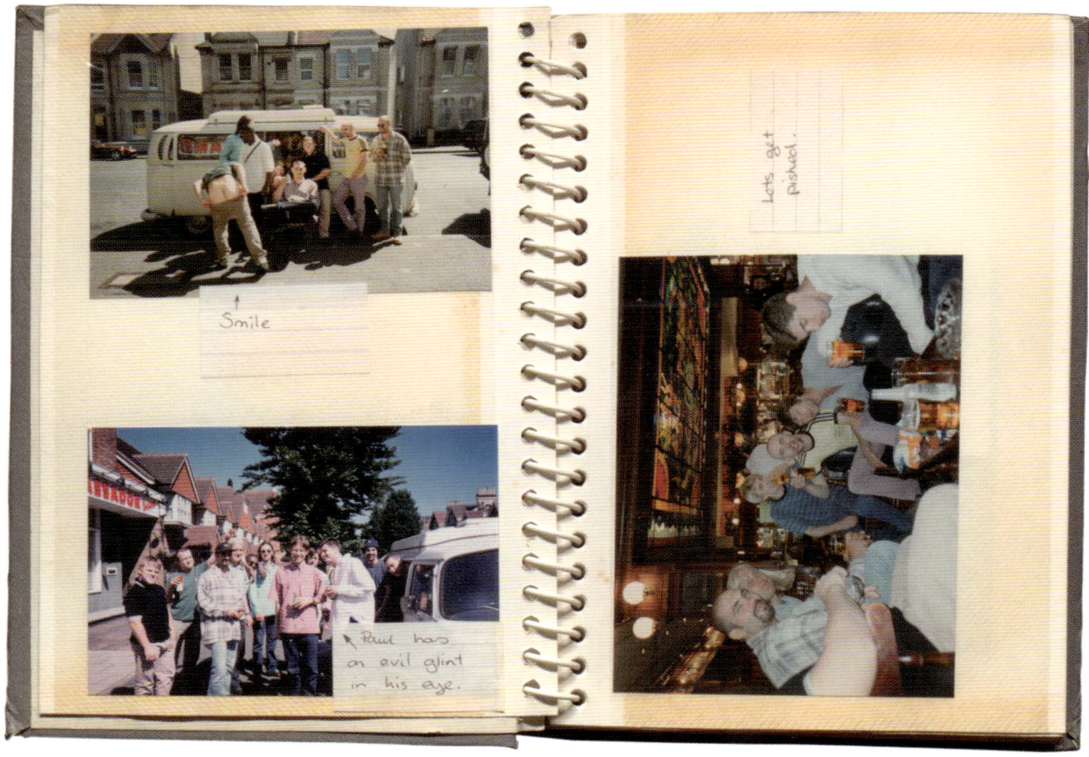
Smile

Paul has
an evil glint
in his eye.

Lets get
Pished.

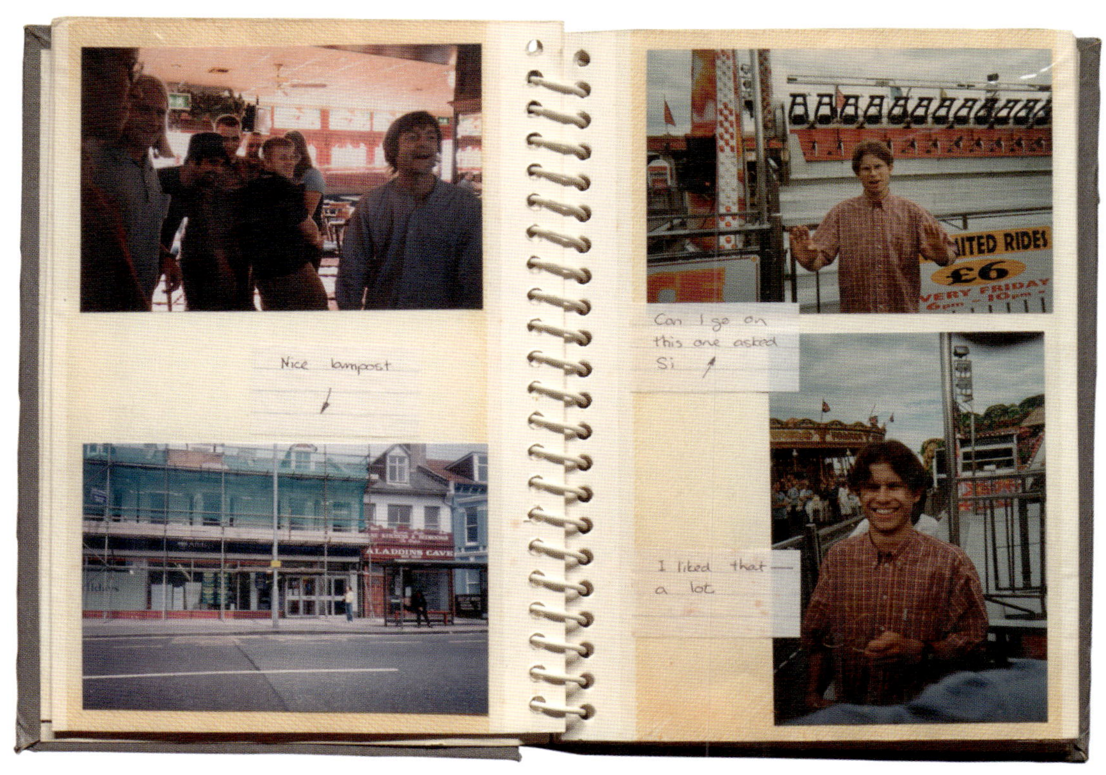
Nice lampost
ALADDINS CAVE
UITED RIDES
£6
VERY FRIDAY
6pm — 10pm
Can I go on
this one asked
Si
I liked that —
a lot

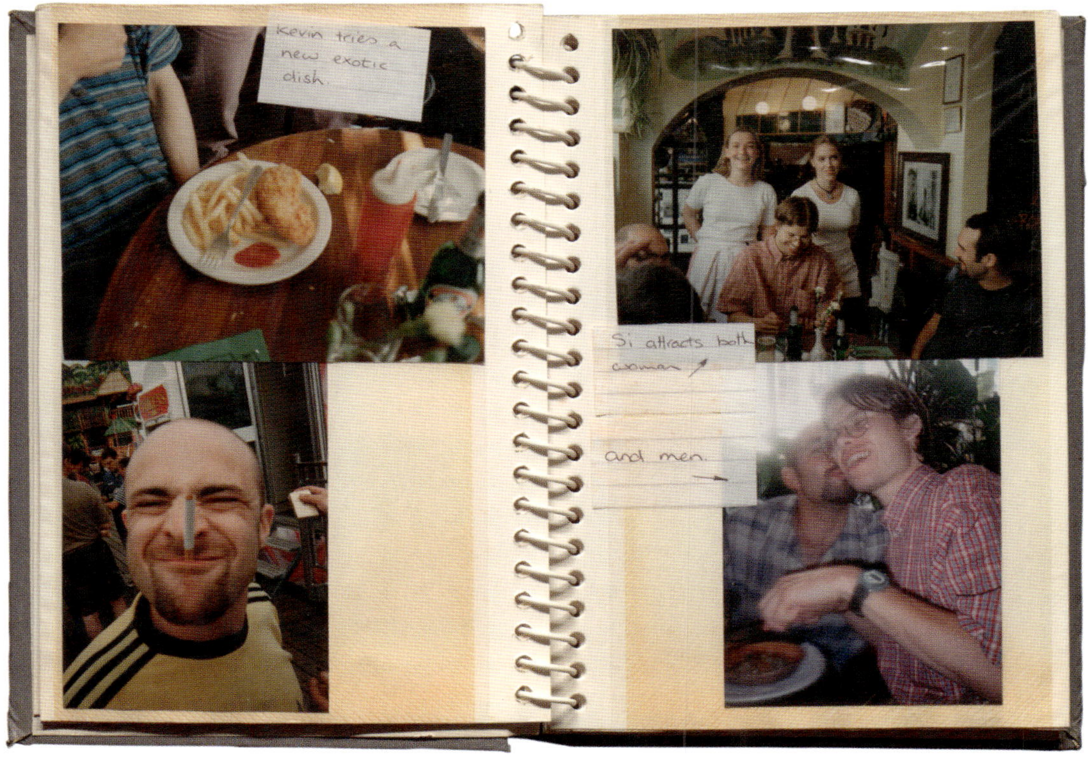
Kevin tries a
new exotic
dish
Si attracts both
women
and men.

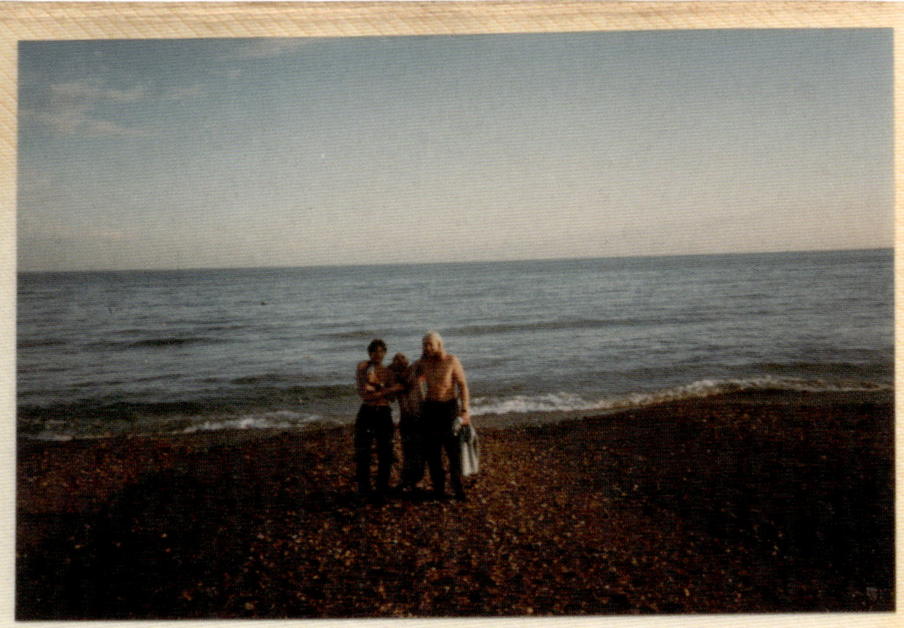

3 queers
take a stroll.

I am a
stud.

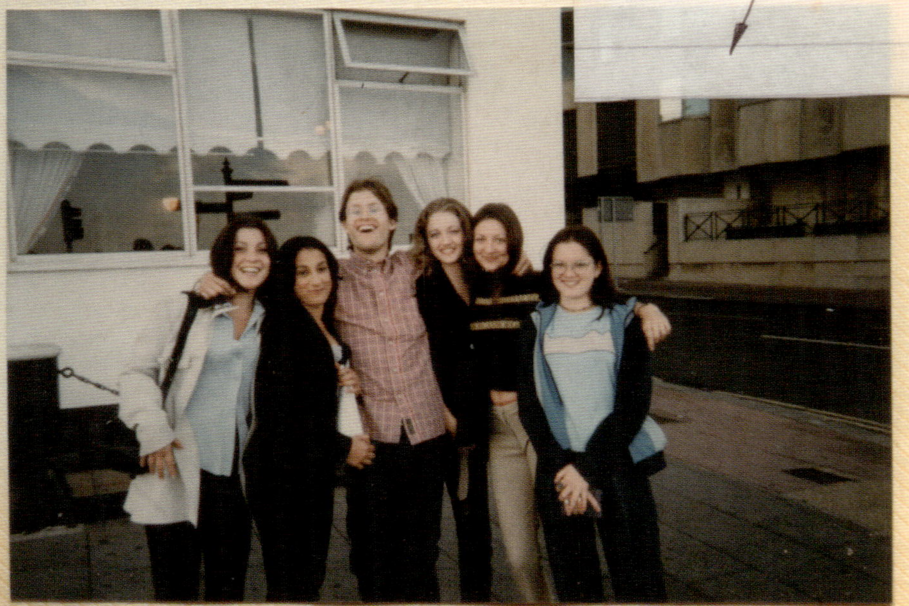

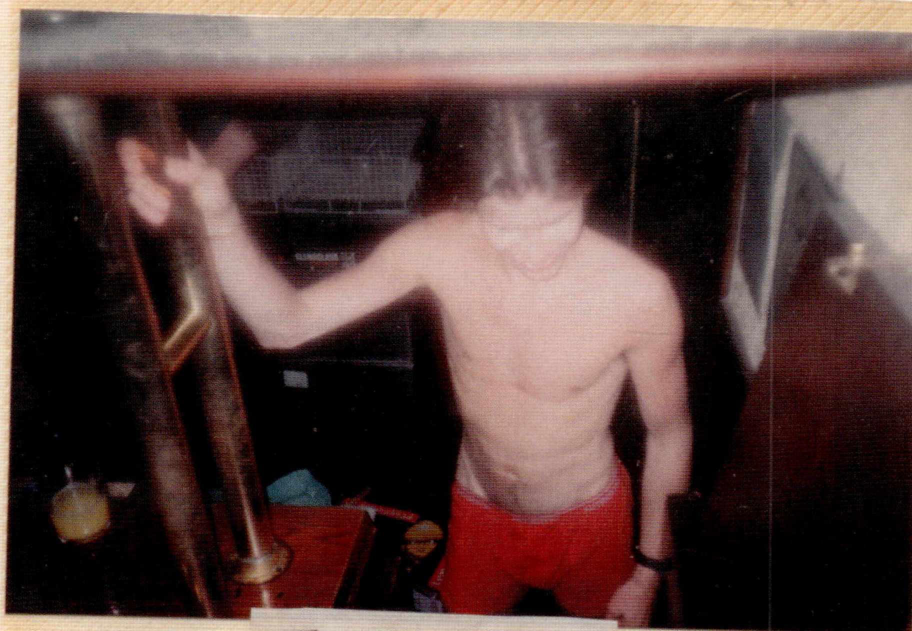

The stripper
arrives

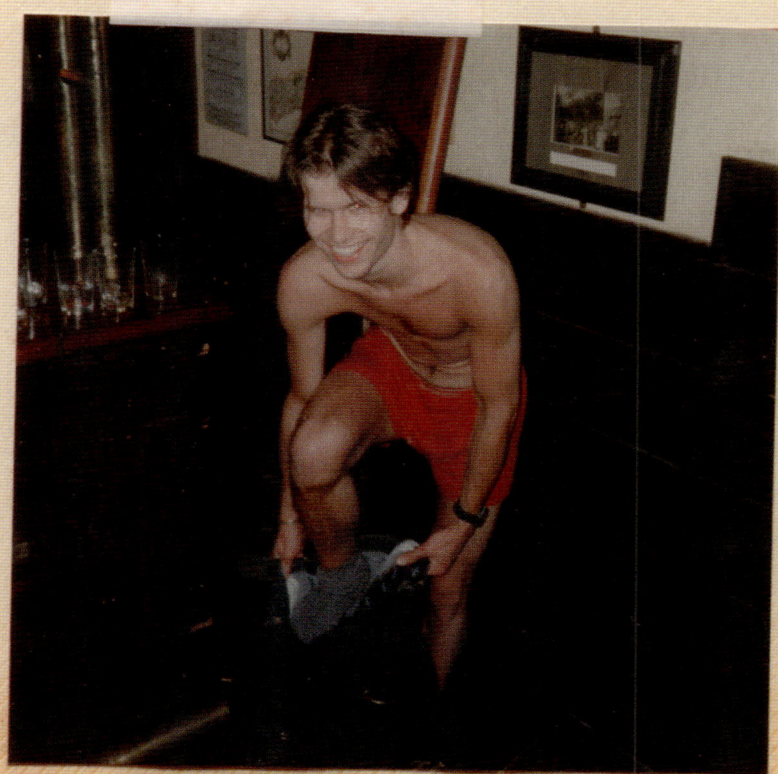

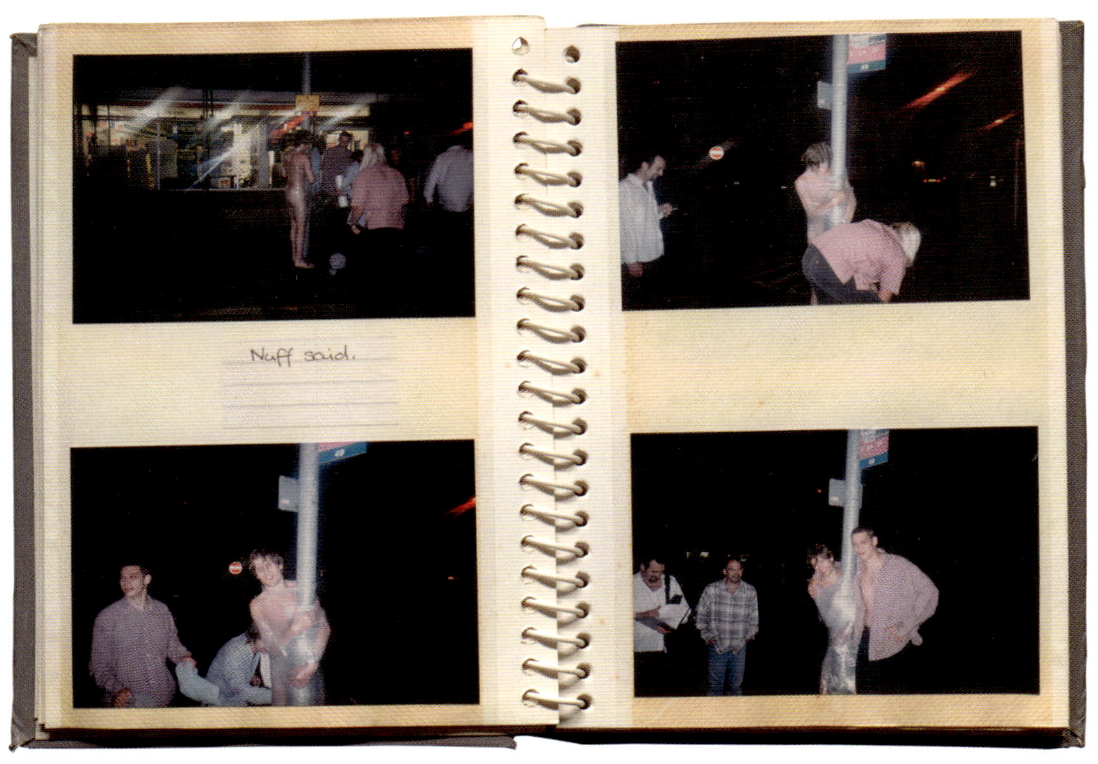
Nuff said.

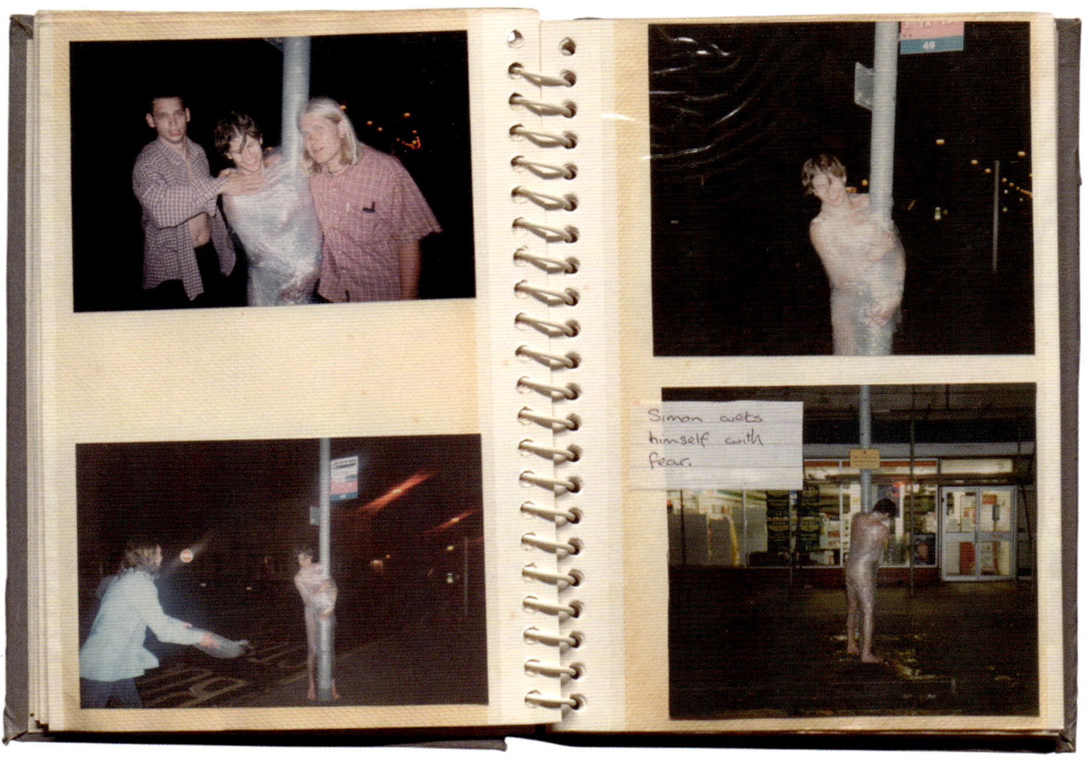
Simon wets himself with fear.

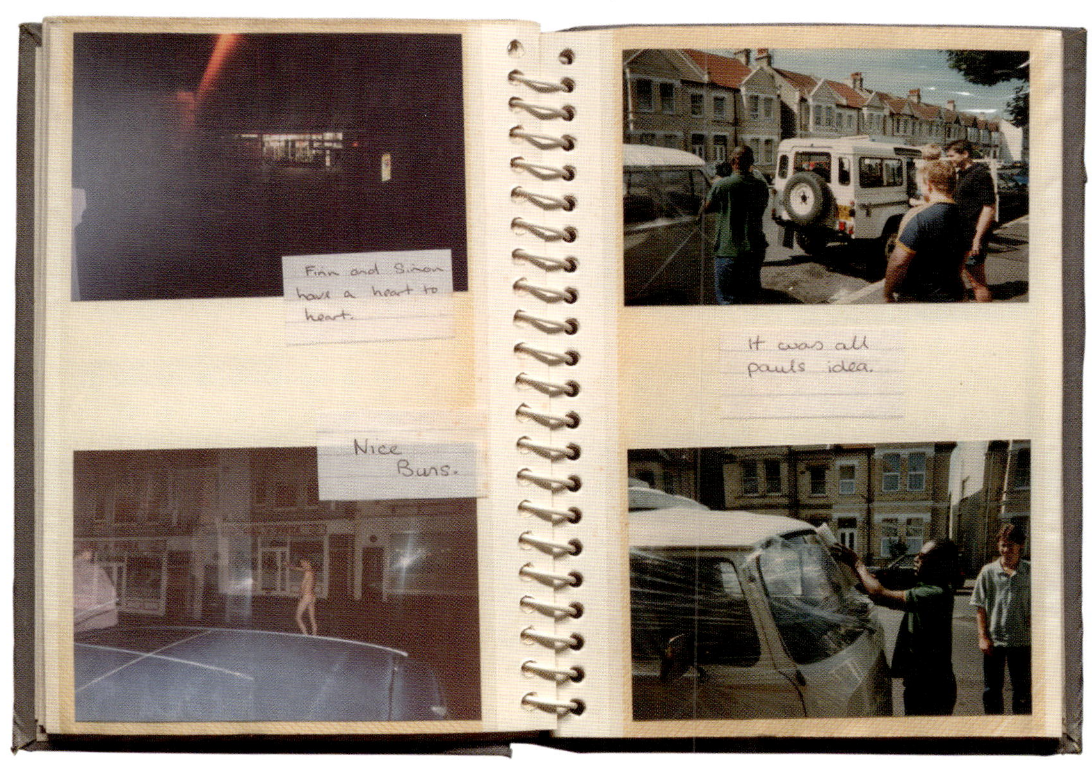
Finn and Simon
have a heart to
heart.

Nice
Buns.

It was all
pauls idea.

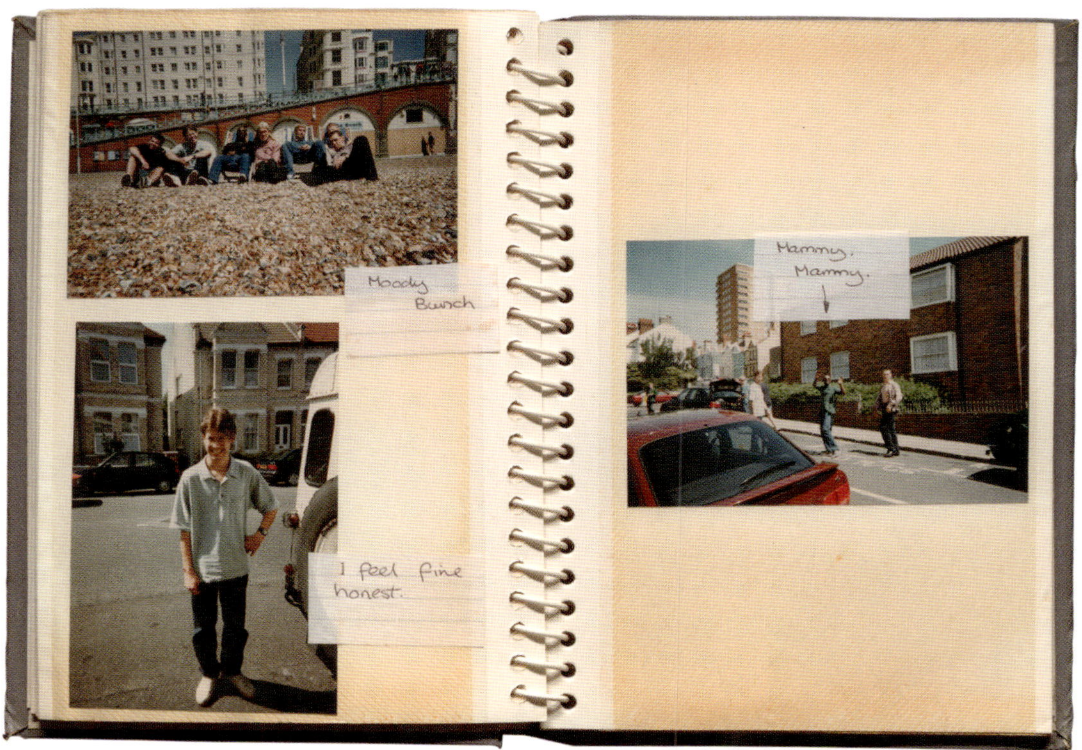
Moody
Bunch

I feel fine
honest.

Mammy.
Mammy.

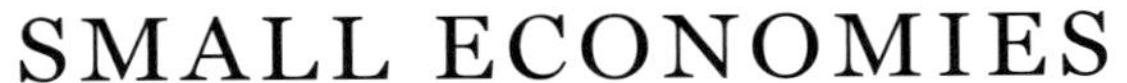

SMALL ECONOMIES

FRUGAL MEALS

DETERMINED CHEERFULNESS

GENUINE BONHOMIE

ECCENTRIC OWNERS

QUIRKY INDIVIDUALISM

ARCHITECTURAL GRANDEUR

WORLDS IN A SMALL ROOM

THE SEASIDE HOTEL

In 2012 photographer Martin Parr was commissioned by community arts organization Multistory to produce photographs and films about the Black Country, a cluster of industrial towns in the West Midlands of England. While researching, he discovered 'Turkey and Tinsel' – low-season bus trips to the seaside for pensioners to celebrate 'Christmas' in a traditional seaside hotel. The film of the same name that Parr created was a comedy about friendship, humour and stoicism, but the real star was the Midland Hotel on the seafront in the declining resort of Weston-super-Mare. There are no material luxuries at the Midland: its managers are stoic, the meals are frugal and everything is done on a shoestring. It is one of thousands of seaside hotels across Britain, keeping their heads above water as tastes and the landscape of tourism change. Parr's film gently captures its ambience: the small economies, out-of-date furnishing, frugal meals and determined cheerfulness, mixed with genuine bonhomie, on the part of its manager and staff.

The seaside hotel is an institution, commemorated throughout fiction, film and photography. As novelist Alison Moore remarked in 2016:

> Through the lens of literature, something interesting happens to the world of sand and sea, harbours and hotels. In fiction, the seaside frequently represents a threshold between order and chaos, society and nature, identity and loss, with a move to the coast signaling a shift from the former to the latter. This undermining of tradition or self is reflected in eroding coastlines, in crumbling houses, in the disintegration of narrative structure itself.[1]

The failing seaside hotel, struggling to keep up with the times, always with an eye on the bottom line, has been the subject of comedy since the 1950s. With their sometimes eccentric owners running businesses that require high levels of customer service, expectations on both sides are not always met. In his seminal study *The British Seaside, Holidays and Resorts in the Twentieth Century* (2000), historian John K. Walton charts the decline of the seaside resort from the 1950s onwards. He notes the difficulties of keeping seasonal businesses afloat, the vagaries of employment, an overwhelming sense of marginality as, cut off from large urban centres and with little industry and invariably incompetent councils, a solid core of permanent employment (particularly for men) did not develop. Seaside populations have been growing older since the 1930s, with many retirees just scraping a living.

The evolution of the small seaside hotel is a complex one – and what we now regard as the traditional boarding house was largely a 1950s phenomenon. Far more usual was the 'Company House', a form of self-catering where the guests bought their own food and the landlady prepared and cooked it.[2]

In his discussion of seaside economies, Walton notes:

> The emblematic figure here was the seaside landlady, whose status as matriarch and businesswoman made her the object of alarm and therefore ridicule, as a powerful woman who dominated husband and guests alike. Her defensive need for rules and regulations, to safeguard visitor comfort, respectability and her own time for cleaning and sleep, was caricatured as dictatorial, and had to be relaxed when cheaper and more informal alternatives began to compete for her customers.[3]

One of postcard artist Donald McGill's favourite subjects was the seaside boarding house, with its formidable landlady and scampering guests.

The small seaside hotel, with its often eccentric proprietors, outdated décor and a sense of time stopped, has occupied a special place in the English imagination. Harold Pinter used a boarding house as the location for menacing scenes in his 1958 play *The Birthday Party*, while in the 1986 British

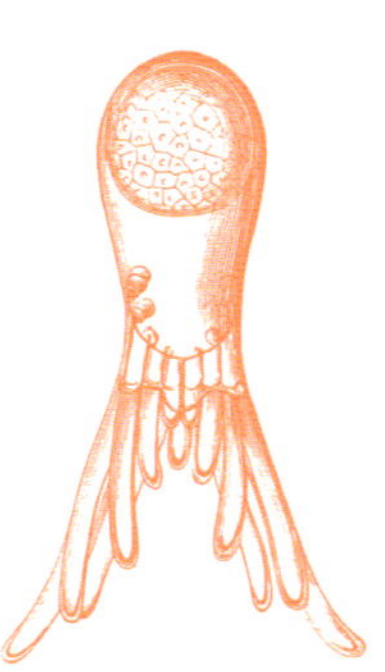

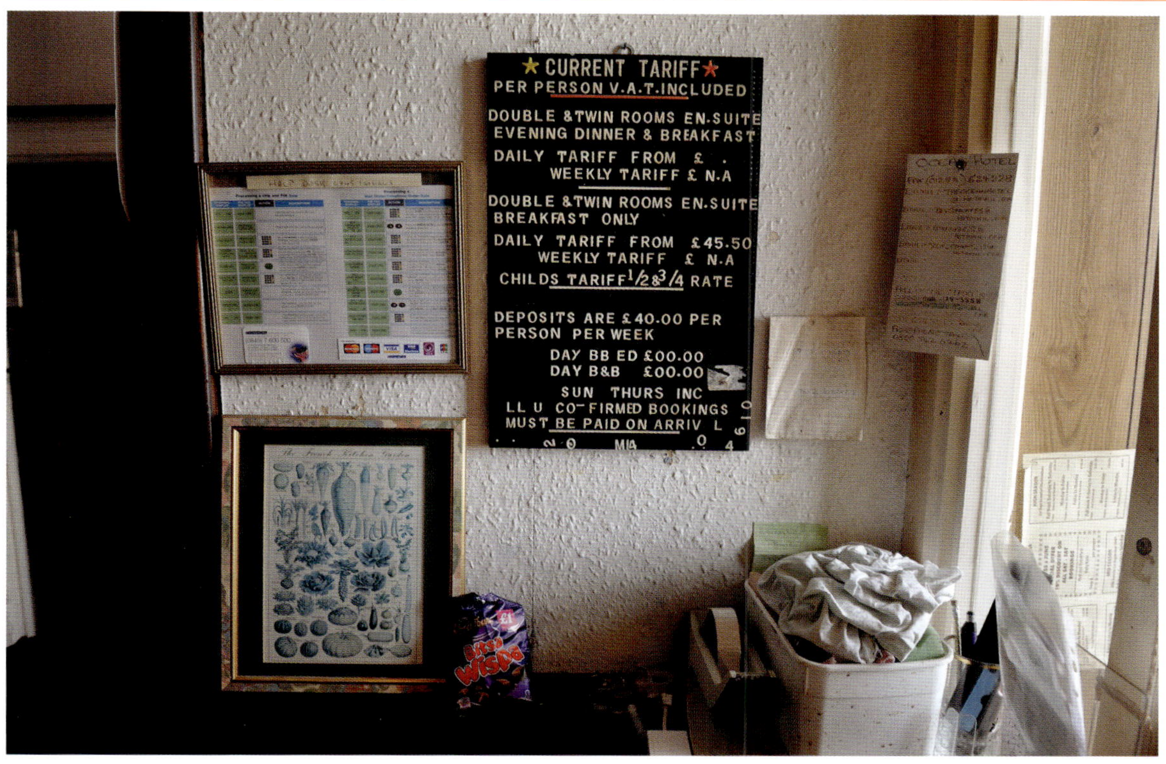
★ CURRENT TARIFF ★
PER PERSON V.A.T.INCLUDED
DOUBLE &TWIN ROOMS EN.SUITE
EVENING DINNER & BREAKFAST
DAILY TARIFF FROM £ .
WEEKLY TARIFF £ N.A
DOUBLE &TWIN ROOMS EN.SUITE
BREAKFAST ONLY
DAILY TARIFF FROM £45.50
WEEKLY TARIFF £ N.A
CHILDS TARIFF 1/2 & 3/4 RATE
DEPOSITS ARE £40.00 PER
PERSON PER WEEK
DAY BB ED £00.00
DAY B&B £00.00
SUN THURS INC
LL U CO-FIRMED BOOKINGS
MUST BE PAID ON ARRIV L

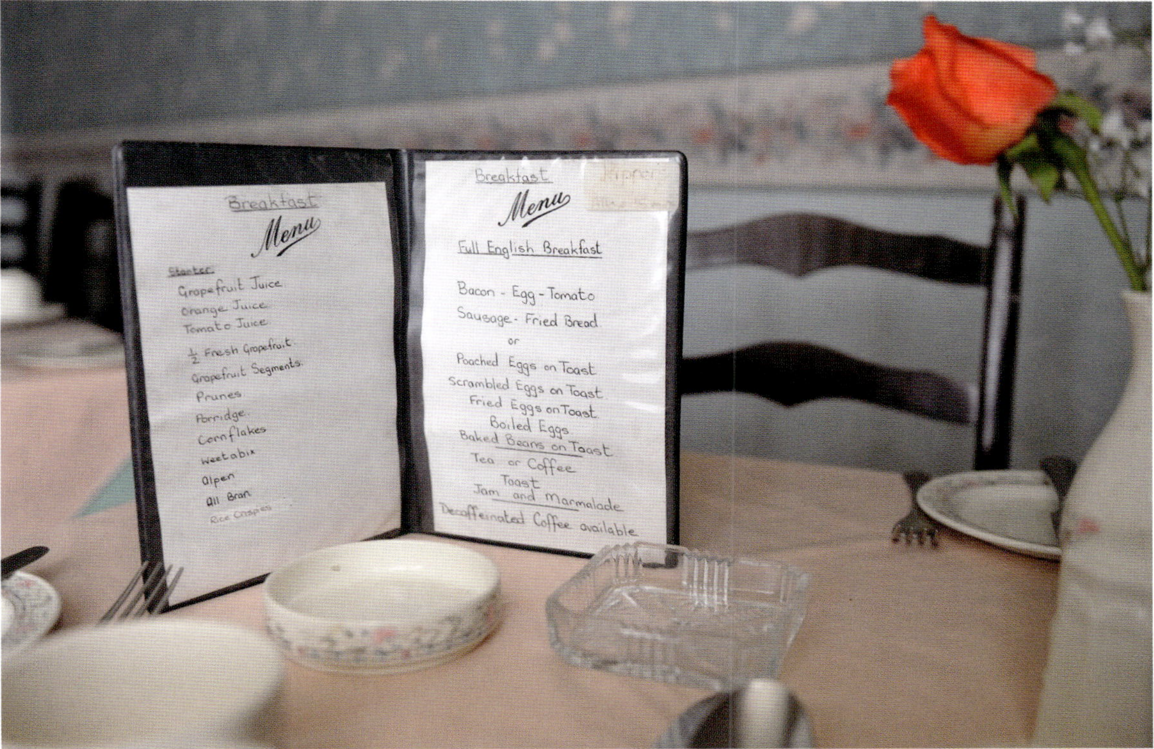
Breakfast
Menu
Starter:
Grapefruit Juice
Orange Juice
Tomato Juice
½ Fresh Grapefruit
Grapefruit Segments
Prunes
Porridge
Cornflakes
Weetabix
Alpen
All Bran
Rice Crispies

Breakfast
Menu
Full English Breakfast
Bacon - Egg - Tomato
Sausage - Fried Bread
or
Poached Eggs on Toast
Scrambled Eggs on Toast
Fried Eggs on Toast
Boiled Eggs
Baked Beans on Toast
Tea or Coffee
Toast
Jam and Marmalade
Decaffeinated Coffee available

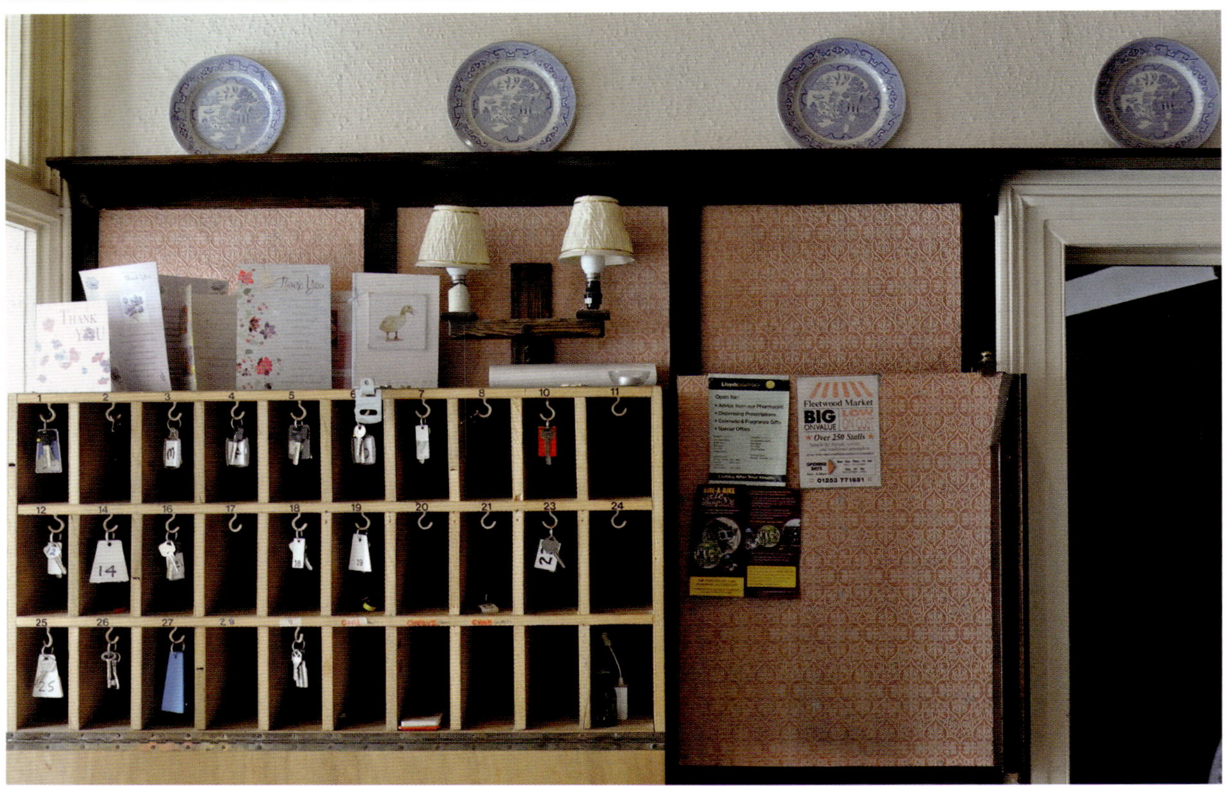

gangster film *Mona Lisa*, the Royal Albion Hotel in Brighton is the setting for the final violent scenes. When Ian McEwan's novel *On Chesil Beach* was made into a film in 2017, the seaside hotel room became a place of trauma and loss.

It is rare, in the twenty-first century, to see a British seaside resort portrayed in a positive light. Working-class resorts such as Blackpool have become particular targets for negativity. In February 2014, the *Daily Mail* newspaper ran a 'Then and Now' story about the decline of seafront Blackpool hotels, which it titled *Welcome to Sad-pool*. Northern press photographer Warren Scott was commissioned to make a series of photographs about what the *Mail* described as

> once the shimmering jewels of a popular holiday resort. But now the grand hotels of Blackpool mark its once-famous Promenade like a mouthful of decaying teeth … Many of the once-proud hotels

and guest-houses overlooking the cold and often fierce Irish Sea are these days only frequented by rats, seagulls, vandals and the homeless … At the height of its success, The Warwick Hotel, with its grand double-fronted vista and indoor heated pool, needed fifty staff to run. But now its doors and windows are boarded shut with MDF panels, its rooms lie unoccupied and its pool slowly festers. Everywhere along the South Promenade air conditioning has given way to smashed windows and curtains fluttering in the wind. Dirt is slowly accumulating on The Royal Carlton; twice named Hotel Of The Year, the briny Blackpool air is now turning its steel window frames to rust.[4]

Four years later, in November 2017, the *Financial Times* ran a similar story about Blackpool in the north-west of England, portraying it as a phantasmagoria of broken lives, poor accommodation and multiple health problems. The working-class seaside resort has always been regarded by suspicion by metropolitan professionals, and in Sarah O'Connor's article, Blackpool is portrayed as a kind of Dickensian place of last resort for the poor and indigent: 'Blackpool exports healthy, skilled people and imports the unskilled, the unemployed and the unwell … The more the economy rots, the more people come.'[5]

For photographer Henry Iddon, the inevitably changing face of the seaside resort provides rich material for documentary photography. Iddon grew up and still lives in Blackpool, and has been making photographs about the town since the 1980s. The Ocean was due to be redeveloped as an art hotel when Iddon began to photograph it (p.153 and opposite):

> There's no doubt that the Ocean Hotel is in an 80s–70s time warp. Places like the Ocean Hotel are full of honesty – no frills accommodation with an odd depth of heritage and no doubt memories that modern corporate hotel providers lack. And that quirky individualism is something to celebrate. I was keen to shoot the Ocean Hotel before it was converted – traditional B&Bs are getting rarer as more venues modernise the décor. I'd been told it was a time warp.[6]

Iddon's photographs were made

> in 90 minutes – shooting on digital SLR and 35mm negative (on Leica M6). It really was an intense time – surrounded by this wonderful time warp of a hotel. In some respects, it was rather sad – but equally wonderful in its aged and empty state. Forty years of Blackpool hotel history in one building, the British seaside B+B distilled. The thank-you cards pinned up by reception – people obviously had happy memories of their stay and were no doubt treated in an

honest and valued way, while on what could have been their main annual holiday.[7]

The photographs document every detail of the Ocean Hotel's interior, empty of guests, but still intact. There is a table laid for breakfast (p.153) with ashtray and handwritten menu slipped into a plastic folder: 'Full English Breakfast, Kippers, allow 15 mins.' There is comfort here and a kind of longing too. In another photograph (p.153), boxes of clutter from the hotel's dismantlement disturb order, but the pricelist for rooms is still nailed up on the woodchip wall: £45.50 for a room with dinner and breakfast included. Next to this is a framed set of instructions for operating a card machine, a faded reproduction of 'The French Kitchen Garden', a dirty sheet, a yellowing list of email addresses and phone numbers and a piece of paper headed 'Lancashire Police'.

At the end of its life as a B&B, the Ocean Hotel was clearly struggling. Exposed to the unflinching gaze of online reviewers, its inadequacies were cruelly exposed – scruffy, dated and eccentrically run. But Iddon's photographs redeem it, as it becomes a stage set of the past, of remembered holidays, of the promise of salt water and sand, the thrill of a hotel breakfast. The detail in these photographs is important, and Iddon's eye is sympathetic – this is a humble place, frayed around the edges but with a kind of dignity. By the room-key hooks, there is a poster for the local pharmacy and a forlorn advertisement for bike hire (opposite). The sense of an ending is acute. More than a just a building, the Ocean is an archive of memories, a dreamcatcher.

For the hardworking people of Bolton, Lancashire, a week in a Blackpool boarding house was an escape from the monotony and arduousness of repetitive and exhausting work in the cotton mills. The annual exodus attracted the attention of Mass Observation in the 1930s, and Humphrey Spender was sent along to photograph in Bolton (Worktown) and Blackpool. Mass Observation employed a number of innovative photographers,

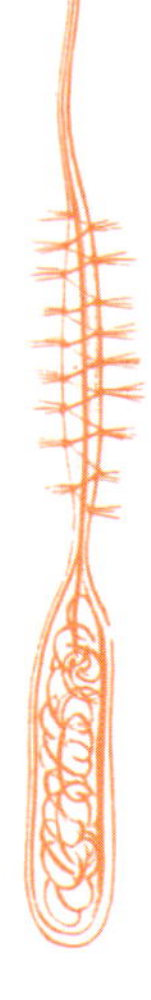

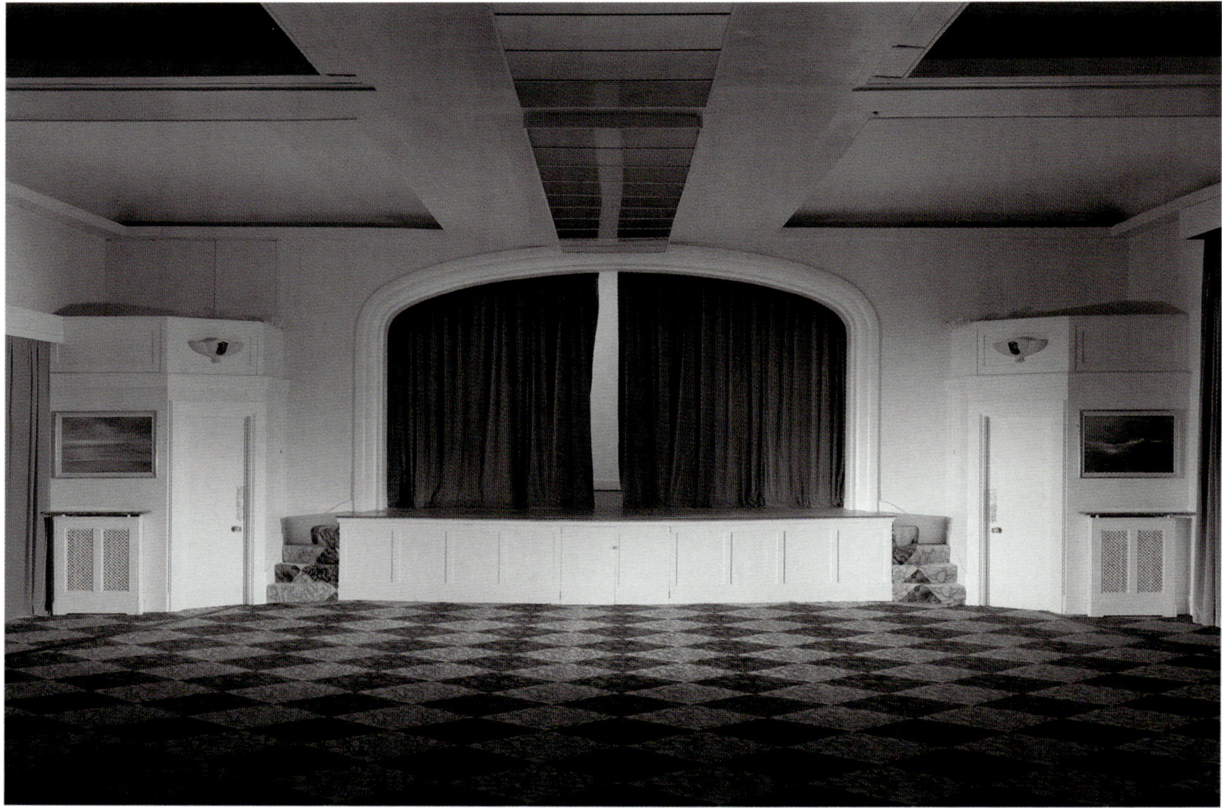

including Spender, Humphrey Jennings and Julian Trevelyan, and most aspects of the holiday were observed, through both written reports and photographs, giving a detailed picture of holiday accommodation used by Worktowners. Reporting back on a Blackpool boarding house, one Mass Observer noted:

> Bedrooms are eight feet by eight, the floor covered with oilcloth, ceiling with leaf wallpaper, the walls with pictures of Dolores Costello, crosses and scrolls bearing the motto 'I know that my Redeemer liveth' (although the proprietors of this house are Jewish) … When visitors want to go to the lavatory, they first peep out of their doors, and when they get in, women average one and a half minutes, men three to four minutes. The visit is usually paid before breakfast. Visitors come down to have breakfast in a room whose

Rowan Whybrew
Untitled, 2014

most compelling decoration is its sheet of rules, ordering noiseless rising, forbidding piano playing before eight o'clock, suggesting an early exit on the day of departure … After breakfast, most people either spend a period sitting on the seat in the garden or go straight out.[8]

The Kent seaside resort of Folkestone is a major site of cultural regeneration on the south-east coast. Supported by businessman Roger de Haan, its Old Town has been revived as a community of artists' studios, and the influential Folkestone Triennial is now an international event. In 2014 sociologist and artist–photographer Rowan Whybrew photographed a series of hotel rooms in the town (above and opposite):

> I am exploring encounters with history and memory in the English landscape.

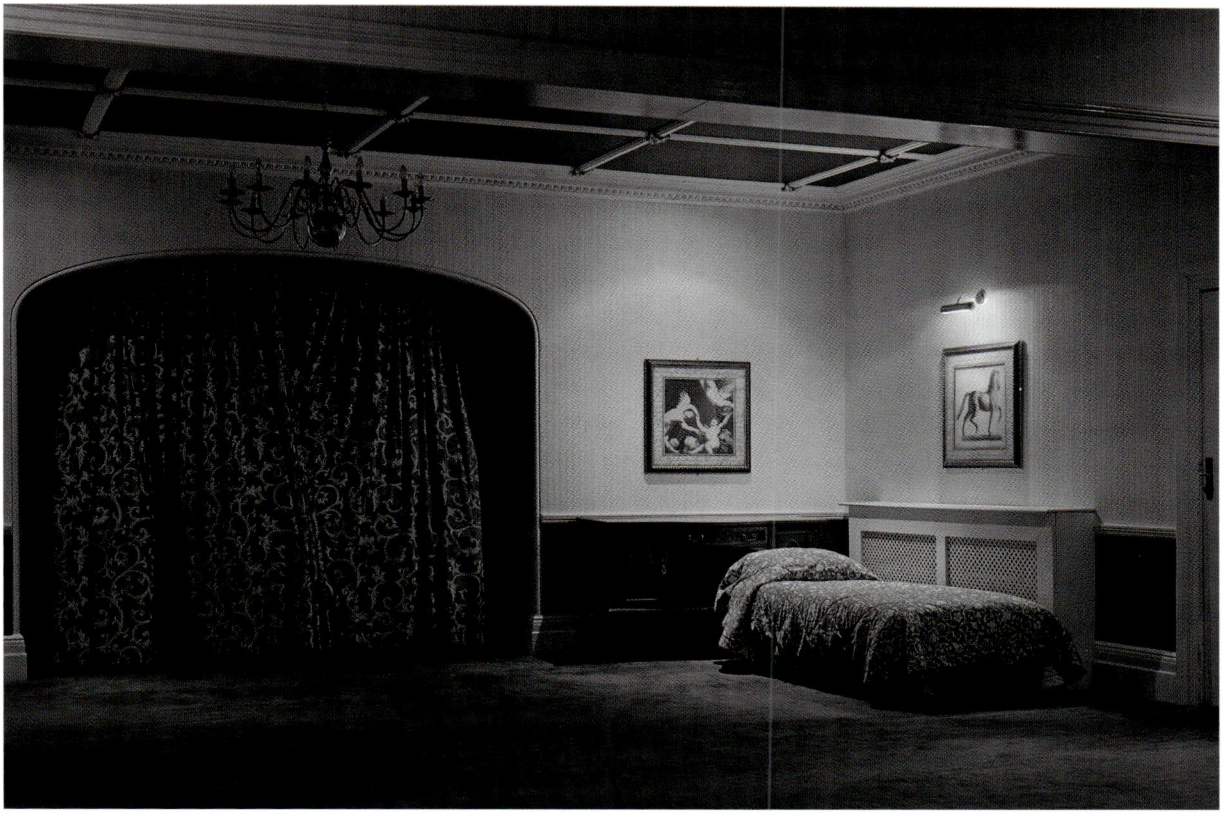

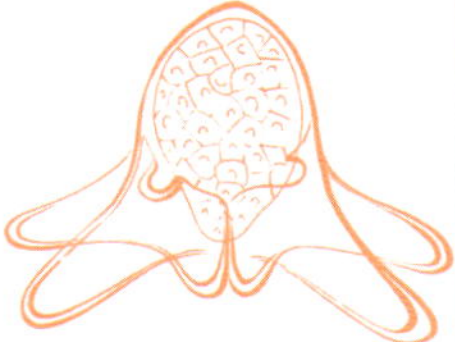

My work is often concerned with the poetics of place, and most recently with the writing and re-writing of historical narrative, and the representation of time and space in photography.[9]

Whybrew came upon the idea of photographing Folkestone hotel rooms while visiting and working in the town. He was interested in the contrasts between its 'architectural grandeur and the social and economic deprivation':

Originally interested in the hotels from a sociological perspective, over numerous visits I became more interested in the places themselves. Their affect, shaped by a multiplicity of histories, I found quite intriguing. My wanting to grasp something of those histories, and the knowledge that I could never do so through their mute foreclosing of the

ROWAN WHYBREW
Untitled, 2014

past, invested the hotels with a sense of presence, absent of historical meaning. To my mind they are places shaped by a historical imaginary and that was something I wanted to explore ...[10]

Whybrew's black-and-white photographs are like theatre sets. The rooms are large, and curtained spaces indicate mystery and promise. Shadowy figures may move in the deep shade that Whybrew documents – there may be a plot – perhaps a Miss Marple or a Morse waiting to solve a crime. They exude a kind of glamour, of better days, of times when Folkestone, with its grand hotels, was proud and prestigious.

Back in Margate, Bob Chicalors made a series of photographs of hotel rooms on an old smartphone (p.159):

At the time, I was documenting a romantic weekend away, which went on to illustrate my zine *Rumours*, where I was reviewing hotels in Margate alongside sexual encounters that took place in them. I love [the English seaside]! There is something uniquely British about a dirty weekend in a rundown seaside town in a rundown B & B. Hotels and guest houses are places that have always held an erotic fascination for me.

In the first issue of *Rumours*, there is a note: 'Have you had sex in a hotel in Margate / Do you remember the carpet? Did it match the curtains? If you can write a completely anonymous erotic review, drop us a line and we might print it.' The first review is of an encounter at the Smiths Court Hotel in February 2015:

His room is sea facing, and with curtains parted, I check out the view. Margate has barely woken up yet. The carpet is a fussy multi-pattern design that could hide all manner of sins, and bizarrely, the framed pictures are of Egyptian Papyrus. One of them is wonky and has slipped down in the frame.

In September 2012 there was an encounter at the Malvern Guest House and Blues Grill:

The first thing you notice about this distinctive B&B is the horrendous statues outside of the Blues Brothers. I don't know how long they've been there but you get the feeling that if Margate was to be inexplicably the target of a nuclear war (just like in [the film] *Threads* [1984]) those two figures would survive like cockroaches.

Another hotel room Chicalors describes is all black and silver like 'a "Next" catalogue has exploded'. *Rumours* is a compilation of encounters, maybe real, maybe fictional, in hotels and bars, set against the background of Margate sea and skies. There are Londoners with hipster rucksacks, guys in Burberrys, tourists. The meetings are almost accidental, chaotic, indecisive, peppered with descriptions of meals, drinks, drugs and sex. Margate seems both desperate and hopeful, a place where things can happen, beyond the dereliction. Chicalors is full of good cheer, buoyant and conscious of the madness of it all:

Think fake period chairs decorated with silver spraypaint, cheap nouveau riche wallpaper, clashing patterns, mirrored replica art deco bedside lamps and huge chenille metalled curtains. I immediately suss out the view, wrestling with the curtains to reveal a view of the Winter gardens, and Margate's famously inspirational sunsets. The windows don't open fully, too low down to be a suicide risk, simply not a wide enough gap to clamber onto the tiny decorative balcony outside the window.

The first issue of *Rumours* also contains a review of the Burlington Hotel:

The view from the room is classic Margate – the back end of some houses, a few overflowing bins, crumbling wooden fences, and a tiny sliver of sea glimpsed through some buildings. We crank the radiator on full blast and leave it. The sunlight does that special trick of making photos glow, and giving the room a royal air. Even though you can lick two walls and spit at the remaining pair without moving, it's enough space for our brief plan getting blind drunk and sleeping there. One of my room mates decorates the bathroom with toilet paper as a garland, and we crack open our deluxe dinner of Doritos and cheap Polish lager.

In this chapter's portfolio (pp.161–9), filmmaker and photographer Danielle Peck has recorded Ivy Gregory's last days at the Cecil Hotel in Cliftonville, Margate, in a series of photographs entitled *Many Original*

ABOVE AND BELOW

BOB CHICALORS
The Malvern Guest Hotel, and Blues Grill
Rumours Review,
September 2012

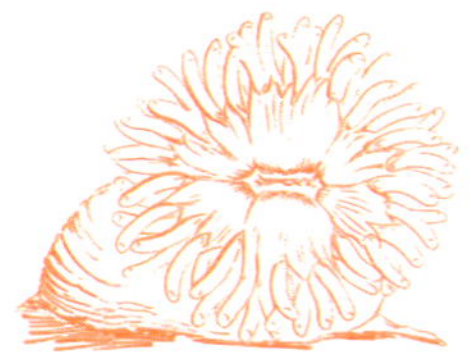

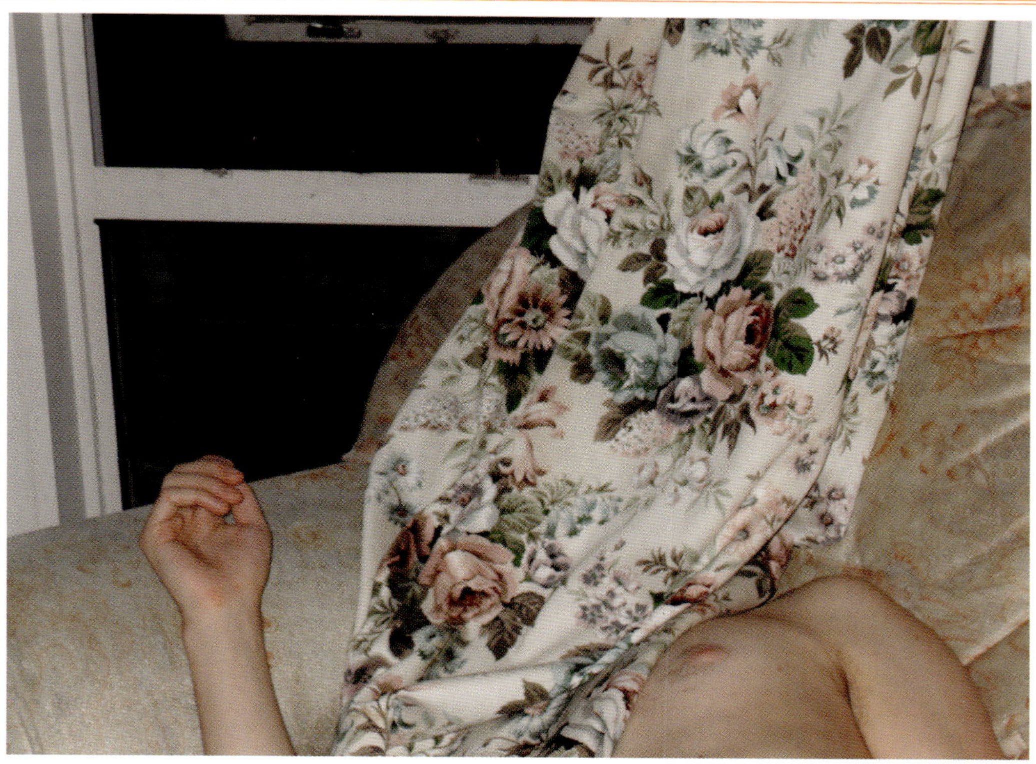

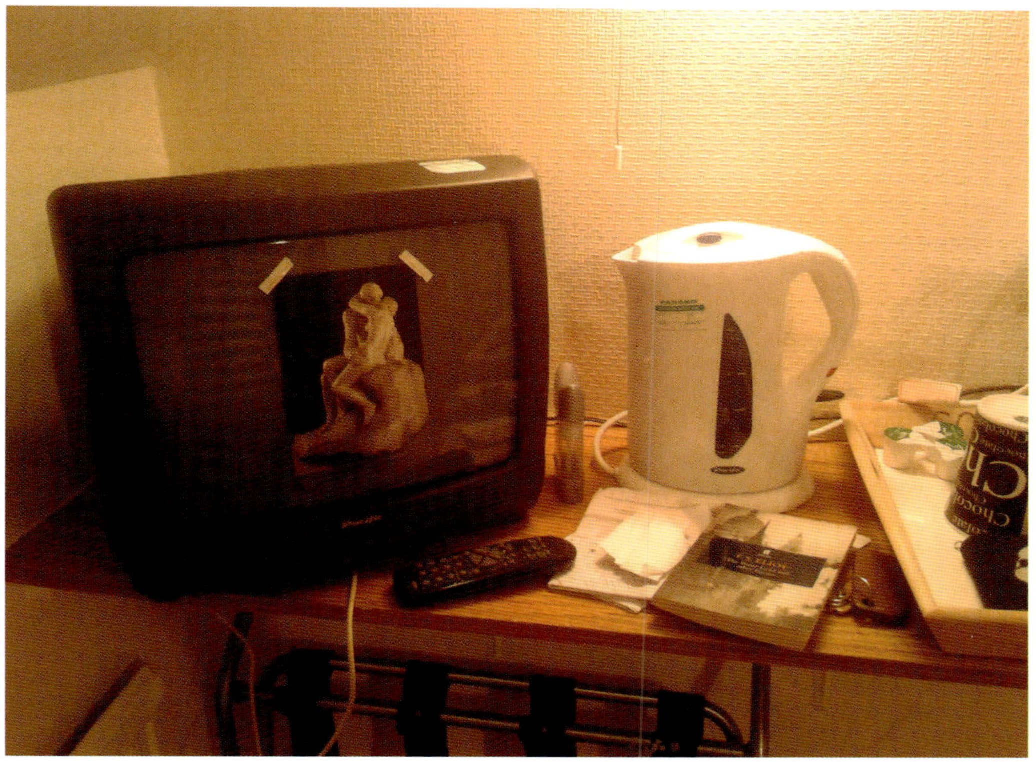

Features. The Cecil was largely untouched since the 1960s, and in its rooms, time stood still. In her photography, Peck seeks out the unconventional, from Afghan Hound racing and same-sex ballroom dancing to the hybrid sport of chess boxing. She has an eye for the joyfully marginal.

Like Iddon, Peck is interested in decline; the Cecil Hotel, at 12 Arthur Road in Margate, once fashionably modern, became a relic, a repository of geometric 1960s wallpapers, patterned fitted carpets, ancient Hoovers, portable televisions, slot machines and hand-written notices. It was built in 1895 and was a private house until 1930, when it became a hotel. Owned by the Gregory family from the 1950s, it was remodelled as holiday flatlets in the 1960s when Margate was booming. Ivy Gregory was the last owner, and the hotel ceased trading in the 1980s.[11]

There is a sense of astonishment in Peck's photographs; suspended in time, the interiors of the Cecil Hotel are subject to the photographer's steady documentary gaze, as histories fragmented and narratives constructed. Ivy Gregory poses calmly for Peck in unoccupied flatlets, shabby now and unused for many years. Her own sitting room is crowded and stacked, a receptacle for memories and the vestiges of the past.

The Cecil continued to be photographed after Ivy Gregory had left and the house was sold. Conservator–restorer Helen Hughes compiled the document: 'Arthur Road – No. 12: Investigation of Decorative Finishes (Exterior and Interiors).'[12] Hughes's photographs are of the empty interiors of the hotel, and show the traces of past occupation and decoration through the discovery of wallpapers and the scientific analysis of paint layers. Throughout its existence, and long before it was a hotel, the Cecil has been documented by photographers, through family photography, the still gaze of the critical documentarist and the cool view of the scientist. Photography layers the past, gives us myriad glimpses into histories that seem so distant. We try in vain to hear, smell or see this place and, in the end, can only imagine it.

The hotel rooms explored here by these photographers are the opposite of what we desire. Iddon rejoices in them because of the memories that they hold and the sheer photogenicness of these fading spaces. He admires their decency and unpretentiousness. Peck uncovers a family history embedded in the very fabric of a building facing transformation, its fraying modernity beyond redemption. Whybrew, in the grand interiors of once-magnificent Folkestone creates a monochrome mystery where something is always hidden, while Chicalors choreographs a rumbustious comedy of youth and chaos.

All that is missing from these seaside rooms are the guests. They are hinted at by Chicalors as partners in sexual encounters, and sometimes we see a partial reflection on a mirror, but elsewhere they are absent. There are traces of their disappointment in the online reviews that live on even when the hotels have closed. Stains and frays, lukewarm water and bad breakfasts. 'Don't stay here,' they implore.

For photographers, however, this is fine material – shabbiness suits photography. Loss and mystery and a glimmer of what used to be, the glance of a stranger, the swish of a curtain, the melancholy handwriting of rules and regulations. We have all stayed in hotels like these – a late booking, a sudden impulse, a series of mistakes, an enveloping gloom. [vw]

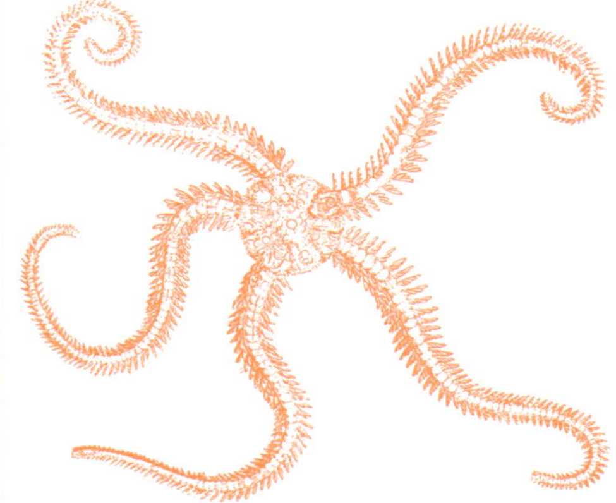

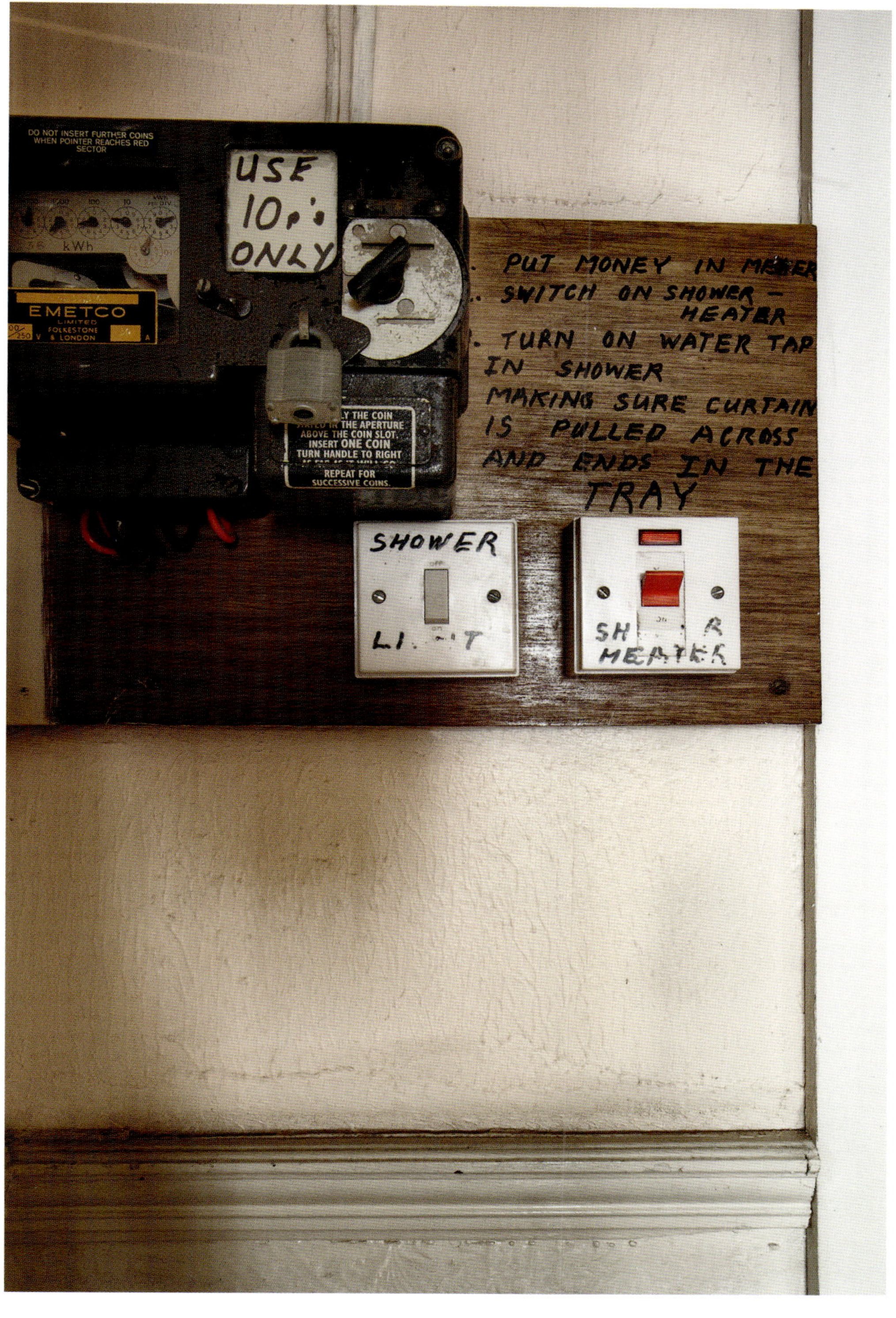
USE
10p's
ONLY
EMETCO
LIMITED
FOLKESTONE
& LONDON
DO NOT INSERT FURTHER COINS
WHEN POINTER REACHES RED
SECTOR
PUT MONEY IN METER
SWITCH ON SHOWER -
HEATER
TURN ON WATER TAP
IN SHOWER
MAKING SURE CURTAIN
IS PULLED ACROSS
AND ENDS IN THE
TRAY
SHOWER
LIGHT
SHOWER
HEATER

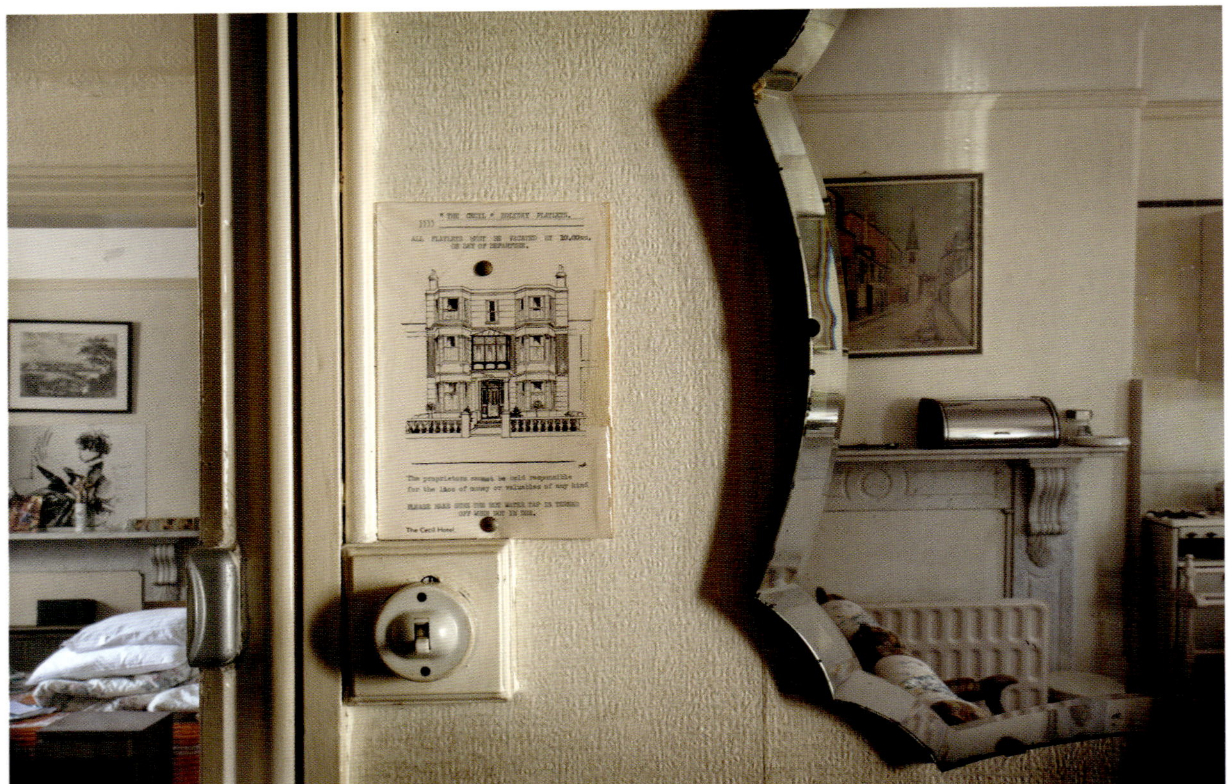

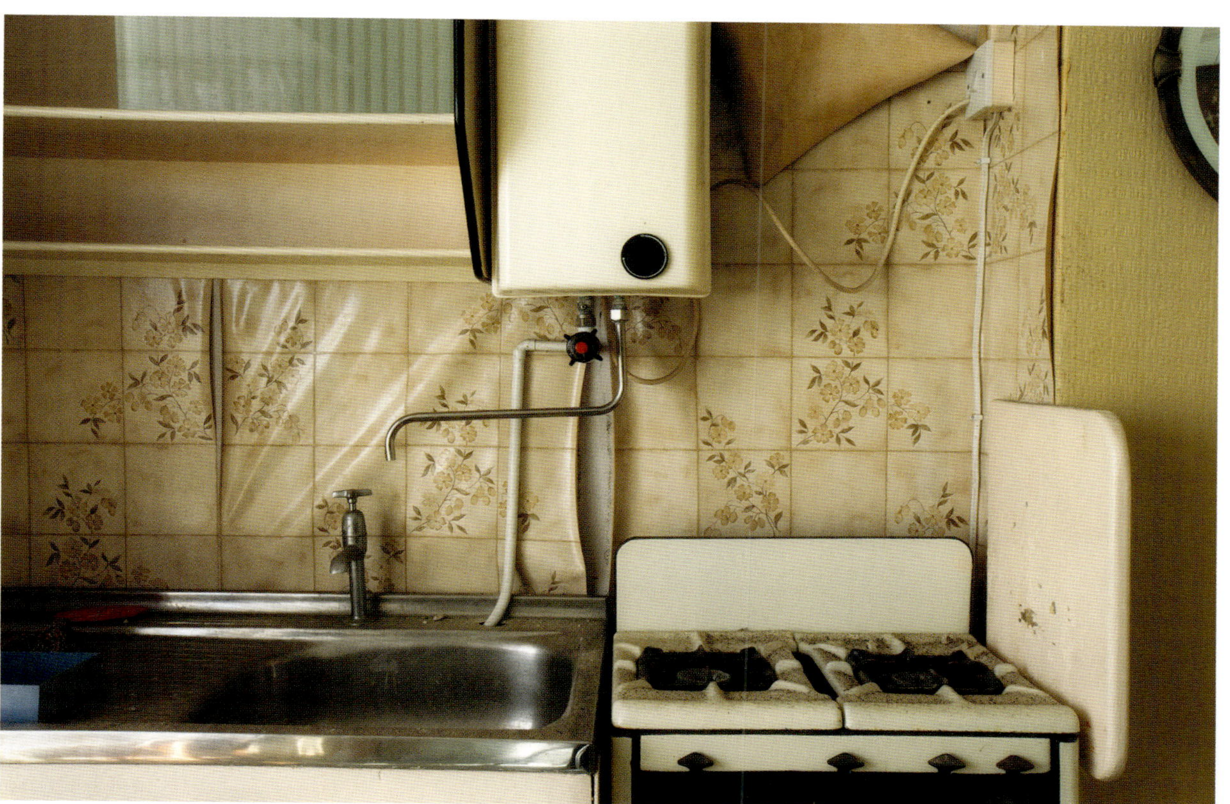

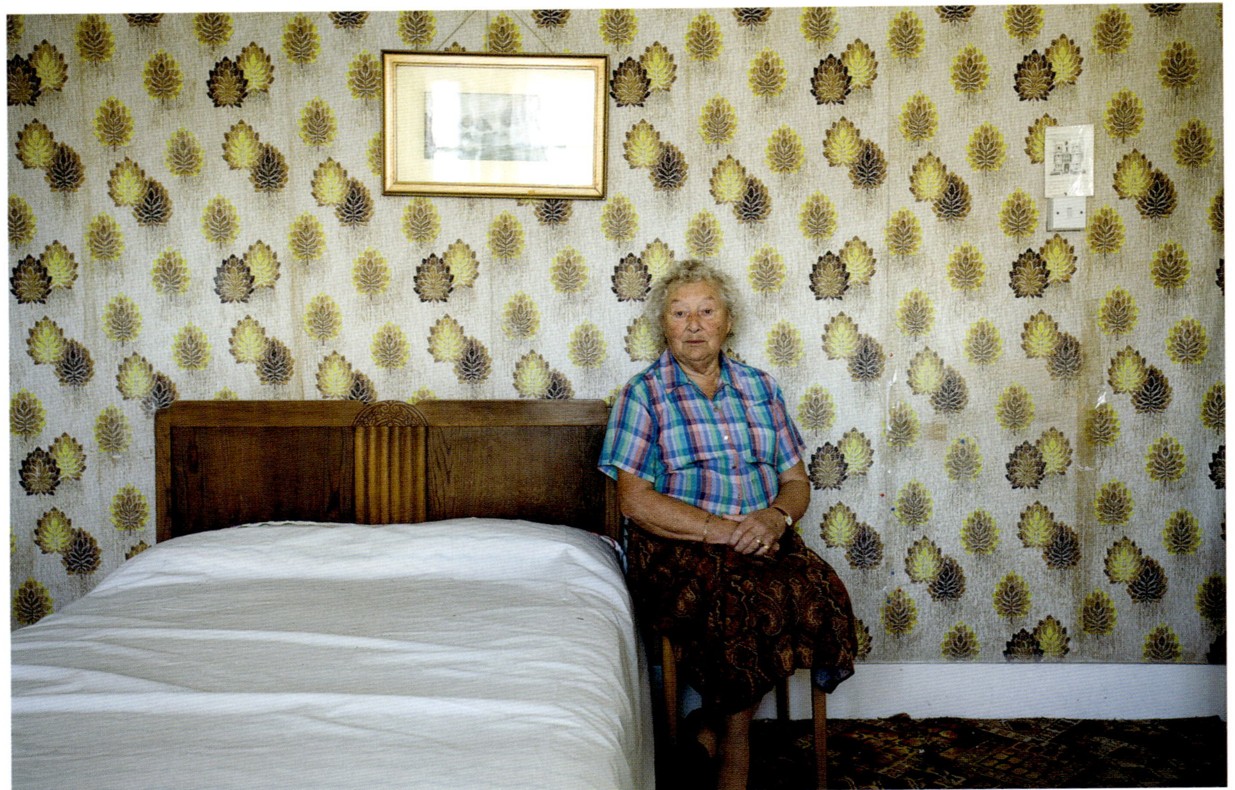

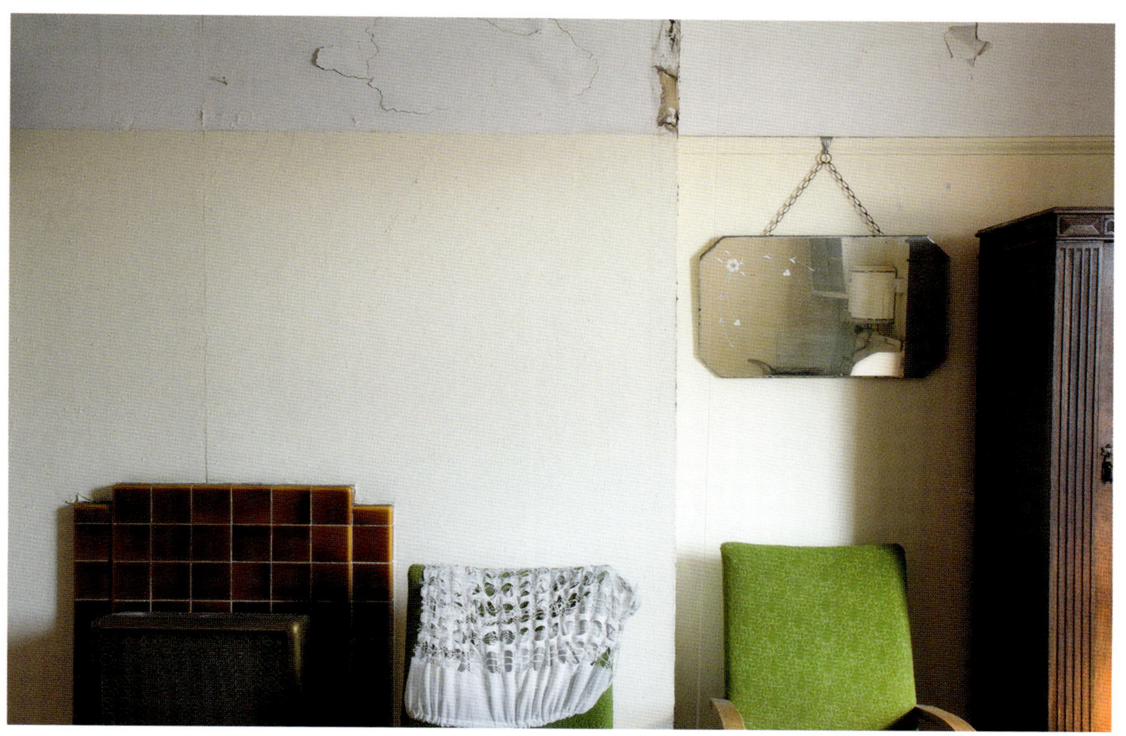

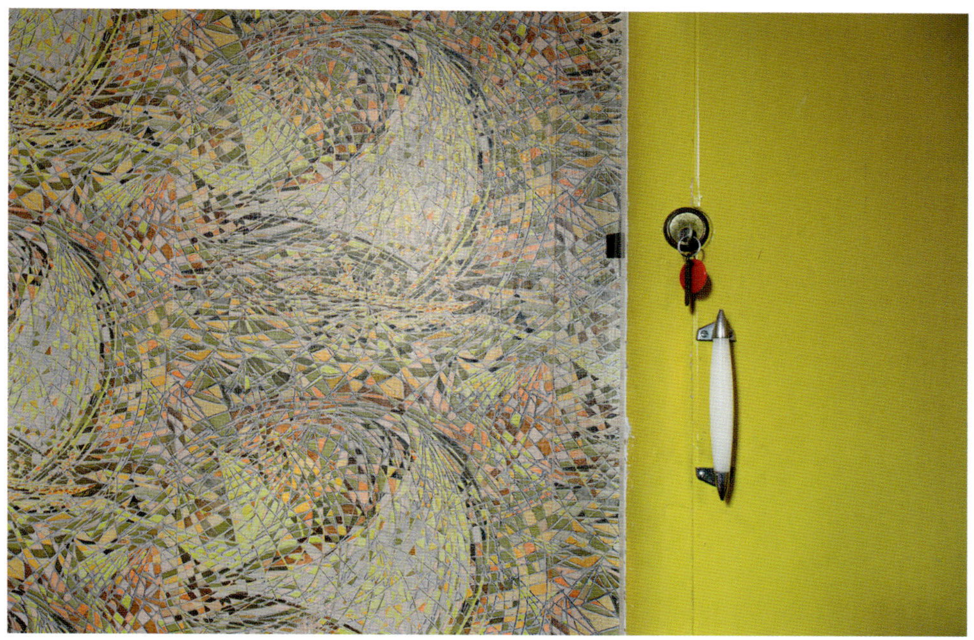

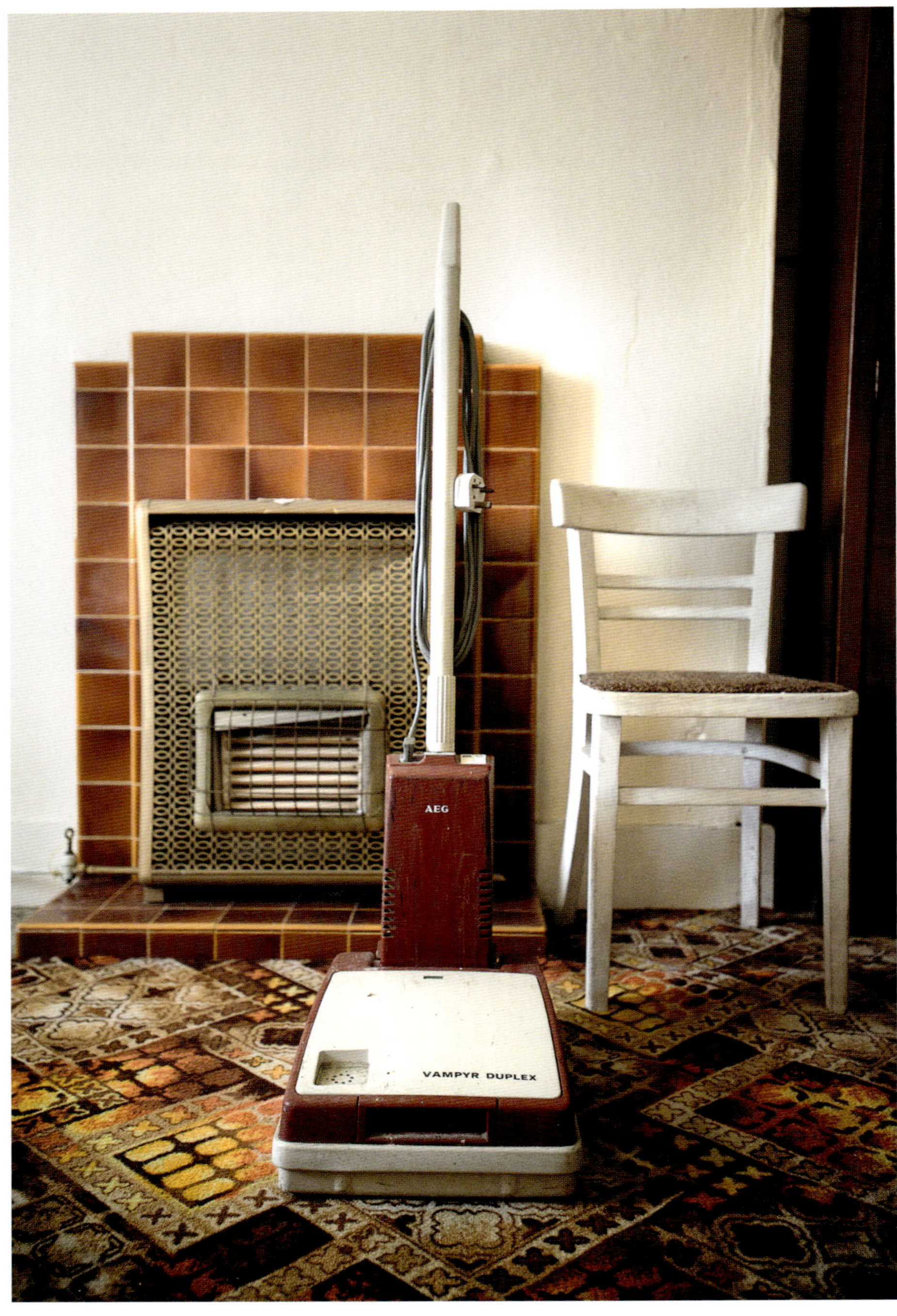
AEG
VAMPYR DUPLEX

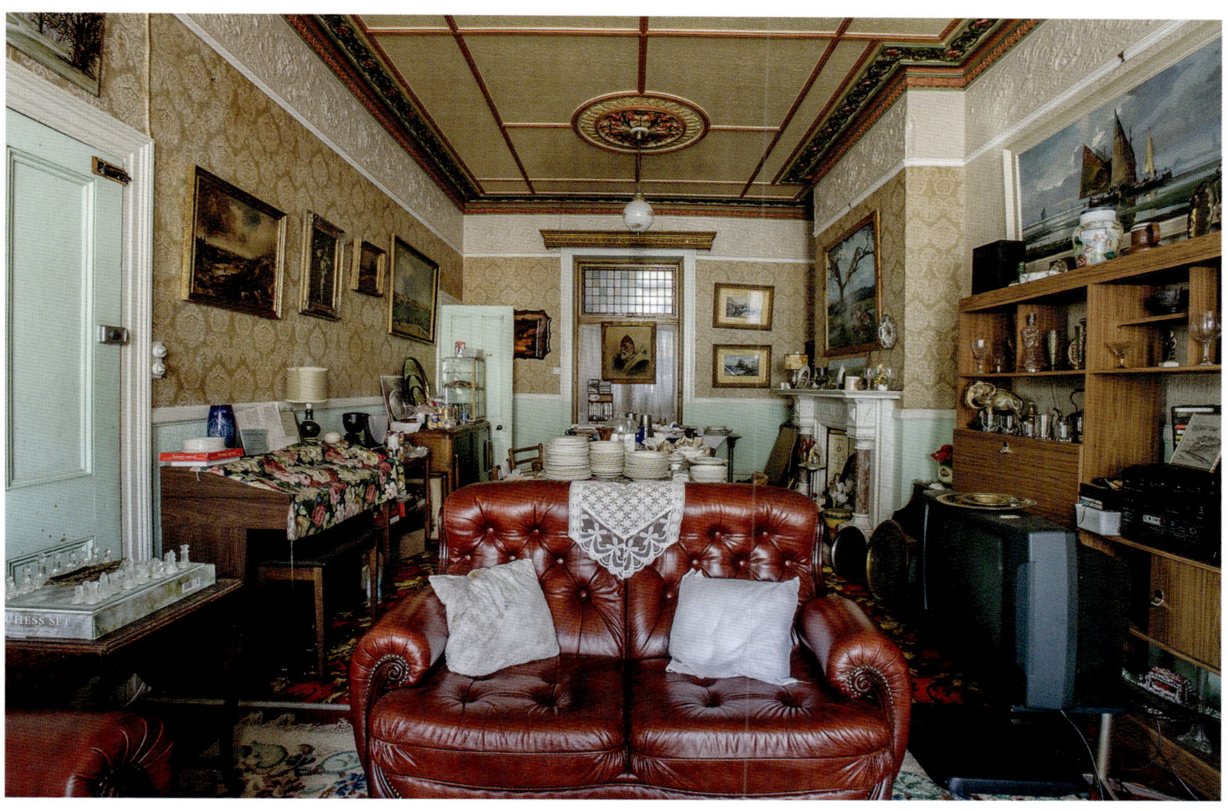

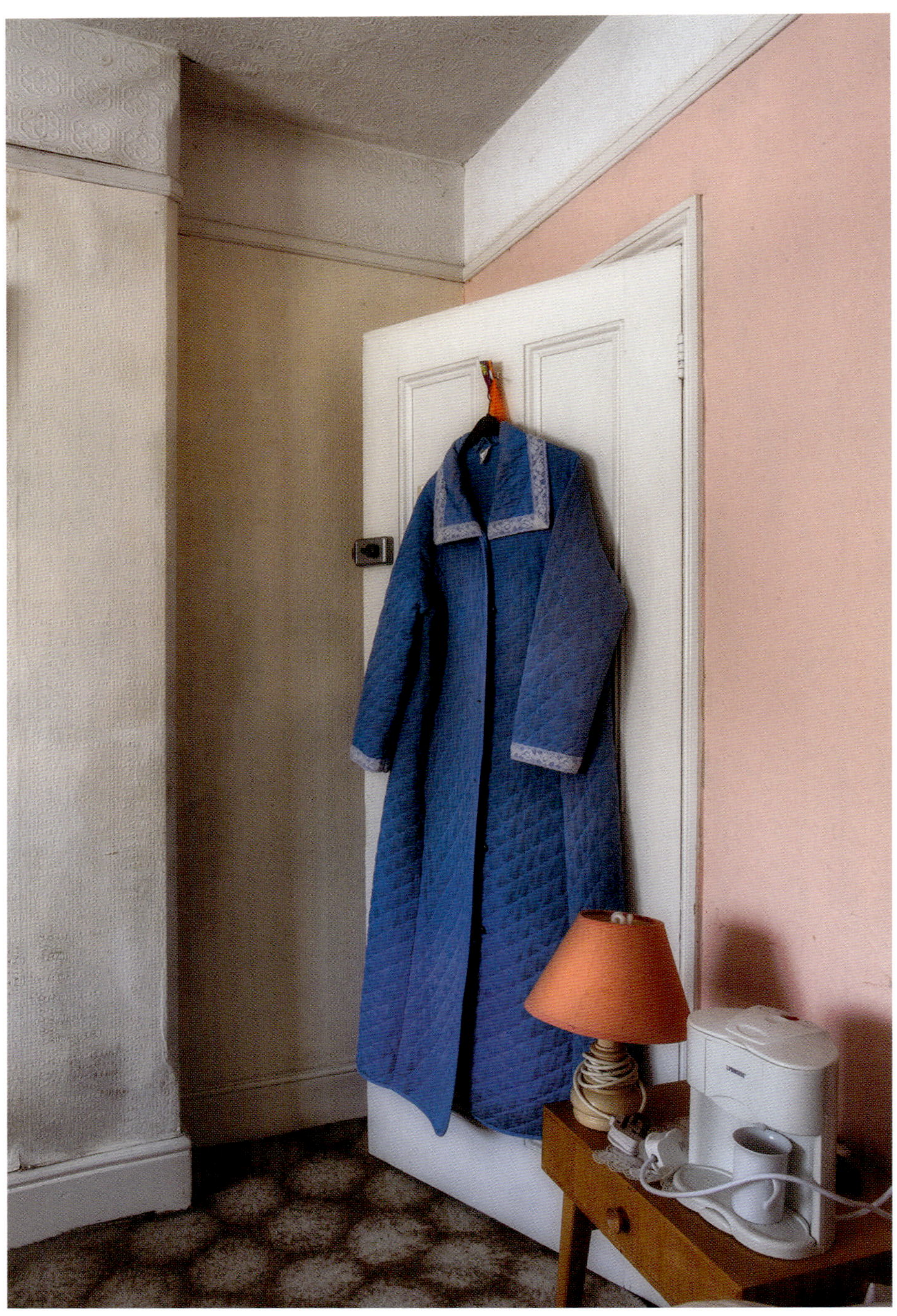

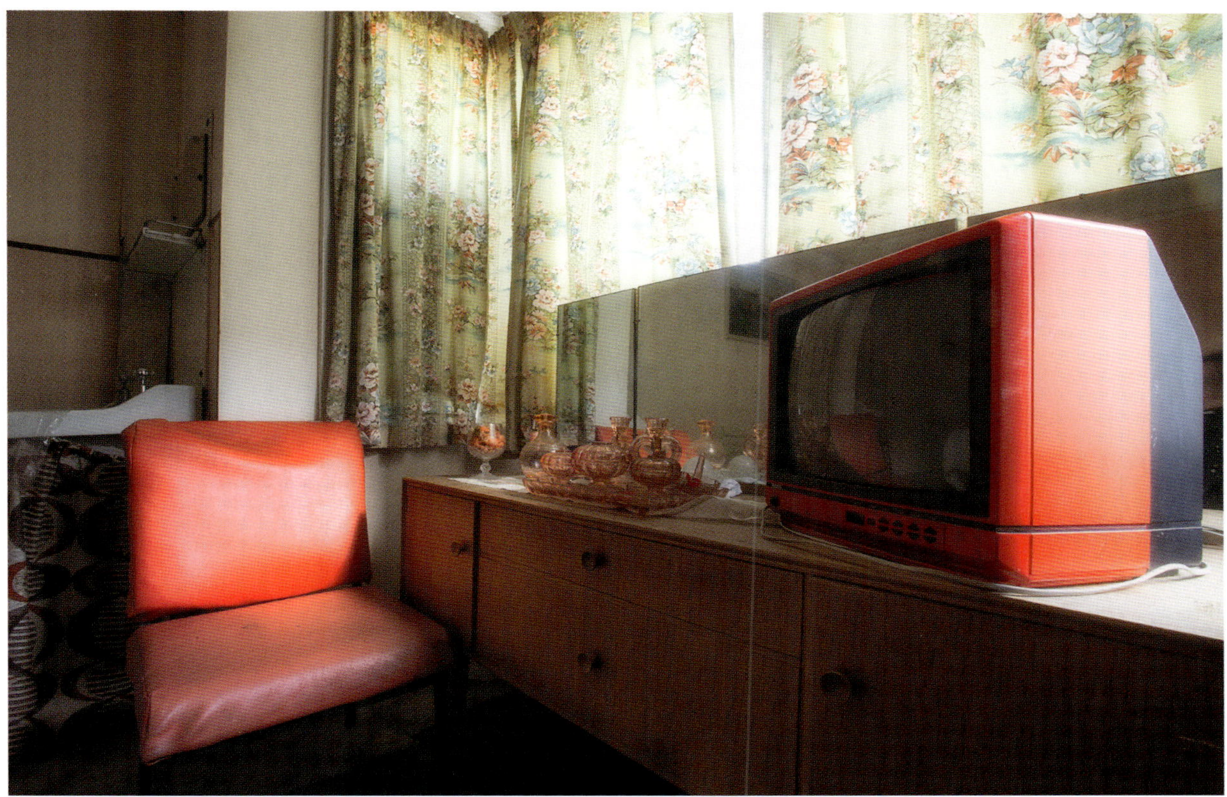

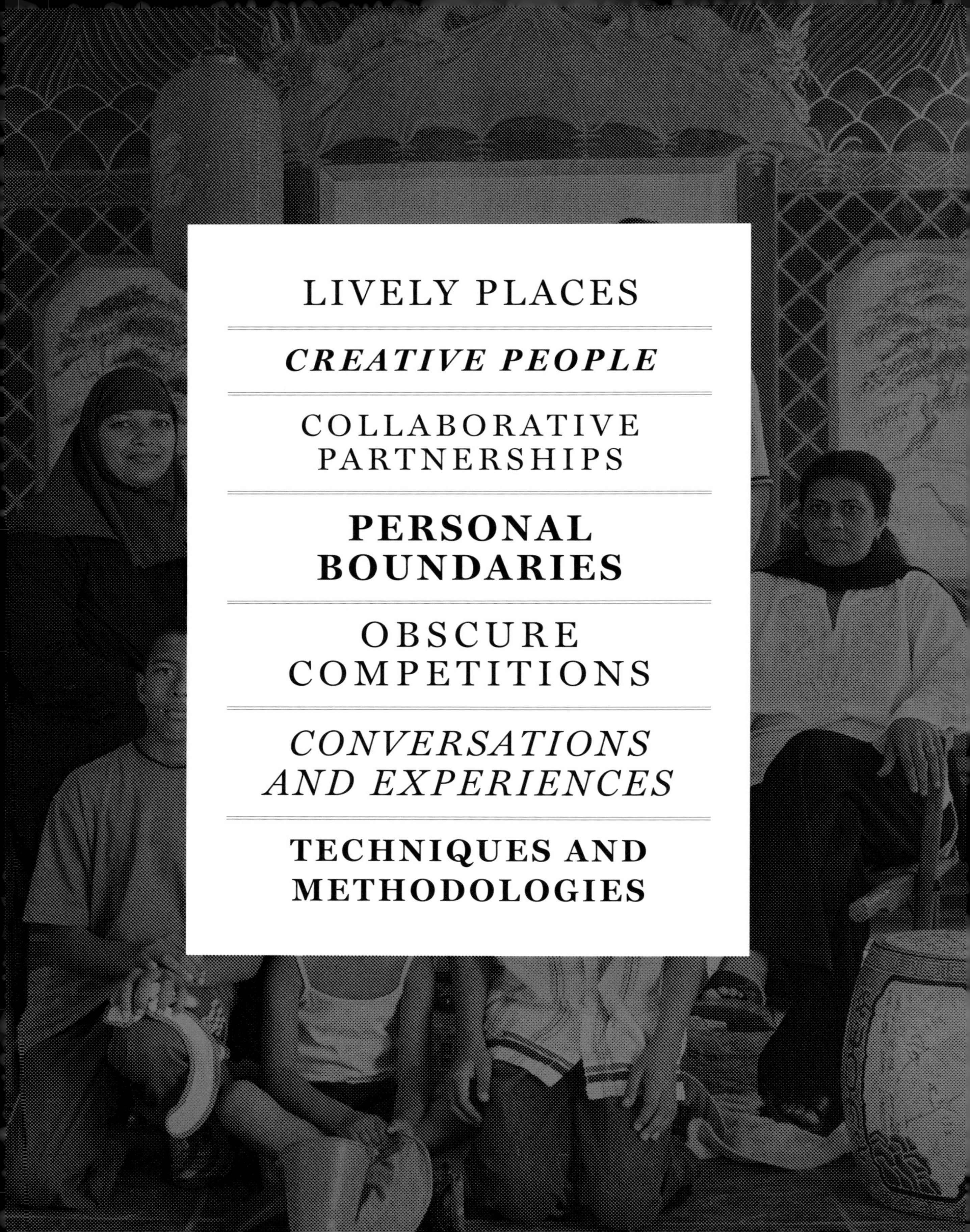

LIVELY PLACES

CREATIVE PEOPLE

COLLABORATIVE
PARTNERSHIPS

PERSONAL
BOUNDARIES

OBSCURE
COMPETITIONS

CONVERSATIONS
AND EXPERIENCES

TECHNIQUES AND
METHODOLOGIES

GAZING UP CLOSE

AND FROM

A DISTANCE

PERFORMING STUDIO PORTRAITURE
IN THE 21ST CENTURY

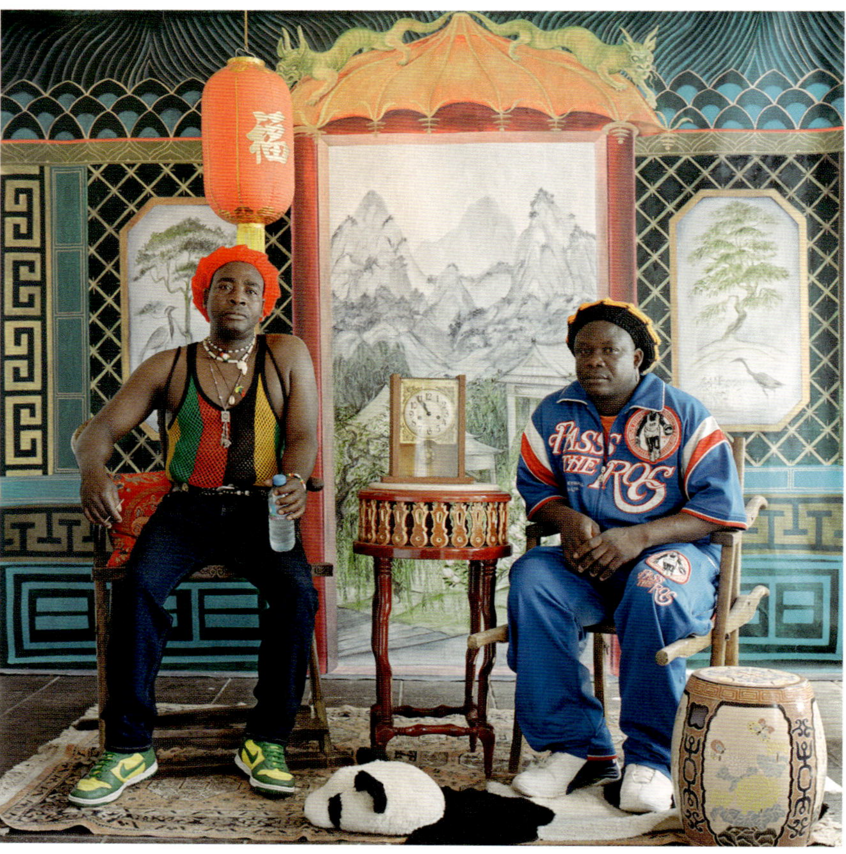

At the beginning of the new century, photographer Grace Lau, who moved (in 1998) from North London to the seaside town of Hastings in Sussex, decided to set up a portrait studio in the community arts facility of St Mary in the Castle, on Hastings seafront. The studio was on a busy route, a few doors away from the Iceland store and the Borough Parking Office, and within viewing distance of the roundabout fountain designed by Sidney Little in the 1950s and on the main route into the tourist draw of Hastings Old Town. When Lau moved there, Hastings was already known as a sympathetic and lively place for creative people to live, and she soon became part of a tight-knit artists' community. Born in China in 1939, Lau settled permanently in North London in 1948. Speaking with photographer Anna Fox in 1995, she remembered the challenges of living in London as a Chinese teenager, attempting to reconcile

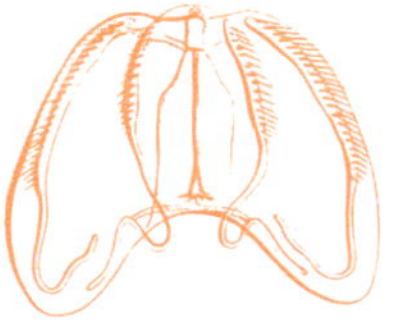

the conflicting demands of her English and Chinese identities.[1]

After a lengthy period of travelling as a young woman, Lau signed up for a photography course at Harrow School of Art, and then, in 1992, enrolled on the legendary Documentary Photography course led by Magnum photographer David Hurn in Newport, Wales. She began to develop her practice of photographing fetishism and a range of sexualities. For her, the notion of colliding cultures was an important one – growing up as a Chinese teenager in England was complex. In the 1980s and 1990s she embraced feminism, soon became involved in emerging women's photography initiatives and set up the Exposures group to create collaborative partnerships around photographing the male nude. The entirety of her work has been about identity, from her book on the history of Chinese photography,

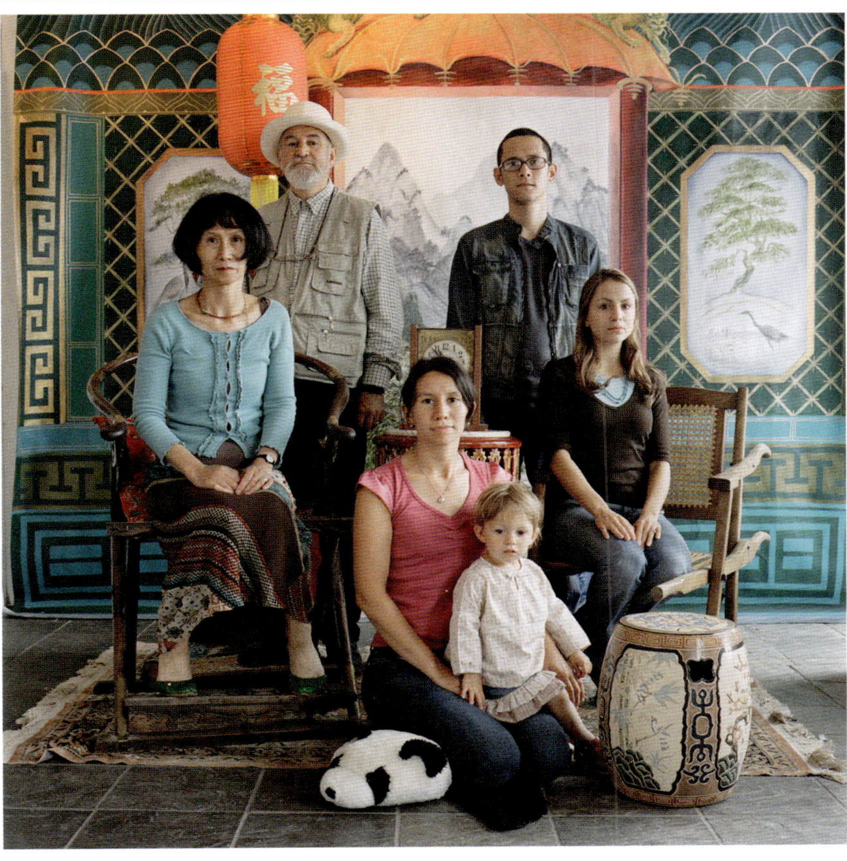

GRACE LAU
Untitled, from the series
21st Century Types,
July/August 2005

and its relationship with the British Empire, to her work on fetish for *Skin Two* magazine.

The Chinese Portrait Studio in Hastings, where she made her series *21st Century Types* (2005), was furnished from Hastings's many secondhand shops to look like a Victorian photography studio, and with a backdrop painted by artist Robina Barson, it explored in a dramatic and complex way the relationships between Chinese and British culture, through medium-format colour studio portraiture. Writing in 2018 about the motivation behind the Chinese Portrait Studio, Lau remembered:

> I had come down to live in Hastings in 1998, having completed my book on the subculture fetish–S&M scene in London [*Adults in Wonderland*, 1997] and feeling slightly jaded by working intimately with a community that defied normal standards of behaviour and roles. The notion of perversity had been questioned in my former work and I had pushed personal boundaries as well as social ones. I had to shift my photographer role to morph into the fantasies that were performed by my subjects for my camera. My personal identity as a Chinese female photographer had been slowly fading into undefined grey, like an under-exposed black-and-white negative.[2]

The portrait studio, free to all comers, was one very clear way in which Lau could set out her identity as a Chinese–British artist and find a defined place in a community that, although by no means hostile to newcomers, had its own rituals and hierarchies. The cultural life of Hastings was very much determined by the notion of spectacle,

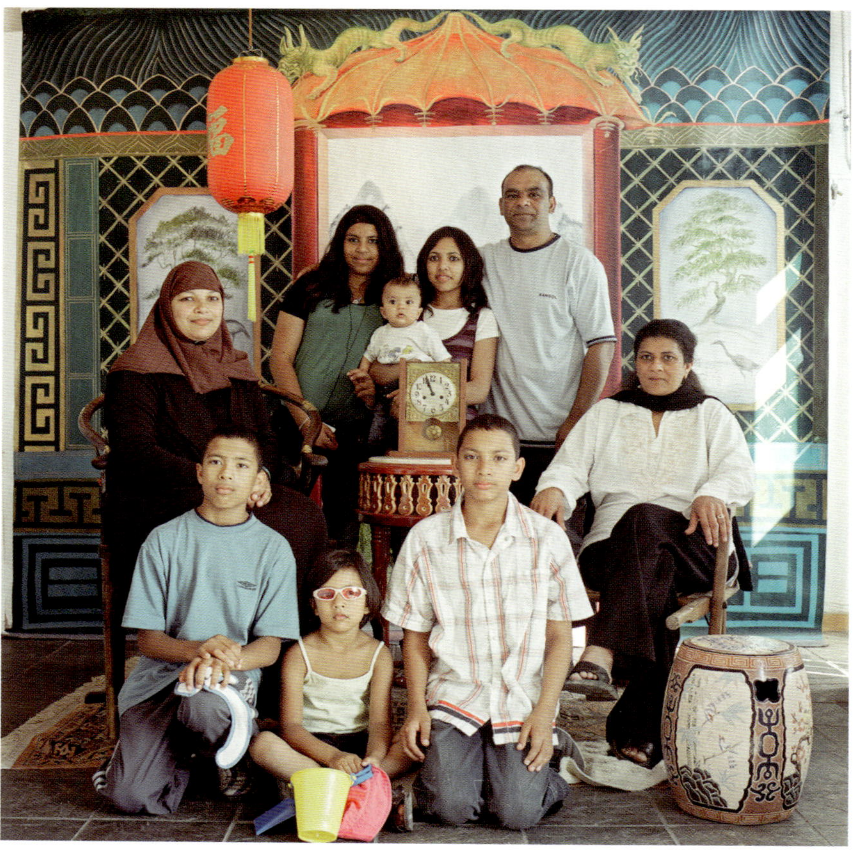

centred around parades, special days, pirates, carnivals, obscure competitions and pub culture. As she remembers: 'After all, they appeared not too different from my fetishists and fantasists in terms of dressing up and presenting a performance. Hastings seaside was as much a stage for theatrical tableaux as a dominatrix dungeon or a fetish rubber ball: A perfect setting for a portrait project.'[3]

As well as traditional day-trippers and a scattering of weekenders, Hastings was attracting a flow of London artists seeking more space and a greater sense of community. The painter John Bratby was a prominent resident for many years, as was the singer–songwriter John Martyn. Surrounded by a large hinterland of villages, Hastings was rapidly becoming a regional centre of entertainment and consumption. But Hastings was nevertheless a monoculture, with poor employment prospects, high levels of child

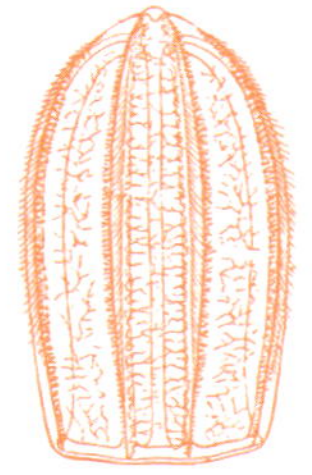

and adult poverty and a notorious 'decanting' process of poor families from London boroughs to decaying private accommodation. A free portrait studio on the seafront could capture some of this:

> I didn't know what to expect when I first arrived at the seaside resort; probably a restful and undemanding home to explore walks in the nearby woods. I glimpsed only a handful of other Asians or black people, apart from those few working in the ubiquitous take-away cafes/shops, so the difference between living in London where being a foreigner was relatively irrelevant to now being an apparently single Asian face here was a vast change. I knew the seaside resort was an alien concept to Asian culture as it represented a place of lower status in comparison to the

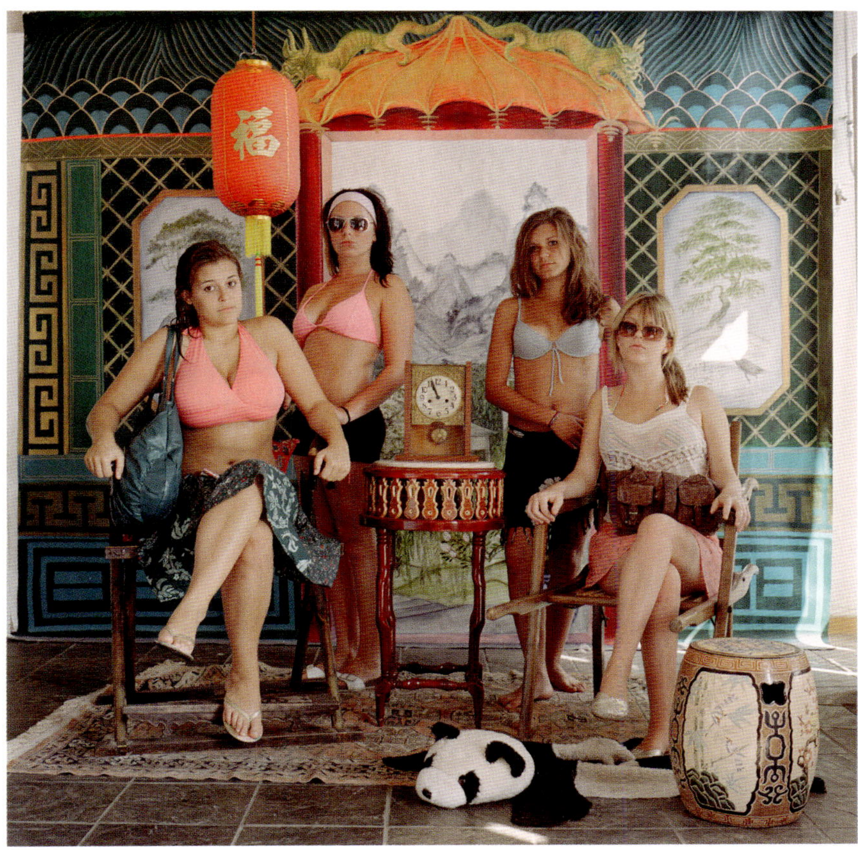

elite urban cities and I felt strangely rather self-conscious. But, in fact, nobody took any notice of my presence and after a few months, I began to feel relaxed amongst the diverse 'tribes' in Hastings.

It had taken me over a year to integrate sufficiently into the fetish scene to allow me freedom of access. Can I now explore my new community and will they be comfortable in front of my camera?[4]

The rationale for the portrait studio was based on August Sander's monumental photograph series 'People of the Twentieth Century', begun in Germany in 1922. Published as *Anlitz de Zeit* (*Face of Our Time*) in 1936, it was divided into seven categories of people and place, and immediately incurred Nazi disapproval. The printing plates were destroyed

GRACE LAU
Untitled, from the series
21st Century Types,
July/August 2005

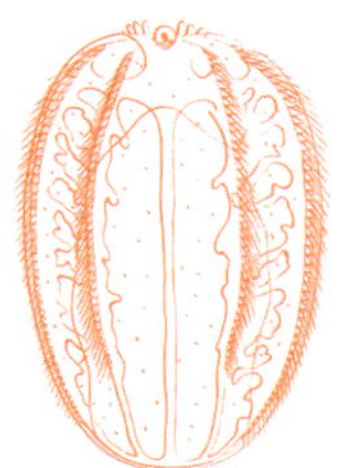

and many thousands of negatives were consumed by fire. For Lau, whose own family had been traumatically displaced by totalitarianism and who, as a teenager in London, had struggled with divided identities, 'People of the Twentieth Century' was a resonant model. Portrait photography is to do with how you look, more than with who you are, and since the early years of photography, studio and itinerant portraitists have laboured to make their subjects look as they want to be seen. Seaside studios, dealing often with people passing through, thrived on novelty, speed and commercial acumen. For Lau, funded by an Arts Council diversity grant, there was no commercial imperative.

It was a sunny summer and Hastings teemed with tourists and local life. It didn't take long before strolling families started to drop in, delighted to find a photography studio to pose in, and to get a free digital print from my assistant. I played the formal photographer, asking them to sit still and look serious while I fussed with focusing and waited for the right shutter second. I also asked them to keep their accessories in the pose, their sunglasses, coke bottles, ice cream, mobiles, souvenirs, sunhats, … plastic bags … all this added a contemporary layer to my old-fashioned studio, compressing history and the present into one eclectic image. Families were squeezed together, yowling babies and barking dogs; couples played up to my camera; macho bikers fidgeted with their helmets; gay couples smooched with their pups and pups tried to pee on my panda rug.[6]

The resulting 400-photograph series, made over six weeks, with everyone who had posed receiving a free digital print, is probably the most extensive and significant portrait study made in post-war Britain. 'Through this project', Lau wrote recently,

I am making an oblique comment on Imperialist visions of the 'exotic' Chinese and by reversing roles, I have become the Imperialist photographer documenting my exotic subjects in the 'Port' of Hastings … Types were recorded by Western missionaries who portrayed beggars, blind orphans and scenes of poverty to raise money from back home for their cause and to 'convert the heathens from their backward ways'. [7]

Although Hastings lacked the multiculturalism of London, Lau showed that diversity could still be discovered within British seaside society of the 1990s. These rich, many-layered, opulent portraits, made in a community centre on a scruffy seafront, by a Chinese feminist photographer more used to portraying the fetish underworld than families with ice creams, are a monument to

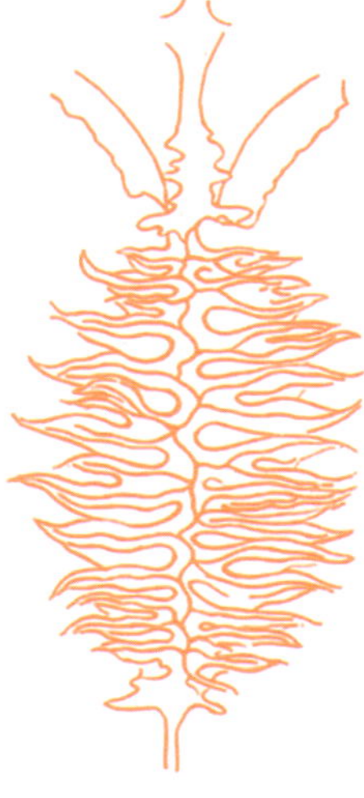

place, race, people and the passing of time, and a direct political comment on the use of photography as propaganda.

Lau's positioning of herself as an outsider photographer, drawn to the south coast of England to photograph the procession of 'types' that passed in front of her camera, was essentially performative – acting the part of the stern Chinese studio portraitist who would not allow her subjects to smile, she created a theatre of photography in which the émigré's drama is played out. All the children in Lau's photographs will now be almost adults, almost all the dogs will have passed away. Partnerships and friendships may have fractured, or still be sound; family groups will have morphed, reformed, grown larger or smaller. Everyone will have a photograph of that day in the summer, five years into the twenty-first century.

Some years later, in 2009, London photographer Jason Wilde drove down to Hastings to set up another free portrait studio on the seafront:

In July 2009, I started the project and spent two weeks on the south coast visiting a variety of towns that included Bexhill-on-Sea, Hastings, Brighton, Margate and Whitstable. After chasing and wrestling my 9ft × 6ft collapsible background along the seaside promenades in windy rain, I decided that an outdoor project was too unpredictable.[8]

The Jason Wilde Portrait Studio in Hastings opened in an empty shop during the Hastings Carnival and is the focus of this chapter's portfolio (pp.180–7). It was very popular, with long queues for the three portrait sessions held over one week, open to all and free. Wilde funded the project himself, and although he did not continue his plans to photograph right along the south coast, the Hastings studio marked the beginning of series of Free Portrait Studios in North London, which continued until 2017 and produced over two thousand photographs.

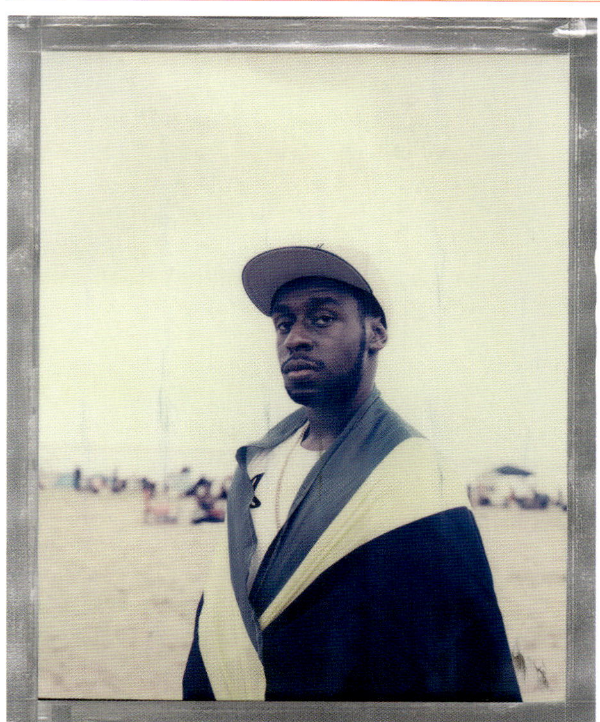

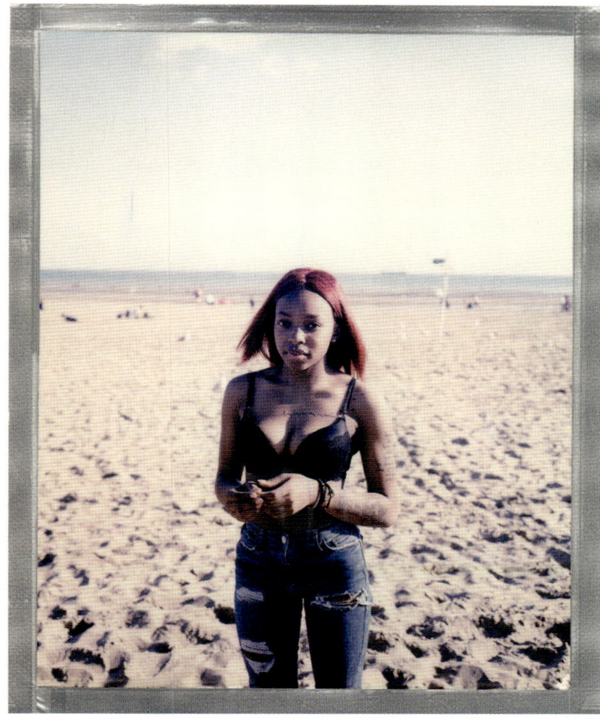

To look back through Wilde's studio portraits, all made against a plain background, is to mark the passing of time, changing faces, a seaside society of the transient and the fixed, assuming identities that we read into them – canvases on which we can impress our thoughts and imaginations. A beautiful woman in a flowing grey dress is a character from Virginia Woolf, and here is a boy straight from *Great Expectations*. A girl in pink is Queen for a week and will ride on a float and will have a glimpse into what it is like to be famous; kind Keith in the straw hat, who had a Roma mother, has not been seen for many years (p.187).

The studio portrait is evidence of a passing through, of a brief partnership between photographer and photographed, where the nature of the contract is clearly understood. No one makes silly faces or clowns around in either Lau's or Wilde's studios. These are serious spaces in which history is made. The props in Lau's studio were significant – in Wilde's there are none, but the gravitas is the same.

Along the coast from Hastings, on the bleak isle of Thanet with its cluster of seaside resorts, photographer Rob Ball has made a series of ferrotypes and polaroids, some on the annual Jamaica Day celebrations in Margate (above). In *Contemporary Itinerant* (2012), Ball set up a number of temporary studios and darkrooms in Margate and Blackpool that would reflect back upon nineteenth-century commercial beach photography. As a thriving seaside resort in the nineteenth century and up until the late 1960s, Margate, like most British seaside towns, was home to many portrait photographers, both fixed and itinerant. Travelling beach photographers lived in horse-drawn caravans or simply camped on the beach, producing wet collodion or ferrotype images.

Itinerant photographers were seen not as artists, but as hawkers – in the United States they were called 'kidnappers' because they offered free portraits of children only to then demand payment for prints.[9] In her remarkable book *Itinerant Photographer: Corpus Christi*,[10] Sybil Miller describes the operation of a travelling photographer in Corpus Christi, Texas, who, in 1934, spent several weeks in the town making photographs of local businesses. When he had supplied the prints, and collected his takings, he moved on, leaving his plate negatives with a local photographer.

In the Australian outback, in the late 1940s, after wartime service on Operation Overlord, English portrait photographer Ursula Powys-Lybbe set up her Touring Camera portrait studio and, with broadcaster Clare Mitchell, travelled around the outback in a Buick with a caravan in tow. As we have seen in the 1970s, Daniel Meadows, Dafydd Jones and Martin Parr all became Butlin's holiday camp 'walkies', making and selling portraits to holiday-makers. In the 1990s, both Wilde and Richard Primrose were employed as travelling photographers and salesmen, canvassing for work on London's outer council estates.

Early beach photographers were low in the hierarchy of studio portraiture and, right up until their eventual demise in the 1980s, 'walkies' were seen as just another ploy to separate punter from money. To the proprietors of the land-based studios in nineteenth-century resorts, they must have seemed little better than hawkers. To their customers, they provided a unique service, a way, through the magical, metallic object of the ferrotype, to create their own memory of their visit to the seaside. Rob Ball decided to revisit itinerant beach photography in 2012:

> The *Contemporary Itinerant* was a reworking of the Victorian beach photographer and saw the creation of photographic beach portraits using the antique and unique ferrotype and Polaroid process. Small mobile darkrooms were built *in situ*, creating a spectacle and allowing viewers to see their portrait shortly after its creation. The work was then displayed in two exhibitions.[11]

By repositioning itinerant photography as art practice, and setting up his touring studio in locations in Margate and elsewhere, Ball explored the way in which photographer and subject collaborate to create portraits. Shorn of the opportunism and gimmickry that entrepreneurial itinerants had to demonstrate as they canvassed among the great seaside crowds of the late nineteenth and early twentieth centuries, Ball offered a partnership, a contemporary way of making this collaborative portraiture:

> People were surprised, engaged, flattered and always willing to take part. The large camera creates a kind of formality to the interaction (hence the often serious poses) and feels more like a collaboration as the sitter has the opportunity to pose/sit as they wish … The added element of the mobile darkroom was used at Walpole Bay/ Jamaica Day – this was me riffing off the Victorian portrait photographer … The plate camera provided a sense of spectacle and the kids enjoyed looking in and seeing each other upside down.[12]

Looking through Ball's *Contemporary Itinerant*, we are taken back into the wonders of early photography. The portrait subjects photographed by nineteenth-century beach photographers must have been amazed by these otherworldly photographs emerging from the wet-collodion process, with its tendency to highlight skin flaws, freckles and the tracery of the human face. Twenty-first-century people stare from Ball's photographs as if they had been transported back to those early days of portraiture, where the magic of photography provided a miraculous likeness. We view the late nineteenth century through the prism of photography, and the people that we see in photographs seem so remote from us, so ancient.

By interrogating techniques and methodologies, Ball has shown us the remarkable facility that photography has to change the real, to imprint on our minds what the camera has seen, rather than what was actually there. In Ball's wet-collodion photographs, there are

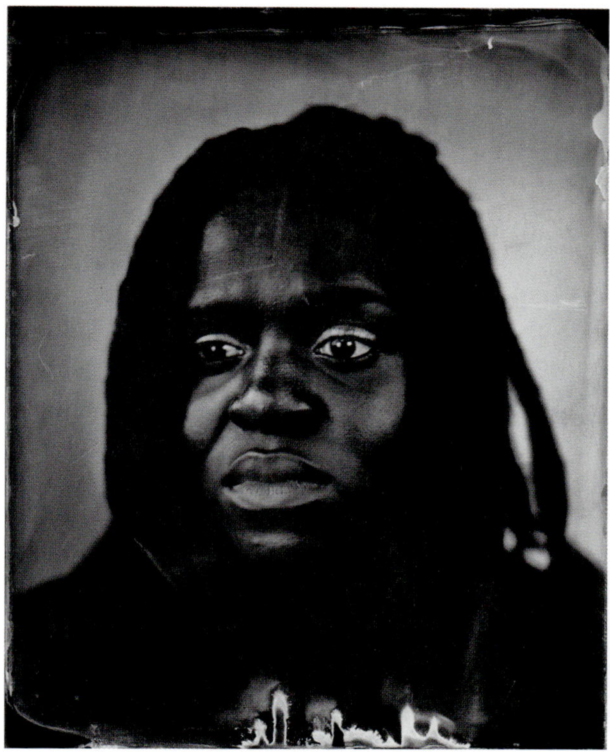

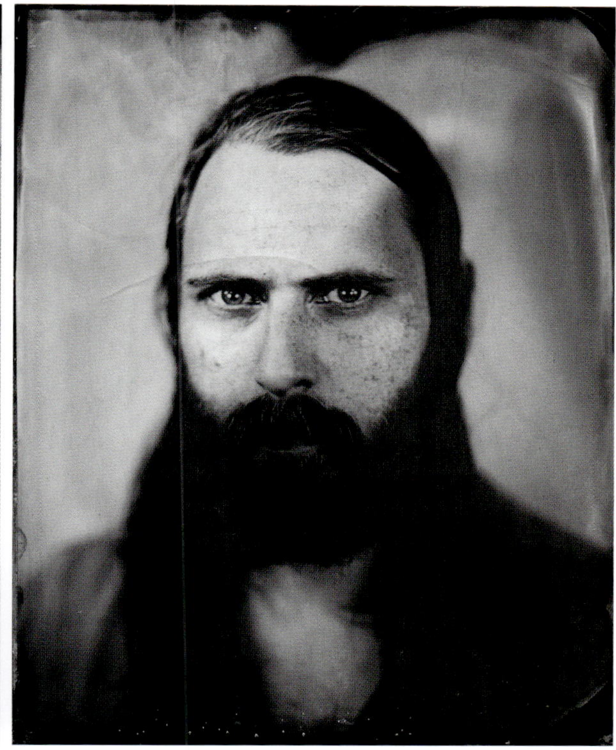

traces of the great local studio photographers of the past – Mike Disfarmer in Heber Springs, Akansas, with his austere photographs of the men women and children who came to his studio, comes to mind. Ball's photographs, like all portrait groups, reflect change – the day-trippers and boarding-house residents of Margate have been joined by a new kind of resident – informed, creative and fashionably dressed. These portraits glimmer like ghosts of the present, the twenty-first century is transposed to the nineteenth and a magical tale is spun.

In their seaside studios, Lau, Ball and Wilde have initiated arenas for the public performance of portraiture, re-enacting the complicitness of photographer and subject. The liminal and repurposed space of the seashore and the shared collective memory of the studio portrait were constituent parts of these photographic experiences. Commercial seaside portrait studios have almost disappeared – by the 1970s, the photo booth, with its primitive and distinctive miniature

LEFT
ROB BALL
Raliat,
Margate Portrait Studio,
June 2013

RIGHT
ROB BALL
Joss,
Margate Portrait Studio,
July 2012

images, had emerged as both a utilitarian and a performance space and now, digital technology has made us all into photographers. The absence of the well-composed, carefully lit studio photograph in our contemporary family histories is a significant one. A sense of order and timelessness has been replaced by more informal mechanisms. We are all, somehow, slightly less grown up. [vw]

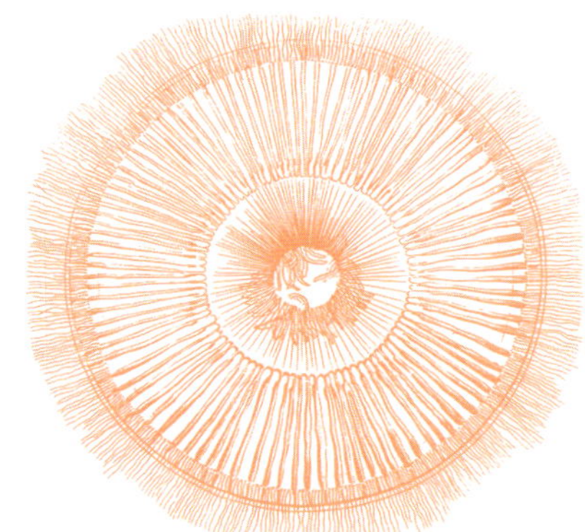

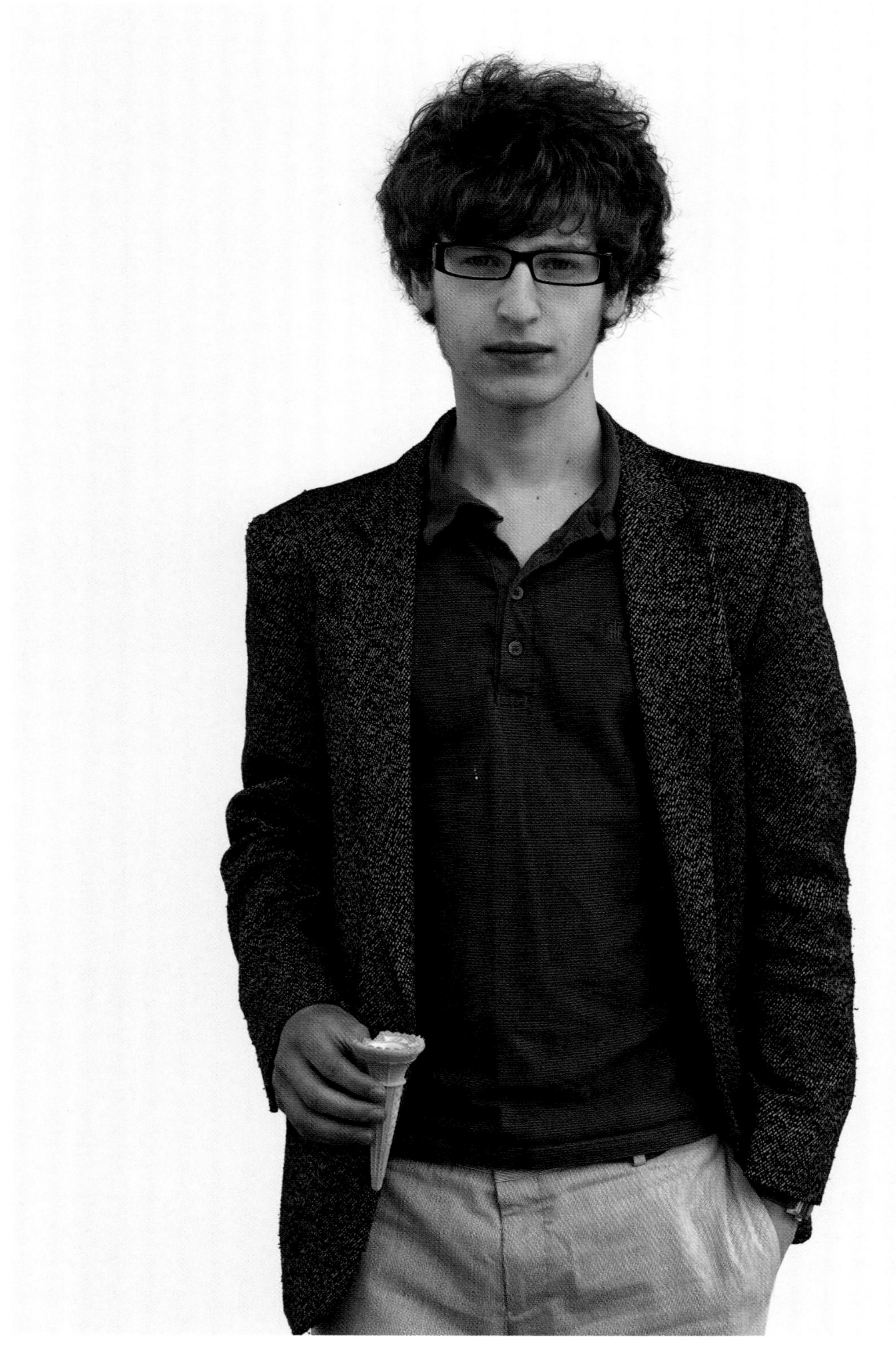

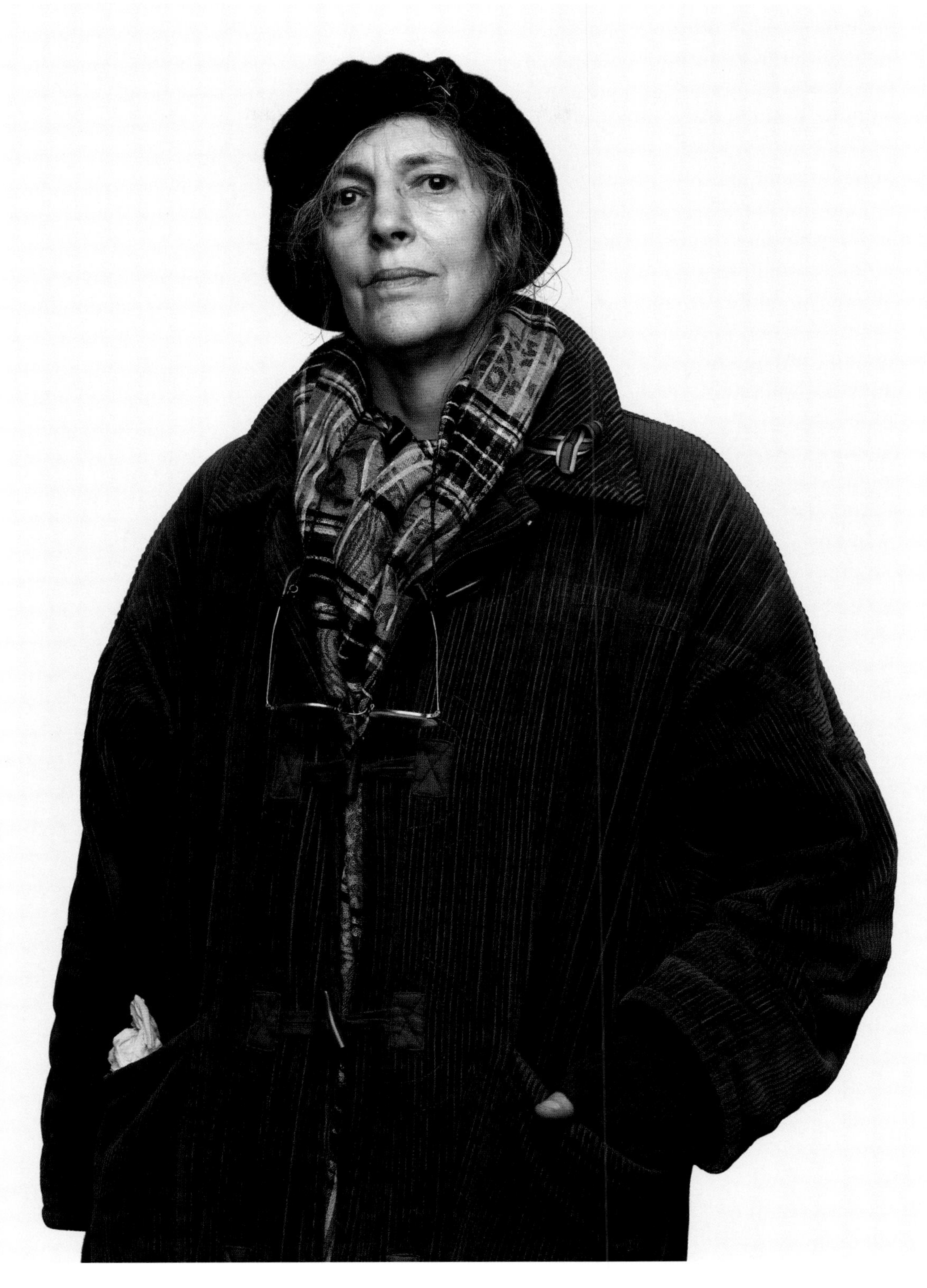

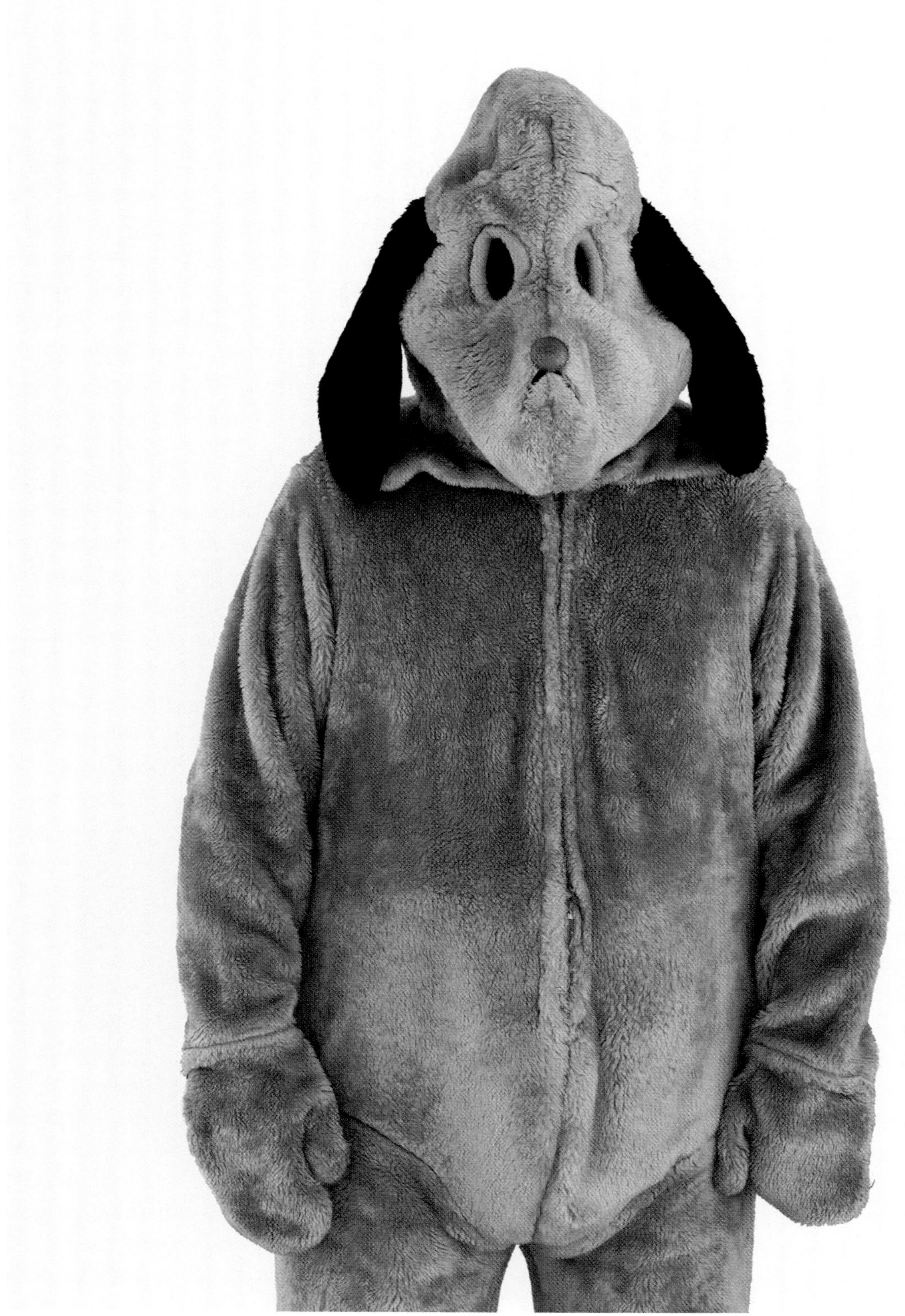

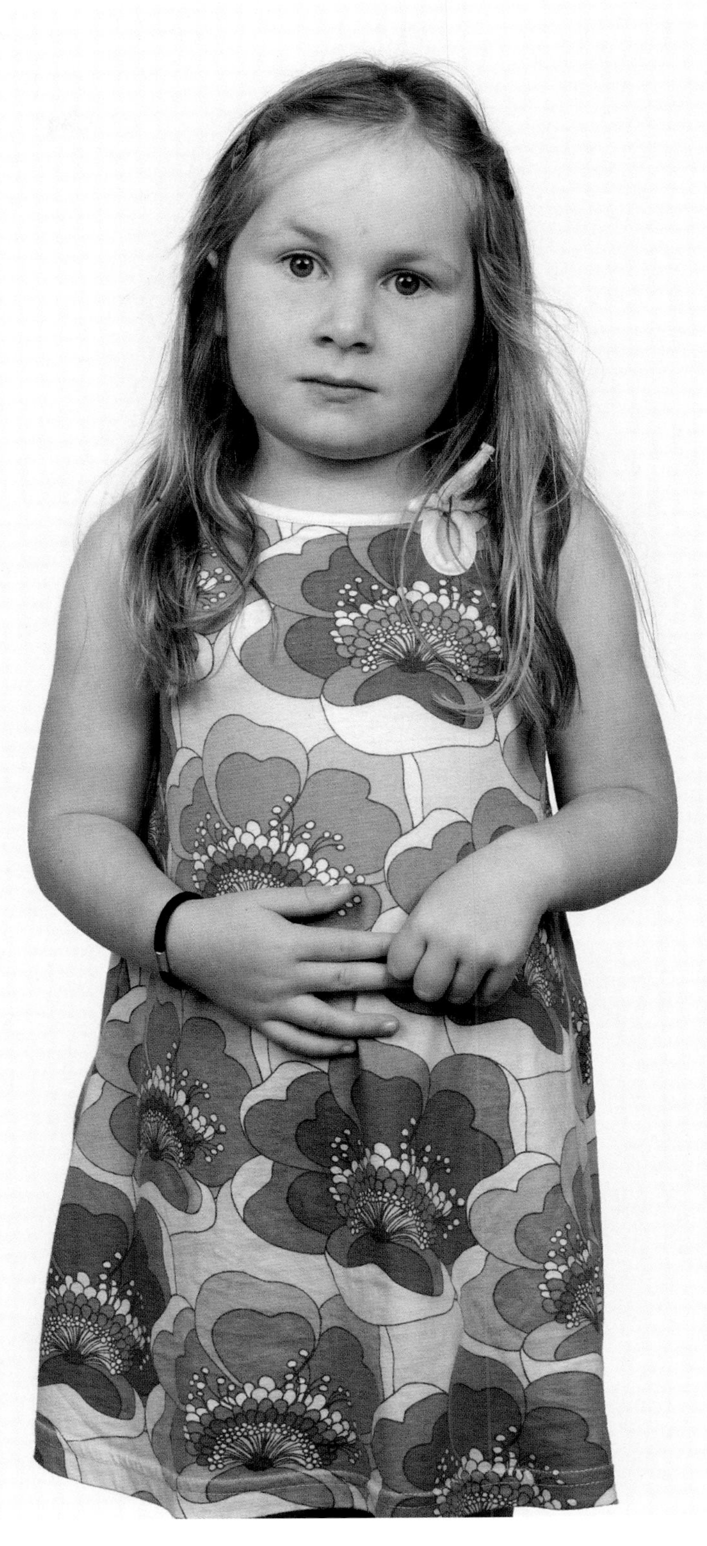

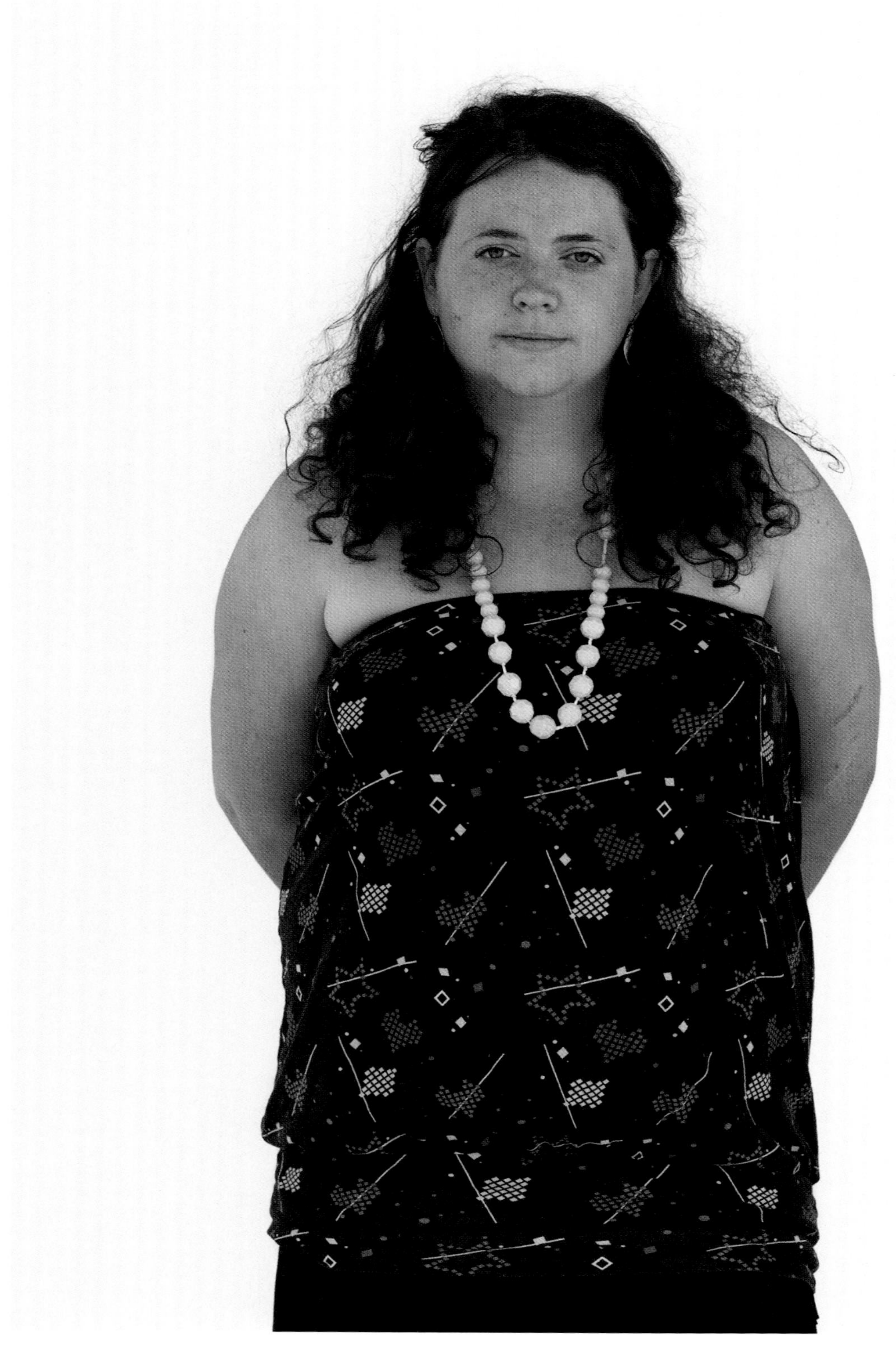

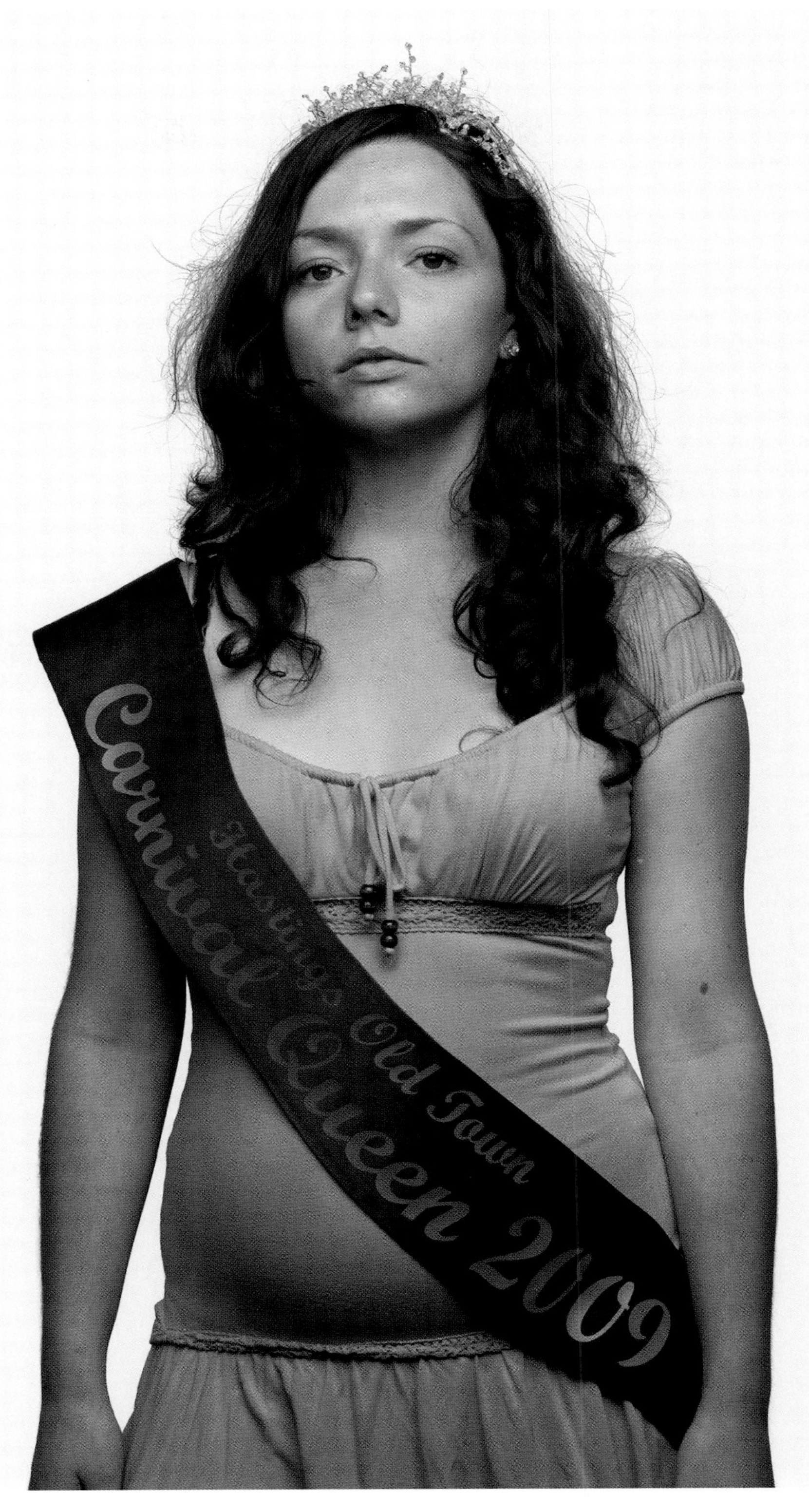
Hastings Old Town
Carnival Queen 2009

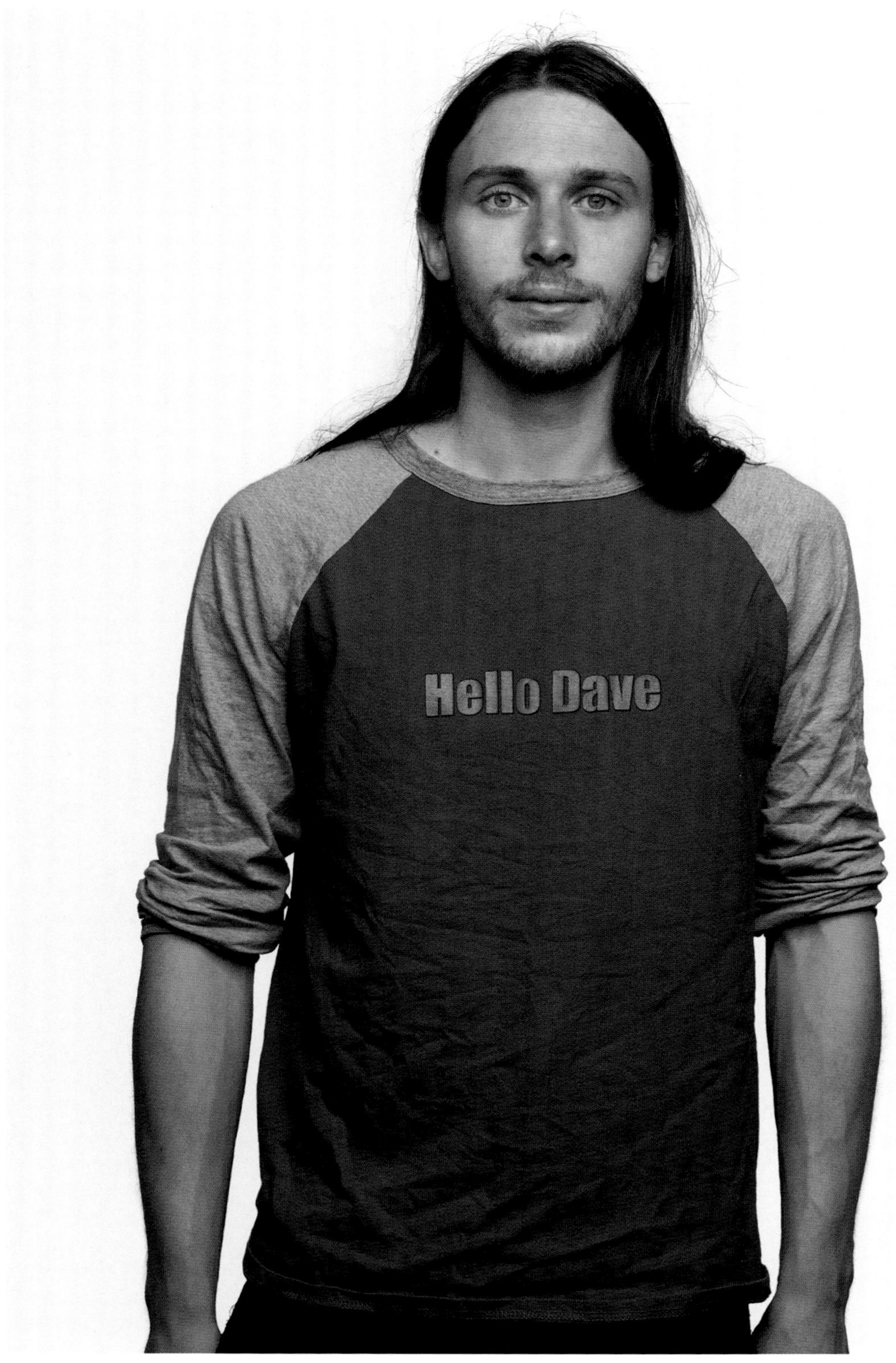
Hello Dave

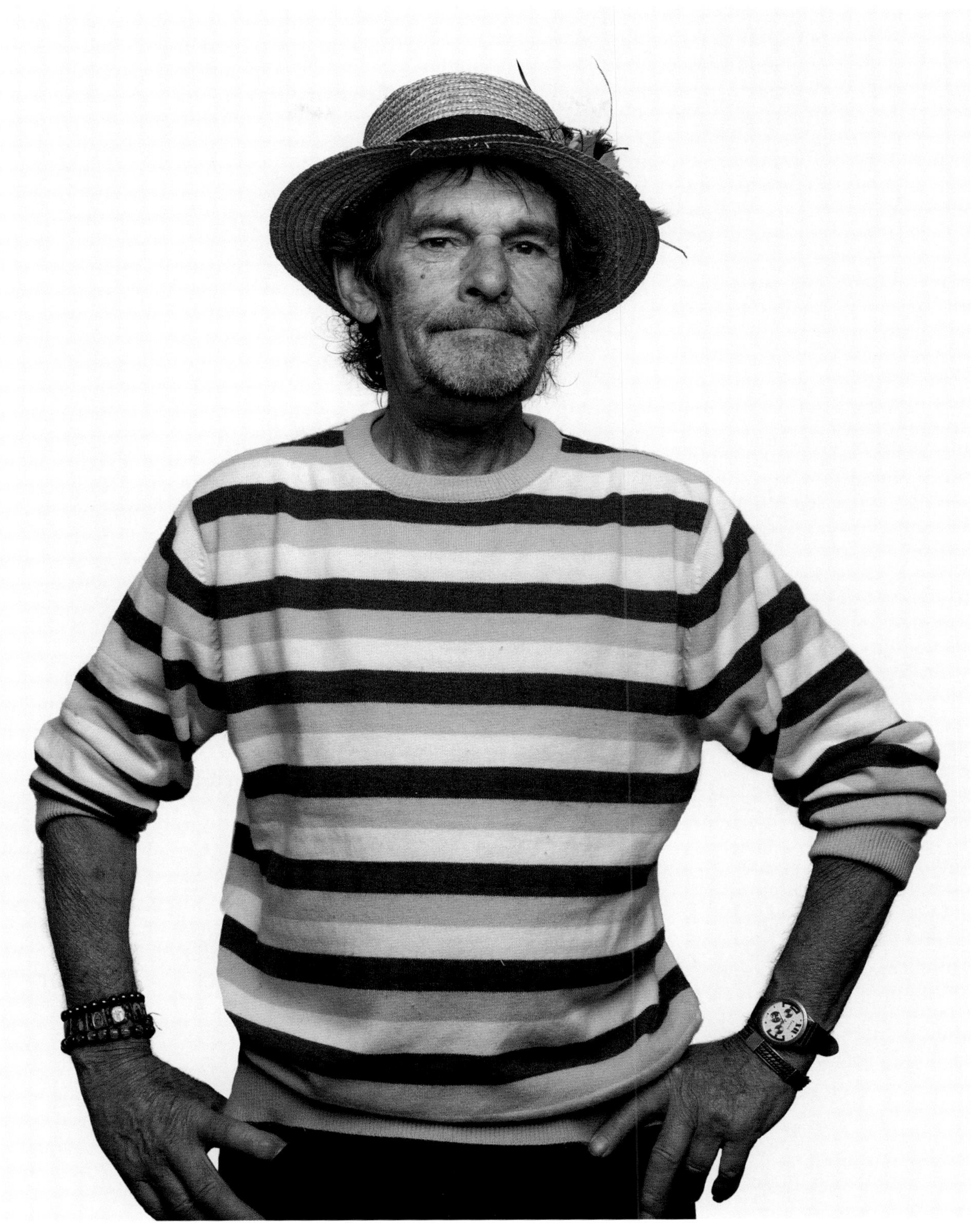

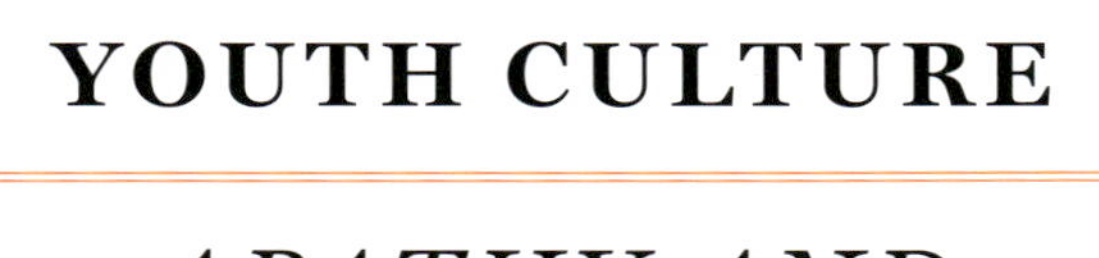

YOUTH CULTURE

*APATHY AND
AIMLESSNESS*

SOUND SYSTEMS

FIRE EXTINGUISHERS

*ALLIANCES AND
ALLEGIANCES*

REPETITIVE BEATS

*ALTERNATIVE
POLITICS*

POPULIST REACTIONS

UNDERCURRENTS

REVISING THE SEASIDE FROM
THE SIXTIES TO THE NINETIES

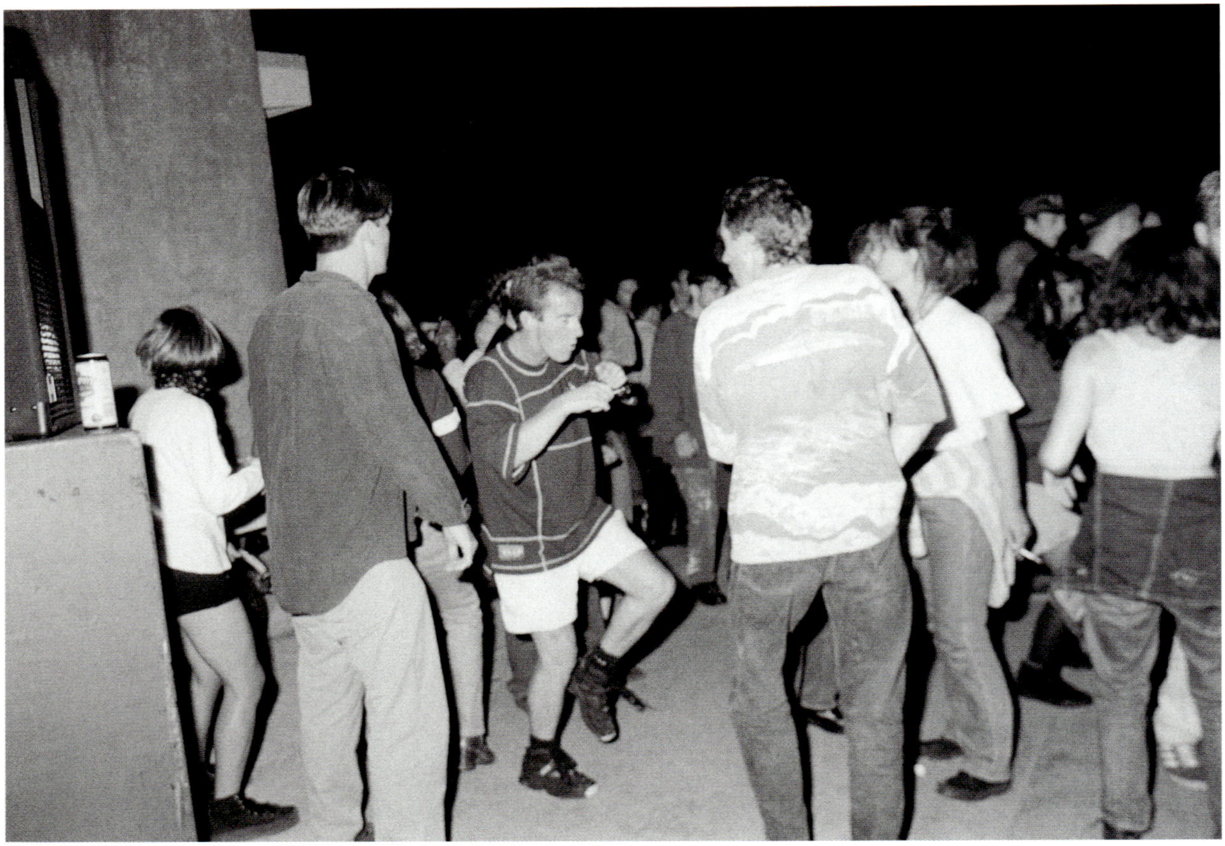

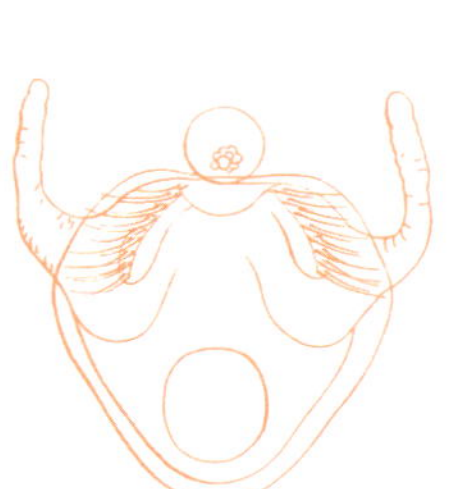

In the early 1990s, Stuart Griffiths, then serving as a Paratrooper and Battalion photographer in the British Army, visited military veteran friends in the English seaside resort of Brighton. He became involved in the emerging rave scene and made a series of photographs that were a continuation of his documentation of life in the barracks and on patrol with the Army in Northern Ireland. In 1993, Griffiths left the Army and moved to Brighton: 'I liked the place a lot, because it was so removed from garrison towns like Aldershot.'[1] In 2011 he began to write a chronicle of his experiences in the Army and the period immediately afterwards, when he became immersed in a rave subculture and Brighton's drug scene.

Griffiths's narrative of early 1990s Brighton is a picaresque and often disjointed description of a journey through rented rooms, chaotic flat shares, often experienced

STUART GRIFFITHS
Illegal Raving in Brighton, Summer 1994

alongside fellow veterans, including Taff, Jock, Geordie and Crosby, through the prism of a culture formed through the extensive and experimental drug use that characterized youth culture in the 1990s. For the former soldiers, attracted by what Griffiths saw as Brighton's 'laid back' atmosphere, the collision with New Age subcultures could be disturbing:

> We all ended up at a party just off Trafalgar Street and stayed in the basement, playing Frank Zappa record … The party itself, no one had a clue whose it was, except Crosby. Everyone there was drugged up and we sat in the basement, talking a load of nonsense. I decided to go on an adventure and see who was around on the other floors, maybe find some action. I'm watching some Indian looking projection moving

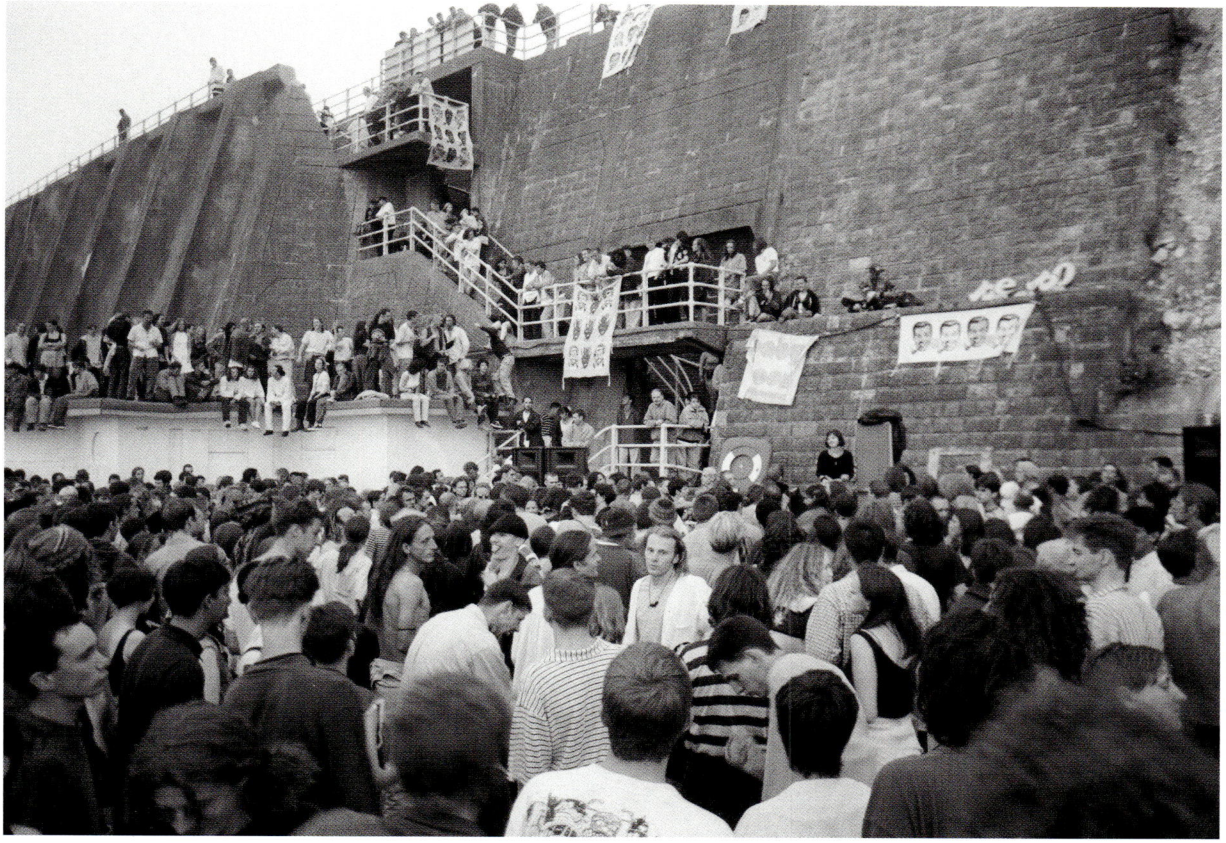

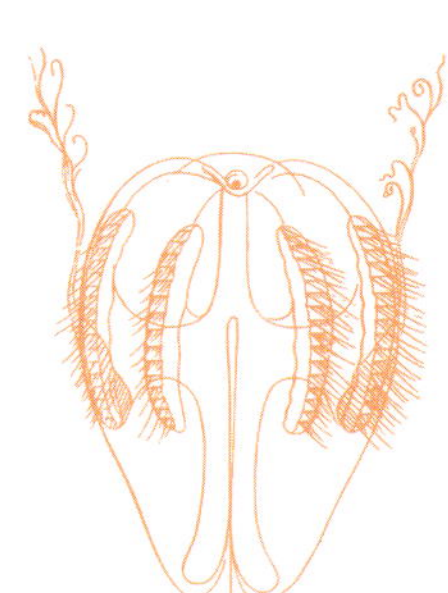

around a wall, when Taff with his big bright red face, grabs me by the arm, looking scared, saying 'This here is devil country, I cannot handle it any longer'. We ended up getting kicked out of the party because Taff nearly torched the kitchen trying to light a cigarette.[2]

Griffiths saw himself as the essential outsider, in common with many Army veterans, and was catapulted into a bewildering cast of characters, from Builder Dave, a small-time drug dealer with whom he lodged when he arrived in Brighton, to the captivating 'Mountain Girl', who he met at a party

packed with mainly crusty looking people, who wore chunky dreadlocks and played bongo drums. Strange eyeballs off this people tonight, as this mescaline is real strong I stare around

the room and see this girl with beautiful but menacing eyes staring back at me. She is wearing Manchester City socks in blue and white … she is Mountain Girl stomping over the mountains of life, taking no shit and each day I'd like her even more.[3]

The veterans did not stay together, and after the group broke up – some were arrested and imprisoned – Griffiths, by now living permanently in Brighton, made contact with the Church of the SubGenius, a Slacker group originating in the USA:

… the presence of Slack, which generally stands for the sense of freedom, independence and original thinking that stops you thinking about personal goals. Slack is about finding satisfaction with what you have and who you are, as opposed to searching for satisfaction in accomplishment ... Slack is about doing nothing and getting what you want anyway.[4]

Richard Linklater's 1990 film *Slacker* made Slacker philosophy widely known: 'We were all part of the Slacker movement', Griffiths remembers:

At weekends, they organized illegal raves at Black Rock and Ovingdean and I decided to be their 'unofficial photographer' and go along and take some photographs. I did not care that people thought I was an undercover cop, my two black eyes [from a mugging] were evidence that I was not working on the other side. We got the sound system in place under cover of darkness and soon many people emerged. I stood on the cliff edge to try and catch the scene in one frame.[5]

Griffiths's progress through the Brighton club and rave scene is like a chronicle of Slacker culture in the early 1990s. He went to the Zap Club, which by the time Griffiths came to Brighton was famous for its acid house parties, especially its Tonka and Protechtion nights, as well as DJs Sasha and John Digweeds's Northern Exposure nights.

Griffiths's years in Brighton, before he enrolled on the BA photography course at Brighton University, were sustained by a succession of casual jobs – he worked as a docker at Shoreham, a cleaner at Gatwick, a kitchen assistant and a bungee jump operative at Hell's Angels rallies and countryside raves:

The raves we worked on, Geordie would get loaded on speed to keep himself sharp. I'd always be the first to test the bungee jump, standing 200 feet high in the cage in a huge field, while the DJ checked the sound system.[6]

In many ways, Griffiths brought the culture that had enveloped him in the Army,

and which he now remembers with antipathy, to the Brighton rave scene. Veterans from army days appear throughout his narrative, displaced and angry in the neo-hippy rave culture of the 1990s, but attracted by its chaos, anarchy and drugs, and its undemanding sense of community.

The artist Tariq Alvi was similarly influenced by the Brighton rave scene of the 1990s, and used art to examine the many contradictions that arose during that decade, as exemplified in his 1996 work *Fucked up with Flyers and Aesthetics*. Justin Kerrigan's 1999 film *Human Traffic* follows a weekend in the lives of a group of Cardiff clubbers. The defining motif of all these different artworks is dysfunction – and Griffiths's narrative, a chaotic tale of tedium, interspersed with hallucinogenic intervals, disillusionment and despair, is no exception. Even the notion of 'community' was a nebulous one as spaces and behaviour, alliances and allegiances were mapped out minute-by-minute in a rapidly shifting social and personal landscape.

Stuart Griffiths's photographs of outdoor raves in Brighton are a rare discovery. While the youth subcultures of the 1980s produced remarkable photo series such as Derek Ridgers's portraits of New Romantics and Punk, there is no equivalent archive for the 1990s. The illegal raves of the early 1990s were difficult spaces for photographers to operate in – the venues were difficult to find and photographers were distrusted. Not sensationalist enough for the mainstream press and not beautiful enough for the style press, the photographs that emerged were taken by insiders. Fashionable wear for 1990s ravers was utilitarian and uniform – boiler suits, smiley-face t-shirts, neon-coloured clothes and luminous vests – not attractive to photographers interested in fashion subcultures.

Continuous clashes with the police and officialdom left little room for concerns about fashion; clothes had to be comfortable, warm and challenge the whole tradition of fashionable dress. Griffiths remembers that he wore: 'a sand-coloured hunting jacket with large pockets, Levi jeans and plimsolls, my

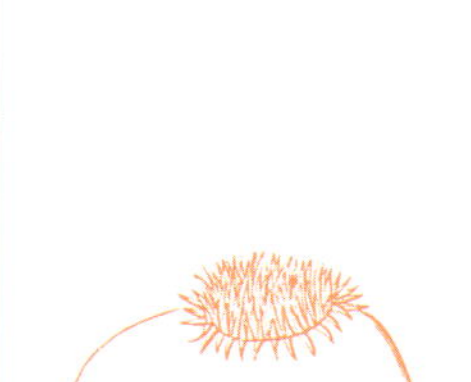

hair was usually short.' The *New York Times* journalist Sam Knight wrote in 2007:

> For four years at the end of the 1980s and the beginning of the 1990s, Britain's youth took to the fields, forests and warehouses, took Ecstasy, wore some of the silliest outfits ever devised – like cricket hats, white gloves and gas masks – and ushered out Thatcherism in a strobe-lighted haze of electronic music that shook the ground they danced on.[7]

If 1980s club and street fashion had been an inventive combination of the customized, handmade and idiosyncratically styled, then the 1990s was about play – bright colours, glow sticks, dummies, Mickey Mouse white gloves, Andy Pandy outfits – combined with utility – hoodies, oversized sweatshirts and legwarmers.

Griffiths's photographs followed the course of the Brighton raves and also documented Army veterans as they encountered a rave culture that could be, and usually was, hostile towards them. Their transgressions on the party scene alienated them from the subculture:

> 'Fuck these savage beats and fuck all Hippies,' Crosby shouted, as loud as he could, making a few heads turn as we pulled out of the mud bath that was Glastonbury for the long drive back home. Mountain Girl attacked me a few weeks later … she poured my beer can over my head and punched me hard in the neck and torso: 'Stay off my case, you fucking weirdo'. She thought I was just a freak.[8]

Made mainly in black and white, Griffiths's photographs from the early 1990s are bleak and laconic; there is no spectacle, just crowds of young people milling around in casual clothes, dressed to survive (pp.190–1), or intimate studies of friends in chaotic kitchens and sparsely furnished flats. People

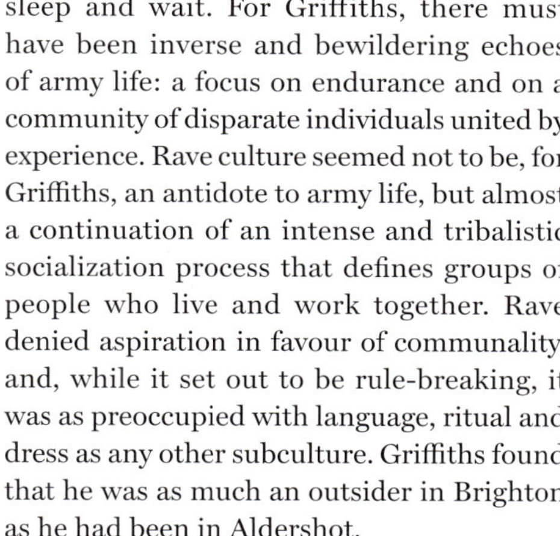

sleep and wait. For Griffiths, there must have been inverse and bewildering echoes of army life: a focus on endurance and on a community of disparate individuals united by experience. Rave culture seemed not to be, for Griffiths, an antidote to army life, but almost a continuation of an intense and tribalistic socialization process that defines groups of people who live and work together. Rave denied aspiration in favour of communality, and, while it set out to be rule-breaking, it was as preoccupied with language, ritual and dress as any other subculture. Griffiths found that he was as much an outsider in Brighton as he had been in Aldershot.

By the mid-1990s the illegal rave scene in Britain was declining. The Criminal Justice and Public Order Act of 1994 prohibited unlicensed gatherings of groups of more than 100 people where 'sounds characterized by the emission of a succession of repetitive beats' were played. The focus of the subculture was now on licensed venues, and the scene was increasingly commodified. For Griffiths, it had been a rite of passage, a journey completed as

> the parties on the beach started to get that bit ugly. Stories of people throwing themselves off cliffs, drug gangs moving in from London with guns, selling crack and heroin. People were not interested in getting high, they just wanted to be completely out of it and get completely numb. I knew this exact feeling one New Year's Eve, sat on my own at Taff's place, listening to The Pogue's 'Dirty Old Town'. I fumbled desperately in the bin for old bits of used tinfoil to smoke. It had now got that bad, I thought. All I needed to do now was to find a needle somewhere to bang into my arm and stagger around the streets like a depraved drunken fool, swigging from a warm can of Tennants Super 9% lager, and my image would be complete.
>
> … I was stone-broke and went for a stroll on the beach, to try and find some

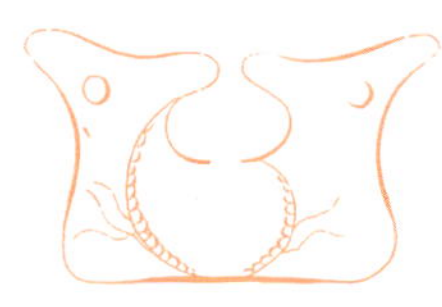

direction, knowing that I needed to be free from the evils. Staring across the Channel, watching waves meander in and out of view. Here by the seaside I was just another piece of driftwood.[9]

For Vinca Petersen, the traveller/rave scene of the late 1980s and 1990s meant freedom. A new kind of photography had emerged in the early 1990s, pioneered by Corinne Day, Wolfgang Tillmans, Jason Evans (Travis), Elaine Constantine and others, a blend of high American documentary and British street style with a definite edge of punk, which captured the new style of grunge. When Corinne Day photographed the young Kate Moss in a dingy bedsit in 1993, for *Vogue*, a new phrase, 'heroin chic', described photography that rejected glamour and gloried in the grungy everyday. Style magazines such as *i-D*, which began publishing in 1980, and *The Face* were joined in the 1990s by *Dazed and Confused*, *Self Service* and many more short-lived publications, moulding the look of a generation.

Petersen left home at the beginning of the 1990s and moved to London. She lived in a squat and became immersed in rave culture and the new fashion. Talking with journalist Sheryl Garratt about the 1990s, she revealed:

> ... [she] got involved in alternative politics as well as the rave/free party scene, and occasionally worked as a model in edgy fashion spreads and music videos. Through this she met the influential photographer Corinne Day, who became a mentor of sorts, occasionally giving Vinca cameras, film and giving her more confidence to continue taking her pictures.[10]

Petersen's photographs of the traveller/rave culture of the early 1990s British seaside show people sleeping, camping in cars, sitting around (opposite). They are like penitents or pilgrims in an ancient procession, besmirched, almost holy, as they place themselves, if only for a moment, on the margins of society. Their

processional is littered with the detritus of casual camping, and they are in thrall to sensation. The British seaside was on the margins too: no urban seaside space was prized, and its physical decline seemed unstoppable.

Long associated with corruption and veniality, and often used as a setting for fiction and documentary that purported to show the social and political underbelly of Britain, the seaside was a no man's land in which diverse cultural phenomena took root and thrived. The liminal spaces that the seaside offered were ideal for rave parties and for photography up until the the passing of the Criminal Justice Act in 1994. Down-at-heel, and with repurposed spaces (including the beach) that could accommodate large crowds, the empty seaside could be refigured into massive dance and music venues.

More than two decades before Petersen and Griffiths began to photograph alternative cultures at the British seaside, other documentarists were interested in emerging seaside youth cultures. Italian photojournalist Enzo Ragazzini, who had played an important part in the re-emergence of British documentary photography in London in the 1960s, travelled down to the south coast in 1970 to photograph the third Isle of Wight Music Festival.

Isle of Wight 1970 was the last festival on the island until 2002. It was host to, among others, Jimi Hendrix, The Doors, The Who, Leonard Cohen, Joni Mitchell and Miles Davis. Chaos ensued as large numbers of people arrived without tickets, and an encampment – known as Desolation Row – soon grew up. Walls were torn down and acts interrupted until the organizers declared the festival free to enter. Rather than photographing the acts, as most of the photographers did, Ragazzini concentrated on the audience, as shown in this chapter's portfolio (pp.198–204).

His photographs, taken in the morning, often of people sleeping, are an enticing combination of tenderness and sharp photojournalistic practice. Litter is everywhere, giant furls of paper are like collapsed sails,

VINCA PETERSEN
Rave Car,
Kent, 1990s

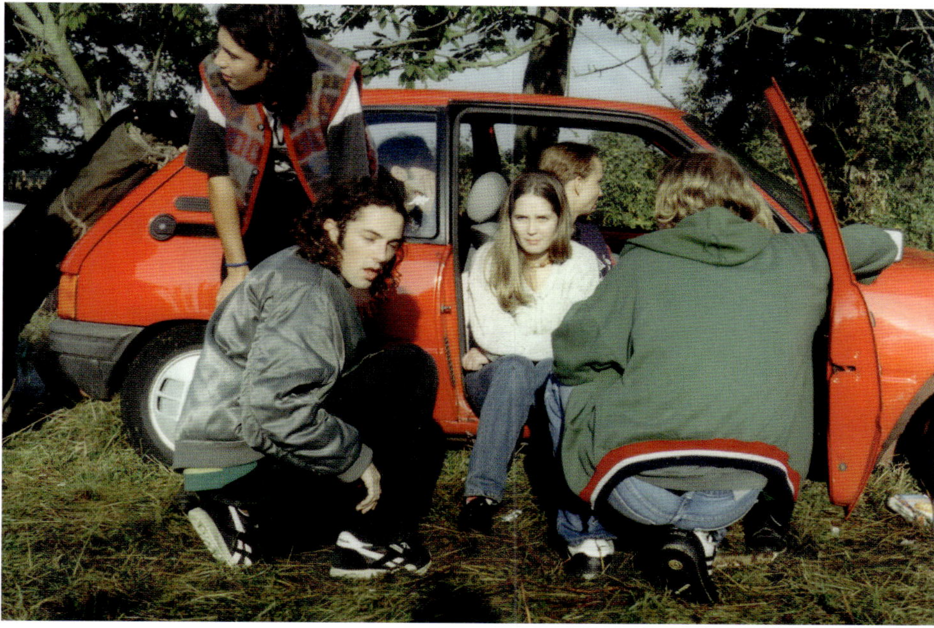

VINCA PETERSEN
Ali and Frizbee,
Norfolk Coast, 1990s

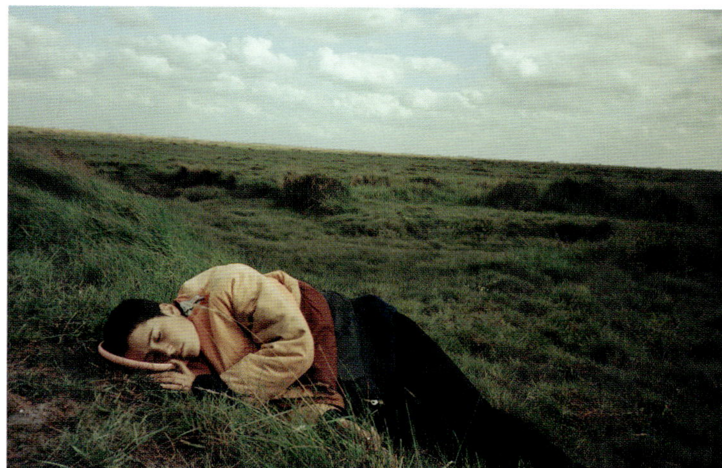

VINCA PETERSEN
Out of Order,
Norfolk Coast, 1990s

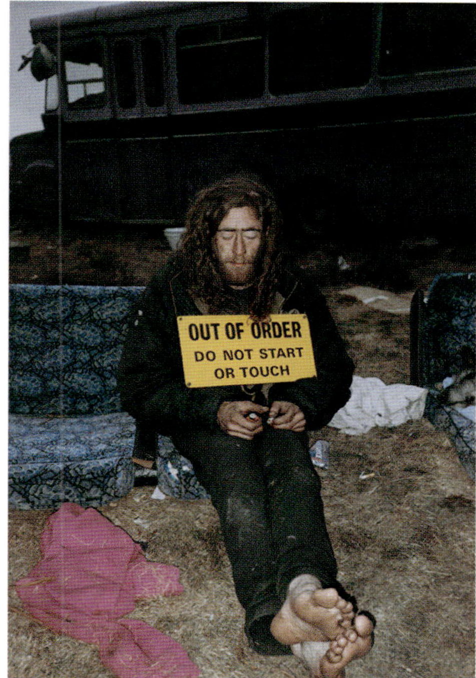

and people wander about in the rubbish like survivors of war. The young men and women he photographed are like angels in the debris, curled in youthful grace, hair flowing. Ragazzini's photographs presented the English seaside as a place where the visual canvas of Britain was altering. The seaside had always been a place of crowds and carnival, and here, as it went into decline, was the modern iteration of this, but discordant and dissolute.

In 1972 sociologist Stanley Cohen published *Folk Devils and Moral Panics*, an examination of youth subculture and populist reactions to it.[11] Cohen was particularly interested in the phenomenon of Mods and Rockers meeting in large numbers on the English seafront on summer Bank Holidays. He examined the reactions of those present and the attitude of the popular press, which dramatized the rowdiness as a kind of skewed war story – the beach as battleground, innocent bystanders and a dissolute rebel army.

Media interest in the procession of Mods and Rockers to the English seafront was intense, with a moral indignation and exaggeration guaranteed to convince the population at large that Britain was in the grip of social malaise on a huge scale. For resorts such as Hastings and Margate, already in decline, the reputational damage was significant. For the press, the symbolism of these scuffles was profound. Memories of the Second World War were still acute – the heroic exploits of Dunkirk, the beach as a fenced danger zone rather than a place of pleasure were all still in living memory. In its use of battleground terms and action photojournalism, the press revived wartime memories and stoked anger.

The coverage by some publications was a little more thoughtful; the photojournalist C. Smith, working for the *Daily Herald* newspaper, made a perceptive photo-essay about Mods, focusing on body language and dress rather than rampaging action (opposite). Most media coverage of Mod and Rocker gatherings in British seaside resorts was hostile and negative – fleeing granddads and screaming toddlers, kickings

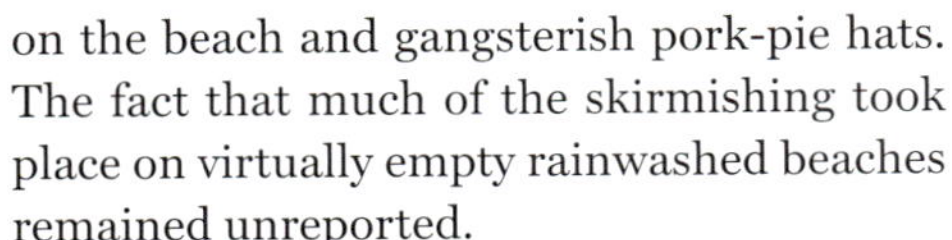

C. SMITH
Disturbances in
Clacton-on-Sea,
Essex, for the
Daily Herald, 1963

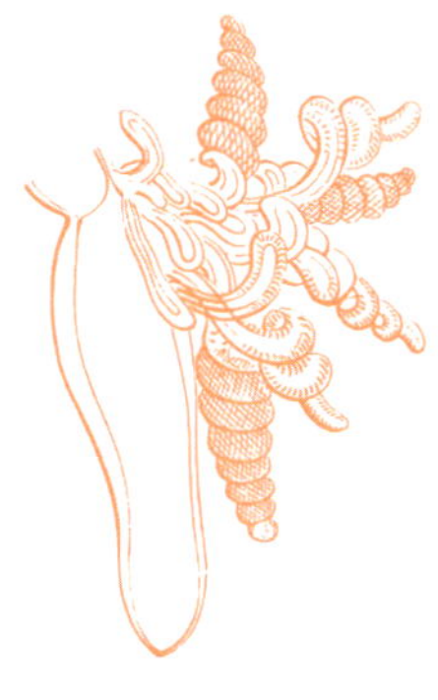

on the beach and gangsterish pork-pie hats. The fact that much of the skirmishing took place on virtually empty rainwashed beaches remained unreported.

Newspapers shamelessly appealed to a wartime generation both nostalgic and traumatized, in mourning for a seaside past of jollity and freedom. By the time the Mods and Rockers met up on British beaches, the seaside was shabby, mostly deserted and deeply unfashionable. For the younger generation, the Mods symbolized a break from the past, and the past included the British seaside. That the Mods had created what Cohen saw as 'Folk Devils and Moral Panic' made them even more alluring. Photographers like C. Smith presented them as a subcultural tribe as well as intriguing fashion icons.

The Mod and Rocker 'battles' of the 1960s, and the appropriation of seaside land by the organizers of the Isle of Wight festivals and their unruly audiences, established the seaside as a vacant space where youth could perform new rituals against the background of an underdeveloped and still-traumatized Britain. Later ritualistic practices – the rave parties and New Age traveller culture of the late 1980s and early 1990s – were the inheritors of an alternative seaside subculture of the 1960s. While seaside Mod culture was photographed primarily by outsiders – mainly press photojournalists – for public consumption, the 1990s party scene – much more aware of the power of reportage than its 1960s forebears was less media friendly. There is very little press documentation of large-scale seaside raves, except by trusted insiders, such as Petersen and Griffiths.

From Ragazzini and Smith in the 1960s to Griffiths and Petersen in the 1990s, the British seaside was a background to photographs that charted profound social change. These are not joyous photographs; their cast of characters wander like lost souls among the debris. For many, they signified the death of the British seaside, the final abandonment of the bucket and the spade. [vw]

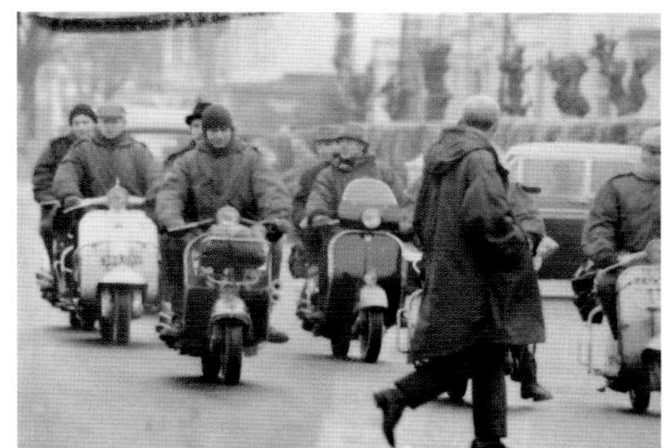
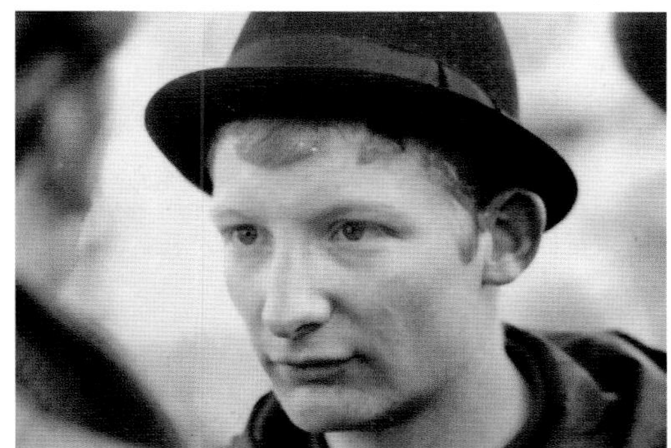
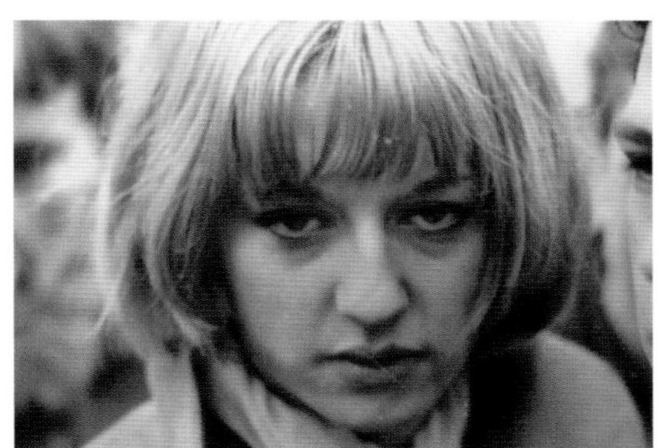
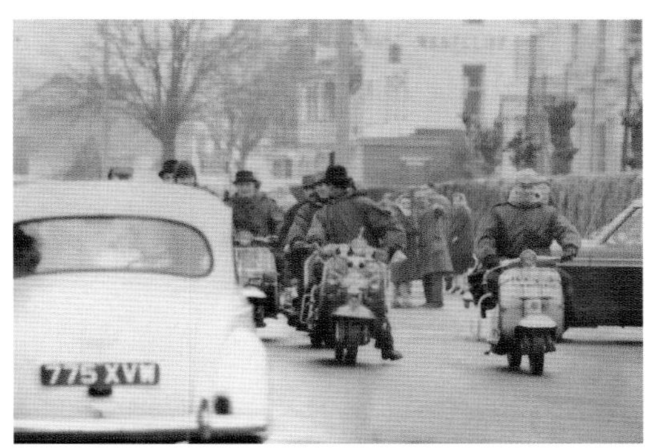
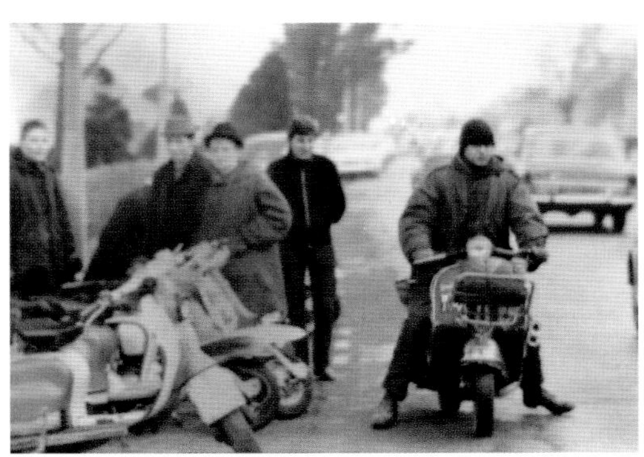
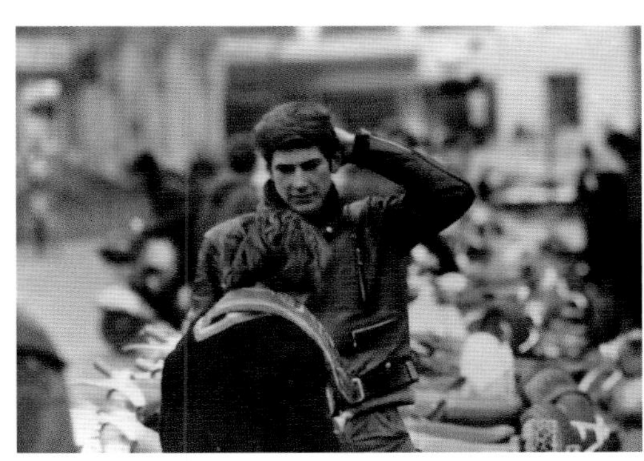
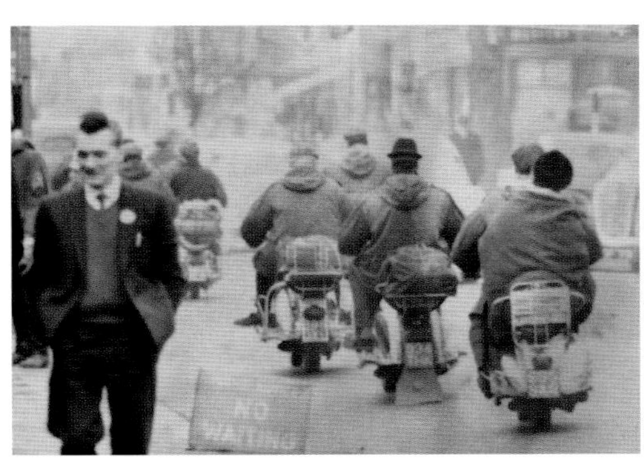
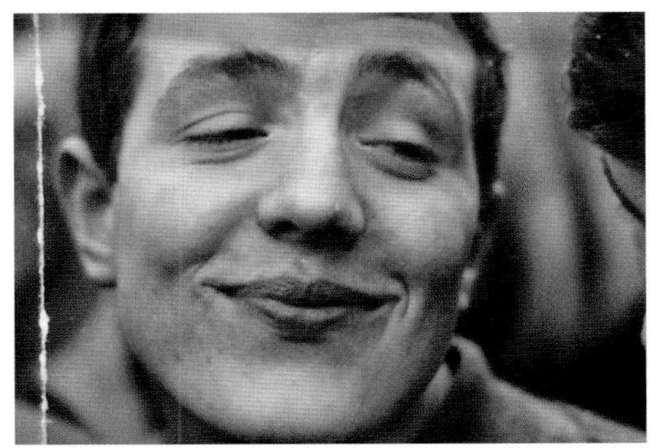

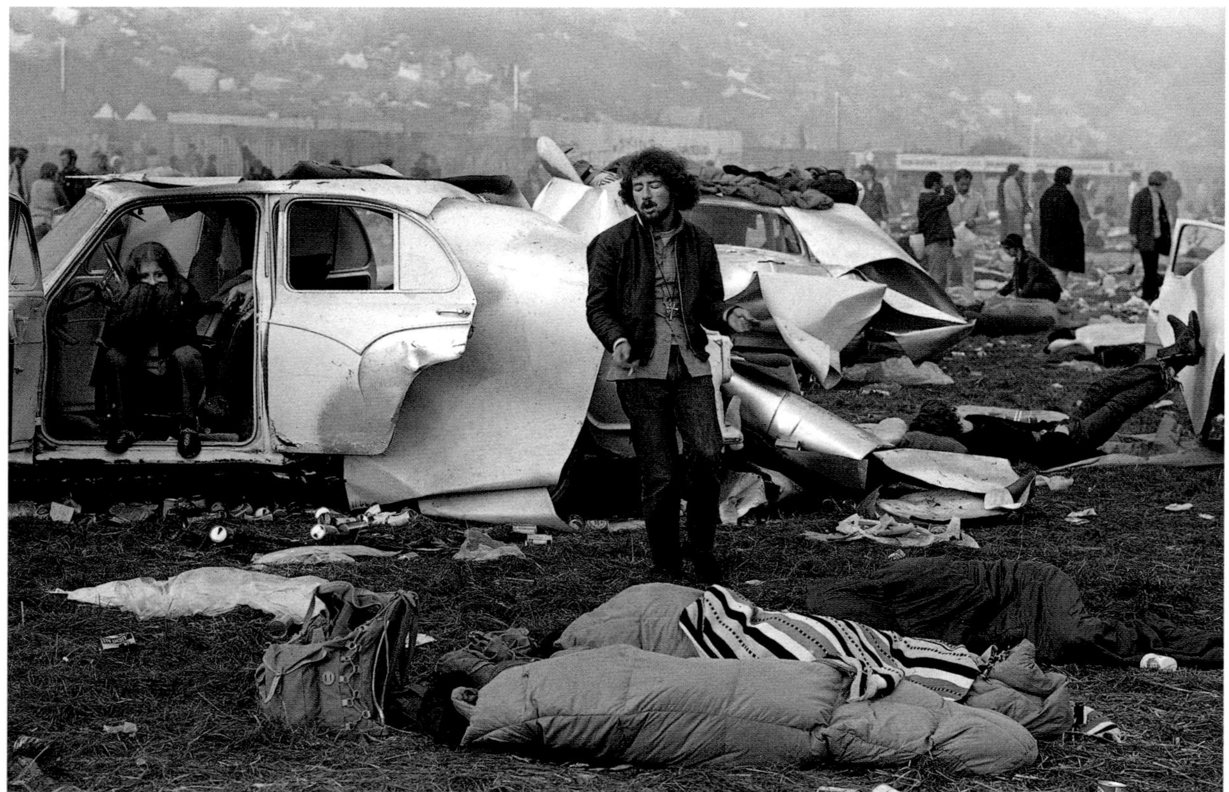

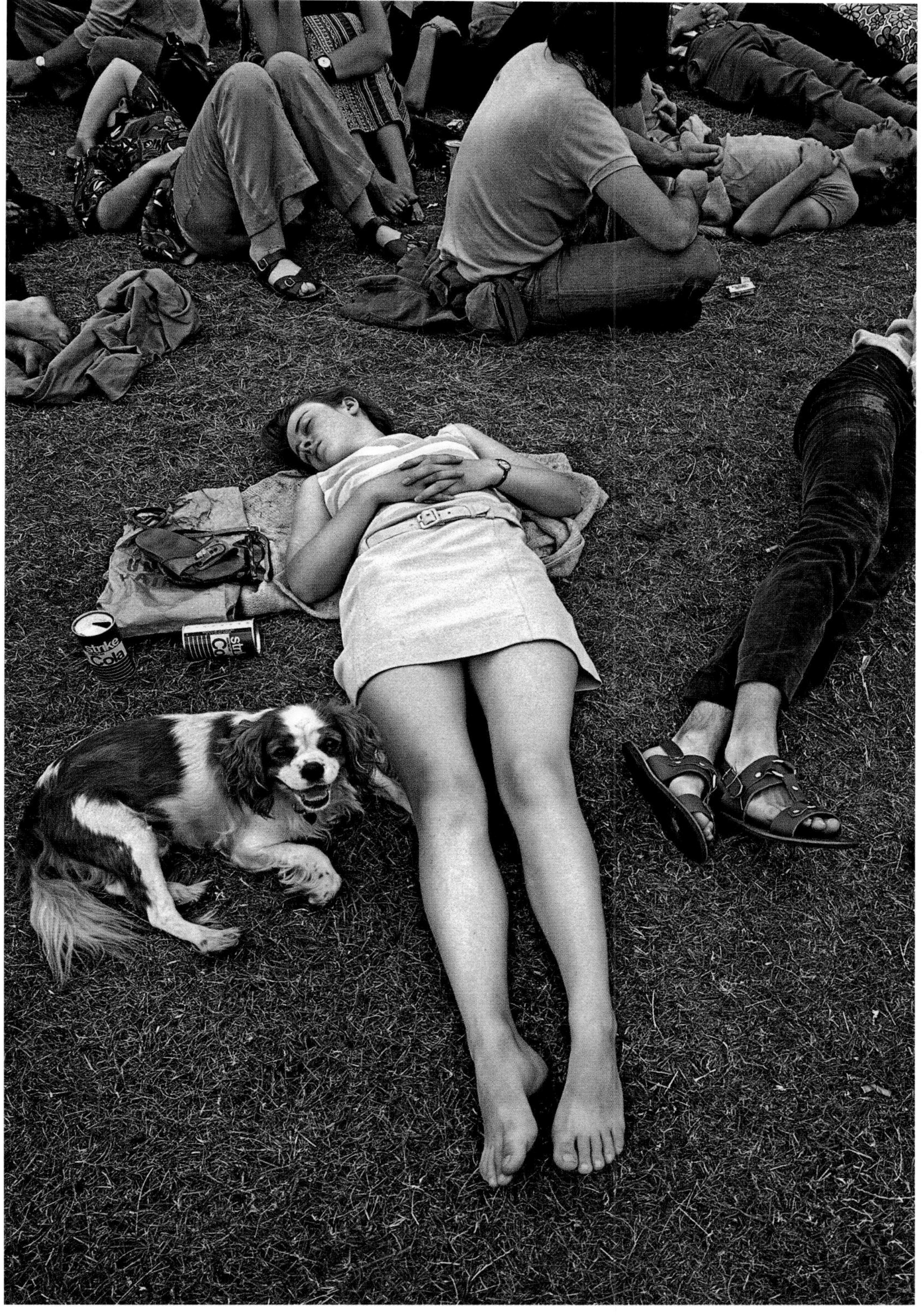

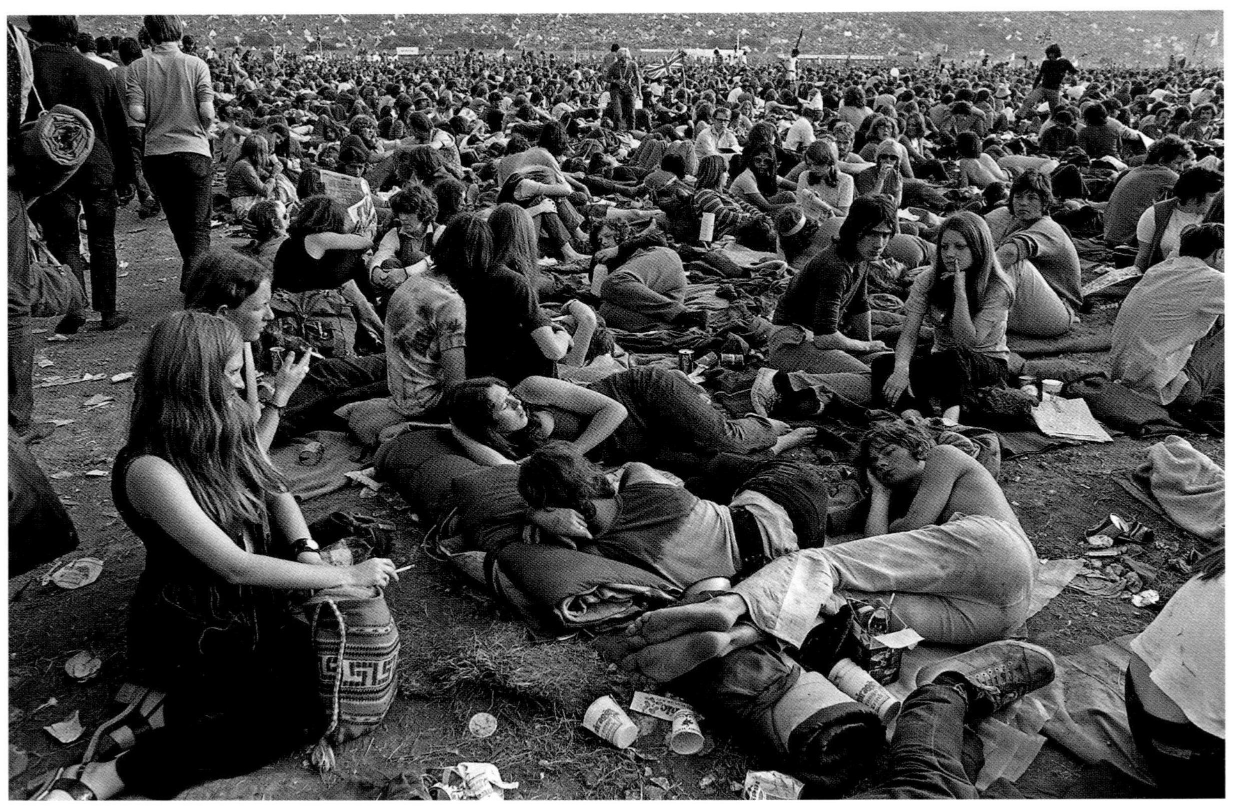

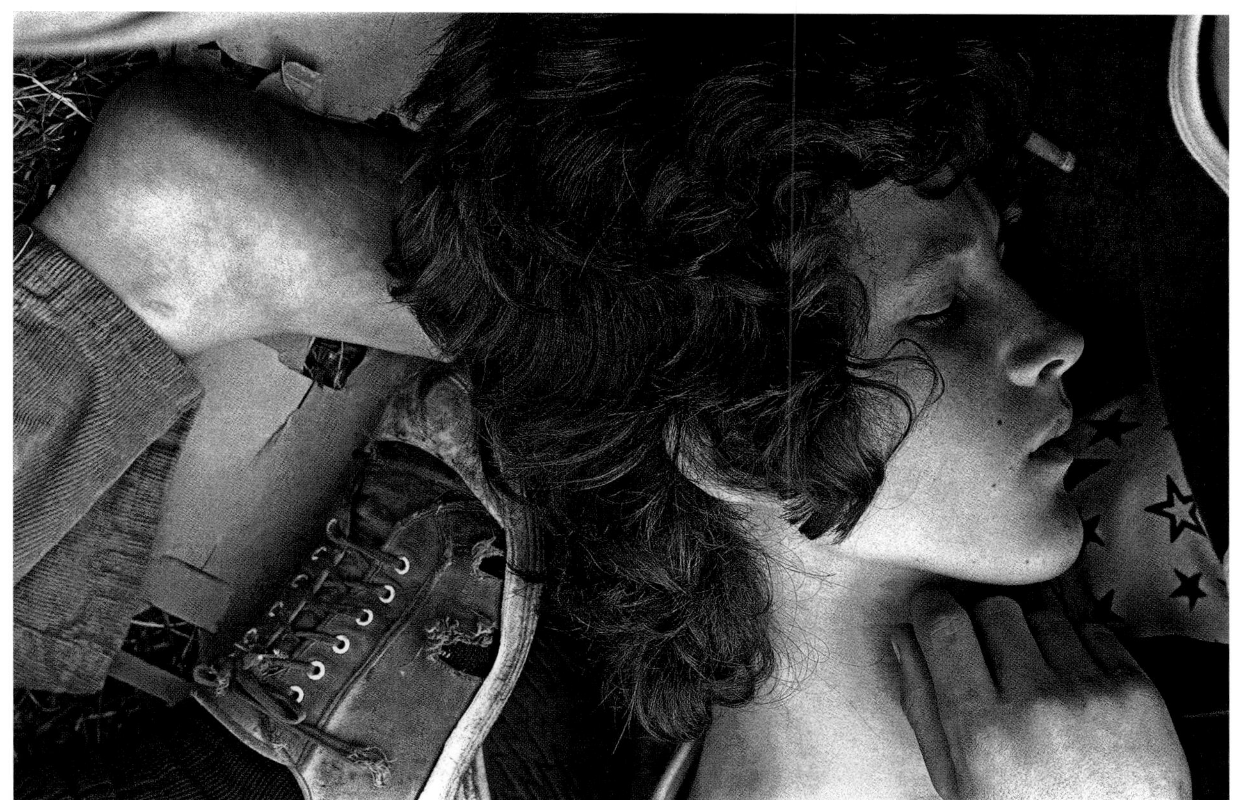

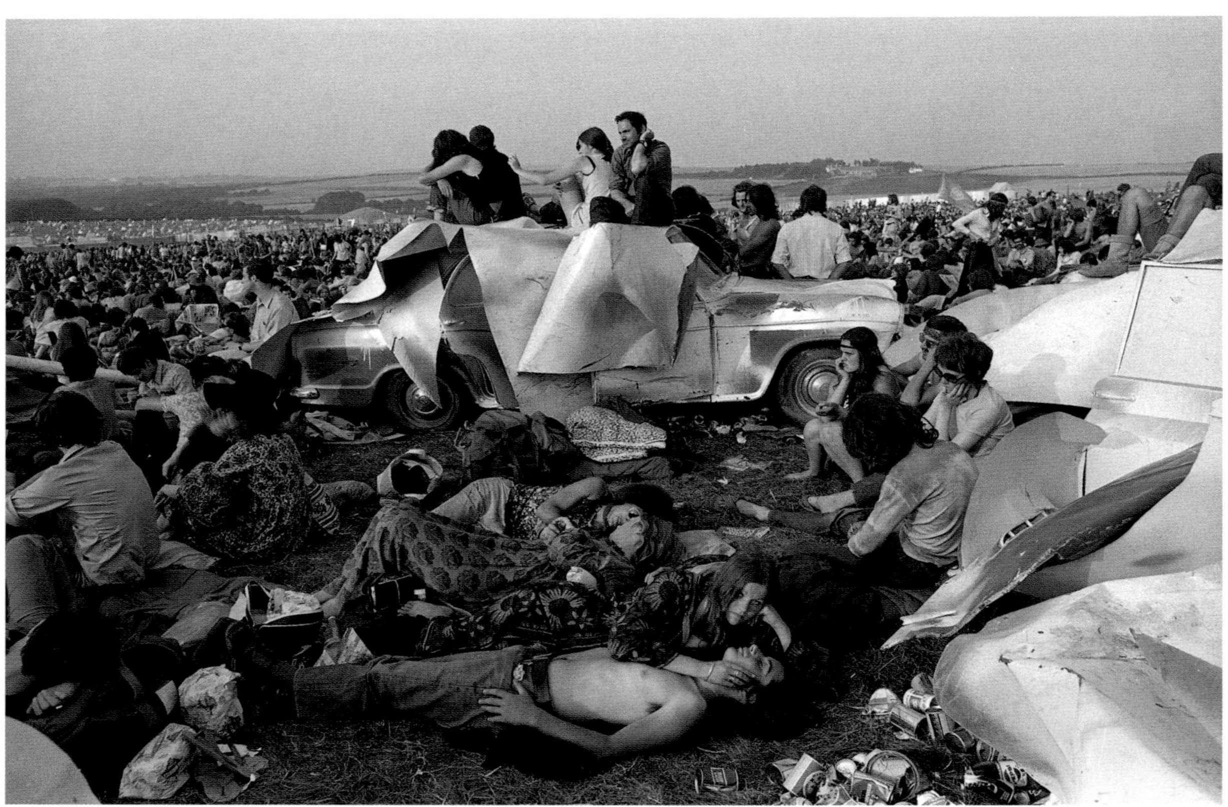

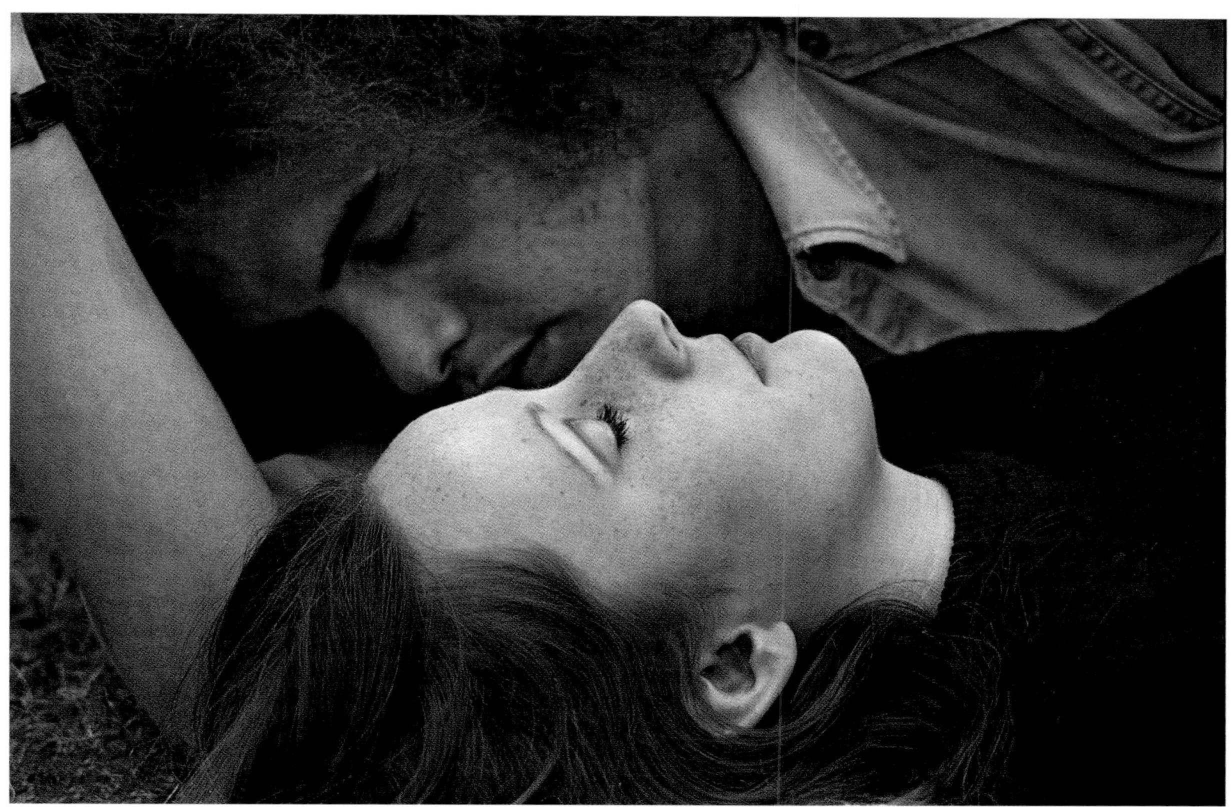

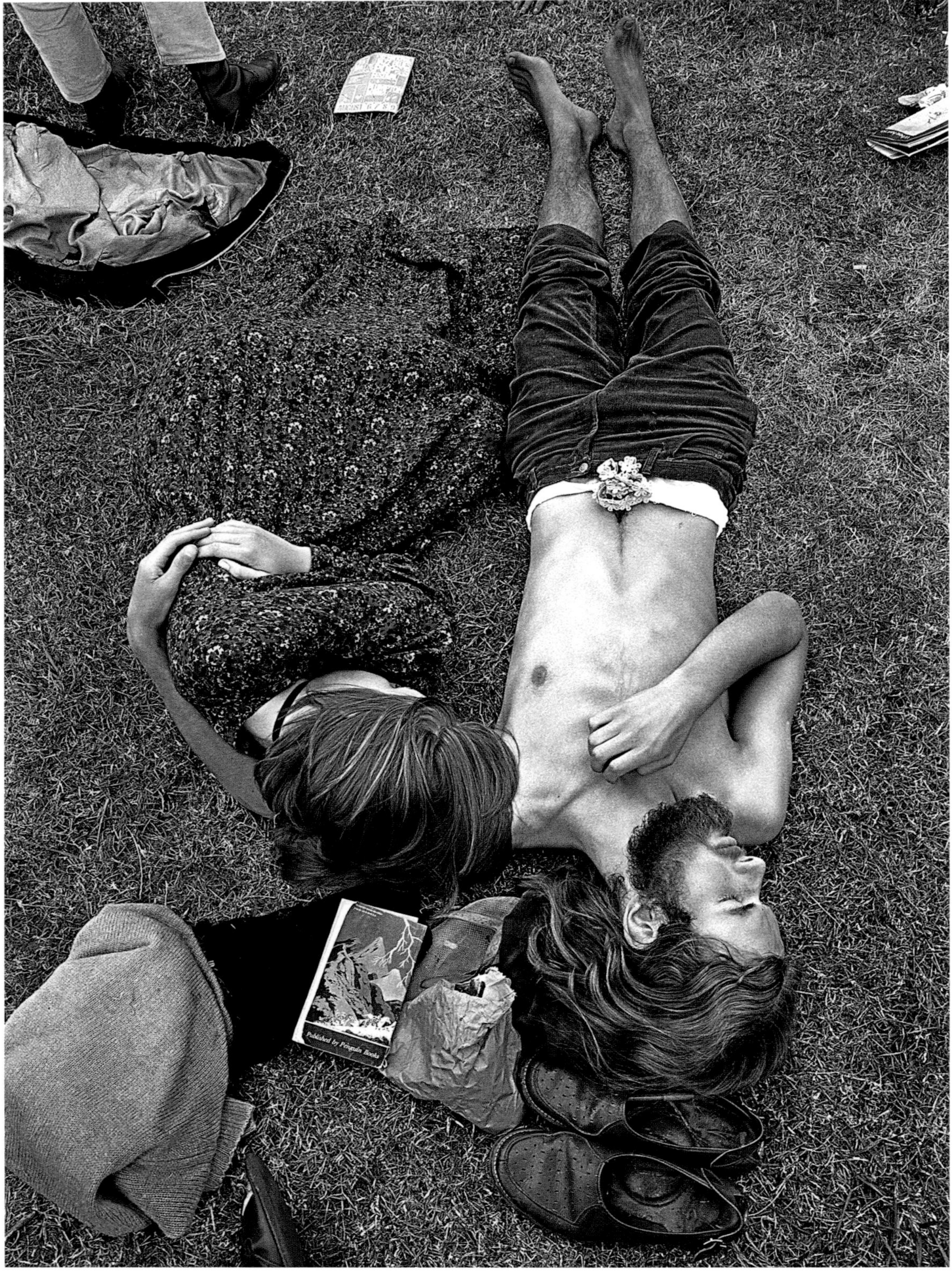

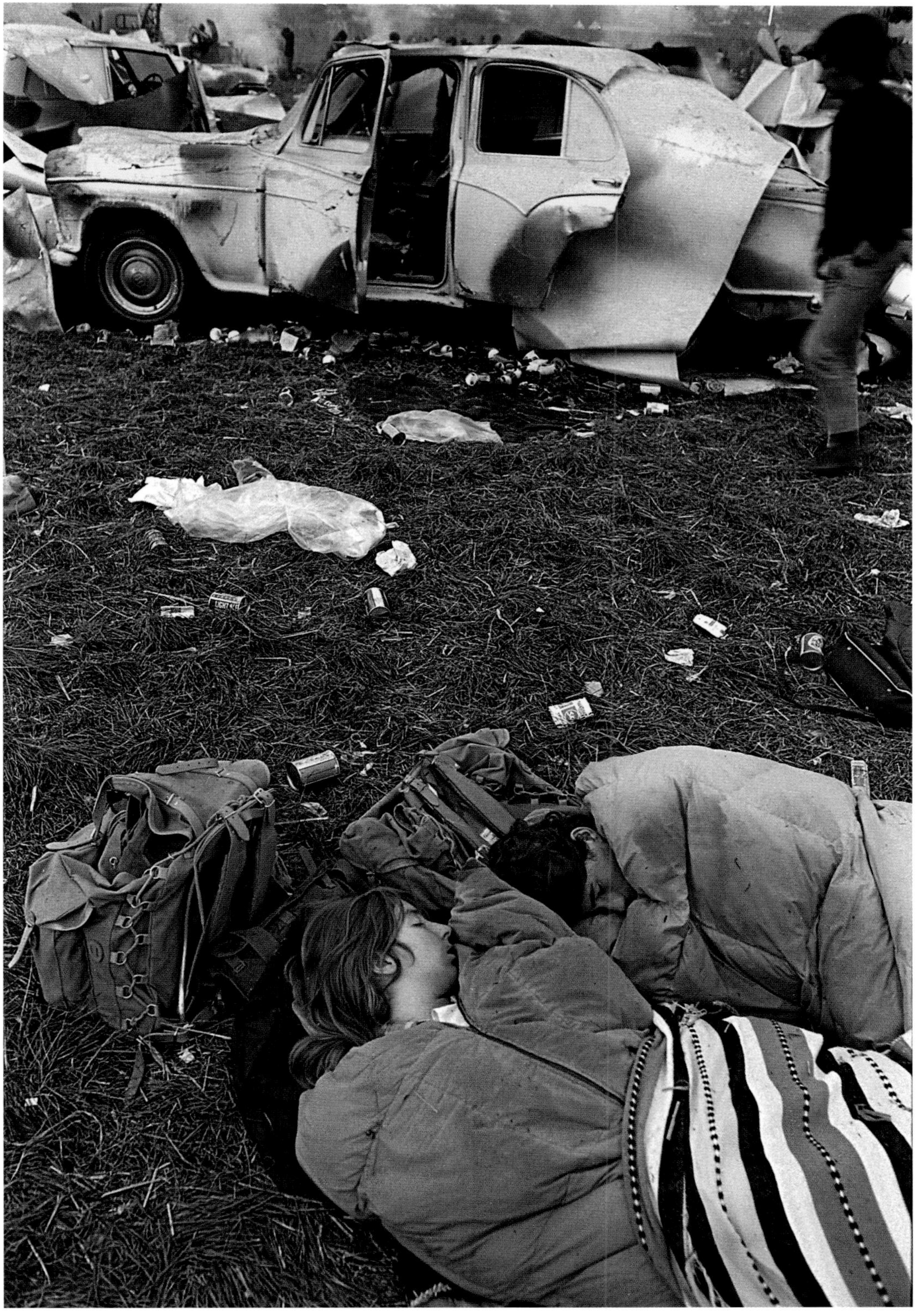

Eileen Agar RA
1899–1991

BORN IN Flores, Buenos Aires, Agar arrived in England in 1911. Her practice encompassed painting, sculpture and photography. She studied in London, first at the Byam Shaw School of Art in 1918, and then at the Slade School of Fine Art 1921–4. In 1933 she had her first show at the Bloomsbury Gallery, London. In the same year she joined the London Group. She was invited to exhibit her work at the 'London International Surrealist Exhibition' in 1936, and two years later at the 'International Surrealist Exhibition' in Amsterdam. After the Second World War she continued to paint. In 1971, a retrospective exhibition of her work was held at the Commonwealth Institute in London.

COLLECTIONS INCLUDE Tate, London; Arts Council Collection, England; National Portrait Gallery, London.

Shirley Baker
1932–2014

BORN IN Salford, Manchester, Baker studied Pure Photography at Manchester College of Technology. Upon graduating, she worked at Courtaulds, the fabric manufacturers, as an in-house photographer, but left to take up freelance work. Throughout the 1960s and 1970s, Baker photographed a range of humanist subjects. In 1986 her photographs came to wider public attention with the exhibition 'Here Yesterday, Gone Today', Salford Art Gallery, a collection of photographs taken within the working-class communities of Salford and Manchester. In 1989 a book was published *Street Photographs: Manchester and Salford*. In 2000, her street photographs were shown in an exhibition to celebrate the opening of the Lowry Centre in Salford. There was an accompanying publication called *Streets and Spaces: Urban Photography*. Ten years later, two retrospective exhibitions took place in Salford and Oldham. Her photographs were included in the exhibition 'Saturday Night and Sunday Morning: the Authentic Moment in British Photography', Nottingham (2012–13). Her first London solo exhibition was in 2015: 'Shirley Baker: Women and Children; and Loitering Men' at the Photographer's Gallery, with a book of the same title being published.

The exhibition toured China (2015), Madrid (2016) and Manchester (2017). As part of Photo London, Photofusion launched 'On the Beach by Shirley Baker' (2016), an exhibition of Baker's beach photographs of Blackpool taken through the 1970s, contrasting sharply with those taken on the beaches of the French Riviera. This exhibition toured to Blackpool (2017) and to Le Lavandou, France (2018).

Rob Ball
b.1977

BRITISH PHOTOGRAPHER Rob Ball was awarded an MA in Photography from the University of the Arts London. He is deputy director of SEAS Photography and senior lecturer at Canterbury Christ Church University, England.

Ball's photographic work is principally based by the coast, where he employs a range of techniques to respond to and find new ways of looking at coastal communities, which form the basis for publications, events, exhibitions and installations. In the summer months Ball creates peripatetic portrait studios on the beach in dialogue with the work made by Victorian portrait photographers, creating both a spectacle and an archive of visitors on a specific day. Ball often works collaboratively under the title Obsolete Studios, where outdated techniques are used within the contemporary context.

His projects have been published and exhibited worldwide, including at The Photographers' Gallery, London; Format Festival, Derby; Illinois State University, Illinois (USA); and the Sidney Cooper Gallery, Canterbury. Publications include *Dreamlands* (2015), *Coney Island* (2017) and *Funland* (2019).

COLLECTIONS INCLUDE University of the Arts London; National Portrait Gallery, London.

Maurice Beck
1886–1960

FOR A NUMBER OF YEARS, Beck lived and worked in Shanghai, China, before returning to England. In the 1920s he worked for Condé Nast Publications, working closely with Helen MacGregor as chief photographers for British *Vogue*. They photographed actors, writers and dancers, such as Cecil Beaton, Virginia Woolf and Sir Osbert Sitwell. Beck's photographs were published in a wide range of magazines and newspapers. In the 1930s Beck worked for a number of companies including Shell-Mex BP Ltd, London Transport and the Underground Group, for which he designed posters (1930–4). In 1937 he was included in the exhibition 'Photography 1839–1937' at the Museum of Modern Art, New York. He contributed photographs to the Shell Guides *Oxon* (1938) and *Oxfordshire (not including the City of Oxford)* (1953), both by John Piper.

COLLECTIONS INCLUDE Victoria and Albert Museum, London; London Transport Museum, London.

Michael Bennett
b.1954

MICHAEL BENNETT received a degree in Fine Art at Leeds. Self-taught in photography from the age of fourteen, he created an intimate project documenting his own family, which was first seen in 1976 at the Impressions Gallery of Photography, York before touring Britain, including the Institute of Contemporary Arts, London, and was the subject of a BBC Arena film. The Victoria and Albert Museum and Arts Council England acquired work from 'The Family', for their permanent collections.

In 1977 Bennett began working for newspapers and magazines, including *The Times*, the *Independent*, the *Sunday Times*, the *Financial Times*, *New Society*, and the *New Statesman*, and *Private Eye* as well as the BBC and the BBC World Service.

He has worked both as a satirical artist, using photomontage (composite printing), and as a documentary photographer. He has taught photography and photomontage at a number of institutions, including photography schools in Madrid and Barcelona, where he showed photomontage in the 1984 Primavera Fotografica.

COLLECTIONS INCLUDE Victoria and Albert Museum, London; Arts Council England and National Portrait Gallery, London.

LUCY BENTHAM
b.1985

LUCY BENTHAM is a fine art and documentary photographer, curator and writer, with an interest in found photography and collecting photographic archives.

HANNAH BLACKMORE
b.1988

HANNAH BLACKMORE is a British photographer and director. Her work explores the identity of individuals and communities, examining how we present ourselves, the ties that bring us together and the impressions we leave behind us.

Blackmore grew up on the Isle of Thanet in Kent, and it is the unique characters and quirks of life there that led to a keen interest in studying people. This interest has continued through Blackmore's work. By talking to her subjects about what is important to them – their interests, hobbies, jobs and loved ones – she creates complex portraits that immerse the viewer in another person's life, providing an opportunity to reflect on our universal concerns, hopes and ambitions.

JANE BOWN
1925–2014

IN THE SECOND WORLD WAR Bown served in the Women's Royal Naval Service (1944–6). After the war she studied photography at the Guildford School of Art (1946–50). She began working for the *Observer* newspaper in 1949 with a commission to photograph Bertrand Russell, and continued to work for the newspaper for her entire career. Although primarily known for portraits of people including actors, writers, artists, politicians and musicians, she also photographed many other assignments. In 1995 she was made a CBE for services to journalism.

Her books include *The Gentle Eye* (1980), *Women of Consequence* (1986), *Men of Consequence* (1987) and *Faces: The Creative Process Behind Great Portraits* (2000).

COLLECTIONS INCLUDE National Portrait Gallery, London; Guardian News & Media Archive (formerly the Newsroom), London; Palace of Westminster, London.

BILL BRANDT
1904–83

BORN HERMANN WILHELM BRANDT in Hamburg, Brandt settled in England in the early 1930s. In 1930 he visited Paris, working as an assistant to Man Ray. In 1940, he was commissioned by the Ministry of Information to take photographs of the air-raid shelters in London. He was employed by the National Buildings Record to record churches and monuments across England in 1941. Brandt's subjects, which were published in books and magazines and shown widely in exhibitions, included portraits, architecture, landscape and the nude.

Brandt had a number of books published of his photographs: *The English at Home* (1936), *A Night in London* (1938), *Camera in London* (1948), *Literary Britain* (1951), *Perspective of Nudes* (1961), *Shadow of Light* (1966). His photographs were also published in a number of magazines: *The Bystander*, *Lilliput*, *Weekly Illustrated*, *News Chronicle*, *Picture Post* and *Harper's Bazaar*.

COLLECTIONS INCLUDE Victoria and Albert Museum, London; Arts Council England; British Council, London; Tate, London; Historic England Archive, Swindon; Bill Brandt Archive, England; National Portrait Gallery, London; The Metropolitan Museum of Art, New York; The J. Paul Getty Museum, Los Angeles.

ANNE BRAYBON
b.1947

BRAYBON IS AN independent creative director and photo historian. She studied graphic design at Hornsey College of Art, London and was a licensed beach photographer on the Brighton seafront during her final student vacation. She worked as an editorial art director in Amsterdam, Paris and London, winning multiple awards, before joining the National Portrait Gallery, London, as a consultant.

In 2005 she produced the first of three themed exhibitions of newly commissioned photographic portraits. In 2009 she was invited to develop the creative approach and produce the gallery's largest and most challenging commission ever. The ensuing BT–NPG 'Road to 2012' was a celebration of the London 2012 Olympic Games. She writes, commissions, lectures and leads courses on photography for the public and private sector, including the National Galleries of Scotland, the Photographers' Gallery, London and PHotoEspaña.

Braybon is a member of the Deutsche Börse Foundation Photography Award Academy, and a committee member for the Royal Photographic Society Awards and the Format International Photography Festival steering group.

VANLEY BURKE
b.1951

ARRIVING IN ENGLAND in 1965, Burke has documented the lives and experiences of migration and settlement of African Caribbeans in Birmingham. His work represents possibly the largest photographic record of the Caribbean diaspora in the UK, and as an avid collector, he continues to connect histories through his substantial archive housed at the Library of Birmingham. In 2007 he was awarded an Honorary Doctorate from Leicester University, and the Wolverhampton School of Art and Design presented him with an Honorary Degree of Doctor of Art in 2009.

From local community organizations to the Victoria and Albert Museum and Whitechapel, London, he has exhibited widely in the UK, and as far afield as New York, South Africa and China.

His exhibitions include 'The Rivers of Birmingham', Midlands Arts Centre (MAC), Birmingham (2012); 'At Home With Vanley Burke', Ikon Gallery Birmingham (2015); 'Watchers, Seekers, Keepers', CONTACT Toronto Photography Festival, Toronto, Canada (2015); 'Three Shadows', Photography Art Centre, Xiamen, China (2016); and 'North: Diversifying a Landscape', Somerset House, London (2017).

COLLECTIONS INCLUDE Library of Birmingham, Birmingham; Arts Council of England; BM&AG, Birmingham; Herbert Art Gallery, Coventry; Walsall Local Study Museum, Walsall; Museum Africa, Johannesburg; Caribbean Cultural Center, New York.

THE CARAVAN GALLERY
2000

THE CARAVAN GALLERY is a collaboration between artists and photographers Jan Williams (b.1961) and Chris Teasdale (b.1951). Founded in 2000, the Caravan Gallery is a mobile exhibition and itinerant space. The travelling venue takes contemporary art to locations across Britain and overseas. The Caravan Gallery engages with the public, depicting diverse and multifaceted views of their home towns through the creation of temporary exhibition spaces and alternative visitor information centres in empty shops. The Caravan Gallery has published widely including *Is Britain Great?* Vols 1–3 (2007, 2009, 2011) and *Extra{ordinary}* (2015).

HENRI CARTIER-BRESSON
1908–2004

BORN IN CHANTELOUP-EN-BRIE, France, Cartier-Bresson began to take photographs from 1932, with his first exhibition in New York at the Julien Levy Gallery in 1933. In the Second World War he was a prisoner of war, escaping in 1943. He photographed the liberation of Paris in 1945 and in the same year directed, with Richard Banks, the film *Le Retour*, which looked at the return of prisoners of war. He went on to direct the films *Impressions of California* (1970) and *Southern Exposures* (1971). In 1947, along with George Rodger, David Seymour, Robert Capa and William Vandivert, he founded Magnum Photos. He travelled to many countries, including USA, India, China, France, and USSR, and visited Britain a number of times, photographing seaside towns, portraits of actors, writers, artists, Eton College and at many events.

His publications include *Images à La Sauvette* (1952), *The Europeans* (1955), *China in Transition* (1956) and *Photographs by Henri Cartier-Bresson* (1963).

COLLECTIONS INCLUDE Victoria and Albert Museum, London; The Museum of Modern Art, New York; The Museum of Fine Arts, Houston; The J. Paul Getty Museum, Los Angeles; Carnavalet Museum, Paris; Bibliothèque Nationale de France, Paris.

NATASHA CARUANA
b.1983

CARUANA IS A London-based artist working across photography, moving image and installation. She is concerned with narratives of love, betrayal and fantasy, drawing from archives, the Internet and personal narratives. She has an MA in Photography from the Royal College of Art, London and is a senior lecturer of photography at the University for the Creative Arts in Farnham, Surrey.

Caruana's works have toured widely across the United States, France, Lithuania, Portugal, India, China, Australia and Saudi Arabia and are included in numerous contemporary photographic catalogues. Recent exhibitions include 'Hooked', Science Gallery, London (2018); 'Timely Tale', Photoworks, Brighton (2017); 'The New Observatory', FACT, Liverpool (2017); 'The Real Thing', Flowers Gallery, New York (2016) and 'Married Man', International Center for Photography Museum, New York (2016). She has undertaken commissions and residencies with the Museum of Broken Relationships, Los Angeles; Photoworks, Brighton and the Open Data Institute, London.

In 2014 Caruana won the BMW Artist in Residence Award at the Nicéphore Niépce Museum, France, which led to solo shows at Les Rencontres d'Arles and Paris Photo and the monograph *Coup de Foudre*. Her work has been nominated for the 2014 Foam Paul Huf Award and the Magenta Foundation Flash Forward Award, 2012.

COLLECTIONS INCLUDE The British Library, London; The Women's Library, London; BMW Art and Culture, France; Nicéphore Niépce Museum, France; Northern Gallery for Contemporary Art, Sunderland; The Kinsey Institute, Indiana.

BOB CHICALORS
b.1982

BOB CHICALORS made his first zine in 1997 and went on to spend a decade writing for *Gay Times* magazine, where he was deputy editor. His performance work includes the queer cabaret punk band Jean Genet, go-go dancing around Europe with The Hidden Cameras and performing as (the now deceased) drag alter-ego 'Tracey Ermine' in venues around Margate, Sink The Pink and a final performance at Tate Britain. Chicalor currently creates *Rumours* zine, is writing a theatrical re-imagining of *Xanadu* for Round In Circles and is studying for an MA in The Contemporary at the University of Kent.

JOHN CHILLINGWORTH
b.1928

CHILLINGWORTH STARTED his career for *Picture Post* aged sixteen, working in the publication's darkroom. Towards the end of the Second World War, he was called up, and returned to the magazine after three years. Although back in the darkroom, he was soon going on assignment as a photographer. As a staff photographer, he would cover all types of subjects, from conflict in Korea to seaside holidays in Blackpool. He left *Picture Post* before it ceased publication, and worked as a freelance photographer for newspapers, magazines and in advertising.

COLLECTIONS INCLUDE Tate, London.

OLIVE COOK
1912–2002

BORN IN CAMBRIDGE, Olive Cook attended Newnham College, University of Cambridge, where she read modern languages. After graduation, she worked for publishers Chatto and Windus, and also, during the Second World War, for the National Gallery. Postwar, she specialized in writing the text for major topographical and architectural books and guides, working often with the photographer Edwin Smith, who she married in 1954. Cook and Smith worked together to produce writing, photography and design concepts for the yearly *Saturday Book*.

ALFRED CRACKNELL

LITTLE IS KNOWN about Cracknell, other than that he was an architectural photographer.

COLLECTIONS INCLUDE Royal Institute of British Architects, London; Historic Environment Scotland, Edinburgh; University of Glasgow, Glasgow.

WILLIAM CROOKES
1832–1919

BORN IN LONDON, Sir William Crookes studied at the Royal College of Chemistry (1848–54) where his scientific knowledge was keenly applied to numerous experimental practices including uranium printing and, later, photography's ability to capture spiritual manifestations. Most probably triggered by the death of his younger brother, his interest in and subsequent writings on spiritualism would lead him to be charged with unscientific practice in 1874. Crookes regularly contributed to *Photographic News*; he was editor of the *Liverpool Photographic Journal* (1856–7) and secretary of the London Photographic Society.

COLLECTIONS INCLUDE National Science and Media Museum, Bradford.

COLIN CURWOOD
b.1951

AT SIXTEEN Curwood worked in a photography studio in South London. Four years later he travelled across Europe to pursue an interest in documentary street photography, returning with a set of pictures that were published in various photography publications including *Creative Camera*. In 1972 Arts Council England invited thirty photographers to submit portfolios for consideration for a project called *Two Views*, in which each photographer was given two towns in Britain to photograph. Curwood was chosen as one of the final eight and, alongside Josef Koudelka, photographed Derby and Kendal. The following year the photographs were exhibited in the chosen towns, as well as at the Photographers' Gallery in London.

In 1975 Curwood published *Religious Goods, Teas and Refreshments (Irelands Holy Places)*, and he took part in the Serpentine Gallery's 'Young British Photographers' exhibition in 1979.

Curwood has worked as a freelancer for a number of UK and US publications including *Nova*, *New Society*, *The Times*, *Design Magazine*, *Now Magazine*, *Honey*, *19* and *Car*, as well as large corporations including Shell, Texaco, Hawker Siddeley and Sea Containers.

COLLECTIONS INCLUDE Victoria and Albert Museum, London.

BRUCE DAVIDSON
b.1933

BORN IN CHICAGO, Davidson studied photography at the Rochester Institute of Technology, 1951–4. In 1955 he studied at Yale University but left to serve as a photographer in the United States Army until his discharge in 1957. After military service Davidson moved to New York and worked as a photographer for a number of magazines such as *Life*, *Esquire*, *Queen* and *Vogue*. In 1958 he joined Magnum as an associate and a year later was made full member. In 1959, for eleven months, he photographed a gang of young men and women known as the 'Jokers' for a project called the *Brooklyn Gang*, which was published in *Esquire* magazine in June 1960. In the same year he visited Britain, travelling across the country; his photographs were published in 'Seeing Ourselves as an American Sees Us: A Picture Essay on Britain', *The Queen* magazine, April 1961. In 1966 he photographed people living in East Harlem; in 1970, *East 100th Street* was published as a book and also exhibited at The Museum of Modern Art, New York.

His publications include *East 100th Street* (1970), *Subway* (1986), *Circus* (2007) and *Bruce Davidson: Los Angeles 1964* (2015).

COLLECTIONS INCLUDE Tate, London; Museum of Modern Art, New York; de Young Museum, San Francisco; New-York Historical Society, New York.

F. GREAVES

LITTLE IS KNOWN about Greaves, other than he was a photographer for the *Daily Herald* in the 1940s and 1950s.

COLLECTIONS INCLUDE National Science and Media Museum, Bradford.

STEVE FERRIER
b.1966

STEVE FERRIER bought his first camera at eighteen, with the proceeds of an evening cleaning job at a military dental school. While working as a graphic designer, he spent three years documenting the coastal resorts between Walton-on-the-Naze, Essex to the east, and Weymouth, Dorset to the west.

Twenty years later he returned to photography and has been working on subjects that deal with our relationship with landscape, notably the transient nature and development of the outer suburbs, and issues of private and public space.

Ferrier self-published the tabloid photobook *Fortune of War* – a lost landmark to a satellite town in Essex – and has released a series of posters focused on the North and South Circular Roads of London.

TERRY FINCHER
1931–2008

BORN IN AYLESBURY, Fincher moved to London when he was young. At an early age, he became interested in photography and between 1945 and 1957, he worked for the Keystone Press Agency, first as a messenger and then as a photographer. He covered the Suez Crisis as a photojournalist and won the World Press Photo Award in 1968 and the British Press Photographer of the Year four times. He worked for the *Daily Herald* in 1957 and in 1960 joined the *Daily Express*. The *Daily Express* gave him his own weekly page: 'The Fincher Files', showing his photographs from around the world, including zones of conflict and war in Vietnam, Northern Ireland, Cyprus and Biafra. In 1969 he started his own news agency called Photographers International, and although best known for his photographs of conflict, he also photographed royalty, actors, sports, and feature stories.

COLLECTIONS INCLUDE Science and Media Museum, Bradford.

ANNA FOX
b.1961

WORKING IN COLOUR, Fox first gained attention for *Work Stations: Office Life in London* (1988), a study of office culture in Thatcher's Britain. She is best known for *Zwarte Piet* (1993–8), a series of portraits taken over five years exploring Dutch black-face folk traditions associated with Christmas. Other projects include *The Village* (1992), a multimedia installation examining the experiences of rural women, and *Friendly Fire* (1995), which records the leisure activity of paint-balling in the manner of war reportage. *Anna Fox Photographs 1983–2007* was published by Photoworks in 2007.

Fox's recent projects *Resort 1 and 2* investigate the contemporary face of Butlin's in Bognor Regis. Her work has been included in international group shows including 'Work, Rest & Play: British Photography from the 1960s to Today', Three Shadows, Beijing (and China tour); 'Centre of the Creative Universe, Liverpool, and the Avant-Garde' at Tate Liverpool and 'How We Are: Photographing Britain' at Tate Britain.

Fox was shortlisted for the 2010 Deutsche Börse Photography Prize and in 2016 was granted a Leverhulme Trust International Networks Award for the project Fast Forward, investigating women photographers across the globe. Fox is professor of photography at University for the Creative Arts in Farnham, Surrey, where she leads the MFA Photography course.

COLLECTIONS INCLUDE Victoria and Albert Museum, London; Museum of London, London; The National Museum of Photography, Film and Television, Bradford; Encontrens Imagen, Portugal; Museum of Contemporary Photography, Chicago; The Pompidou Centre, Paris.

STUART GRIFFITHS
b.1972

STUART GRIFFITHS is a UK-based lens-based artist who first began taking photographs as an Airborne Infantryman during the Northern Ireland 'troubles'. In 2010 Griffiths was winner of the Brighton Photo Fringe Open for his exhibition 'Closer'. In 2011 and 2013, two monographs were published based upon his soldier photographs from his days in the British Army: *The Myth of the Airborne Warrior* and *Pigs' Disco*. Griffiths is currently finishing his PhD 'The Soldiers Camera: Barrack rooms to the Battlefields' at Ulster University.

'Illegal raves in Brighton' are photographs that Griffiths took a year after leaving the Parachute Regiment. It was then that Griffiths became the unofficial photographer for the 'Church of the Sub-Genius', photographing revellers who gathered together for 'raves' on a Saturday night to dance through to early Sunday morning. Later that same year, these very 'after-parties' of more than ten people became illegal after The Criminal Justice and Public Order Act 1994 outlawed such 'repetitive beat' gatherings.

COLLECTIONS INCLUDE Imperial War Museum, London; Archive of Modern Conflict; National Science and Media Museum, Bradford.

PAT GWYNNE / JO MURRAY
1915–96 / b.1969

GWYNNE WAS BORN in Dublin and grew up with his twin brother in an orphanage, and at fourteen both were moved to a Barnardo's home in North London. Pat was apprenticed as a printer and in the 1960s moved to Ditchling in Sussex to work for Hilary Pepler who was a member of the Arts and Crafts Group that included Eric Gill. Gwynne eventually set up his own press in Hurstpierpoint, West Sussex.

Jo Murray has been archiving the colour slides of her grandfather Pat Gwynne, who photographed his family over many decades. Murray is an artist living and working in Margate. She is an Open School East 2017 alumna and graduated from Fine Art Sculpture at Brighton University in 2005. Her practice is multimedia, includes film and performance, and is wide ranging in subject matter. Murray has exhibited abroad and in the UK, including *Mrs Teasmaid* in the group show 'In the Violet Hour' at the Nayland Rock, Turner Contemporary's offsite Waste Land programme, in 2018. Alongside her own practice, Jo Murray is co-curator and programmer at Crate in Margate.

SUSAN HILLER
b.1940

SUSAN HILLER'S practice encompasses photography, painting, installation, video and writing. She studied film and photography at the Cooper Union, New York, and anthropology at Hunter College, New York. After working in anthropology, she decided to become an artist. Her first exhibition was at the Gallery House, London, in 1973; since then she has had numerous solo and group exhibitions in Great Britain and in many other countries. In 2011 she had a retrospective exhibition of her work at Tate Britain.

COLLECTIONS INCLUDE Tate, London; Victoria and Albert Museum, London; Arts Council England; Henry Moore Sculpture Collection, Leeds; Akzo Nobel Art Foundation, Amsterdam; Museum of Modern Art, New York; Augustín and Isabel Coppel Collection, Culiacán, Mexico.

JULIA HORBASCHK
b.1976

BORN IN MÜNSINGEN, near Stuttgart, Julia Horbaschk is an artist, photographer and self-taught filmmaker. After studying Editorial Photography at Brighton University, she went on to acquire a MA in International Photojournalism, and trained as a teacher at University College London.

Her works have appeared in BBC World News; *Marie Claire*; *Location, Location, Location*; *Wavelength Magazine*, *Hotshoe International* and the *British Journal of Photography*. Commissions include interviewing Magnum photographers Alec Soth, Chris Steele-Perkins and Rupert Grey for Ideas Tap and Brighton's Big Screen.

Horbaschk has delivered workshops and talks for adult education, community groups and in gallery settings, including Morley College, London; London Metropolitan University; City of Westminster College, London; Greater Brighton Metropolitan College; Brighton and Hove Museums; Brighton Digital Festival; and Montefiore Hospital, Hove. She is a disability arts and outsider art advocate. Her work has been shown in galleries and Photo Festivals including Brighton Photo Fringe; Ningbo Photo Festival (China); Goethe Institute, London; CNova Edinburgh; Jerwood Space, London; Brighton Media Centre and Hastings ArtsForum.

CHARLES HOWELL
1866–1943

ACTIVE FROM THE 1910s to the 1940s Howell had photographic studios in Belfast, Dublin and Blackpool. He was the official photographer of Blackpool Pleasure Beach, photographing the holidaymakers and day-trippers to Blackpool.

COLLECTIONS INCLUDE Greater Manchester County Record Office, Manchester.

DAVID HURN
b.1934

THE SELF-TAUGHT HURN became a photographer on leaving the British Army. He began his career at Reflex Agency in 1955, which he left in 1957. In 1956 he photographed the Hungarian revolution, with the photographs published in *Life* magazine. On leaving Reflex Agency, Hurn worked as a freelance photographer, and his work was published in a variety of magazines. He joined Magnum as an associate in 1965, becoming a full member two years later. Between 1972 and 1977, he was a member of the Photography Committee of Arts Council England. In 1973 Hurn was head of Film and Photography at Gwent College of Higher Education in South Wales and was instrumental in founding the School of Documentary Photography in Newport, for which he was director. In 1979–80 he was the Distinguished Visiting Artist and Adjunct Professor at Arizona State University.

His publications include the exhibition catalogue for 'Wales in Black and White', (1974), *David Hurn Photographs 1956–1976* (1979), *On Being a Photographer: A Practical Guide* (with Bill Jay; 1997) and *Wales: Land of My Father* (2000).

COLLECTIONS INCLUDE Arts Council England; Welsh Arts Council, Cardiff; International Museum of Photography, George Eastman House, Rochester, New York; Museum of Modern Art, New York.

KURT HUTTON
1893–1960

BORN KURT HÜBSCHMANN, Hutton settled in England in 1933 and a year later he worked for the magazine *Weekly Illustrated*. In 1938 Hutton began to work for *Picture Post* as a freelance photographer until interned in a camp in 1940. On his release in 1941, he again worked for *Picture Post* but as a staff photographer. In 1951, due to his health, he moved with his wife to Aldeburgh, Suffolk. On occasion he continued to work on stories for *Picture Post* and photographed the Aldeburgh Festivals. Hutton wrote about his work as a photojournalist in the book *Speaking Likeness* (1947), part of Focal Press's series, Master of the Camera.

COLLECTIONS INCLUDE National Portrait Gallery, London; Britten-Pears Foundation, Aldeburgh; The Hyman Collection, London; Tate, London.

HENRY IDDON
b.1969

IDDON IS A Blackpool-based photographer who has been documenting the town since the early 1980s. His work has also included curating and mentoring young homeless people, documenting their experiences of the town. He has received two major individual grants from Arts Council England in 2006 for *Spots of Time* and in 2016 for *Instanto Outdoors*. Iddon was artist in residence at Forton Motorway Services on the M6, Lancashire, in 2015–16, and was nominated for the National Media Museum Bursary Award (UK), shortlisted for the And/Or Book Awards and long listed for the 2014 Aesthetica Art Prize. His work has been shown in galleries and at photography festivals in Brazil, Italy, Nepal, Syria and the UK.

COLLECTIONS INCLUDE Banff Centre for Mountain Culture, Alberta, Canada; Centre for Contemporary Photography, University of Tucson Arizona, USA; George Eastman House, Kodak Museum, Rochester, USA; Kraszna-Krausz Collection, National Science and Media Museum, Bradford; Scottish National Screen Archive, Edinburgh; State Library of New South Wales, Sydney; The North West Film Archive, Manchester Metropolitan University, Manchester; The Wordsworth Trust, Cumbria; Keswick Museum and Art Gallery, Cumbria.

DAFYDD JONES
b.1956

JONES STUDIED FINE ART and is a self-taught photographer. After college he was employed at Butlin's holiday camp, Minehead, as a photographer. In 1981 he won a prize for his photographs 'Bright Young Things' in a photographic competition organized by the *Sunday Times* magazine. Soon after, he was employed to photograph various balls, dances and weddings for *Tatler* magazine. In 1989 he moved to New York, working for the *New York Observer*, *Paper* magazine and *Vanity Fair*.

COLLECTIONS INCLUDE National Portrait Gallery, London.

SIRKKA-LIISA KONTTINEN
b.1948

BORN IN FINLAND, Konttinen studied filmmaking in London and became a founder member of the Amber Film and Photography Collective, based since 1969 in Newcastle upon Tyne. Her documentation of Byker, the close-knit community of Newcastle where she lived for seven years, was recognized as a key photographic and filmic account of a rich working-class culture on the eve of its destruction.

Long-term projects, developed as exhibitions, books and/or films, include 'Byker' (1980 – exhibition); *Byker* (1983 – book); *Keeping Time* (1983); 'Step by Step' (1989); *Letters to Katja* (1989); *Writing in the Sand* (2000 – book); 'The Coal Coast' (1998–2002); *Byker Revisited* (2009); *Today I'm With You* (2010); and *Song For Billy* (2017). The companion films *Byker* (1983) and *Writing in the Sand* (1991) have won numerous awards at international film festivals.

In 1980 Konttinen's 'Byker' exhibition was the first photographic exhibition from the UK to be taken to China by the British Council after the Cultural Revolution. In 2016 Tate Modern acquired the *Byker* series for its permanent collection and displayed it as part of its inaugural show at the Switch House extension. In 2011 Konttinen's photography and Amber's films were inscribed in the UNESCO UK Memory of the World Register as being of outstanding national value and importance to the UK.

COLLECTIONS INCLUDE Finnish Museum of Photography, Helsinki; Museum of Fine Arts, Houston; New York Public Library, New York; Tate, London; The Side Photographic Collection, Newcastle upon Tyne; Victoria and Albert Museum, London.

GRACE LAU
b.1939

BORN IN LONDON of Chinese parentage, Lau is a practising photographer, artist, writer and lecturer. She has a MA in Photography and Culture from University of the Arts London. She has exhibited widely, including at the National Portrait Gallery and Tate Britain in London, Photofusion London and Aberystwyth Arts Centre, Wales.

In 2005 Lau received an Arts Council England grant to recreate a nineteenth-century Chinese portrait studio in Hastings, in which she invited residents and visitors to pose for their portraits, in a reverse situation to that of Victorian photographers in China during the 1800s. Her project resulted in an archive of contemporary *21st Century Types*.

Lau's published books include *Adults in Wonderland* (1997) and *Picturing the Chinese: Early Western Photographs and Postcards of China* (2008).

COLLECTIONS INCLUDE National Portrait Gallery, London; Michael Wilson Collection; Sarah and David Kowitz Collection; Asia Culture Institute, Korea.

RAYMOND CONRAD LAWSON
1928–2006

LAWSON WAS BORN the second of five children to a Scottish father and an English mother in Canada. When Raymond was five years old, the family returned to London, England. Lawson was largely self-taught, but did study briefly via a series of lectures under Baron Adolph de Meyer, a celebrity portrait photographer. He attended both the 1948 London Olympics at Wembley and the Festival of Britain in 1951 at the South Bank in London. Lawson photographed varying aspects of both events using a Rolleiflex and later a Pentax camera.

Attending his brother's wedding in Whitstable, Kent, in 1954 as best man, Ray was so taken with the maid of honour (his future wife Alma) that within 36 hours they were engaged. The marriage was long and fruitful, and they had five sons between the years of 1956 and 1965. From the late 1950s they were an integral part of the local Catholic community, with Ray taking over as the parish photographer, liaising with the infant and primary school of St Mary's at such events as the class photo or the children's First Holy Communion.

Lawson photographed the parish and documented the changing face of Whitstable for over forty years.

BARRY LEWIS
b.1948

BARRY LEWIS studied photography at the Royal College of Art, London and is a London-based photographer and film-maker and founder of the agency Network Photographers. Lewis has worked internationally for books and magazines including *Life* magazine and the *National Geographic*. As well as photojournalism and portraiture, Lewis has directed over twenty documentaries, commercials and art films. His work has been exhibited at the Victoria and Albert Museum, the Museum of London, the Photographers' Gallery and Modern Art Oxford. Exhibitions and awards include 'Positive Lives' (1993), a book and international exhibition about living with AIDS, and the World Press Award's Oscar Barnac Medal for humanitarian photography (1990). In 2010 Barry worked with musician David Toop and singer Elaine Mitchener to produce the mixed-media production *Of Leonardo da Vinci* for the Teatro Fondamenta Nuove, Venice. A new version, choreographed by Dam Van Huynh, now tours internationally and was performed at the Purcell Room on the South Bank in September 2018.

Lewis's recent books include *Miami Beach 1985–2000*; *Vaguely Lost in Shangri-la: Photographs from the Glastonbury Festival* (2011); *Blackpool 1984–1989* (2017) and *Soho 1990* (2018).

PAUL MARTIN
1864–1944

BORN IN HERBEUVILLE, France, Martin and his family moved to London in 1872. In 1880 he was apprenticed, for three years, to Paul Douet, a wood engraver, staying with him until 1886. His interest in photography began in the mid-1870s, and in 1884 he purchased a camera, taking photographs, some of which he sold to his employer. Martin, with others, founded the West Surrey Amateur Photographic Society in 1888. In his spare time and on holidays, he photographed the streets during the day and at night, and at the seaside. Martin was awarded a gold medal for his night scenes of London, exhibited at the Annual Exhibition of the Royal Photographic Society in 1896. He took up photography full-time, entering into partnership with

H. Dorrett to form the company Dorrett and Martin in 1898. After the company ceased to operate in 1926, Martin continued to photograph, travel, lecture and exhibit his photographs.

COLLECTIONS INCLUDE Victoria and Albert Museum, London; Museum of Modern Art, New York; Harry Ransom Center, The University of Texas at Austin.

CHLOE DEWE MATHEWS
b.1982

CHLOE DEWE MATHEWS is an award-winning photographic artist based in St Leonards-on-Sea. After studying fine art at Camberwell College of Arts, London and the University of Oxford, she worked in the feature-film industry before dedicating herself to photography.

Her work is internationally recognized, exhibiting at Tate Modern, the Irish Museum of Modern Art, Museum Folkwang and Fotomuseum Antwerp, as well as being published widely in newspapers and magazines such as the *Guardian*, the *Sunday Times*, the *Financial Times*, *Harpers* and *Le Monde*. She has also been commissioned to make new work by institutions such as the Contemporary Art Society, University of Oxford and Photoworks.

Her awards include the *British Journal of Photography* International Photography Award, the Julia Margaret Cameron New Talent Award and the Royal Photographic Society Vic Odden Award, and her nominations include the Deutsche Börse Photography Prize, the Prix Pictet and the Paul Huf Award.

Matthew's first monograph *Shot at Dawn* was published in 2014, and in the same year she became the Robert Gardner Fellow in Photography at the Peabody Museum of Archaeology and Ethnology, Harvard University.

COLLECTIONS INCLUDE the British Council Collection, London; the Irish State Art Collection; National Library of Wales.

IAIN MCKELL
b.1957

MCKELL FIRST STARTED taking photography seriously as a fine art student in 1976 while studying at Exeter Art College. The project was called *Private Reality*. During the summer holidays in his hometown of Weymouth, he worked as a seaside photographer. After college in 1979 he moved to London, where he photographed the Skinhead–Mod revival. He went on to photograph the New Romantic scene and began working for *i-D* magazine and *The Face*, and taking on commissions from record and advertising companies. Shooting Madonna's first magazine cover in 1982, he began working for *Vogue Italia* and *L'Uomo Vogue*. Since 2012 he has returned to the seaside, with trips to numerous seaside towns with a personal perspective on a subject he understands. In addition he has collaborated with Kate Moss, going on the road for two days shooting fashion with the New Gypsy travellers in 2011.

His publications include *Sub Culture* (1979) about the Skinhead–Mod revival; *The New Gypsies* (2011); *Fashion Forever* (2004); and *Beautiful Britain* (2012).

McKell has had numerous exhibitions in New York, London, Paris and Milan.

DANIEL MEADOWS
b.1952

PHOTOGRAPHER, DOCUMENTARIAN and digital storyteller, Meadows has spent a lifetime recording British society. He challenges the status quo by working in a collaborative way to capture extraordinary aspects of ordinary life through pictures, audio recordings and short movies. He is best known for his 10,000-mile journey around England in the Free Photographic Omnibus (1973–4), a project he revisited twenty-five years later for the series *National Portraits: Now & Then* (1997). His pioneering work of participatory media, BBC Capture Wales (2001–8), encouraged many hundreds of people to embrace the digital age in pop-up workshops, making their own two minutes of television by framing their memories and pictures into digital stories. Capture Wales won a BAFTA Cymru in 2002.

Meadows taught Documentary Photography in Newport (1983–94) with David Hurn; also photojournalism (1994–2001) and digital storytelling (2000–12) at Cardiff School of Journalism, Media and Cultural Studies, where he completed his PhD (2005). In the 1990s he taught photojournalism workshops in the emerging democracies of eastern Europe. After 2000 he travelled repeatedly to Australia and the USA, lecturing.

His photographs and short films have been exhibited widely both in the UK and Europe. Solo shows include ICA London (1975), the Photographers' Gallery, London (1987) and National Science and Media Museum, Bradford (2011). Group shows include the Serpentine Gallery, London (1973) and Tate Britain, London (2007).

In addition to his own five books, there is a scholarly overview of his early work by Val Williams, *Daniel Meadows: Edited Photographs from the 70s and 80s* (2011).

A Café Royal Books boxed-set edition, *Eight Stories* (2015), celebrates the work he did while artist in residence in northeast Lancashire in the 1970s. The Daniel Meadows Archive was acquired by the Bodleian Library at the University of Oxford in March 2018.

COLLECTIONS INCLUDE Bodleian Library, University of Oxford, Oxford; Victoria and Albert Museum, London.

LEE MILLER
1907–77

BORN IN Poughkeepsie, New York, Miller was a model and photographer. After education in Paris, she returned to New York in 1926 and studied at the Art Students League. She was also in demand as a fashion model, working for *Vogue* magazine. In 1929 she went back to Paris and met and worked with Man Ray in his studio. While in Paris Miller opened her own photography studio, but returned to New York in 1932, where she opened another successful studio. In 1939 she settled in England and a year later began working as a photographer for *Vogue* magazine in London, taking portrait and fashion photographs. Miller also photographed war-torn London, with some of her photographs published in the book *Grim Glory: Pictures of Britain under Fire* (1941). In 1942 she became an accredited US Forces War Correspondent, covering the war in Europe. After the war she continued for a short time to photograph for *Vogue* magazine, and also for her husband Roland Penrose's biographies on artists.

COLLECTIONS INCLUDE Lee Miller Archives, Sussex; Victoria and Albert Museum, London; Philadelphia Museum of Art, Philadelphia.

LÁSZLÓ MOHOLY-NAGY
1895–1946

BORN IN Borsód, Mohol Puszta, Hungary, Moholy-Nagy served as an officer in the Austro-Hungarian army during the First World War. After the war he returned to his law studies but decided to become an artist. In 1920 he moved to Berlin and by 1922 began to experiment with photograms. At the invitation of Walter Gropius, he taught at the Bauhaus from 1923 to 1928. He left Germany at the rise of the Nazi regime in the 1930s, eventually moving to England in 1935.

While living in London, Moholy-Nagy worked as a photographer and designer, photographing the markets of London and its architecture. He worked on a film by director Alexander Korda and designed issues of the *Architectural Review*. He lived in London until 1937 until moving to the USA to be head of the New Bauhaus American School of Design, in Chicago. In 1939 he founded the School of Design (later the Institute of Design, 1944).

Moholy-Nagy's publications include *The Street Markets of London* (1936), *Eton Portrait* (1937) and *An Oxford University Chest* (1938).

COLLECTIONS INCLUDE Royal Institute of British Architects, London; Victoria and Albert Museum, London; Tate, London; Solomon R. Guggenheim Museum, New York; The J. Paul Getty Museum, Los Angeles.

FRANCIS MORTIMER
1874–1944

BORN IN Southsea, Portsmouth, Mortimer became an articled clerk and passed his Law Society exams. In 1902 he worked for *Amateur Photographer* writing articles, and in 1904 he was assistant editor of the *British Journal of Photography*, but he left in 1906 to work at the *Photographic News*. In 1908 Mortimer took up the editorship of what would become *Amateur Photographer and Photographic News*, a position he held until his death in 1944.

In 1908 he became a member of the Linked Ring brotherhood of photographers and was known as Bromoiler. Mortimer joined the Royal Photographic Society in 1904 and later became its president from 1940 to 1942. He was a member and later president of the Camera Club, London from 1938 to 1944.

While Mortimer photographed a variety of subjects, he was primarily known for his photographs of the sea, for which he received considerable acclaim. In 1942 he was made a CBE for his contribution to photography. He died in July 1944, as a consequence of his injuries sustained a month earlier during a flying bomb attack on London.

COLLECTIONS INCLUDE Royal Photographic Society Collection, Victoria and Albert Museum, London; the Camera Club, London; Art Gallery, New South Wales.

HELEN MUSPRATT
1907–2001

BORN IN INDIA, Muspratt came to England as a child and quickly became interested in photography. She trained at Regents Street Polytechnic in London, and in 1929 opened her first studio in Swanage, Dorset. She photographed arts and cultural figures in Swanage, as well as being an all-round family portraitist. In 1930, she opened a studio in Cambridge with Lettice Ramsey, and later opened a second studio in Oxford.

Muspratt was an innovator and experimentalist, and was one of the pioneers of solarization in Britain. The Swanage studio was managed by Muspratt's sister Joan for many years. In 1986 her work was included in 'The Other Observers: Women's Photography in Britain' exhibition at the National Museum of Photography in Bradford, and her legacy has been preserved by her daughter Jessica Sutcliffe in her book *Face: Shape and Angle* (2016).

EDMUND NÄGELE
b.1950

BORN IN 1950, Nägele began his career in advertising in Munich. He joined the John Hinde Company in the mid-1960s, and has become well known for his remarkable highly coloured tableaux of life at Butlin's holiday camps, and his large-format photography across Britain and Europe. John Hinde was a pioneer of colour photography in Britain, who recruited a talented group of photographers from Europe and the UK to be part of his team.

PAUL NASH
1889–1946

BORN IN London, Paul Nash was an artist whose practice encompassed a range of mediums: painter, writer, designer and photographer. In 1910 he attended the Slade School of Art but left after one year. At the start of the First World War, he enlisted in the Artists' Rifles Regiment, later receiving a commission in the Hampshire Regiment. In 1917 he was invalided home but later that year returned to the conflict as an official war artist. In 1918 he returned to England and continued to paint, exhibiting his drawings and paintings of the conflict at the Leicester Galleries, London.

In the 1930s Nash began to use photography as a source for his paintings and to illustrate articles he had published. He contributed articles that he illustrated with his own photographs to magazines such as the *Architectural Review*. He was commissioned by John Betjeman to write a Shell Guide to Dorset (1936). He founded Unit One, a group of artists and architects, and in the Second World War he once again become an official war artist.

COLLECTIONS INCLUDE Tate, London; Imperial War Museum, London; Arts Council England; Manchester Art Gallery, Manchester.

MARTIN PARR
b.1952

THROUGHOUT HIS CAREER Parr has exhibited, published, curated and collaborated extensively.

Following graduation from Manchester Polytechnic (1973) where he studied photography, Parr moved to Yorkshire where 'Home Sweet Home' was shown at Impressions Gallery, York (1974). Two years later Parr's 'Beauty Spots' was exhibited at Impressions Gallery, York (1976) as well. The 1980s saw Parr produce some of his key series including: 'Bad Weather' (1982) and 'The Last Resort' (1986), the latter produced in New Brighton and exhibited at the Serpentine Gallery, London (1986). The 1980s also saw Parr join Magnum Photos (1988), where he was the collective's president from 2013 to 2017.

Parr's exhibitions have included 'Three Perspectives on Photography', Hayward Gallery, London (1979); 'The Non-Conformists', Camera Work, London (1981); 'Bad Weather', Photographers' Gallery, London (1982); 'The Cost of Living', Royal Photographic Society, Bath (1989); 'Signs of the Time', Janet Borden, New York (1992); 'Autoportrait', Tom Blau Gallery, London (2000); 'Cruel and Tender', Tate Modern, London (2002); 'Martin Parr Photoworks 1971–2000', Barbican Art Gallery, London (2002); 'Black Country Stories', Light House Media Centre, Wolverhampton (2011) and 'Life's a Beach', Aperture, New York (2013).

He has been guest curator for Arles Festival (2004) and the Brighton Photo Biennial (2010). In 2016 Parr curated 'Strange and Familiar' at the Barbican Art Gallery, London.

Val Williams's book *Martin Parr* was published in 2002. Parr's own publications include *The Cost of Living* (1989), *Sign of the Times* (1992), *From A to B* (1994), *Small Worlds* (1995), *Boring Postcards* (1999), *Common Sense* (1999) and *Think of England* (2000) and his edited publications include *Our True Intent Is All For Your Delight* (2002), *Lodz Ghetto* (with Timothy Pruss, 2004), *The Photobook: A History* – Vol. I (2004), Vol. II (2006) and Vol. III (2014), all with Gerry Badger, and *The Chinese Photobook: From the 1900s to the Present* (2016) with WassinkLundgren.

Martin Parr was awarded the Sony World Photography Award for Outstanding Contribution to Photography in 2017, and in that same year the Martin Parr Foundation was opened in Bristol, UK.

COLLECTIONS INCLUDE Arts Council England; Victoria and Albert Museum, London; Tate, London; Museum of Modern Art, Tokyo; Museum of Modern Art, New York; Kodak, France.

ERIC PATTERSON

ERIC PATTERSON'S abandoned archive was discovered by artist Jess Kohl in Canonbury in North London. Patterson was a cabinet-maker and keen photographer. The archive of transparencies, ranging from holiday photos to gay erotica, was found in a flat that had remained untouched since the 1960s.

DANIELLE PECK
b.1966

PECK STUDIED for a MA in Documentary Photography and Photojournalism at the London College of Communication. She has been immersed in documentary story-telling for nearly thirty years, primarily as an international award-winning television documentary producer for the BBC. Much of her photography looks at curious hobbies: Afghan hound racing, same-sex ballroom dancing and the utterly bizarre but captivating sport of chess boxing. She also worked with Actionaid International, shooting globally for their campaigns and smaller NGOs in Ghana and Madagascar to build their image libraries.

Peck has worked as Head of Pictures at the BBC, running the BBC's photography department, which commissions and manages programme-related photography. In October 2013 Peck was selected to join the prestigious Eddie Adams Workshop in New York for an intense and exhilarating four days where America's photojournalism elite share their experience and wisdom with one hundred new professionals from around the world.

VINCA PETERSEN
b.1973

BORN IN South Korea, Petersen now lives in Kent. Her recent photographic work has been featured in *AnOther*, *True*, *AnOther Man* and *Aperture* magazines. She is best known for her book *No System* (1999), which documented her years travelling with European sound systems. In 2010 she created Future Youth Project, which has run charity projects in Romania, Ukraine and Africa. Currently she engages in collaborative creative projects with a wide range of people using photographs and ephemera from her extensive archive. One such project was published in 2018 as *Future Fantasy*.

COLLECTIONS INCLUDE Victoria and Albert Museum, London; The Monsoon Collection, London.

JOHN PIPER
1903–92

BORN IN Epsom, John Piper's practice encompassed a range of mediums: painting, photography, tapestry, stain glass, writing and theatre design. He studied art at Richmond School of Art (1927–8) and then the Royal College of Art, London (1928–9). In 1937 he met John Betjeman, editor of the Shell County Guides, who asked him to write a book on Oxfordshire, which he illustrated with a number of his photographs. Piper also wrote and illustrated articles on church sculpture and on the built environment for the *Architectural Review*. During the Second World War, he was commissioned as a war artist, creating paintings of churches damaged by bombing.

His publications include *Oxon* (1938), *Romney Marsh* (1950), *Shropshire: A Shell Guide* (1951), *Oxfordshire, not including the City of Oxford* (1953) and *A Painter's Camera: Buildings and Landscapes in Britain 1935–1985* (1987).

COLLECTIONS INCLUDE Tate, London; Royal Institute of British Architects, London.

ENZO RAGAZZINI
b.1934

BORN IN Rome, in 1934, Ragazzini studied architecture at the University of Rome. A self-taught photographer, he works as a freelancer in Rome and London. He taught photography at the Hornsey College of Art, London (1969–71) and in 1969 he was part of the photography exhibition 'Spectrum: the Diversity of Photography' at the Institute of Contemporary Arts in London.

His publications include *Conversazione in Sicilia* (1973), *Arno* (1974) and *Photographs of Bomarzo* (1980).

MARC RIBOUD
1923–2016

BORN IN Saint-Genis-Laval, France, Riboud began to take photographs when he was fourteen years old. He studied engineering at the Ecole Centrale, Lyon from 1945 to 1948. By 1951 he had decided to become a photographer and two years later he was invited to join Magnum. From the 1950s to the 2000s, he visited many countries, working on stories. During 1954 he spent time in England, where he photographed in Blackpool, London and Southend.

His publications include *Women of Japan* (1959) and *Into the Orient* (2012).

COLLECTIONS INCLUDE The Pompidou Centre, Paris.

GRACE ROBERTSON
b.1930

ROBERTSON'S PHOTOGRAPHIC CAREER began in 1947 working with Simon Guttmann at Report Agency. Robertson is best known for her significant work with *Picture Post* magazine, where she remained a contributor until 1957 when the publication closed. In the late 1960s, Robertson began a career as a primary school teacher, but her photographic practice continued and gained recognition. Her work was featured in 'The Other Observers: Women's Photography in Britain' exhibition at the National Museum of Photography, Bradford, and in the 1990s Robertson exhibited her series on nonagenarians at the Royal National Theatre, London.

Other exhibitions include '1989', Zelda Cheatle Gallery, London (1990), Cathleen Ewing Gallery, Washington, DC and the National Gallery of Wales (1994). Publications include *Grace Robertson: Picture Post Photographer* (1989) and *A Sympathetic Eye* (2002).

COLLECTIONS INCLUDE the National Gallery of Australia, Sydney; Scottish National Portrait Gallery, Edinburgh; Victoria and Albert Museum, London and National Science and Media Museum, Bradford.

BARNET SAIDMAN
1913–93

BARNET SAIDMAN came from a family of photographers, learning his trade in the studio of his father George in Blackpool. At the age of sixteen, he worked for the *Bristol Evening World*. In the mid-1930s he joined the *News Chronicle*, covering news stories and features. In the Second World War, he joined the RAF as a flight lieutenant in the photographic unit. After the war he rejoined the *News Chronicle* but left the newspaper in 1960 to work freelance. He was a fellow of the Royal Photographic Society.

COLLECTIONS INCLUDE National Science and Media Museum, Bradford; Imperial War Museum, London; London College of Fashion, University of the Arts London.

REUBEN SAIDMAN
1906–67

REUBEN SAIDMAN came from a family of photographers, learning his trade in the studio of his father George in Blackpool. He worked for the local papers in Blackpool, later working for the *Daily Herald* and *Illustrated*. In the Second World War he was a war correspondent, covering Europe and the Far East. He was a member of the Royal Photographic Society.

COLLECTIONS INCLUDE National Science and Media Museum, Bradford; National Portrait Gallery, London.

REGINALD SLADER
1920–2002

AFTER THE SECOND WORLD WAR, Slader worked mainly for the civil service. In 1953 he married Doreen King and went on his one and only flight to Austria. Although he loved sharing adventures, he preferred trains and boats to planes. While this might seemingly have limited the scope of his explorations, he always felt the British Isles had so much to offer he would never see it all. His son Tim pointed out that Slader particularly enjoyed the coast because of its extreme diversity: from the wild seas around Cornwall to the Jurassic cliffs in Devon, from the holiday beaches of Kent to the wind-swept sands of Northumberland.

Slader always took his camera with him searching for patterns and character, constantly looking for inventive ways to visually interpret so that his photographs were not simply snaps but told a wider story. His interest in photography continued after the birth of his sons, when he switched from monochrome to colour photography. Slader continued to be involved in the arts and photography throughout his life, passing on this creative spirit to both his children.

Slader was a member of the Friern Barnet & Totteridge Camera Club in North London for many years, winning several awards for his portraiture and landscape work. He died following a stroke in 2002. His son Tim Slader cares for the archive.

C. SMITH

LITTLE IS KNOWN about C. Smith, other than that he was a photographer for the *Daily Herald* in the 1960s.

COLLECTIONS INCLUDE National Science and Media Museum, Bradford.

EDWIN SMITH
1912–71

AGED EIGHTEEN, Smith won a scholarship to the Architectural Association in London but due to family circumstances did not complete his studies. He worked as an architectural draughtsman until 1935, when he became a freelance photographer. He photographed not just architecture but also the landscape, topography and gardens in Britain and other countries.

Numerous books were published which included Smith's photographs, many of which were collaborations with writers, most notably his wife Olive Cook. These include *English Cottages and Farmhouses* (1954), *English Abbeys and Priories* (1960), *The Wonders of Italy* (1965) and *English Cathedrals* (1989).

Smith's publications include *Phototips on Cats and Dogs Not for Beginners Only* (1938), *All the Photo-tricks: Ways and Ideas Off the Beaten Track* (1940), *English Parish Churches* (1952) and *England, Photographed by Edwin Smith* (1957).

COLLECTIONS INCLUDE Royal Institute of British Architects, London; Victoria and Albert Museum, London; Tate, London; Fry Art Gallery, Saffron Walden.

COLIN THOMAS
b.1950

BORN IN Aberystwyth, Wales, Thomas is a self-taught photographer whose first body of work *Event* was inspired by the work of British documentary photographers such as Tony Ray-Jones and David Hurn. *Event* was exhibited at the Open Eye Gallery, Liverpool in 1985 and Thomas has since worked on projects in Merseyside, mid Wales and Shropshire. His photographs have been exhibited in England, Wales and France, and he has had four photobooks published.

KEITH VAUGHAN
1912–77

BORN IN Selsey, England, Vaughan was a self-taught painter and during 1930 set up a darkroom at his home, enabling him to print his photographs of the landscape and friends. Between 1931 and 1938, Vaughan worked for the advertising agency Lintas. In the later years of the 1930s, before the outbreak of the Second World War, he spent time at Pagham beach photographing friends, which he later assembled into an album called *Dick's Book of Photographs*. In 1941 Vaughan joined the Pioneer Corp and worked as an interpreter in a German prisoner-of-war camp in Yorkshire. Directly after the war, Vaughan taught at Camberwell School of Arts and Crafts (1946–8) and then Central School of Art (1948–57), both in London. He also taught at the Slade School of Fine Art, London.

In 1942 he exhibited drawings at the Reid and Lefevre Gallery, London, with an exhibition of paintings four years later. In 1962 the Whitechapel Art Gallery, London held a retrospective exhibition. In 1964 Vaughan was made an honorary fellow at the Royal College of Art, London and in 1965 he was awarded a CBE.

COLLECTIONS INCLUDE Tate, London; School of Art Gallery and Museum, Aberystwyth University, Aberystwyth.

ROWAN WHYBREW
b.1975

WHYBREW STUDIED SOCIOLOGY at the University of Bristol and Fine Art at University of the Arts London and Wimbledon College of Art, London. Currently, Whybrew is a Fine Art MPhil–PhD candidate (by practice) at the Royal College of Art, London. Prior to art school, he worked as a graphic designer, and it was through working with other people's photographs that he developed an interest in the lure of images. That interest, initially underpinned by a curiosity to understand how images govern experience, how they represent the world and how they do or do not signify meaning, shaped his early art practice and still informs some of his work today. Though not bound to any particular medium, he works predominantly with photography.

He is currently a research student and is exploring encounters with history and memory in the English landscape. His work is often concerned with the poetics of place, and, most recently, with the writing and rewriting of historical narrative and the representation of time and space in photography.

JASON WILDE
b.1967

JASON WILDE is a photographer born and based in London, England. He received a MA in Photography at the London College of Printing, London. Along with a number of solo shows, he has exhibited in venues that include Tate Modern, London, the National Portrait Gallery, London, the Museum of London and the Guernsey Museum. In 2015–16 he was the artist in residence for the Guernsey Museum and Guernsey Photography Festival.

In 2017 Wilde set up a small independent publishing company called Butchers Hook Books, which has since published *Vera & John* (2017), *JWFPS 01* (2017), *Guerns!* (2018) and *JWFPS 02* (2018).

COLLECTIONS INCLUDE Museum of London, London; Guernsey Museum, Guernsey.

DO YOU WISH YOU WERE HERE?

1. Elborough, Travis, *Wish You Were Here* (Sceptre, London, 2010), p.10.

SHELL STORIES

1. Heathcote, David, *A Shell Eye on England: The Shell County Guides 1934–1984* (Libri Publishing, Faringdon, 2011).
2. Ibid., p.16.
3. Spalding, Frances, *John Piper, Myfanwy Piper: Lives in Art* (Oxford University Press, Oxford, 2009), p.135.
4. Fraser Jenkins, David, *John Piper: A Painter's Camera* (Tate Publishing, London, 1987), pp.11–12.
5. Accessed 26 November 2018: www.earlyphotography.co.uk
6. Fraser Jenkins, David, *John Piper: A Painter's Camera* (Tate Publishing, London, 1987), p.17.
7. Accessed 26 November 2018: https://en.m.wikipedia.org/wiki/Ferrania
8. Spalding, Frances, *John Piper, Myfanwy Piper: Lives in Art* (Oxford University Press, Oxford, 2009), p.36.
9. Piper, John, *Buildings and Prospects*, *Architectural Review*, 1948, p.11.
10. Accessed 26 November 2018: www.ryemuseum.co.uk
11. Causey, Andrew, *Paul Nash's Photographs: Document and Image* (Tate Publishing, London, 1973), p.11.
12. Tate Archive.
13. Tate Archive.
14. Tate Archive.
15. Nash, Paul, 'Swanage or Seaside Surrealism', *Architectural Review*, 1936.
16. Ibid.
17. Denton, Pennie, *Seaside Surrealism: Paul Nash in Swanage* (Peveril Press, Swanage, 2002), p.18.
18. Ibid.
19. ND quoted in Denton, Pennie, *Seaside Surrealism. Paul Nash in Swanage* (Peveril Press, Swanage, 2002), p.51.
20. John Betjeman, *Cornwall: A Shell Guide* (Faber and Faber, London, 1964). p.7.
21. Ibid., p.100.
22. Cook, Olive and Edwin Smith, 'Beside the Seaside', *The Saturday Book*, (Hutchinson, London, 1952).
23. Fraser Jenkins, David, *John Piper: A Painter's Camera* (Tate Publishing, London, 1987), pp.9–10.

WAVES ON THE BEACH

1. The railway station at Ramsgate main sands opened in 1863.
2. Mortimer, F. J., 'On a Rocky Coast' in *The Amateur Photographer*, Vol. XXXVIII, No. 992, 8 October 1903, pp.292–6.
3. Ibid., p.293.
4. Ibid., p.294.
5. Susan Hiller cited in Gallagher, A. (ed), *Susan Hiller* (Tate Publishing, London, 2011), p.30.
6. Burnett, Charles, J., 'On the application of Uranium and other matters to Photography' in *Photographic Notes*, 2, 1858.

SEASIDE BOHEMIAS

1. For the information about Helen Muspratt's work in Purbeck, I am indebted to Jessica Sutcliffe's illustrated biography *Face: Shape and Angle* (Manchester University Press, Manchester 2016).
2. Ibid., p.91.
3. Ibid., p.123.
4. Lee, Hermione, *Penelope Fitzgerald: A Life* (Chatto and Windus, London, 2013), p.128.
5. Hastings, Gerald, *Keith Vaughan: The Photographs* (Pagham Press, London, 2013).
6. Ibid., p.72.

REPORTING BACK

1. R. Mortimer in Brandt, Bill, *The English at Home* (B. T. Batsford, London, 1936), p.8.
2. The phrase 'creative treatment of actuality' was coined by film-maker John Grierson in a paper discussing documentary cinema. See Grierson, J., 'The Documentary Producer', *Cinema Quarterly*, 2 (1), 1858, pp.7–9.
3. Delaney, P., *Bill Brandt: A Life* (Jonathan Cape, London, 2004), p.112.

4. Saidman, R., 'Black as Night', *Popular Photography*, October 1946, pp.50–1 and pp.150–4.
5. Grace Robertson interviewed by Pulver, A., 'My Best Shot', *Guardian*, 19 May 2010.
6. Quoted in Robertson, G., 'Mother's Day Off', *Picture Post*, 25 September 1954, 64(13), p.14.
7. Robertson, G., *Grace Robertson, Photojournalist of the 50s* (Virago Press, London, 1989), p.23.
8. B. Davidson cited in Riefe, J., 'A Passing Era: Two Americans' Visions of Britain and Ireland in the 1960s', *Guardian*, 1 December 2010.
9. Hurn, D. and B. Jay, *On Being A Photographer: A Practical Guide*, (Lensworks, Anacortes, WA, 2007, 3rd edition), p.66.
10. Cartier-Bresson, H., *The Decisive Moment* (Simon and Schuster, New York, NY, 1952), p.3 of foreword.

HALCYON DAYS

1. Thomas, Dylan, *Holiday Memory* (J. M. Dent & Sons Ltd, London, 1972), no pagination.
2. Sheriff, R. C., *The Fortnight in September* (Persephone Books, London, 2017. First published Victor Gallancz, London, 1931), p.128.
3. Ibid., p.162.
4. Germaine Greer in Bown, J., *Unknown Bown* (Observer Books, London, 2007), unpaginated.
5. Jane Bown cited in Bown, J., *Unknown Bown* (Observer Books, London, 2007), p.75.
6. Baker, S. cited in Douglas, A., *Shirley Baker: Women and Children; and Loitering Men* (The Photographers' Gallery, London, 2015), p.152.
7. Thomas, Dylan, *Holiday Memory* (J. M. Dent & Sons Ltd, London, 1972), no pagination.

ROAD TRIPS

1. Walton, John K. (2000), *The British Seaside: Holidays and Resorts in the Twentieth Century* (Manchester University Press, Manchester), p.27.

2. Cited in Kuhn, A and K. E. McAllister (eds), *Locating Memory: Photographic Acts* (Berghahn Books, Oxford and New York, NY, 2006), p.55.
3. See Roberts, R., *Tony Ray-Jones* (Chris Boot Ltd, London, 2004), p.37.
4. David Hurn in video interview, March 2018. Accessed 26 November 2018: https://www.youtube.com/watch?v=Ru-Y3V5oCXY
5. Theroux, P., *The Kingdom by the Sea* (Penguin, London, 1985), p.47.
6. Hall, S., 'Vanley Burke and the "Desire for Blackness"' in Sealy, M. (ed), *Vanley Burke: A Retrospective* (Lawrence & Wishart, London, 1993), pp.12–15.
7. Stephen Ferrier to the author, May 2018.
8. Cited in Ward, C. and D. Hardy, *Arcadia for All: The Legacy of a Makeshift Landscape* (Five Leaves Publication, Nottingham, 1984), p.38.

WHO'S LOOKING AT THE FAMILY?

1. Theroux, Paul, *The Kingdom by the Sea* (Penguin, London, 1983), p.52.
2. Theroux, Paul, *The Kingdom by the Sea* (Penguin, London, 1984), p.199.
3. Jackson, Tom, *Postcard from the Past* (4th Estate, London, 2017), p.16.
4. Ibid., p.26.
5. Ibid., p.41.
6. Ibid., p.106.
7. Ibid., opposite title page.
8. Meadows, Daniel, Fieldstudy, UAL Photography and the Archive Research Centre, 2011.
9. Barry Lewis to the author, 2015.
10. Daffyd Jones to Bob Pullen, 2017.
11. All biographical information about Raymond Lawson was given to the authors by Nick Cordès.
12. Tim Slader to the authors, 2017.
13. Theroux, Paul, *The Kingdom by the Sea* (Penguin, London, 1983), p.67.
14. Dennis, Peter, Beccie Mannall and Linda Pointing, *Daring Hearts* (Brighton Ourstory Project and QueerSpark Books, Brighton, 1992).
15. E-mail to the author from Natasha Caruana, 2018.

WORLDS IN A SMALL ROOM

1. *Guardian*, 24 August 2016.
2. For an in-depth description of the seaside landlady and the different iterations of seaside accommodation, see Susan Barton's *Working-class organizations and popular tourism 1840–1970* (Manchester University Press, Manchester, 2005).
3. John K. Walton, *The British Seaside, Holidays and Resorts in the Twentieth Century* (Manchester University Press, Manchester, 2000), p.149.
4. Accessed 26 November 2018: www.dailymail.co.uk/news/article-2570386/Pictures-Blackpools-proud-hotels-sit-boarded-sad-reminder-seaside-towns-faded-glory-days.html
5. I am grateful to Henry Iddon for drawing my attention to this article in the *Financial Times*, 16 November 2017.
6. 'Letter to the author', 11 July 2018.
7. Ibid.
8. Cross, Gary (ed.), *Worktowners at Blackpool; Mass-Observation and popular leisure in the 1930s* (Routledge, London, 1990), p.67.
9. Letter to the author, July 2018.
10. Ibid.
11. Press Release. Studio Sam Causer, Margate, ND.
12. Written in *c.*2015.

GAZING UP CLOSE
AND FROM A DISTANCE

1. Grace Lau interviewed by Anna Fox for the British Library National Sound Archive Oral History of British Photography in 1995.
2. Grace Lau to the author, January 2018.
3. Grace Lau to the author, April 2018.
4. Ibid.
5. Ibid.
6. Ibid.
7. Accessed 26 November 2018: www.gracelau.co.uk
8. Letter to the author, June 2018.
9. Accessed 26 November 2018: www.norman.hrc.utexas.edu/itinerant/introduction.cfm
10. Miller, Sybil, *Itinerant Photographer: Corpus Christi*, (University of New Mexico, Albuquerque, NM, 1987).
11. Letter to the author, 28 June 2018.
12. Ibid.

UNDERCURRENTS

1. Stuart Griffiths in conversation with the author, 2013.
2. Ibid.
3. Ibid.
4. Ibid.
5. Ibid.
6. Ibid.
7. Knight, Sam, 'I hope you Saved Your Glow Stick', *New York Times*, 21 January 2007.
8. Stuart Griffiths in conversation with the author, 2013.
9. Ibid.
10. Accessed 26 November 2018: www.vincapetersen.com, ND
11. Stanley Cohen's PhD thesis was first published as *Folk Devils and Moral Panics: The Creation of the Mods and Rockers* (MacGibbon and Kee, London, 1972).

ACKNOWLEDGMENTS

Seaside Photographed is curated and written by Val Williams and Karen Shepherdson in partnership with Turner Contemporary, Margate on the occasion of the exhibition of the same title organized by Turner Contemporary, Margate, with financial support from Arts Council England. The curators are grateful for the support from: Canterbury Christ Church University; London College of Communication; and University of the Arts London.

With thanks to
All the artists and lenders to the exhibition

Special thanks to
Anne Braybon · Valeria Carullo · Sarah French · Paul Gambin · Trevor Gigg · Graham Goldwater · Melanie Hough · James Hyman · Colin Harding · Grace Lau · Sally Minogue · Bob Pullen · Jessica Sutcliffe · Shaun Vincent

At Turner Contemporary, Margate
Victoria Pomery · Sarah Martin · Kate Boys-Layton

SUPPORTERS

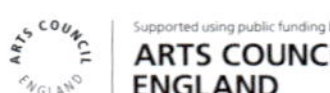 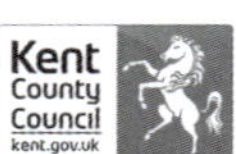

PICTURE CREDITS

a = above   c = centre   b = below   l = left
r = right

2 Charles Howell. Courtesy Bob Pullen; **6, 12, 13** © Julia Horbaschk; **8, 31bl, 40, 41, 42, 43** Architectural Press Archive/RIBA Collections; **9** *Architectural Review* (July, 1936)/Private collection; **10** © Hannah Blackmore; **11** © Eric Patterson. Courtesy Jess Kohl; **14** © Chloe Dewe Mathews; **15** The Caravan Gallery: © Jan Williams and Chris Teasdale; **16, 17, 18, 19, 20, 21, 22, 23, 104, 105** © Iain McKell; **24, 26, 27** The Architectural Press, London (1934)/Private collection; 29, **30, 31, 33** The Architectural Press, London (1936)/Private collection; **34, 35, 36, 37, 38, 39** Hutchinson, London, 1952/Private collection; **40, 41, 42, 43** © The Piper Estate/DACS 2019; **44, 47, 48, 54, 55, 56, 57, 58, 59, 60, 61** Courtesy SEAS Photography; **46** W. W. Russell. Courtesy SEAS Photography; **49** © Victoria and Albert Museum, London; **50, 51** Art Gallery of New South Wales, Sydney, Gift of Molly Roberson (née Mortimer) 1996; **52** © Susan Hiller. All Rights Reserved, DACS 2018; **53, 80, 81, 197** National Science and Media Museum, Bradford and Science & Society Picture Library; **62, 69, 72, 73, 74, 75** Aberystwyth University School of Art Museum and Galleries. © The Estate of Keith Vaughan. All Rights Reserved, DACS 2018; **64, 66, 67** © Helen Muspratt Estate. Courtesy Jessica Sutcliffe; **65al** Hood & Co/Private collection; **65ar** H. Mumford/Private collection; **65cl** L. B. Bradshaw/Private collection; **65cr** Houghton Photo/Private collection; **65bl, 65br** Photographer unknown/Private collection; **68** Courtesy Britten-Pears Foundation; **60, 69, 72, 73, 74, 75** © The Estate of Keith Vaughan. All rights reserved, DACS 2019; **71** © Lee Miller Archives, England 2018. All rights reserved; **76, 83** © John Chillingworth/Getty Images 78 B. T. Batsford, London (1936)/Private collection; **82** © *Daily Herald* Archive/National Science and Media Museum, Bradford and Science & Society Picture Library; **84** © Grace Robertson; **85** © Marc Riboud/Magnum Photos; **86** © Bruce Davidson/Magnum Photos; **87** © David Hurn/Magnum Photos; **88, 89, 90, 91, 92, 93** © Foundation Henri Cartier-Bresson; **94, 98** © Anne Braybon; **97** © Jane Bown, *Guardian* News & Media Ltd 2018; **99** © Shirley Baker. Courtesy Shirley Baker Estate; **101** © Sirkka-Liisa Konttinen. Courtesy Amber/L. Parker Stephenson Photographs; **102, 108, 109** © Steve Ferrier; **106, 107** © Vanley Burke. Courtesy Vanley Burke; **110, 111** © Anna Fox. Courtesy James Hyman Photography, London; **112** © Colin Curwood; **113** © Colin Thomas; **114, 115, 116, 117, 118, 119, 120, 121, 122, 123** © Michael Bennett; **124, 130, 131** © Barry Lewis; **127** © Martin Parr/Martin Parr Foundation/Magnum Photos; **129** © John Hinde Archive; **132** © Daniel Meadows; **134, 135, 136, 137** © Dafydd Jones; **138** Courtesy Lucy Bentham; **139** © Raymond Conrad Lawson. Courtesy the Estate of Raymond C. Lawson; **140, 141** © Reginald Slader. Courtesy Tim Slader; **143** © Pat Gwynne. Courtesy Joanna Murray; **144, 145, 146, 147, 148, 149** Courtesy Natasha Caruana; **150, 161, 162, 163, 164, 165, 166, 167, 168, 169** © Danielle Peck; **153, 154** © Henry E. Iddon; **156, 157** © Rowan Whybrew; **159** © Bob Chicalors; **170, 172, 173, 174, 175** © Grace Lau; **177, 179** © Rob Ball; **180, 181, 182, 183, 184, 185, 186, 187** © Jason Wilde; **188, 195** © Vinca Petersen; **190, 191** © Stuart Griffiths; **197** © C. Smith, National Science and Media Museum, Bradford and Science & Society Picture Library; **198, 199, 200, 201, 202, 203, 204, 205** © Enzo Ragazzini.

CHAPTER OPENERS

6 Detail of Julia Horbaschk, *Worthing Palms*, July 2017 (see p.13); **24** Detail of Paul Nash's photograph in *Dorset: A Shell Guide*, 1936 (see p.33); **44** Detail of Anonymous, cased ambrotype, possibly Hastings, *c*.1900 (see p.60); **62** detail of Keith Vaughan, *Dick's Book of Photographs*, *c*.1939 (see p.73); **76** Detail of John Chillingworth, *Blackpool Nightlife*, July 1954 (see p.83); **94** Detail of Anne Braybon, *Sweater Weather, Brighton*, 1969 (see p.98); **102** Detail of Steve Ferrier, *Jaywick*, 1989 (see p.108); **124** Detail of Barry Lewis, *Butlin's Holiday Camp, Skegness*, 1982 (see p.130); **150** Detail of Danielle Peck, *Untitled* from *Many Original Features*, 2013 (see p.162); **170** Detail from Grace Lau, *Untitled* from the series *21st Century Types*, July/August 2005 (see p.174); **188** Detail from Vinca Petersen, *Rave Car*, Kent, 1990s (see p.195, above).

Karen Shepherdson

KAREN SHEPHERDSON [KS] is a photographer, curator and writer. She is reader in Photography at Canterbury Christ Church University, co-editor for the *Journal of Photography and Culture* and the founder director of the UK's South East Archive of Seaside (SEAS) Photography. Shepherdson has received a number of funding awards and regularly creates national and international partnerships for practice and exhibition.

Shepherdson's research and practice focuses on coastal communities that have endured chronic cultural and social underinvestment and considers how common ground can be used as sites for potential wellbeing and community repair.

Shepherdson was director of the Old Lookout Gallery in Broadstairs (2010–15), curated several festivals including Folkestone's Salt: Festival of the Sea and Environment and in 2012 curated 'Beyond the View: New Perspectives on Seaside Photography'. Karen's own photographic work has been exhibited in the UK, Scandinavia and the USA.

Val Williams

VAL WILLIAMS [VW] is a curator and writer based in London and Hastings, and is Professor of the History and Culture of Photography at the University of the Arts London, founder director of the Photography and the Archive Research Centre (2003–18) and of the Moose on the Loose Biennale of Research (2009–16). She is also a founder editor of the *Journal of Photography & Culture* and member of the board of Fast Forward: Women in Photography, and co-convener of its biannual conference. She teaches on the MA Photography course at London College of Communication, London.

Val was the founder director of Impressions Gallery of Photography in York in the early 1970s, founded and co-directed two series of the Shoreditch Photo Biennale with Anna Fox in the 1990s and established the Oral History of British Photography with the British Library National Sound Archive, London. She was curator of exhibitions and collections at the Hasselblad Foundation in Gothenburg (Sweden) in the late 1990s.

Curated projects include 'How We Are' (Tate Britain); 'Daniel Meadows: Early Photographs' (Library of Birmingham and touring); 'Warworks' (Victoria and Albert Museum and touring); 'Martin Parr Retrospective' (Barbican Art Gallery, London and touring); 'The Dead' (National Media Museum and touring); 'Who's Looking at the Family?' (Barbican Art Gallery, London): 'Look at Me: Fashion and Photography in Britain' (British Council and touring); 'Ken: To be Destroyed' (Schwules Museum, Berlin and touring); 'Soho Archive and Soho Nights' (Photographers' Gallery, London) and 'Tish Murtha' (Photographers' Gallery, London).

Val Williams has also written extensively for newspapers and magazines. Major essays include 'No Nostalgia', on the work of Swedish photographer Sune Jonsson, and in 'Youth Unemployment: Photographs by Tish Murtha', in the Paul Reas monograph *Fables of Faubus*. She has written lengthy texts on the work of photographers including Martin Parr, Anna Fox and Daniel Meadows. Val has curated and co-curated *Seaside Photographed* with Karen Shepherdson.

This book is dedicated to Pete James (1958–2018), writer and curator.

First published *in* the United Kingdom *in* 2019 *by* THAMES & HUDSON LTD 181A High Holborn, London WC1V 7QX

Published to accompany the exhibition 'Seaside Photographed', curated by Val Williams and Karen Shepherdson in partnership with Turner Contemporary, Margate.

EXHIBITION DATES

Turner Contemporary, Margate
25 May–8 September 2019

John Hansard Gallery, Southampton
25 January–22 March 2020

Grundy Art Gallery, Blackpool
4 April–20 June 2020

Newlyn Art Gallery
and the Exchange, Newlyn
11 July–3 October 2020

British Library Cataloguing-in-Publication Data. A catalogue record for this book is available from the British Library.

ISBN 978-0-500-02206-1

Biography text *by* BOB PULLEN

Designed *by* JONATHAN ABBOTT

Edited *by* CAROLINE BROOKE JOHNSON

Printed and bound *in* China *by*
1010 PRINTING INTERNATIONAL LTD

To find out about all our publications, please visit **www.thamesandhudson.com**. There you can subscribe to our e-newsletter, browse or download our current catalogue, and buy any titles that are in print.

FRONT COVER
RAYMOND CONRAD LAWSON
Left to right: *David Wood, Sheila Wood and Alma Lawson,*
1959 (see p.139)

TITLE PAGE
CHARLES HOWELL
Blackpool postcard portrait, 1939

BACK COVER
JASON WILDE
Hastings Free Portrait Studio portrait, 2009 (see p.180)